"Christians want, and sometimes lack, assurance of their salvation. Finding salvation and finding assurance are not quite the same thing. Eric Lehner sheds light on this problem by reading Jonathan Edwards's *Religious Affections* as a treatise on assurance. By setting Edwards against his historical, philosophical, and theological background, this reading provides fresh insight into one of the most widely read works of Christian theology and devotion. Lehner's contribution, while narrow, is important for a full understanding of Edwards."
—**Kevin T. Bauder**, Research Professor of Systematic Theology, Central Baptist Theological Seminary, Minneapolis

"Eric Lehner's academic *tour de force* hits two birds with one stone. First, it elucidates Edwards's view of assurance in the context of his Puritan ancestors, demonstrating his exegetical and pastoral sensitivity. Second, it explores how one of America's most brilliant minds integrated sources ranging from the Holy Scriptures to the philosophy of John Locke under a coherent theological methodology. Lehner's monograph makes a valuable contribution to the study of the premier pastor-theologian in the First Great Awakening."
—**Joel R. Beeke**, President, Puritan Reformed Theological Seminary

"I love it when scholars provide a close reading of a text! Dr. Lehner examines *Religious Affections* with a prodigious eye to detail, and he asks bigger questions about the theological method adopted in Edwards's exposition of Christian assurance and authentic spiritual experience. With clarity, common sense, and appeal to context, Lehner draws together the skills of theologian and historian to remind us that it is not how we set out on the journey that really counts but signs of progress along the way."
—**Rhys Bezzant**, Dean of Missional Leadership, Director of the Jonathan Edwards Center, Ridley College, Australia

I0808012

"Sympathetic to Jonathan Edwards's own vision, enviably well-versed in the relevant literature, and carefully documented, *Marks of Saving Grace* is a significant new study of *Religious Affections*. Dr. Lehner's discussions range from a careful assessment of Edwards's theological method to a valuable and balanced assessment of his use of proof texts, and an illuminating analysis of his source material. This is an important contribution to the increasingly massive corpus of Jonathan Edwards scholarship. Given its subject matter, it merits the attention not only of scholars and students, but also of those who—like Edwards himself—are working pastors."
—**Sinclair B. Ferguson**, Professor of Systematic Theology, Redeemer Seminary

"Lehner's work fills a clear void in Edwards scholarship. After meticulous examination of *A Treatise Concerning Religious Affections*, Lehner concludes: Let Edwards be Edwards—a Bible-centered theologian and churchman passionate to defend Christian assurance first and foremost from Scripture and, only after thus proved, to support and illustrate the doctrine by philosophical and historical means. Lehner's careful study advances our understanding of Edwards's theological method and commends his doctrine of assurance for the good of the church."
—**Kenneth M. Gardoski**, Assistant Director, Ph.D. Studies, Associate Professor of Systematic Theology, Clarks Summit University

"To bring new, significant insight to an already robust understanding and appreciation of Edwards's classic treatise on the doctrine of assurance is not an easy accomplishment. Yet this is indeed what Dr. Lehner has accomplished. He has succeeded in paying careful attention to contextualizing Edwards, offering the general reader, as well as the scholar, a dizzying composite of information with perceptive interpretation. Though a doctoral dissertation (evidenced by the mass of scholarly footnotes and conversations), the work is a delightful introduction to the mind of Edwards. It is also a serious antidote

to false ideas about the doctrine of God and the nature of redemption, and the consequent lifestyle of desires, passions, and priorities. I highly recommend this intriguing study, regardless of readers' previous acquaintance with Mr. Edwards."
—**John D. Hannah**, Distinguished Professor of Historical Theology, Research Professor of Theological Studies, Dallas Theological Seminary

"Few books are more needed for pastoral reflection than Jonathan Edwards's *Religious Affections*. Not only does Edwards help us pastors think through the nature of true conversion and assurance, he also warns us about the reality of hypocrisy and self-deception in ways that remain pastorally relevant. In addition, as the historian Perry Miller noted, Edwards offers the most wide-ranging and valuable textbook on religious psychology in recent times. Eric Lehner's treatment in *Marks of Saving Grace* offers something not only for Edwards specialists, but for pastors and leaders wrestling with the nature of assurance and saving faith. It proves to be a valuable addition to the literature on *Religious Affections*."
—**Sean Michael Lucas**, Professor of Church History, Reformed Theological Seminary, Jackson

"When Jonathan Edwards and his contemporaries emphasized conversion and the new birth in the eighteenth century, their preaching brought with it the question, "How can I know that I have been born again?" In *Marks of Saving Grace*, Eric Lehner takes up the crucial question in Edwards's thought about how one can distinguish between true and false conversions. Beginning with Edwards's own struggle over whether he had truly been converted, and then moving on to discuss how Edwards grappled with history, Scripture, and epistemology, this book offers a comprehensive look at Edwards's theology on a question that has been vital to evangelicals ever since at least the eighteenth century. Whether readers come to this book with historical questions or theological questions, they will benefit from

reading Edwards with Lehner as their guide."
—**Lincoln A. Mullen**, Assistant Professor, Department of History and Art History, George Mason University

"Professor Lehner has offered here an outstanding contribution to our understanding of Edwards, his doctrine of assurance, and his theological method, riding a wave of recent work on Edwards's biblical exegesis. I am happy to recommend it."
—**Douglas A. Sweeney**, Professor of Church History and the History of Christian Thought, Director of the Jonathan Edwards Center, Trinity Evangelical Divinity School

Marks of Saving Grace

Reformed Academic Dissertations

A Series

Series Editor

John J. Hughes

Marks of Saving Grace

Theological Method and the Doctrine of Assurance in Jonathan Edwards's A Treatise Concerning Religious Affections

Eric J. Lehner

P&R
PUBLISHING
P.O. BOX 817 • PHILLIPSBURG • NEW JERSEY 08865-0817

Marks of Saving Grace: Theological Method and the Doctrine of Assurance in Jonathan Edwards's A Treatise Concerning Religious Affections. Eric J. Lehner, Ph.D, Th.M., M.Div., B.A. Submitted to Baptist Bible Seminary, Clarks Summit, PA, 2012, for the Ph.D. degree. Supervisor: Kenneth M. Gardoski.

Italics within Scripture quotations indicate emphasis added.

Printed in the United States of America

ISBN: 978-1-62995-268-0 (pbk)
ISBN: 978-1-62995-269-7 (ePub)
ISBN: 978-1-62995-270-3 (Mobi)

To Anna

Contents

Analytical Outline ix
Series Introduction xvii
Foreword by John D. Hannah xix
Preface xxv
Acknowledgments xxxi

1. The Puritan Model of Assurance 1
2. Edwards's Quest for True Religion 33
3. The Question of Edwards's Theological Method 50
4. The Illustrative Power of Metaphysics and Epistemology in *Religious Affections* 87
5. The Confirmation of History in *Religious Affections* 131
6. The Supremacy of Scripture in *Religious Affections* 158
7. Edwards's Theology of Assurance in *Religious Affections*: A Synthesis 190
8. Theological Method and the Doctrine of Assurance in *Religious Affections*: An Appraisal and Appropriation 221

Conclusion 258
Appendix 1. Distribution of Historical Sources in *Religious Affections* 266
Appendix 2. Reference to Thomas Shepard in *Religious Affections* 267
Appendix 3. Reference to Solomon Stoddard in *Religious Affections* 271
Appendix 4. Reference to John Flavel in *Religious Affections* 273

Appendix 5. Reference to Minor Historical Sources in *Religious Affections* 275
Appendix 6. Citations of Biblical References in *Religious Affections* 278
Bibliography 282
Index of Scripture 319
Index of Subjects and Names 323

Analytical Outline

1. The Puritan Model of Assurance
    a. The Essential Idea of Puritanism
        i. Interpretations of the Essence of Puritanism
        ii. Conversion as the Essence of Puritanism
        iii. The Vision for Establishing the Holy Community
        iv. The Logic for Attaining the Holy Community
    b. The Impetus for the Puritan Doctrine of Assurance
        i. Support for the Reformers' Doctrine of Justification
        ii. Unresolved Problems in the Reformers' Doctrine of Assurance
        iii. Pastoral Considerations
    c. Distinct Features in the Puritan Understanding of Christian Assurance
        i. The Nature of Assurance: An Experience Independent of the Essence of Faith
        ii. The Meaning of Assurance: Certainty of Personal Election
        iii. The Extent of Assurance: An Experience Attained by Degree
        iv. The Basis of Assurance: Spirit, Word, and Sanctification
    d. Distinct Features in the Puritan Appropriation of Christian Assurance
        i. The Use of Syllogism
        ii. The Use of Preparation
        iii. Approaches to Preparation

(a) Passive Preparation
(b) Active Preparation

2. Edwards's Quest for True Religion
  a. Edwards's Difficult Path to Assurance
    i. The Gospel According to Timothy Edwards
    ii. Jonathan Edwards's Account of Assurance Problems
    iii. Jonathan Edwards's Account of Conversion and Assurance
    iv. The Significance of the "Personal Narrative"
  b. The Occasion for *Religious Affections*
    i. Controversy Concerning the Authenticity of the Awakening
    ii. Edwards's "Faithful Narrative"
    iii. Edwards's "Distinguishing Marks"
    iv. Edwards's "Some Thoughts Concerning the Revival"
  c. Summary

3. The Question of Edwards's Theological Method
  a. The Challenge of Assessing Theological Method
    i. Resolving the Problem of Anachronism
    ii. Resolving the Equivocation in the Definition of *Theological Method*
  b. The Interpretation of Edwards's Theological Method
    i. A Survey of Interpretations of Edwards's Theological Method
    ii. The Inadequacy of Philosophical Interpretations
      (a) An Inadequate Account of Edwards's Biblical Interest
      (b) An Unjustified Disqualification of Christian Historiography
    iii. The Inadequacy of Central Interpretive Motif Interpretations
      (a) The Problem of Reductionism
      (b) The Problem of Decontextualization

iv. The Inadequacy of a Categorical Systematic Theology Approach
c. Edwards's Theological Method as a Regulated Matrix
i. Evangelical Approaches to Theological Method
(a) A Stratified Approach
(b) An Integrative Approach
(c) A Regulated Matrix Approach
ii. The Value of Assessing Edwards in Terms of a Regulated Matrix
(a) The Epistemological Value of a Regulated Matrix
(b) The Historical Value of a Regulated Matrix
d. Summary

4. The Illustrative Power of Metaphysics and Epistemology in *Religious Affections*
a. The Role of Metaphysics in the Theological Method of *Religious Affections*
i. The Nature of the Affections
(a) The Affections in Terms of Faculty
(b) The Affections in Relation to the Body
(c) The Affections Distinguished from Passions
(d) The Affections in Relation to Actions
(e) The Significance of the Nature of the Affections for Edwards's Theological Method
ii. The "Simple Idea"
(a) Edwards's Use of Locke's "Simple Idea"
(b) Interpretations of Edwards's Use of Locke's "Simple Idea"
(c) The Significance of the "Simple Idea" for Edwards's Theological Method
b. The Role of Epistemology in the Theological Method of *Religious Affections*
i. The Problem of Perception
(a) The Problem of Object and Eye

- (b) The Problem of Self-Deception
- (c) The Significance of Perception Problems for Edwards's Theological Method
- ii. "The New Sense"
  - (a) "The New Sense" Prior to *Religious Affections*
  - (b) "The New Sense" in *Religious Affections*
  - (c) Interpretive Approaches to "The New Sense"
  - (d) The Significance of "The New Sense" for Edwards's Theological Method
- c. The Significance of Philosophical Categories for Edwards's Theology of Assurance
  - i. Philosophical Categories in Historical Context
  - ii. Philosophical Categories in Rhetorical Context
    - (a) Metaphysics and Assurance
    - (b) Epistemology and Assurance
- d. Summary

5. The Confirmation of History in *Religious Affections*
   - a. Edwards's Prior Use of Historical Sources in the Defense of the Revival
     - i. Edwards's Use of Historical Sources in "Distinguishing Marks"
     - ii. Edwards's Use of Historical Sources in "Some Thoughts Concerning the Revival"
     - iii. Chauncy's Response in *Seasonable Thoughts*
   - b. Edwards's Use of Historical Sources in *Religious Affections*
     - i. Edwards's Apologetic Use of Historical Sources
       - (a) Source Distribution within the Structure for Apologetic Purposes
       - (b) The Debate with Chauncy
     - ii. Edwards's Polemic Use of Historical Sources
       - (a) General Stylistic Elements for Polemic Purposes
       - (b) Special Use of Thomas Shepard for Polemic Purposes

c. The Significance of Historical Sources for the Doctrine of Assurance in *Religious Affections*
i. Theological Themes Concerning the Subject of Spiritual Perception
ii. Theological Themes Concerning the Object of Spiritual Perception
d. Summary

6. The Supremacy of Scripture in *Religious Affections*
a. Edwards's View of Scripture in *Religious Affections*
i. The Sufficiency of Scripture
ii. The Essential Clarity of Scripture
iii. The Self-Authentication of Scripture
b. Edwards's Use of Scripture in *Religious Affections*
i. Edwards's Indirect Use of Scripture
(a) The Use of Biblical Allusion
(b) The Use of Scripture in General
(c) The Use of Theological Generalization
ii. Edwards's Direct Use of Scripture
(a) The Use of Biblical Exegesis
(b) The Use of Proof-Texting
c. The Significance of Biblical Sources for the Doctrine of Assurance
i. Scripture as the Measure of Assurance
ii. Scripture and Signs
iii. Scripture and Preparation
iv. Scripture as a Ground for Assurance
d. Summary

7. Edwards's Theology of Assurance in *Religious Affections*: A Synthesis
a. The Nature of Assurance: Not of the Essence of Faith
i. The Nature of Assurance as Expressed in *Religious Affections*

ii. The Nature of Assurance as Clarified in the Gillespie Correspondence
b. The Basis of Assurance: The Spirit, the Word, and Sanctification
i. The Witness of the Spirit
ii. The Testimony of Scripture
iii. The Role of Sanctification
iv. The Relationship Among the Spirit, the Word, and Sanctification
c. The Accessibility of Assurance: Attainable and Normative
i. The Loss of Assurance as the Consequence of Sin
ii. The Gain of Assurance as the Normative Reward of Sanctification
d. The Means of Assurance
i. The Means of Self-Examination
ii. The Means of Action
iii. Ordinary Means of Grace

8. Theological Method and the Doctrine of Assurance in *Religious Affections*: An Appraisal and Appropriation
a. Reconsidering the Central Interpretive Motif in the Task of Theology
i. A Review of the Central Interpretive Motif in the Appraisal of Edwards's Theology
ii. An Assessment of the Use of the Central Interpretive Motif in the Task of Theology
b. Reconsidering the Use of Proof-Texting in the Task of Theology
i. Proof-Texting and the Protestant Cause
ii. A Qualified Case for Proof-Texting
iii. Proof-Texting in *Religious Affections*
c. Reconsidering Assurance Theology in Terms of the Believer's New Nature

i. Edwards's Portrayal of the Change Attending the New Creation
ii. Appraisal and Appropriation
d. Summary

9. Conclusion

10. Appendices
a. Distribution of Historical Sources in *Religious Affections*
b. Reference to Thomas Shepard in *Religious Affections*
c. Reference to Solomon Stoddard in *Religious Affections*
d. Reference to John Flavel in *Religious Affections*
e. Reference to Minor Historical Sources in *Religious Affections*
f. Citations of Biblical References in *Religious Affections*

Series Introduction

P&R Publishing has a long and distinguished history of publishing carefully selected, high-value theological books in the Reformed tradition. Many theological books begin as dissertations, but many dissertations are worthy of publication in their own right. Realizing this, P&R has launched the Reformed Academic Dissertation (RAD) program to publish top-tier dissertations (Ph.D., Th.D., D.Min., and Th.M.) that advance biblical and theological scholarship by making distinctive contributions in the areas of theology, ethics, biblical studies, apologetics, and counseling.

Dissertations in the RAD series are *curated*, which means that they are carefully selected, on the basis of strong recommendations by the authors' supervisors and examiners and by our internal readers, to be part of our collection. Each selected dissertation will provide clear, fresh, and engaging insights about significant theological issues.

A number of theological institutions have partnered with us to recommend dissertations that they believe worthy of publication in the RAD series. Not only does this provide increased visibility for participating institutions, it also makes outstanding dissertations available to a broad range of readers, while helping to introduce promising authors to the publishing world.

We look forward to seeing the RAD program grow into a large collection of curated dissertations that will help to advance Reformed scholarship and learning.

John J. Hughes
Series Editor

Foreword

With age, aggression is often replaced with reflection. As a student of the past, one seeking to squeeze from dusty tomes and dark archives timeless truths that, though contextually dated, possess a ring of relevancy and, hence usefulness, I have come to at least four conclusions as I increasingly reflect upon the task of mining the past for contemporary wisdom. First, the structure of past relevancies may be the seedbed of irrelevancy in a contemporary setting; there is a danger in "glorifying the past." As much as one ought to consistently disagree with Gotthold Lessing, the replication of the past is really tricky business. This I believe is so because of the tendency to read into the past contemporary concerns and insights that were unknown or unanticipated by the original audience. Bringing perceived insights from the past into the present, consequentially, can be distortive and misleading. This is because of the second lesson I have observed through reflection. It is this; we are not objective creatures. A subjective bias prevails even in those who arduously seek to avoid it, or at least are aware of its potency. This is, at least in part, because we are subject to preconditioned insights that form a sort of lens through which we see. What we often think we see most clearly is only a subject-impression reflectively garnered through an undetected mirror. What is the lesson in all of this philosophical meandering? It is that we are shaped in our perceptive faculties by the past, by inherited social experiences that have made an indelible imprint on us without knowing it.

The third conclusion is that humans often see value in the context of contrast; in fact, positive value has been frequently perceived through the lens of negative avoidance. We are creatures that swing as a pendulum living our lives according to the relative virtue of seeking to minimize pain while maximizing the pleasurable. The fourth is this. We live our lives seeking to correct the impact and presence of the negative by constructing mechanisms of correction that have within them inherently the seeds of disappointment because we see value in contrast to the negative, but fail to see the negative potential of our corrective measures. Life seems to explode before us grasping yet not obtaining, avoiding but only temporally acquiring, acquiring only to later discover the fallacies of the benefit. I am sounding somewhat like the writer of Ecclesiastes who I once thought was a dire pessimist but now think was a realist and optimist. He lived in what the literary figure C. S. Lewis called "Narnia," but, like Abraham, we look expectantly for a city whose builder and maker is God.

As a Christian, pursuing the art of historical analysis as a professional endeavor within the academy, I practice my discipline through the lens of acknowledged biases and assumptions. For example, it is my conviction that the world we perceive through the collective capacity of the senses, assembled into a cognitive fabric through mental reflection, is real, but a mere shadowy reflection of a reality that is far greater and vastly more beautiful, so that the senses and mental activity can only vaguely comprehend being inadequate for the task of knowing beyond the material, though there are clues that the whole is greater than the sum of the parts. To truly begin to grasp the other, more real, existence requires "a sixth sense," a concept addressed by the British-American cleric Jonathan Edwards. To this brilliant man, situated in parish ministry in rural 18th century Massachusetts, the volume of natural revelation came close to the volume of special revelation of which he made a life-long, serious pursuit. The natural world, a "Book of Shadows," pointed to a greater world, a profoundly more prolific and magnificent reality. He entered more deeply into that world with a perception and precision as few before or since.

FOREWORD

One of the most insightful comments concerning the mental life of Jonathan Edwards came from Paul Ramsey, expressed in his Introduction to the eighth volume of the Yale edition of Edwards's works. "One studies the times and backgrounds of some men in order to understand them. Others have such rare greatness that one studies *them* in order to understand their times, or even to comprehend the deepest meaning of the intellectual and other influences that were effectual upon them. Jonathan Edwards was such an original (*Ethical Writings*, WJE 8:12)." When one reads Edwards, at least I have concluded, you encounter a man that thought deeply on the issues of his day but in such a manner that he serves as an insightful bridge into the issues of our day. He was well aware of the inroads of the Enlightenment, but wrote with such insight that his answers, at least in the realm of epistemology, have a postmodern relevancy. American Evangelicalism, more frequently than not saturated by Enlightenment assumptions of measurability, progress, and triumphalism, would very much be the target of his polemics. Though a man of his time in many ways, such as in his aristocratic approach to ecclesiastical authority in his Northampton church, his devotion to a timeless book caused many of his insights to have the ring of relevance that transcends time, cultures, and geo-political structures.

Thus, we come now to the relevancy of the work before us. Though the author has ventured into a realm that has been traversed by scholars before him, Eric Lehner provides fresh insight into the mind of Edwards that has a gripping relevance for Christ-followers struggling with an increasingly apathetic culture, graying church constituencies, and not-to-infrequent approaches to renewal that appear at times more culture-conforming than radically gospel impassioned.

The context in which Edwards wrote *A Treatise Concerning Religious Affections* (1746) has a ring of continuity as well as remarkable contrast to today's American brand of popular Christianity. The point of similarity concerns the issue of the nature of genuine conversion. As in Edwards's day, a degree of superficiality is often observable of those who claim to be known of Christ. Profession without Christ-likeness presents a dilemma for most pastors seeking to fulfill their ministry as shepherds of the flocks of God. Many in our churches appear to give lip service to the Savior, but do not seek identification with him in any consistent manner. Edwards feared empty professions in the enthusiastic excesses he witnessed, particularly in the 1740s Awakening, to such an extent that he became increasingly skeptical of many aspects of it. American Christianity, often focusing upon the subjective and personal rather than focusing on the person and claims of Jesus Christ, has been deeply influenced by the 19th century revivalist tradition and the political ethos of democratic volunteerism (i.e., Christianity as a personal choice rather than on the wonder of God's discriminatory and unmerited grace).

The contrast between Edwards's day and Christianity in the 21st century is that in his day the Bible was profoundly respected, the cleric central in community life, the church the foremost institution, and theological literacy widespread. The average parishioner was well aware and knowledgeable of his/her creed and catechism. Biblical literacy by contrast is in decline among the general laity in contemporary churches. Edwards struggled with a head knowledge that did not seem consistent with the nature of biblical regeneration; it is all-too-apparent that contemporary Christianity is often psychologically emotive but intellectually shallow. When head and heart, the intellect and the affections, function in discontinuity, can the profession of faith be genuine? In Edwards's day the problem was often intellectual orthodoxy, but affectional heterodoxy; in ours it tends to be quite the opposite, with the result of weakening the intellectual content of biblical faith by stressing the subjective experience of faith. This is the tension that underscores Edwards's discourse, found in several of his writings, but culminating in the work before us. Edwards attempted to bring the mental and the affectional together into a non-bifurcated unity.

The structure of Edwards's work is twofold: first, he described twelve signs or evidences that are not necessarily ground of a genuine redemptive experience. The list is shocking, Edwards arguing that, if the devil can duplicate the same, it is impossible to base assurance of divine mercy upon such manifestations. Second, Edwards sets forth twelve signs that the devil cannot duplicate and these are evidences of a genuine work of God. Among the positive evidences of a genuine work of God, Edwards describes the nature of the Spirit's regenerative work, the initial positive signs. His point is that an effect participates in the nature of its cause. The nature of biblical rebirth is that it is a mighty work of the Spirit of God, who by divine mandate applies the benefits procured by Jesus Christ. The essence of the Spirit's redeeming work fundamentally acts upon the faculty of the affections, affections actuated by alluring insight (the utter beauty and unparalleled magnificence of Jesus's atoning sacrifice). The miracle of the overwhelming revelation of the love of God incites the affections and transforms priorities in everyone who is privileged to behold the ravishing beauty of God. Hence, for Edwards, profession of faith without moral conformity to the supposed object of faith is false faith. The basic principle seems to be two: first, the choices we make are predicated on two interconnected principles, the minimalizing of pain and the maximizing of pleasure. Second, choices are made freely (meaning we want to do it), but not without prevailing stimuli or prior options. While Christ is freely chosen, the embrace is because Christ is seen as the high object of our pleasure. It is the work of the Spirit in conformity to the good pleasures of God to reveal the Son. This transforming vision of Jesus is truly that—transforming. Edwards goes on to describe the nature of that transformation, recounting several realities that the devil cannot enduringly duplicate. Among these are admiration for Jesus Christ and the bearing of Christlikeness, fruit being the cardinal evidence of regeneration.

This brings me to Eric Lehner's *Marks of Saving Grace*. While the work rehearses Edwards's argument for the grounds or evidences of a genuine work of God, it is makes a unique contribution to Edwardian scholarship. One of the neglected areas of such studies has been the biblical foundation of Edwards's insights; scholars of the not-to-distant past have recognized that he operated from the sphere of the church and the pulpit, but they approached him through the lens of his intellectual accomplishments, some suggesting that he wasted his brilliant mind on archaic, worn-out topics such as religion. Dominated by secular assumptions, experts have rooted his scholarly attainments in the philosophical and social sciences, as a fruit of almost anything but the Bible. That trend has been reversed in the works of Stephen Stein, Robert Brown, and a growing host of interpreters. Lehner's work continues the positive trend using *A Treatise Concerning Religious Affections* to demonstrate the point that Edwards was preeminently a biblically-oriented cleric who read widely but only to validate and elucidate the Bible, the starting and ending point locus of knowledge.

I think the topic of the genuineness of Christian profession is a timelessly relevant topic for the serious pastor seeking to understand his flock, as in the case of Edwards, providing wise insight that does not trivialize the potency of the simplicity of child-like faith in Jesus, but at the same time does so with the firm conviction that belief without the regenerating reorientation of the Spirit is not saving faith at all. Thus, Dr. Lehner's work is important to the scholar, enlarging our perspective on a truly profound biblical thinker, the pastor struggling with the fact that regeneration does not cure human nature and yet desirous to comfort the troubled but unwilling to support a myth, and the informed Christian who wants to be a realist when it comes to struggling with sin and yet possess hope.

John D. Hannah
Distinguished Professor of Historical Theology
Research Professor of Theological Studies
Dallas Theological Seminary
Dallas, TX
22 July 2016

Preface

Of the many works of Jonathan Edwards, *A Treatise Concerning Religious Affections* ranks as one of the most widely read and appreciated of his writings.[1] Prized for its astonishing intellectual and spiritual content, *Religious Affections* has been examined, analyzed, and acclaimed since 1760, when it was first publicly assessed.[2] With such an extensive body of commentary already available, one may question the place for yet another analysis of *Religious Affections*. Two considerations suggest such a place. First, recent literature has filled many voids in our understanding of *Religious Affections* while at the same time introducing new questions regarding Edwards's doctrine of assurance and the larger question of understanding his theological method. Second, a steady stream of leading evangelicals continues to address the persistent challenge of postmodernity to the proclamation of gospel truth. Postmodernity may be passé in the academy, but its influence in the culture remains potent. The church continues to grapple with the task of boldly affirming gospel certainty, not only to a culture that views doubt, ambiguity, and epistemological fog as the best evidence of humility, but also to a church that has adopted the

[1] According to Smith, "It has unquestioningly been Edwards's most widely read book." John E. Smith, "Editor's Introduction," in *The Works of Jonathan Edwards*, ed. Perry Miller, vol. 2, *Religious Affections* (New Haven: Yale, 1959), 78.

[2] For the first public comment on *Religious Affections*, M. X. Lesser cites Joseph Bellamy's *A Careful and Strict Examination of the Covenant* (New Haven: Thomas and Samuel Green, 1760), 184, in his *Reading Jonathan Edwards: An Annotated Bibliography in Three Parts, 1729–2005* (Grand Rapids: Eerdmans, 2008), 53.

culture's outlook on notions of certainty and propositional truth. This too suggests that a new examination of the subject of assurance within *Religious Affections* is timely.

Recent Literature

The major theme of *Religious Affections* is the subject of "defining the soul's relation to God."[3] Or, as Ava Chamberlain puts it, "Edwards's aim in this treatise was specifically to discriminate between gracious and counterfeit affections in order to establish a firm foundation for personal assurance."[4] It would seem, then, that the subject of Edwards's theology of Christian assurance would represent a significant portion of scholarship concerning this treatise. Surprisingly, this assertion has not been the case. There are, however, several relevant works worthy of note, both unpublished and published.[5]

Edwards's theology of Christian assurance is addressed to some degree in several unpublished works. Kilboi's M.A. thesis "The Assurance of Salvation in the Theology of John Calvin, Jonathan Edwards, and John Wesley" endeavors to show how the various perspectives of these three on the matter of assurance can actually be combined to form a more satisfying and comprehensive approach to the doctrine.[6] Calvin Malefyt's 1966 dissertation on "The Changing

[3] Smith, "Editor's Introduction," WJE 2:1.

[4] Ava Chamberlain, "Self-Deception as a Theological Problem in Jonathan Edwards's 'Treatise Concerning Religious Affections,'" *Church History* 63, no. 4 (December 1994): 546.

[5] Verification of scholarship in the form of published works and dissertations, which is provided in the following section, is based on data provided by three sources: the online services of ProQuest/UMI, M. X. Lesser's exhaustive bibliographic work mentioned above, and the somewhat dated but still valuable bibliographic study by Richard S. Sliwoski, "Doctoral Dissertations on Jonathan Edwards," *Early American Literature* 14, no. 3 (Winter 1980): 318–27.

[6] John Michael Kilboi, "The Assurance of Salvation in the Theology of John Calvin, Jonathan Edwards, and John Wesley: Toward a Cumulative Case Argument," M.A. thesis (University of St. Michael's College, 2005).

Concept of Pneumatology in New England Trinitarianism, 1635–1755" devotes a chapter to *Religious Affections* and the role of the Holy Spirit in assurance.[7] Douglas Harrison, in his "Toward a Theology of Experience," offers a psycho-analytical solution to the dilemma of "belief and incapacity" in Calvinism, transcendentalism, and pragmatism, as represented by Edwards, Emerson, and James respectively.[8] Lowery's dissertation attempts to analyze Wesley's doctrines of assurance and perfection by examining his selective use of Edwards's *Religious Affections*.[9] David Clark's dissertation entitled "Leveling Mountains, Drying Up Rivers" argues that Edwards's belief he was living in the millennial era moved him to adjust his theology of preparationism which in turn impacted his doctrine of assurance.[10]

Other dissertations include those by Atchison, Lamborn, and Nichols. Atchison endeavors to demonstrate how Edwards's trinitarianism is a useful device for articulating the doctrine of Christian assurance from 1 John.[11] Lamborn's study "Blessed Assurance?" is an attempt to explain how New England Puritan theologians could reconcile the possibility of assurance with the belief of remaining sin in the regenerate amidst the ever-present danger of self-deception.[12]

[7] Calvin Sterling Malefyt, "The Changing Concept of Pneumatology in New England Trinitarianism, 1635–1755" (Ph. D. diss., Harvard University, 1966).

[8] Douglas Harrison, "Toward a Theology of Experience: Belief and Incapacity in Edwards, Emerson, and William James" (Ph. D. diss., Washington University, 2005).

[9] Kevin Twain Lowery, "Constructing a More Cognitivist Account of Wesleyan Ethics" (Ph. D. diss., University of Notre Dame, 2004).

[10] David Edward Clark, "Leveling Mountains, Drying Up Rivers: Jonathan Edwards' Historiography Applied" (Ph. D. diss., Westminster Theological Seminary, 2001).

[11] Thomas F. Atchison, "Towards Developing a Theology of Christian Assurance from 1 John with Reference to Jonathan Edwards" (Ph. D. diss., Trinity Evangelical Divinity School, 2004).

[12] James Spencer Lamborn, "Blessed Assurance? Depraved Saints, Philosophers, and the Problem of Knowledge for Self and State in New England, 1630–1820" (Ph. D. diss., Miami University, 2002).

Stephen Nichols's "An Absolute Sort of Certainty" argues that Edwards's theology of Christian assurance functions for him as the basis of his apologetic and epistemology.[13] However, none of these fine unpublished works seeks to address the assurance theology of Edwards within *Religious Affections* as the main subject, nor do any of these consider the role of theological method with respect to either assurance or *Religious Affections*.

Published material on the themes of Edwards's assurance theology is also quite limited. According to Lesser, the first published work to address Edward's assurance theology in any thematic sense was John Gernster's *Steps to Salvation* in 1960, but this work discusses Edwards's assurance theology as a subset of his larger conversion theology.[14] In fact, to date no major published work exists dedicated solely to the assurance theology of Edwards. Published discussions of Edwards's theology of assurance are relatively few, variable in degree of directness, and limited to articles, chapters in edited works, and brief discussions within broader works.[15] Furthermore, none but

[13] Stephen J. Nichols, "'An Absolute Sort of Certainty': The Holy Spirit and the Apologetics of Jonathan Edwards" (Ph.D. diss., Westminster Theological Seminary, 2000). This work was subsequently published as *An Absolute Sort of Certainty* (Phillipsburg, N.J.: Presbyterian and Reformed, 2003).

[14] John H. Gerstner, *Steps to Salvation: The Evangelistic Method of Jonathan Edwards* (Philadelphia: Westminster Press, 1960); Lesser, *Reading Jonathan Edwards*, 220–21; 675.

[15] The most noteworthy of these include C. C. Goen, *Revival and Separatism in New England, 1740–1800: Strict Congregationalists and Separatist Baptists in the Great Awakening* (New Haven: Yale, 1962), 13–15, 45–46; Robert Clifton Whittemore, "Jonathan Edwards," in *Makers of the American Mind* (New York: William Morrow, 1964), 32–45; Norman Pettit, *The Heart Prepared: Grace and Conversion in Puritan Life* (New Haven: Yale, 1966) 208–12; Terrence Erdt, *Jonathan Edwards, Art, and a Sense of the Heart* (Amherst, Mass.: University of Massachusetts, 1980); Henry H. Knight, III, "The Relation of Love to Gratitude in the Theologies of Edwards and Wesley," *Evangelical Journal* 6 (Spring 1988): 3–12; William J. Abraham, "Predestination and Assurance," in *The Grace of God, the Will of Man*, ed. Clark H. Pinnock (Grand Rapids: Academie, 1989), 231–42; Volume 3 of John H.

Chamberlain directs a study of assurance with respect to *Religious Affections*.[16]

Currents in Evangelical Theology

Presently, Reformed theology is experiencing a resurgence within much of English-speaking evangelicalism and a consequent renewed attention to the historic doctrines of grace. Simultaneously, broader philosophical and cultural currents suggest that notions of certainty are illusory at best and arrogant at worst. Consequently, the doctrine of Christian assurance and the discipline of theological method have become subjects of renewed interest in evangelicalism. The Lordship Salvation controversy of the 1990s and the resurgence of Calvinism in American evangelicalism appear to have contributed to the former.[17] Interest in the latter may be attributed to the larger philosophical currents which have called into question the notion of foundational categories of thought. As a consequence, renewed interest in epistemology has compelled evangelical scholarship to revisit the subject of theological method.[18] The heightened attention paid to both of these subjects—the doctrine of assurance and theological method—attests to the impact of postmodernity in the academy, the church, and the culture at large.

Gerstner, *The Rational Biblical Theology of Jonathan Edwards*, 3 Vols. (Powhatan, Va.: Berea, 1993); Michael J. McClymond and Gerald R. McDermott, *The Theology of Jonathan Edwards* (Oxford: Oxford, 2012), 371–72.

[16] Chamberlain, "Self-Deception as a Theological Problem," 541–56.

[17] The Lordship Salvation controversy of the 1990s centered on John MacArthur's *The Gospel According to Jesus* (Grand Rapids: Zondervan, 1988); the resurgence of Calvinism in American evangelicalism is succinctly captured in Collin Hansen's *Young, Reformed, and Restless* (Wheaton, IL: Crossway, 2008).

[18] See, for example, Stanley J. Grenz and John R. Franke, *Beyond Foundationalism: Shaping Theology in a Postmodern Context* (Louisville: Westminster John Knox, 2001), 11–15.

An attentive reading of *Religious Affections* will lead the reader to concur with John E. Smith that it "contains his [Edwards's] most acute and detailed treatment of the central task of defining the soul's relation to God."[19] As such, *Religious Affections* remains Edwards's most complete treatment on the subject of Christian assurance. The question of assurance is epistemological in nature; assurance speaks not only to the idea that one can know his or her standing before God but also to the ground of that knowledge. In other words, a theology of assurance must contain its own justification in order for it to provide the assurance of which it speaks. Therefore, an explanation of Edwards's theology of assurance is incomplete if it simply conveys the immediate rationale for that theology; it must also account for the epistemological ground that serves as the foundation for that rationale.

The proposition of this study—that Edwards's theological method in *Religious Affections* is best viewed as a matrix of informing sources with Scripture as the primary and governing source—is significant, for it challenges the validity of two ideas basic to many interpretations of Edwards. The first is the idea that Edwards's thought was fundamentally governed by the philosophical categories of the Enlightenment. The second is the idea that Edwards's entire corpus is governed by a central interpretive motif. If principles such as these govern his entire corpus, then a careful analysis of any one of his prominent works would supply confirming evidence. However, a close examination of *Religious Affections* indicates otherwise: this key work is governed by biblical, not philosophical, categories; furthermore, *Religious Affections* is also formulated apart from a larger controlling motif of either its content or argument. These conclusions are borne out in the method that Edwards employs in *Religious Affections* and the result of that method as expressed in his theology of assurance.

[19] Smith, "Editor's Introduction," 1.

Acknowledgments

I am truly indebted to many who are mentors, supporters, and encouragers, all of whom in one way or another have been instrumental in the completion of this book: Dr. Rolland McCune, Dr. Michael Windsor, and Dr. Michael Stallard, for remarkable mentorship in the areas of systematic and historical theology; Dr. Ken Gardoski and Dr. David Mappes, for constructive insights and suggestions throughout the writing process; Dr. John Hannah, for specialized direction in the study of Jonathan Edwards; Dr. Judi Coats, for patient proofing of the manuscript; Mr. John Hughes of P&R Publishing, for expert guidance throughout the publishing process; and the board of Virginia Beach Theological Seminary, for providing a generous sabbatical directed to the completion of this project. Finally, I would like to thank my lovely wife Anna; my children, Mark and Grace; and my parents, Joseph and Kareen Lehner, for the faithful love and encouragement that supported me throughout my years in seminary and during the writing of this project.

1

The Puritan Model of Assurance

A Treatise Concerning Religious Affections speaks directly to the individual and experiential aspect of the Christian faith, so not surprisingly, the degree of attention the church has given to the work spans over two centuries. Furthermore, *Religious Affections* is especially valued because it addresses that one question which is more significant than any other: how can a person avoid self-deception regarding one's own profession of faith and know that one's own faith is genuine and saving? *Religious Affections* seeks to answer the question of Christian assurance in terms that are definitive and theological. *Marks of Saving Grace*, in turn, seeks to understand Edwards's answer to that question as well as the method he used to justify his answer.

Several layers of context, moving from the general to the specific, overlap one another to bring a clear picture of Edwards's background and his motivation for writing. First, the doctrine of assurance was a substantial component of the overall Puritan idea, and as such the essential idea of Puritanism itself is critical for understanding *Religious Affections*. Second, it is important to account for the early Puritan motivations for the development of the doctrine of assurance. Building on these two principles, necessity then demands the examination of the substance of the Puritan doctrine of assurance; this third step will establish the theological context of *Religious Affections*. Fourth, the doctrinal components of syllogism and preparation, which the

Puritans employed to enhance their theology of assurance, are key to understanding Edwards's approach to assurance.

The Essential Idea of Puritanism

Efforts to define *Puritanism* have typically assessed the concepts, agendas, values, or ideas which were essential to the movement. A number of single governing motifs have been suggested, as have certain combinations of motifs, in order to explain what Puritanism really consisted of.

Interpretations of the Essence of Puritanism

Interpretations of Puritanism have varied considerably over the last hundred years or so. A concise analysis by Joel Beeke and Randall Pederson[1] documents competing definitions of *Puritanism* which center upon single governing ideas such as predestination,[2] covenant,[3] conversion,[4] politicized socio-economics,[5] and anti-Anglicanism.[6] Additionally, Edmund Morgan proposes that separatism was the central idea that propelled Puritanism.[7] Andrew Delbanco's work is typical of the socio-political interpretation in which New England Puritanism is viewed as the key to comprehending the moral and religious fabric that is unique to the American mind set.[8]

[1] Joel R. Beeke and Randall J. Pederson, *Meet the Puritans* (Grand Rapids: Reformation Heritage, 2006), xvi.

[2] William Haller, *The Rise of Puritanism* (New York: Harper, 1938), 83.

[3] Perry Miller, *Errand Into the Wilderness* (New York: Harper and Row, 1956), 48–49.

[4] Alan Simpson, *Puritanism in Old and New England* (Chicago: University of Chicago, 1955), 2.

[5] Christopher Hill, *Society and Puritanism in Pre-Revolutionary England* (London: Panther, 1964).

[6] John S. Coolidge, *The Pauline Renaissance in England: Puritanism and the Bible* (Oxford: Clarendon, 1970).

[7] Edmund S. Morgan, *Visible Saints* (Ithaca, NY: Cornell, 1963), 139–52.

[8] Andrew Delbanco, *The Puritan Ordeal* (Cambridge: Harvard University, 1989), 25–27.

An alternative approach, however, has emerged: one which suggests that Puritanism should be understood in terms of a multifaceted rubric. Beeke and Pederson see Puritanism as a movement comprised of a combination of theological, practical, political, and experiential components.[9] J. I. Packer defines *Puritanism* as "that movement in sixteenth- and seventeenth-century England which sought further reformation in the Church of England than the Elizabethan settlement allowed." This movement enveloped clergy, laity, and powerful public figures who found common cause in resisting Anglican formalism, embracing Presbyterian causes, promoting Calvinist forms of theology and practice, and employing the legal system for the purpose of establishing societal norms compatible with their values.[10] Francis Bremer likewise takes a synthetic view but with a pronounced emphasis on the theological element.[11] Alan Simpson seems agreeable to such an approach when he suggests that the various groups in the movement were united by the conversion experience, the establishment of a holy community, an apocalyptic view of their destiny, and the shared community experience.[12]

Conversion as the Essence of Puritanism

When considering the essence of Puritanism from the Puritan perspective, it appears that the idea of conversion rises to the place of prominence. The idea of conversion accounts not only for particular claims of certain Puritans,[13] but, more importantly, it explains the

[9] Beeke and Pederson, *Meet the Puritans*, xvi–xviii.

[10] James I. Packer, *A Quest For Godliness* (Wheaton, IL: Crossway, 1990), 35.

[11] Francis J. Bremer, *The Puritan Experiment: New England Society from Bradford to Edwards*, rev. ed. (Lebanon, NH: University Press of New England, 1995), 15–28.

[12] Simpson, *Puritanism in Old and New England*, 17–22.

[13] Cromwell's acceptance of Presbyterians, Anabaptists, and Independents was on the basis of conversion and was expressed in terms which historians have often recalled: "Though a man be of any of those three judgments, if he have the root of the matter in him, he may be admitted." Oliver Cromwell,

logical relationship the Puritans maintained between the community and the individual. The importance of this relationship is seen in the Synod of 1662 and its consequent "Half-Way Covenant." These two events illustrate how Puritans perceived conversion to be the key to uniting the individual to the holy community, so conversion became the priority that defined the existence and purpose of Puritanism.

The Vision for Establishing the Holy Community

The vision of the New England Puritans was to succeed where the Puritans of Old England had failed. The attempt to establish a holy state under the Cromwell regime rapidly degenerated into a failed cause, but the Puritans did not abandon all hope. The colonial enterprise on the other side of the Atlantic promised another opportunity. America, it seemed, promised the Puritans a blank slate for the establishment of a pure community.

Perry Miller's definitive *Errand into the Wilderness* unfolds this visionary element of the Puritan enterprise. The book's title, and its governing thesis, is drawn from the sermon delivered by Samuel Danforth on May 11, 1670 entitled *A Brief Recognition of New England's Errand into the Wilderness.*[14] Miller is convinced that Danforth intentionally used the term *errand* with a double meaning: that of having a purpose of business to accomplish and that of performing a duty in obedience to a higher power. Miller convincingly argues that the "Puritans did not flee to America; they went in order to work out that complete reformation which was not yet accomplished in England and Europe, but which would quickly be accomplished if only the saints back there would have a working model to

---

Oliver Cromwell's Letters and Speeches, ed. Thomas Carlyle (New York: Harper and Brothers, 1851), 2:340.

[14] For a critical introduction to the sermon, see A. W. Plumstead, *The Wall and the Garden: Selected Massachusetts Election Sermons, 1670–1775* (Minneapolis: University of Minnesota, 1968), 47–52. Text for the sermon immediately follows.

guide them."[15] In the words of John Winthrop, "Wee must Consider that wee shall be as a Citty upon a Hill, the eies of all people are uppon us."[16] New England, then, would have a divine purpose:

> A society despatched upon an errand that is its own reward would want no other rewards: it could go forth to possess a land without ever being possessed by it. . . . For once in the history of humanity (with all its sins), there would be a society so dedicated to a holy cause that success would prove innocent and triumph not raise up sinful pride or arrogant dissention.[17]

Of course, the success of this enterprise was not guaranteed; it "would come about if the people did not deal falsely with God."[18] But the errand failed; the Puritans failed to set up the kingdom, and their kingdom theology could not adequately explain their failure. For this reason, says Miller, the theology of Puritanism was abandoned, and the "errand" was redefined by man to serve his own interests.

The Logic for Attaining the Holy Community

As important as the realization of the holy society was, the spiritual condition of the individual was the prerequisite for such a society. Without the conversion of the individual, the purpose and the logic of the Puritan agenda was lost. So essential was the conversion of the individual that, by 1660, the issue of conversion had plunged New England Puritanism into crisis. While the Restoration had sealed the demise of the Puritan community in Old England, New

[15] Miller, *Errand Into the Wilderness*, 11.

[16] Cited by Miller in *Errand Into the Wilderness*, 11. For text of the sermon, see John Winthrop, "A Modell of Christian Charity," in *The Literatures of Colonial America: An Anthology*, ed. Susan P. Castillo and Ivy Schweitzer (Oxford: Blackwell, 2001), 245–50. The "city on a hill" expression has been viewed as paradigmatic for the Puritan agenda; see Bremer, *The Puritan Experiment*, 55–72.

[17] Miller, *Errand Into the Wilderness*, 6.

[18] Ibid.

England Puritans were discovering that the holy community was rapidly suffering a disintegration of its own. The second and third generation offspring of the original colonists were not giving sufficient evidence of conversion and its attending holiness, precipitating a dilemma which threatened the very existence of the Puritan vision of a holy church-state.

In keeping with the recently established Westminster Confession (1646), the sacrament of baptism carried the significance of circumcision, requisite to acceptance in the covenant community. The first generation of American Puritans professed conversion and received baptism. They baptized their children, making the second generation external participants in the covenant community; the children were committed to God with the anticipation that God would bring them to conversion. These were not to participate in communion until such a time that they could profess godliness (conversion). Therefore, until they evidenced conversion, they were, in effect, half-members.

Some of these children, those of the second generation, grew to adulthood without evidencing or professing conversion. Should their children be permitted to be baptized? If the answer was "no," then the vision of an undivided church-state community was compromised. If the answer was "yes," then the vision of a pure church was compromised. The Puritans, then, were forced to choose between (a) an undivided Christian community and (b) a pure church comprised of regenerate membership.

The Synod of 1662 addressed the conundrum. The signatories implemented a compromise designed to buttress the fragile church/state union while maintaining a semblance of church purity. The compromise became known as "the Half-Way Covenant,"[19] because it permitted baptism (the first half of the covenant) for the children of the unconverted, but not communion (the second half).

[19] Simpson, *Puritanism in Old and New England*, 35–36; George M. Marsden, *Jonathan Edwards: A Life* (New Haven: Yale, 2003), 29–30.

Thus the covenant of grace was taken to be one that extended through generations even if only as a gateway to salvation.

Although numerous interpretations have been proposed concerning the essence of Puritanism, the collective action of the New England community in 1662 gives compelling evidence that, in their view, the conversion of the individual was the decisive component of Puritanism. Both Simpson and Packer, who prefer a synthetic definition of Puritanism, are nevertheless willing to concede that the matter of individual conversion is the pre-eminent element.[20]

Puritanism, then, was variegated in agenda, but its essential and foundational principle was the conversion of the individual. The regeneration of the person was the single element from which the variety of Puritan expression found its motive to collective action, whether toward a united national church or toward a separated one.[21]

The Impetus for the Puritan Doctrine of Assurance

With conversion in the foreground of the Puritan mind, it comes as no surprise that three important factors converged to motivate the Puritans to aggressively focus on the doctrine of assurance. The first is the very close proximity, both in time and in topic, of Puritan soteriology to the Reformer's work on justification. The second is the variety of opinion concerning the essence of assurance that extended without a clear resolution from the Reformation into the Puritan period. The final factor that motivated the Puritans to develop their understanding of assurance was their commitment to the effective function of the pastor, especially as it concerned his role as spiritual counselor to those seeking to know their spiritual state.

[20] Simpson, *Puritanism in Old and New England*, 2; Packer, *A Quest For Godliness*, 35–36. Packer qualifies this central idea as "revival," which entails both the conversion of the unbeliever and the reinvigorating work of sanctification of the believer.

[21] Simpson, *Puritanism in Old and New England*, 15.

Support for the Reformers' Doctrine of Justification

The fact that the Puritans made much of assurance is due largely to the fact that this doctrine was the unfinished business of the Reformers' soteriology. If the Elizabethan Settlement is accepted as the catalyst of Puritanism, then the birth of Puritanism is little more than four decades removed from the *Ninety-Five Theses*, suggesting a significant overlap between maturing Reformation doctrine and initial Puritan thought.[22]

The first and second generation Reformers, typically represented by Luther and Calvin, were keenly aware of the implications that extended from their theology of justification. A definition of *justification* as given by the Reformers entailed a radical departure from Rome on the subject of assurance.[23] In the effort to redefine *justification*, the Reformers had moved the seat of authority from the church to the text of Scripture, the act of redemptive mediation from the clergy to Christ alone, and the means of grace from the sacraments to the faith of the individual. As a consequence of this systematization, all that salvation entailed—from its epistemological ground to its means to its personal realization—was redefined. This comprehensive and systematic redefinition of salvation enveloped the subject of assurance, which

[22] R. N. Frost, "Puritanism," in *The Dictionary of Historical Theology*, ed. Trevor A. Hart (Grand Rapids: Eerdmans, 2000), 441–43. While there is a high degree of unanimity among scholars regarding the beginning of Puritanism, its point of termination is not agreed upon. Bremer's perspective is comprehensive, beginning with the Act of Supremacy in 1534 and ending with the death of Edwards in 1758; see Bremer, *The Puritan Experiment*, xi–xxvi.

[23] The position represented here is that the Reformers, and most notably Luther and Calvin, were in essential agreement regarding the doctrine of assurance and that their differences were peripheral. However, this is not the traditional opinion of critical historians. Randall Zachman's recent work argues against the traditional view and in favor of essential agreement between Luther and Calvin. See Randall C. Zachman, *The Assurance of Faith: Conscience in the Theology of Martin Luther and John Calvin* (Minneapolis: Fortress, 1993); Martin I. Klauber, "Review of *Assurance of Faith* by Randall C. Zachman," *The Sixteenth Century Journal* 24, 4 (Winter 1993): 997–98.

included objective certainty regarding the authority, ground, means, and personal application of salvation. If, as the Reformers asserted, salvation was objectively grounded in the promise of the Word of God and obtainable by faith, the logical consequence was objective certainty.[24]

Rome, on the other hand, claimed that salvation was proprietary to the church and to the sacraments and insisted that assurance was, at best, a matter of probability. The Tridentine statement cemented that position firmly, anathematizing opinions to the contrary. Notions of certain assurance, according to Rome, were dangerous, in that they engendered independence from circumspect living, the church, and the sacraments.[25]

Unresolved Problems in the Reformers' Doctrine of Assurance

While the Reformers were unified in maintaining that assurance was attainable, certain, normative, and grounded in the Spirit and the Word, they were by no means uniform in other aspects. Considerable debate ensued between the Protestants concerning the precise nature of assurance. The debate concerned various issues including whether or not assurance was itself the essence of faith, whether or not assurance was always consciously experiential, and whether authentic assurance entailed absolute certainty or was obtained in degrees. Other questions remained: the question regarding in what sense the Holy Spirit was a means of assurance, the question concerning in what sense Christ served as grounds of assurance, the question regarding what role syllogism played in the formulation of assurance, the question as to what extent assurance was subjective vis-à-vis

[24] Allister E. McGrath, *Studies in Doctrine* (Grand Rapids: Zondervan, 1997), 390–97.

[25] Joel R. Beeke, *The Quest for Full Assurance: The Legacy of Calvin and His Successors* (Edinburgh: Banner of Truth, 1999), 9–15. Especially helpful is Beeke's analysis of assurance theology as articulated by the Council of Trent, 14–15.

objective, and the question as to what relationship the act of assent (of the mind) had to the act of trust (of the will).[26]

The rise of Puritanism as a movement grounded in Reformation theology meant that the movement adopted the assets and the liabilities of its theology. By embracing Reformation soteriology, Puritanism committed itself to sustaining its views of assurance in the face of traditional Roman dogma. It also committed itself to completing the unfinished business of defining the nature of Christian assurance in terms that the heirs of the Reformation could agree upon. The Puritans engaged these unresolved issues, and in so doing sustained the momentum of the work initiated by the Reformers.

Pastoral Considerations

A third impetus that motivated the Puritans to define *assurance* was pastoral in nature. The central message of Puritanism was conversion—what it meant, why it was so important, and how it was obtained. To this end, pastors proclaimed the danger of sin and the consequent eternal wrath of God. The anxiety that followed was intended as the means to move the sinner to repentance. However, Puritan pastors also noted that the work of Satan and the evil propensity of the sinner complicated the matter by introducing the possibility of self-deception into the equation. As a result, the capacity for self-deception and the danger of false conversion was another major theme in Puritan preaching as was the consequent call to self-examination.[27] Anxiety and self-examination were considered appropriate when produced by a conscience that perceived a gap between one's own self and God.[28] Yet the Puritans saw the temporary sufferings of the

[26] William Cunningham, *The Reformers and the Theology of the Reformation* (1862; repr., Edinburgh: Banner of Truth, 2000), 113–26; Beeke, *The Quest for Full Assurance*, 16–81; Gregg R. Allison, *Historical Theology* (Grand Rapids: Zondervan, 2011), 550–57; R. Michael Allen, *Reformed Theology* (New York: T&T Clark, 2010), 87–88.

[27] Beeke, *The Quest for Full Assurance*, 120–21.

[28] Thomas Shepard, *God's Plot: Puritan Spirituality in Thomas Shepard's Cambridge*, ed. Michael McGiffert, rev. ed. (Amherst, MA: University of

anxious soul to be an ultimate mercy, and they regarded gentle preaching to be the instrument of ultimate harm, in that it neglected the duty to warn those in peril of losing their souls.[29]

Regardless of what the Puritans may have intended, the very fact that Puritan pastors sought to create anxiety in the minds of anyone is considered by some to be inexcusable by any standard. According to Perry Miller,

> The doctrine of regeneration caused the founders of New England to become experts in psychological dissection and connoisseurs of moods before it made them moralists. . . . . It is often difficult to see how Puritan divines could believe that they offered battered humanity any more of a haven than the priests, for in practice he who was justified by faith was taken from the rack of fear only to be strapped to the wheel of doubt.[30]

Miller's critique is worthy of note because it represents a significant segment of critical Puritan scholarship.[31] Yet the critical perspec-

---

Massachusetts, 1994), 19–21. This work is Shepard's autobiography accompanied by the editor's commentary.

[29] G. A. Hemmings, "The Puritans' Dealings with Troubled Souls," in *Puritan Papers*, ed. J. I. Packer, vol. 1, *1956–1959* (Phillipsburg, NJ: P&R Publishing, 2000), 32–34; Bremer, *The Puritan Experiment*, 21.

[30] Perry Miller, *The New England Mind: The Seventeenth Century* (Cambridge: Harvard University Press, 1939), 53. Miller's final comment here requires some explanation. William Stoever's observation, which elaborates on the problem of assurance in Thomas Shepard's journal, is helpful: "This document evokes the full range and intensity of spiritual anxieties to which the Puritan saints were subject. Indeed, it suggests that the Protestant *sola fide*, while rescuing the individual from endlessly having to earn sufficient merit to cover his daily sins, in Puritan hands might deliver him to seemingly endless pursuit of firm evidence of his justification." See William K. B. Stoever, *'A Faire and Easie Way to Heaven': Covenant Theology and Antinomianism in Early Massachusetts* (Middleton, CT: Wesleyan University, 1978), 148.

[31] In addition to the works of Perry Miller, see Delbanco, *The Puritan*

tive of Miller, which passes judgment on the Puritan system of belief and practice, does so having already presupposed a non-Biblical world view with its standard of morality. The Puritan clergy embraced a world view defined by the Bible and centered upon the need for humanity to reconcile with God by means of conversion. For this reason, the pastoral emphasis was to guide each member of the flock from a place to doubt to a place of peace and assurance.[32]

Distinct Features in the Puritan Understanding of Christian Assurance

Understanding Edwards on the subject of assurance requires some understanding of the Puritans on assurance. The Puritans prioritized conversion and consequently established significant motivation for framing the doctrine of Christian assurance. A full exposition of this subject is beyond the scope of *Marks of Saving Grace* and would require a substantial volume.[33] However, for the sake of

---

Ordeal; Simpson, *Puritanism in Old and New England*; Theodore Dwight Bozeman, *The Precisionist Strain: Disciplinarian Religion and Antinomian Backlash in Puritanism to 1638* (Chapel Hill, NC: University of North Carolina, 2004); *The Cambridge Companion to Puritanism*, ed. John Coffey and Paul C. H. Lim (Cambridge: Cambridge University, 2008). John Coffey, in his contribution to *The Cambridge Companion* entitled "Puritan Legacies," provides an orderly account of the extent to which scholarship looks to Puritanism as "an explanatory tool" for understanding America, its incurably religious character, and its embrace of capitalism, American exceptionalism, sexism, morally motivated politics, intolerant attitudes, and the various evils of modernity. See John Coffey, "Puritan Legacies," in *The Cambridge Companion to Puritanism*, ed. John Coffey and Paul C. H. Lim (Cambridge: Cambridge University, 2008), 327–40.

[32] It should also be noted that anxiety was not the only theme by which Puritan pastors exhorted their parishioners to seek assurance. Themes such as the joy of salvation, the love of Christ, and the blessings of fruitfulness in the Christian life were also employed to this end. See, Michael G. Hall, *The Last American Puritan: The Life of Increase Mather, 1639–1723* (Hanover, NH: Wesleyan University, 1988), 102.

[33] To date such a work does not exist. The most thorough examination to

establishing the theological context for Edwards on the subject of assurance, surveying the distinctive elements of Puritan assurance theology remains vital.

The doctrine of assurance gained stability under the care of the Puritan divines. By the time the Westminster Assembly had convened in 1643, a high degree of unanimity prevailed as to how the doctrine should be expressed. Although the doctrine of assurance was a significant component of the Confession, the Assembly did not address the subject until 1646. When it finally addressed the doctrine, it did so for two days in February, and another two days in July.[34] The doctrine of assurance was not addressed again by the Assembly although it continued to convene until February of 1649 for a total of 1,163 sessions.[35] Such minimal attention on the part of the Assembly

---

date of the Puritan doctrine of Christian assurance has been conducted by Joel Beeke in two separate works. Beeke's aforementioned *Quest for Full Assurance* (1999) devotes its major portion to the doctrine of assurance in the Puritan era, yet the work is constrained by the limits of the design of the project which examines, by means of comparison and contrast, select representatives of English Puritanism and the Dutch Second Reformation. Beeke's recent publication of "The Assurance Debate" is a brief but thoroughly researched accounting of the major issues attending the Puritan discussion of this doctrine. See Joel R. Beeke, "The Assurance Debate: Six Key Questions," in *Drawn Into Controversie: Reformed Theological Diversity and Debates Within Seventeenth-Century British Puritanism*, ed. Michael A. G. Haykin and Mark Jones (Göttingen, Germany: Vandenhoeck and Ruprecht, 2011), 263–83.

[34] Based upon Beeke's analysis of the Assembly's minutes in "The Assurance Debate," 264; minutes referred to are published in *Minutes of the Sessions of the Westminster Assembly of Divines*, ed. Alex F. Mitchell and John Struthers (London: Blackwood and Sons, 1874).

[35] Adam Loughridge, "Westminster Assembly," in *The New International Dictionary of the Christian Church*, ed. J. D. Douglas, rev. ed. (Grand Rapids: Zondervan, 1978), 1039; F. L. Cross and E. A. Livingstone, eds., "Westminster Assembly," in *Oxford Dictionary of the Christian Church*, 2nd ed. (Oxford: Oxford University, 1974), 1472; Philip Benedict, *Christ's Churches Purely Reformed: A Social History of Calvinism* (New Haven: Yale, 2002), 200–202. It should be noted that the date of the Confession's completion has been variously represented, ranging from December of 1646 to April of 1647.

should not be taken as a token of disinterest: the Confession devoted an entire section to the doctrine of assurance; and of the 159 members of the Assembly, no fewer than twenty-five wrote works dedicated to the subject of Christian assurance.[36] The relatively short period of time devoted to a significant section of the Confession testifies to the harmony of the members of the Assembly. This harmony is confirmed by the general consensus of opinion expressed in the body of Puritan writings devoted to assurance.[37]

Assurance was understood, first and foremost, as a matter of individual experience. The Puritan theologians typically served in pastoral capacities; therefore, they were motivated to define *assurance* in terms that accounted for both the Scriptures *and* their pastoral observations. As a result of this dynamic, the Puritan doctrine of assurance entailed an experientially-oriented definition that accounted for its nature, meaning, extent, basis, and appropriation.[38]

The Nature of Assurance: An Experience Independent of the Essence of Faith

The most significant feature of the Puritan doctrine of assurance is its affirmation that Christian assurance is not of the essence of

[36] John M. Frame, "Westminster Confession of Faith," in *Evangelical Dictionary of Theology*, ed. Walter A. Elwell, 2nd ed. (Grand Rapids: Baker, 2001), 1271; Beeke, "The Assurance Debate," 264.

[37] For the sake of restricting the length of this discussion, it is not within the scope of this study to examine the pertinent primary sources. The following summary is based on competent engagement and synthesis of primary sources as represented by the secondary sources cited in this section.

[38] Other delineations of the salient points of Puritan doctrine of assurance have been offered. The Westminster Confession outlines four: 1) the possibility of assurance, 2) the foundation of assurance, 3) the cultivation of assurance, and 4) the renewal of assurance. WCF, 18.1–4. Joel Beeke also proposes a four-fold set of distinctives: 1) the distinction of saving faith from assurance, 2) assurance by the agency of the Holy Spirit, 3) assurance on the basis of the covenant of grace and the work of Christ, and 4) the provisional and incomplete character of assurance as normative. See Beeke, *The Quest for Full Assurance*, 113–19.

saving faith. The consequence of such a view was the possibility for a person to believe in Christ and be truly saved without actually possessing assurance of his/her salvation.[39] The significance of this stance is that it appears to be a reversal of the doctrine taught by the early Reformers, many of whom stressed that assurance was of the very essence of faith. In other words, they affirmed that the character of saving faith was such that it comprehended both certainty concerning the truth of the gospel *and* the knowledge of its actual saving application to the one who believes. Though the question was clearly unsettled during the last half of the 16th century, the first half of the 17th century gives clear evidence of a consolidation of opinion.[40] The Westminster Confession was unequivocal in its position separating assurance from faith, and subsequent confessions confirm that the Confession's influence on this subject was decisive.[41]

Why did the Puritans depart from the Reformers on this point? In Cunningham's estimation, the Reformers took up the view that assurance was of the essence of faith for two reasons. First, full and immediate assurance was the norm that was experienced and witnessed by the Reformers. Cunningham argues that this phenomenon should be interpreted as one of temporary experience: the Reformers and those who followed them were granted an extraordinary measure of grace by God so that they might persevere through the spiritual

[39] Beeke, *The Quest for Full Assurance*, 87–88; Packer, *A Quest for Godliness*, 181–82.

[40] According to Stoever, "by about 1630, the notion that justifying faith is properly assurance had become an issue with elements of English nonconformity that even the more extreme Puritans regarded as excessively radical." Stoever, *'A Faire and Easie Way to Heaven,'* 130. However, Stoever observes that the shift of opinion was general in nature and that some Puritans continued to closely associate the two. See 129–37.

[41] Cunningham, *The Reformers and the Theology of the Reformation*, 111–27. Though the Confession's influence was indeed the watershed for the main body of the non-Conformist faiths, the Confession's interpretation was not accepted by all as the Marrow Controversy demonstrated. See D. Beaton, "'The Marrow of Modern Divinity' and the Marrow Controversy," *Princeton Theological Review* 4, 1 (January 1906): 327–31.

conflict at hand. Second, the Reformers were contending for an absolute form of assurance in order to buttress justification by faith in the face of criticism from Rome. Cunningham asserts that in the heat of the contention, the Reformers overstated their case; as a consequence, they involved themselves in contradictory and untenable statements concerning the nature of assurance.[42] As the decades passed, the accumulation of pastoral experience and theological reflection tempered the overstatement of the Reformers.[43]

[42] Cunningham, *The Reformers and the Theology of the Reformation*, 113–25. In an alternative interpretation, Joel Beeke argues for a substantial continuity between Calvin and the Westminster Confession. Joel R. Beeke, "Does Assurance Belong to the Essence of Faith? Calvin and the Calvinists," *The Master's Seminary Journal* 5, 1 (Spring 1994): 43–71.

[43] Cunningham's argument is not altogether sustainable. The subjectivity involved in his first point is evident: "The Reformers . . . seem to have enjoyed usually an assurance of being in a state of grace and of being warranted to count upon salvation. God seems to have given to them the grace of assurance more fully and more generally than He does to believers in ordinary circumstances. And this is in accordance with the general course of his providential procedure. The history of the church seems to indicate to us that two positions are true, with references to this matter, viz.— 1st, That assurance of salvation has been enjoyed more fully and more generally by men who were called to difficult and arduous labours in the cause of Christ, than by ordinary believers in general. And 2dly, that this assurance, as enjoyed by such persons, has been frequently traceable to special circumstances connected with the manner of their conversion as its immediate or proximate cause. So it certainly was with the Reformers." While Cunningham's proposition sounds plausible, he supplies no data to sustain the assertion that *history* indicates that God supplies more assuring grace in times of duress. Second, the attempt to explain the Reformers' view of assurance on the basis of experience is not presented clearly. It is not clear whether, in Cunningham's estimation, the Reformers were leaning on their own personal experience of conversion, or depending upon their overall acquaintance with the conversion experiences of others. In any case, it appears that he places considerable confidence in the noble character of the leaders of the Reformation. On this point Cunningham's work (first published in 1862) seems to have imbibed a measure of the "Great Man" historiography typical of 19th century European historians. See Alan Edelstein, *Everybody's Sitting on the Curb: How and Why America's Heroes Disappeared* (Westport, CT: Praeger, 1996), 33. Cunning-

The Meaning of Assurance: Certainty of Personal Election

The question as to whether or not assurance was of the essence of saving faith was somewhat complicated in that the term *assurance* was applied to more than one subject within general discussion of the doctrine. *Assurance* often was a reference to certainty concerning the objective work of Christ and the propositional content of the gospel. At other times, the term was used in reference to the subjective, experiential sense of certainty that the self was truly converted and belonged to the elect.[44] This equivocation, when not clearly distinguished, contributed to a degree of confusion since at times the content of the assurance being referred to was the former objectivity, and at other times it was the latter subjectivity.

The separation of assurance from the essence of faith was in fact a recognition that the question of the content of faith was not being clearly addressed. The reason that assurance could not be of the essence of saving faith was that the content of saving faith differed from that of assurance. The content of saving faith was confidence in the propositional message of the sufficiency of Christ on behalf of sinners; the content of assurance was confidence that Christ's sufficiency had been applied to the self.

The Puritan view of *assurance*, then, was that of "a God-given conviction of one's standing in grace, stamped on the mind and the heart by the Spirit."[45] Or, in the words of Brooks, it was the "reflex act of a gracious soul, whereby he clearly and evidently sees himself in a gracious, blessed and happy state; it is a sensible feeling, and an experimental discerning of a man's being in a state of grace."[46]

---

ham's second line of reasoning is more reliable, sustained on the grounds of the documentation of the debate. Cunningham correctly observes that the Reformers overextended themselves in attempting to objectify the agency of the Spirit in assurance. Cunningham, *The Reformers and the Theology of the Reformation*, 113–25; for quotation, see page 113.

[44] R. M. Hawkes, "The Logic of Assurance in English Puritan Theology," *Westminster Theological Journal* 52, 2 (Fall 1990): 249–50.

[45] Packer, *A Quest for Godliness*, 182.

[46] Thomas Brooks, *Heaven on Earth: A Treatise on Christian Assurance*

The Extent of Assurance: An Experience Attained by Degree

The extent of assurance was taken by the Puritans as one of degree; assurance was not possessed in absolute terms. A low state of assurance was possible among the truly regenerate; many Puritan commentators suggested that even those professors who claimed to be devoid of any assurance whatsoever actually possessed assurance in some incipient form.[47] Though such a professor found the comfort of assurance beyond his/her grasp, yet the impulse to persevere in faith gave evidence that some seed of assurance was present.

On the other end of the spectrum was "full assurance," a certainty that was a "heaven on earth," a joy to which every believer was spiritually entitled and a source of strength for holy living so remarkable as to be described as a "second conversion." The true convert could experience any degree of assurance, from a low state in which assurance seemed non-existent, to a very high state in which one's election was perceived as certain.[48]

The Basis of Assurance: Spirit, Word, and Sanctification

The experience of assurance was regarded by the Puritans as having its foundation in the Spirit, the Word, and in sanctification. This complex basis was an attempt to explain both the objective and the subjective elements of assurance that were attested to in the Scriptures.[49] Although assurance was seen to be objectively grounded in the

---

(1654; repr., Edinburgh: Banner of Truth, 1982), 14.

[47] Beeke, *The Quest for Full Assurance*, 91.

[48] Packer, *A Quest for Godliness*, 181; John Spurr, *English Puritanism* (London: Macmillan, 1998), 157–58.

[49] The idea of the Puritan "ground of assurance" has been interpreted in a variety of ways. Stoever maintains that "this private seal [of the Spirit] is the true foundation of assurance." Miller and von Rohr argue that the Covenant served the Puritans as the basis of assurance. See Stoever, "*A Faire and Easie Way to Heaven*," 120; Miller, *The New England Mind: The Seventeenth Century*, 389; John von Rohr, "Covenant and Assurance in Early English Puritanism," *Church History* 34, 2 (June 1965): 195–203.

promise of the Word of God,[50] the Scriptures also attested that assurance was a sovereign work of the Holy Spirit and that assurance also maintained a direct relationship to personal holiness.[51]

All the Puritans agreed that it was the Holy Spirit who, according Romans 8:15–16, assumed the role of bringing the comfort of salvation to believers. However, the precise manner in which the Holy Spirit performed this work was the subject of some disagreement among the Puritans. Stoever suggests that Richard Sibbes is representative of Puritan opinion on the manner of the Spirit in bringing assurance. Sibbes saw a fourfold "sealing" work of the Spirit in which he directly communicates words of comfort, moves the heart of the believer to prayer, imparts Christ's image to the soul, and supplies joy in triumph over temptation. This view saw the work of the Spirit as primarily immediate, though not exclusively so.[52]

This immediate view of the Spirit's work seemed to be not unlike the doctrine of Rome, which insisted assurance was not possible apart from special revelation. For this reason, Puritans who held to a more immediate approach were careful to explain that the Spirit employed providential means, rather than miraculous ones. In this way, the Puritans believed they were able to maintain sufficient distance from the Catholic position. Yet the practicality of the Puritan culture demanded that its theologians explain how such an immediate view of the Spirit's work manifested itself in the life of the church and in the life of the individual. The explanation inevitably reverted to external forms that indicated that the Spirit's work was not quite as immediate in practice as suggested in theory.[53]

Miller is convinced that neither Sibbes nor the Puritans should be interpreted as basing assurance in the work of the immediate and subjective workings of the Spirit but in the objectivity of the Cove-

[50] Beeke, *The Quest for Full Assurance*, 124–30.
[51] Spurr, *English Puritanism*, 163.
[52] Stoever, *'A Faire and Easie Way to Heaven,'* 121–23.
[53] Ibid.

nant.[54] A more balanced interpretation is offered by Packer, who suggests that Sibbes is in essential agreement with Thomas Brooks, Thomas Goodwin, and John Owen. According to Packer, these men represent the best of Puritan thought on the subject of the Spirit and assurance, when in the course of their writing,

> They take the text [Rom. 8:16] as referring to two distinct modes of witness, the first being inferential . . . and the second being that of the Spirit testifying, no longer indirectly, but immediately and intuitively; not merely by prompting us to infer our adoption, but by what Goodwin calls an "overpowering light" whereby he bears direct witness to the Christian of God's everlasting love to him, of his election, and his sonship, and his inheritance.[55]

The Spirit's testimony—whether direct or indirect—was subjective in nature. However, the Spirit's testimony was not the exclusive basis for assurance. The promises of the Word of God also functioned as a basis for assurance, one which the rational mind could appeal to. Such an appeal to the subjective and to the objective simultaneously did not present a situation that was contradictory, but rather one that was complementary:

> Because they speak of an operation of the Spirit within human reason, it is possible to present the Puritans as either anti-intellectual or rationalistic. Thus, we find Thomas Brooks saying that "reason's arm is too short to reach this jewel of assurance." Yet John Preston asserts that "there is no grace that any man hath, but it passeth in through the understanding." There is no conflict here. Rather, the Puritans regard reason,

[54] Miller, *The New England Mind: The Seventeenth Century*, 388–89; for a similar view see von Rohr, "Covenant and Assurance in Early English Puritanism," 195–203.

[55] Packer, *A Quest for Godliness*, 184.

> though helpless on its own, as a ready instrument by which the Spirit may, across time and through experience, establish an assured faith.[56]

The subjectivity of the Spirit and the objectivity of the Word, then, are complementary because the latter functions as the instrument of the former. Packer, referring to Goodwin's doctrine, concurs:

> The Spirit witnesses to the truth of the Word of God and its application to the individual. In creating faith, he convinces the sinner that the conditional promises of the gospel are held out by God to him . . . and prompts him to make the appropriate response, i.e., to trust. In giving assurance, he convinces the Christian that the absolute promises of Scripture include him in their scope . . . and moves him to make the appropriate response, i.e., to rejoice.[57]

In short, "the Spirit applies words and thoughts of Scripture to the heart so powerfully and authoritatively that the believer is left in no doubt that they are being spoken by God to him."[58]

In addition to the testimony of the Spirit and the Word of God, the Puritans were convinced that the Scriptures attested to a third basis of assurance: the evidence of sanctification within the professing believer. True Christians give evidence of conversion in the form of holy dispositions, words, and actions. This third element, though objective in nature, was notoriously difficult to interpret. Self-deception could distort one's interpretation of the evidence. Certain attitudes and behaviors might prove to be, upon close inspection, inconclusive for ascertaining the holiness that attended conversion.

[56] Hawkes, "The Logic of Assurance in English Puritan Theology," 255. This quotation cites Thomas Brooks, *Heaven on Earth*, 109; John Preston, *The New Covenant or Saints Portion* (London, 1630), 451.

[57] Packer, *A Quest for Godliness*, 185.

[58] Ibid.

But self-deception was not inevitable. Safety from this danger was found in the testimony of the Spirit and the Word. These served as the frame of reference by which the claims of a changed life could be introduced as reliable evidence into the court of conscience.[59]

For the Puritans, the Spirit, the Word, and sanctification worked in unison by means of an interdependent relationship. The Word stimulates sanctification; and in a "living spiral of assurance," sanctification appeals to the Word for authenticity so that "the reflective act combines the internal evidence of a Christian with the infallible revelation of Scripture to arrive at a full assurance. Thus, the Christian spirals upward in a knowledge of God, turning from Scripture to endeavor, from endeavor back to a scriptural evaluation."[60] And both the Word and the evidences of sanctification are authenticated by the testimony of the Spirit. Thus, in the Puritan perspective, the three grounds of assurance did not compete, nor contradict, but cohered into a unified, consistent, and reliable ground of assurance.[61]

Distinct Features in the Puritan Appropriation of Christian Assurance

All of the theological substance behind the doctrine—the nature, meaning, extent, and basis of assurance—culminated in practical implementation. Such was the objective of all Puritan theology. The question of how the believer was to practically pursue and obtain assurance reduced to two basic components. One component involved

[59] This relationship between the Spirit, the Word, and sanctification points to a priority of the Spirit and the Word, given that the Spirit and the Word served as both the cause of sanctification and the measure of its authenticity. Similarly, it may be argued that the relationship between the Spirit and the Word points to a priority of the Spirit, given that the Spirit (as agent) is the source of the Word, as well as the agent who employs the Word (as instrument).

[60] Hawkes, "The Logic of Assurance in English Puritan Theology," 256, 258.

[61] Beeke, "The Assurance Debate," 280–81.

the use of reason by way of syllogism so that the rational nature of truth might unfold in such a way as to instruct and comfort the troubled conscience. A second component involved an examination of the history of events which preceded the time of supposed conversion. A series of events which were of a certain kind and order were considered holy preparation by the Spirit of God for authentic conversion and were considered to be in and of themselves a mark of true conversion. These two exercises—examination by syllogism and examination of preparation—were means by which the doubting soul could receive assurance.

The Use of Syllogism

The Puritans employed syllogistic reasoning as the instrument by which one could reliably demonstrate the relationship between the propositions of Scripture and the self. The syllogism enabled questions regarding the witness of the Spirit, the promises of Scripture, and the reality of sanctification to find answers grounded, at least in part, outside one's own personal senses. The promises of Scripture served as this basis, and Scripture's reliability proceeded from the very faithfulness of its Divine Author. Confidence in Scripture was thus reckoned as confidence in God Himself.[62]

The Puritans' use of the syllogism for cultivating assurance brought the authority of the Word of God to bear on the reality of the evidences of sanctification. The value of this usage was that it established a trustworthy arbiter for determining whether or not such evidences were produced by the Spirit of God and should be taken as His witness. Beeke suggests the following example as typical of the Puritan approach:

[62] Beeke, "The Assurance Debate," 271–72; Hawkes, "The Logic of Assurance in English Puritan Theology," 254–55.

> *Major premise*: According to Scripture, only those who possess saving faith will receive the Spirit's testimony that their lives manifest the fruits of sanctification and good works.
>
> *Minor premise*: I cannot deny that by the grace of God I have received the Spirit's testimony that I manifest the fruits of sanctification and good works.
>
> *Conclusion*: I am a partaker of saving faith.[63]

Use of the formal syllogism was applied to both the outward evidences of grace and the inward evidences of grace. The former, a practical syllogism, worked in conjunction with those passages of Scripture, such as those contained in 1 John and James, which link true regeneration with outward manifestations of holiness. The latter, a mystical syllogism, pointed the conscience to biblical texts which relate authentic salvation to a substantive internal change of attitudes, dispositions, and affections. Both forms are clearly expressed in the Westminster Confession (16.2 and 18.2 respectively).[64]

Beeke's discussion on this subject of syllogistic usage becomes especially pertinent to the examination of Edwards's doctrine with the following observation:

> By the 1640's, Puritans were using both mystical syllogisms and practical syllogisms. Consequently, mid-seventeenth-century Puritan preachers often answered the question "How do I know whether or not I am a believer?" by offering a combination of signs containing the good works of the practical syllogism as well as the inward evidences of grace of the mystical syllogism. For example . . . Burgess delivers eight messages on the true signs of grace and fifteen on the false signs of grace. True signs include obedience, sincerity, opposition

[63] Beeke, *The Assurance Debate*, 274.
[64] Ibid., 273–75.

> against and abstinence from sin, openness to divine examination, growth in grace, spiritual performance of duties, and love to the godly. Signs that fall short of saving grace include outward church privileges; spiritual gifts; affections of the heart in holy things; judgments and opinions about spiritual truth; great sufferings for Christ; strictness in religion; zeal in false worship; external obedience to the law of God; belief in the truths of religion; a peaceable frame of heart and a persuasion of God's love; outward success; prosperity and greatness in the world; and an abandonment of gross sins.[65]

The sign, then, is an instrument for implementing the syllogism. Edwards's use of signs, both positive and negative, will play a significant role in his approach to assurance, first in "Distinguishing Marks," and then in *Religious Affections*.[66]

The Use of Preparation

In addition to the use of the syllogism, which concerned evidences of grace following conversion, the Puritans also appealed to personal experiences preceding conversion. Such experiences were

[65] Ibid., 275–76.

[66] It is important to observe that the use of the syllogism, which involved a cyclical relationship between the Word and the life, between faith and works, is that very feature which has been the occasion for so much criticism. For the Puritans, this cycle was a logical spiral upwards, sustained by the grace of God, to the end of accomplishing a glorious end for the believer. For critics of the Puritan way, this cycle was a tyrant, a downward vicious spiral entrapping those who embraced its twisted logic. See Hawkes, "The Logic of Assurance in English Puritan Theology," 253, 256–61. Hawkes cites Miller as representative of the critical opinion: "Perry Miller, in a statement which may be equally applied to all of Puritanism, echoes the complaint of four centuries when he asserts the Puritan theology 'devolves upon man the responsibility for fulfilling moral terms in return for irresistible grace.' Miller presents Puritan logic as illogic: if God saves, why do the Puritans bother us with obedience?" Ibid., 253; citation of Miller from *The New England Mind: The Seventeenth Century*, 391.

regarded as the preparatory work of the Spirit and as valuable evidence because they themselves could be assessed. If the character and order of these experiences proved to be of a divine character, then the conversion experience in question could also be considered to be authentic.

The Puritan practice of examining the preparatory experiences had its origins in the importance attached to the *ordo salutis*. This delineation of the doctrine of salvation concerned ultimate and proximate cause-and-effect relationships, which in turn had implications for assurance. To the degree the nature of the cause was certain, the effect could be considered certain. Since the matter of certainty was the currency that Christian assurance traded in, the relationship between the *ordo salutis* and Christian assurance seemed natural.

The number, order, and nature of each aspect of salvation along with the relationship that each sustained to one another was the subject of intense debate in the late 16th and early 17th centuries. The Protestant scholastics, leaning on Ramist logic, developed increasingly complex models of the *ordo salutis*. William Perkins supplied a chart to accompany his version of the order of salvation (the "golden chaine"), without which his description bordered on the incomprehensible.[67]

All of these details regarding number, order, and nature were highly significant to the assurance discussion. When the framers of Dort (1618) committed to a theology that saw God as the ultimate cause, the certainty that proceeded from God's character was imputed to the rest of the order of salvation.[68] Since the aspects of salvation functioned in a logical (even causal) relationship, two conclusions could be drawn concerning assurance. First, God's sovereignty in the decree of election brought certainty to the success of the entire sequence of salvation. Second, the very fact that salvation entailed a sequence meant that each built upon the other, meaning that authen-

[67] Felicity Heal, *Reformation in Britain and Ireland* (Oxford: Oxford University, 2003), 342–44.

[68] Ibid., 342.

tic salvation not only had to include all the pieces of the sequence, but that each piece had to follow another in the proper order.

Because the *ordo salutis* was a sequential explanation, it was natural to refer to its practical aspects in terms of "steps." The steps not only attributed to God his causation of salvation aspects, but it also explained how man's responses related to God's sovereign workings. It is not difficult, then, to see the close proximity among the ideas of sequence, salvation, and assurance. God's sovereign causation of these steps was, for the Puritans, his means of preparing the soul for conversion. Since God's means and God's ends attended one another, one could safely conclude that the presence of one signaled the presence of the other.[69]

Consequently, the *ordo salutis* evolved into a primary instrument for ascertaining the true state of one's soul. The urgent need for assurance in the Puritan community placed pressure on its pastors to refine their exposition of the order of salvation, as Stoever explains:

Because the question of assurance was an urgent one for the Puritans, they devoted much space to delineating steps toward, and degrees of, rebirth, which steps and degrees might be experienced in time. These gradations, however, insofar as they belong to a coherent scheme, were not understood necessarily or primarily as a temporal sequence. Puritan discussion of "stages" and "morphology of conversion" (in the idiom of modern interpretation), while exceedingly useful in preaching, pastoral care, and personal devotion, was chiefly a description of an order of causes and only secondarily of a series of historical events.[70]

Moreover, as Puritanism matured, its view and its use of the *ordo salutis* became increasingly sophisticated. The *ordo salutis* began as a model that was basic in form, closely tied to biblically defined categories and causes and reflective of the logical order of God's decrees. It evolved into complicated sub-steps, developed ties with experiential

[69] Stoever, *'A Faire and Easie Way to Heaven,'* 123–26.
[70] Ibid. 124–25.

causes, and increasingly reflected temporal order rather than logical order.[71] Furthermore, earlier exponents of preparatory steps were reluctant to embrace preparatory steps in any dogmatic form since "it was evident from pastoral experience that the marks of regeneration were rarely all together and were not likely to be experienced always in the same order."[72] However, the later Puritans, in addition to introducing complexity, experience, and temporal elements, became increasingly dogmatic concerning the model's necessary place in obtaining assurance.

Why did the later Puritans lean on the *ordo salutis* so heavily as to freight it with preparatory steps that were experiential, temporal, and uniform for all conversions? In short, the later generations of Puritans were alarmed at the lack of piety and the rise of antinomianism in the holy community. True conversion was at the heart of Puritanism, and preparatory steps provided the means for objectifying whether or not a profession of faith was authentic. By appealing to the preparatory steps, false professions were more easily exposed. True conversion would be further promoted and the cause of the holy community upheld.[73] Here we see a phenomenon that recurs in the context of *Religious Affections*: the effort to comprehend and to influence the spiritual state of the community by comprehending and influencing the spiritual state of the individual.

[71] Ibid.

[72] Ibid., 125.

[73] This development of preparationism, essentially an American phenomenon, is most thoroughly addressed in Norman Pettit, *The Heart Prepared: Grace and Conversion in the Puritan Life* (New Haven: Yale, 1966). The second half of this volume narrates the Puritan dilemma in terms of the role preparationism played and how its rigid use for preserving ecclesiastical purity contributed to the tensions that led to the Half-Way Covenant as well as to Solomon Stoddard's reversal of communion standards. See also Stoever, '*A Faire and Easie Way to Heaven*,' 193.

Approaches to Preparation

Most Puritan theologians on both sides of the Atlantic agreed that some form of soul preparation necessarily preceded a genuine conversion experience.[74] Preparation of the soul for conversion was more than simply a matter of spiritual counsel; it was part of the truth of the gospel inasmuch as it hung on the implications of the doctrine of total depravity. But what this preparation consisted of was a matter of debate. As in many a theological disagreement, the matter hinged on how one viewed the tension between divine sovereignty and human responsibility.

Passive Preparation. Conversion was considered by many Puritans to be a matter that required passivity, not activity.[75] The doctrine of total depravity meant that man could do absolutely nothing to bring about his own conversion.[76] Rather, he was to wait for the effectual call of God to bring about his conversion.[77] The Puritans believed that a mark of a person under the convicting hand of God was his cry, "What must I do to be saved?"[78] Yet they would not simply reply "Believe in the Lord Jesus Christ, and thou shalt be saved." Perry Miller, speaking of John Cotton, illustrates:

> He believed it obvious that the gulf between nature and grace is absolute: "A man is passive in his Regeneration, as in his

[74] The doctrine of preparation can be traced to the earliest stages of covenant theology. "A large portion of the Reformed community" was convinced that the nature of the covenant was such that children who were consecrated to its community were to be assumed as elect until proven otherwise. "This view of covenant children clearly helped produce Puritan preparation for regeneration." This preparation was deemed necessary because "the distinction between regenerate and unregenerate covenant children was almost totally obscured." John H. Gerstner and Jonathan Neil Gerstner, "Edwardsian Preparation for Salvation," *Westminster Theological Journal* 42:1 (Fall 1979): 7.

[75] Simpson, *Puritanism in Old and New England*, 4.

[76] Miller, *The New England Mind: The Seventeenth Century*, 17.

[77] Simpson, *Puritanism in Old and New England*, 27.

[78] Ibid., 3.

> first generation." Only when the spirit has burned up, "root and branch," our legal righteousness are we "fit for any duty." There might be something called a "saving preparation," but as Pemble has said, this was not an antecedent but a consequence, and "for our first union, there are no steps to the Altar." "Drowsie hearts" do not open upon the knocking of Christ "unless he be pleased to put the finger of his spirit into our hearts, to open an entrance for himselfe." A blind man cannot prepare to see, and the supreme refinement of false faith is the self-induced resolution to stand ready: "Here is still the old roote of Adam left alive in us, whereby men seek to establish their own righteousness."[79]

Though they certainly affirmed that the call to "believe on the Lord Jesus Christ" was the call to salvation, they could not conceive of salvation being granted by God in response to a "decision." A sinner was simply not able to make a decision for Christ. The depraved condition of man rendered him incapable of responding.[80] But when God sovereignly regenerated him, he would necessarily believe by virtue of his new life. This, in the logic of the Puritan mind, eliminated the need for the call to believe: man's total depravity made such a call irrelevant, and God's effectual call made it unnecessary.[81]

Active Preparation. Thomas Hooker disagreed with passivity in preparation, contending that depravity did not mean that the sinner

[79] Perry Miller, *The New England Mind: From Colony to Province* (Boston: Beacon, 1953), 58.

[80] Thomas Goodwin considered the conversion experience to be one in which a person "is completely passive, for this is a Divine power exerted on a soul which is incapable of helping itself." Simpson, *Puritanism in Old and New England*, 4–5.

[81] So passive is this view of preparation than some historians have interpreted this view as a stance against preparation. Morgan associates Edwards with this passive view. See Edmund S. Morgan, *The Puritan Dilemma*, ed. Oscar Handlin (Boston: Little, Brown, and Co., 1958), 136–37.

could do nothing on his own behalf or was free of responsibility.[82] Speaking of self-preparation,[83] Hooker asserted, "Undoubtedly that soule which hath this worke upon it, shall have faith poured into it."[84] To the person desiring conversion, Hooker replied with the following:

> If you ever thinke to share in the salvation that Christ hath purchased . . . if you would have him dwell with you, and doe good to you, either prepare for him, or else never expect him . . . Christ is marvellous ready to come, only he watcheth the time till your heart be ready to receive and entertaine him . . . If the whole soul be broken and humbled, he will come presently.[85]

To engage in preparation meant to put one's self "in an attitude of receptivity" so that he would not "turn down the covenant when it seem[ed] to be offered to him."[86] This attitude adjustment is what Nathaniel Vincent apparently had in mind when he offered "some directions as to how to become sincere converts."[87] These directions included reflection on one's own sins, the justice of hell, "the vanity of former excuses," forsaking evil company, attending to preaching, and

[82] Miller, *Errand Into the Wilderness*, 87n154. On the other side of the Atlantic, Stephen Charnock concurred, calling seekers to anticipate the sovereign work of God by pursuing every possible means for the preparation of their hearts. Stephen Charnock, *The Doctrine of Regeneration*, (1840; repr., Grand Rapids: Baker, 1980), 210–14.

[83] Thomas Hooker and John Cotton, though divergent on their views of preparation, are considered to be the two individuals most influential in transplanting the doctrine to New England. Gerstner and Gerstner, "Edwardsian Preparation for Salvation," 9.

[84] Thomas Hooker, *The Soules Preparation* (London, 1632), 155, in Miller, *Errand Into the Wilderness*, 87n154.

[85] Thomas Hooker, *The Soules Implantation* (London, 1637), 47, in Miller, *Errand Into the Wilderness*, 87n154.

[86] Miller, *Errand Into the Wilderness*, 87.

[87] Nathaniel Vincent, "The Conversion of a Sinner," in *The Puritans on Conversion*, ed. Don Kistler (Ligonier, PA: Soli Deo Gloria, 1990), 157.

readiness to obey the conviction of the Holy Spirit. Only then would the soul be ready to "lay hold upon and plead the Lord's covenant" in expectancy of the Lord's sovereign regenerating work.[88] Preparation also included self-examination on a daily basis (comparing the state of one's soul with the evidences of conversion),[89] exposure to preaching, the influence of godly people, and even the Lord's Table.[90]

Fear of self-deception among professing believers justified the development of preparation and its increasing sophistication. The practical value was irresistible as it served to enhance discernment among the New England clergy as they dealt with troubled souls in their congregations. By employing the powers of observation and the powers of induction so prized by the Enlightenment mind, pastors could detect patterns which, they concluded, were reliable indicators for identifying a genuine conversion. The doctrine of preparation, in its active sense, became increasingly defined. In some circles, preparation for conversion involved particular steps and even particular steps in a particular order.

[88] Ibid., 157–63.

[89] Miller, *The New England Mind: The Seventeenth Century*, 53.

[90] Admittance of unbelievers to the Lord's Table was advocated (to the extreme disapproval of his contemporaries) by Edwards's grandfather and predecessor in Northampton, Solomon Stoddard. Stoddard was motivated by evangelistic zeal, being convinced that the ordinance was a means by which the sinner could be prepared for conversion. Marsden, *Jonathan Edwards*, 122–23.

2

Edwards's Quest for True Religion

In addition to the larger context of Puritanism, the immediate context of Edwards's conversion and assurance supplies an important element for understanding his theology of assurance in *Religious Affections*. As a final component of historical context, the occasion for the writing of *Religious Affections* will be integrated into this study. These layers of historical context will properly position us to understand how and why *Religious Affections* articulates the doctrine of assurance in the way that it does.

Edwards's Difficult Path to Assurance

The fact that Edwards wrote so directly and so passionately concerning the assurance of the believer is cast in a new light when the biographical element is introduced. The agonizing journey to find his own assurance left an indelible imprint on Edwards, one that would impact him for the rest of his life and one that arguably imprinted his theology of assurance.

The Gospel According to Timothy Edwards

Jonathan's father, Timothy Edwards, preached the gospel in the old Puritan form: the good news of salvation in Christ came to the individual sinner by the sovereign electing work of God; man in his inability was utterly helpless to effect his own salvation. The appropriate path for the sinner who would be saved was to adopt an attitude of passivity, to engage in preparation of the heart, and to begin a journey down the path of holiness while awaiting the sovereignly bestowed conversion experience. While the sinner was incapable of saving himself, he was, on account of his own depravity, quite capable of deceiving himself. Deeply concerned about the possibility of self-deception, Timothy would acknowledge no profession of conversion without attending and persevering evidences.[1]

Timothy Edwards valued the empirical evidence that preparationism supplied and the assistance that it provided to the minister of the gospel whose business it was to shepherd souls into eternal life. The doctrine was both a prescription to those desiring salvation as well as an instrument for measuring it.[2] His own view of preparation was well-defined but simple and involved a three-step process of conversion, one which was fairly typical of the Puritan divines. First, the sinner must come under "conviction," which meant a sense of eternity and one's unpreparedness for it. The second step was humiliation: "Normally, following the first enthusiasm of their awakening, they would experience a backsliding into sin that would lead them to realize the terribleness of their sins and that God would be entirely just in condemning them to hell.[3] Sometimes this stage was described as involving a sense of 'terror.'"[4]

The final step was God's sovereign regenerating work, an experience of illumination of the soul with genuine faith and repentance bringing about a radical change of life.[5] Timothy applied these steps to each of his parishioners as he carefully considered their spiritual

[1] George M. Marsden, *Jonathan Edwards: A Life* (New Haven: Yale, 2003), 28.

[2] Ibid., 26.

[3] Making reference to the step of terrors, Marsden notes that "Puritan authors offered many complex lists of steps, and Timothy's standard was relatively flexible and simple in emphasizing only three essential steps—but he does seem to have insisted on these, particularly this one." *Jonathan Edwards*, 27–28.

[4] Ibid., 27.

[5] Ibid., 28.

condition, even keeping written records on each concerning evidences of their spiritual condition.[6] Undoubtedly, Timothy was intensely concerned for and attentive to the spiritual condition of his son.

Jonathan Edwards's Account of Assurance Problems

Jonathan was as concerned for his own soul as his father could have wished for him to be. Reflecting upon the regular exhortations of his father Timothy, he was for several years tormented with the thought of being deceived concerning the state of his soul. Following the advice of his father, he subjected himself to the most rigorous self-examination. Local revivals in his home town of East Windsor impacted him greatly at the age of nine and again at the age of twelve.[7] Yet he made no profession during either of these times since the very act of profession was considered inappropriate if it occurred prior to the steps of preparation and the appearance of the persevering fruit of holiness. Consequently, Edwards would not reckon either of these two spiritual events as the time of his conversion.

The defining moment came during his senior year at Yale and the first year of his M.A. degree, the years being 1720–21.[8] A spiritual struggle took place which, according to Edwards, was different than the others and the one that culminated in his conversion:

> Indeed, I was at some times very uneasy, especially towards the latter part of the time of my being at college. Till it pleased God, in my last year at college, at a time when I was in the midst of many uneasy thoughts about the state of my

[6] Ibid., 26.

[7] Sereno Edwards Dwight, "Memoirs of Jonathan Edwards," in *The Works of Jonathan Edwards*, ed. Edward Hickman (1834; repr., Edinburgh: Banner of Truth, 2005), 1:liv; Iain H. Murray, *Jonathan Edwards: A New Biography* (Edinburgh: Banner of Truth, 1987), 19.

[8] Murray, *Jonathan Edwards*, 32–37; Kenneth P. Minkema, "A Chronology of Edwards' Life and Writings," The Jonathan Edwards Center, accessed April 5, 2016, http://edwards.yale.edu/research/ chronology.

> soul, to seize me with a pleurisy; in which he brought me nigh to the grave, and shook me over the pit of hell.
>
> But yet, it was not long after my recovery, before I fell again into my old ways of sin. But God would not suffer me to go on with any quietness; but I had great and violent inward struggles: till after many conflicts with wicked inclinations, and repeated resolutions, and bonds that I laid myself under by a kind of vows to God, I was brought wholly to break off all former wicked ways, and all ways of known outward sin; and to apply myself to seek my salvation, and practice the duties of religion: but without that kind of affection and delight, that I had formerly experienced. My concern now wrought more by inward struggles and conflicts, and self-reflections. I made seeking my salvation the main business of my life. But yet it seems to me, I sought after a miserable manner: which has made me sometimes since to question, whether ever it issued in that which was saving; being ready to doubt, whether such miserable seeking was ever succeeded. But yet I was brought to seek salvation, in a manner that I never was before. I felt a spirit to part with all things in the world, for an interest in Christ. My concern continued and prevailed, with many exercising things and inward struggles; but it never seemed to be proper to express my concern that I had, by the name of terror.[9]

These observations, contained in his "Personal Narrative," were made almost twenty years after the fact.[10] At the time, however,

[9] Jonathan Edwards, "Personal Narrative," in *Letters and Personal Writings*, ed. George S. Claghorn, The Works of Jonathan Edwards, vol. 16 (New Haven: Yale, 1998), 791.

[10] The manuscript for Edwards's "Personal Narrative" is not extant; Claghorn establishes this time frame by referencing the testimony of Samuel Hopkins, who originally published the account in 1765, and comparing this

Edwards was not confident that this new spiritual experience was indeed true conversion. He reveals this in a spiritual diary which he began in December of 1722 and maintained sporadically another for three years. The very first entry discloses his lack of assurance and the reasons for it:

> Dec. 18. This day made the 35th Resolution. The reason why I in the least question my interest in God's love and favor, is, 1. Because I cannot speak so fully to my experience of that preparatory work, of which divines speak: 2. I do not remember that I experienced regeneration, exactly in those steps, in which divines say it is generally wrought: 3. I do not feel the Christian graces sensibly enough, particularly faith. I fear they are only hypocritical outside affections, which wicked men may feel as well as others. They do not seem so sufficiently inward, full, sincere, entire, and hearty. They do not seem so substantial, and so wrought in my very nature, as I could wish. 4. Because I am sometimes guilty of sins of omission or commission.[11]

Furthermore, the issue of preparation and the order in which that work was supposed to have occurred headed the list of those

---

to a letter from Aaron Burr to Edwards in March of 1741, which suggests that the "Personal Narrative" may have originally been contained in a letter to Burr. Burr exclaimed, "I desire to bless God that he inclined you to write and especially to write so freely of your own experiences; I think it has been much blessed to my spiritual good. Though I have often heard and read of others' experiences, I never [met] with'm anything that had the like effect upon me. It came in a most seasonable time, and was the means of clearing up several things that I was in the dark about." See George S. Claghorn, "Introduction to Personal Writings," in *Letters and Personal Writings*, ed. George S. Claghorn, The Works of Jonathan Edwards, vol. 16 (New Haven: Yale, 1998), 747.

[11] Jonathan Edwards, "Diary," in *Letters and Personal Writings*, ed. George S. Claghorn, The Works of Jonathan Edwards, vol. 16 (New Haven: Yale, 1998), 759.

items that occasioned the doubting. This lack of evidence produced doubt that persisted into the following year. His journal entry on August 12, 1723 bears this out:

> Monday morning, Aug. 12. The chief thing, that now makes me in any measure to question my good estate, is my not having experienced conversion in those particular steps, wherein the people of New England, and anciently the dissenters of Old England, used to experience it. Wherefore, now resolved, never to leave searching, till I have satisfyingly found out the very bottom and foundation, the real reason, why they used to be converted in those steps.[12]

Marsden speculates that it was this issue of preparatory steps that became a source of open contention between Jonathan and his father Timothy. The evidence is compelling, even if circumstantial. First, Edwards was living with his parents in that summer of 1723, having completed brief pastoral service in New York City earlier that April. Second, Jonathan's spiritual experience was such that Timothy in all probability would have denied Jonathan the privileges attending communicant status, namely, participation in the Lord's Supper.[13] Third, Edwards, the day after making the August 12 entry in his journal (see above), confessed in his August 13 entry a sin against his parents, the need to study the Bible more thoroughly, and his duty to be submissive to the authority God had ordained over him.[14]

[12] Ibid., 16:779.

[13] Marsden, *Jonathan Edwards*, 55–58. The likelihood of Timothy enforcing such a stringent standard upon is own son is reinforced by earlier family history: Timothy's own wife Esther dared not present herself as qualified for communicant status until she was 44. Esther had endured years of internal struggle before being sufficiently assured that her conversion experience met the standard which was required for making a profession of faith and receiving the Lord's Table. See Murray, *Jonathan Edwards*, 9–10, 19.

[14] Marsden, *Jonathan Edwards*, 56.

Journal entries that follow indicate that he continued wrestling with his assurance for some time afterward. One of his last entries, May 28, 1725, shows that the issue remained unsettled:

> Friday, May 28. It seems to me, that whether I am converted or not, I am so settled in the state I am in, that I shall go on in it all my life. But, however settled I may be, yet I will continue to pray to God, not to suffer me to be deceived about it, nor to sleep in an unsafe condition; and ever and anon, will call all into question and try myself, using for helps some of our old divines, that God may have opportunities to answer my prayers, and the Spirit of God to show me my error, if I am in one.[15]

Judging by this series of journal entries, it would seem that Edwards did not attain assurance of salvation at a particular point in time. If this is indeed the case, his assurance came gradually as the doctrine of preparation was checked by the doctrine of perseverance.[16] On this interpretation, Edwards could identify in some measure with those who found the attainment of assurance so difficult that "many, even those who preached the gospel for years, died in despair, spending the final months agonizing over the process of repentance and assurance."[17]

Jonathan Edwards's Account of Conversion and Assurance

However, evidence does intimate that Edwards did attain assurance at a time, or at least in a season of life, which he could objectively

[15] Edwards, "Diary," WJE 16:788.

[16] Edwards's willingness to reject the doctrine of his father as an unbiblical position was a glimpse of things to come. His revered grandfather Solomon Stoddard had established a policy—opposite of Jonathan's father—of open communion in Northampton, a doctrine which Jonathan would also reject as unbiblical. See Marsden, *Jonathan Edwards*, 352.

[17] David S. Dockery, "Review of *The American Pietism of Cotton Mather* by Richard F. Lovelace," *Grace Theological Journal* 2, 2 (Fall 1981): 343.

point toward. Once again, his "Personal Narrative" fills in the gap. In the paragraphs which immediately follow the one in which he "was brought to seek salvation" he makes reference to a sequence of experiences: First, "I remember the time very well, when I seemed to be convinced, and fully satisfied, as to this sovereignty of God, and his justice in thus eternally disposing of men, according to his sovereign pleasure."[18] The testimony continues by emphasizing the contrast between this persuasion and his former objection to God's sovereignty, coupled with the observation that he was never able to ascertain the means that brought him to this persuasion.

Second, he recalls,

> The first that I remember that ever I found anything of that sort of inward, sweet delight in God and divine things, that I have lived much in since, was on reading those words, 1 Tim. 1:17, "Now unto the King eternal, immortal, invisible, the only wise God, be honor and glory forever and ever, Amen." As I read the words, there came into my soul, and was as there were diffused through it, a sense of the glory of the divine being; a new sense, quite different from anything I had ever experienced before.[19]

He notes, however, that at the time, he did not believe "that there was anything spiritual, or of a saving nature in this."[20] Yet he places this event within the series of experiences which, twenty years later, he ascribes to his conversion experience. The third item in the series also makes reference to this same general period: "From about that time, I began to have a new kind of apprehensions and ideas of Christ, and the work of redemption, and the glorious way of salvation by him."[21] He elaborates on this by describing once again his new

[18] Edwards, "Personal Narrative," WJE 16:792.
[19] Ibid.
[20] Ibid., 16:793.
[21] Ibid.

"sense," his new engagement in meditation upon and reading of the things of Christ, and the great pleasure that he experienced in these things.

At this point in the narrative, Edwards pauses to observe, "Not long after I began to experience these things, I gave an account to my father."[22] The significance of this accounting cannot be underestimated. Given what is known of Timothy Edwards, very likely, Jonathan regarded his father's judgment in matters of salvation to be uncompromising. The outcome of that conversation was that Jonathan was "pretty much affected by the discourse we had together."[23] Although this statement sounds inconclusive, the context suggests that Edwards's testimony to his father served to confirm, rather than invalidate, the authenticity of his experiences. Edwards returns to the narrative, explaining how his "sense of divine things gradually increased,"[24] to the point that he testifies to his assurance: "I felt then a great satisfaction as to my good estate."[25]

Edwards notes that his "sense of divine things seemed gradually to increase, till I went to preach at New York; which was about a year and a half after they began."[26] Edwards moved to New York in August of 1722. Therefore, Edwards's experience of conversion and the growing sense of assurance that attended it, began in the early spring of 1721, at which time Edwards is residing in New Haven and completing the first year of his Master of Arts degree. However, this initial period of assurance would be short-lived; beginning at the end of 1722, Edwards entered yet another period of spiritual turmoil before finally gaining a lasting peace in 1726.[27]

[22] Ibid.
[23] Ibid.
[24] Ibid.
[25] Ibid., 16:794.
[26] Ibid., 16:795.
[27] This will be discussed further in chapter 5.

The Significance of the "Personal Narrative"

Edwards's story of assurance is significant as it gives the reader of *Religious Affections* insight regarding a number of key points. First, Edwards's perspective on assurance matured over time as would be expected. The many years that elapsed between his conversion and the composition of his "Personal Narrative" granted the luxury of retrospect. Free from the emotions of uncertainty in a previous stage of life, seasoned in his theological outlook, and armed with two decades of life and ministry experience, Edwards was better positioned to accurately assess his own spiritual journey.

Second, the "Personal Narrative" suggests that Edwards's theology matured in conjunction with his personal experience. Edwards writes his "Personal Narrative"—his only known written testimony of conversion—in March of 1741, at a time in which the Awakening is nearing its height. Within the next six months, Edwards will preach his famous sermon at Enfield, witness the greatest response to the revival in his own congregation, and deliver the commencement address at Yale entitled "Distinguishing Marks of the Work of the Spirit of God." "Distinguishing Marks" proved to be a prototype for *Religious Affections*, a fact which establishes the conclusion that by 1741, Edwards's understanding of his own salvation experience had matured alongside his understanding of the doctrine of assurance. The significance lies in the coincidence of Edwards's experiential progress and his theological progress; one may infer from such a coincidence that Edwards's theology was shaped by his experience—or vise-versa. If such is the case, this coincidence is a factor which must be accounted for when considering Edwards's theological method.[28]

Third, we may observe that Edwards continued to follow the Puritan pattern of mingling conversion and assurance. As marks of personal change increased, so did assurance. Assurance in his "Personal Narrative" is directly associated with such change by means of

[28] Marsden, *Jonathan Edwards*, 45.

assessing "marks" or signs of genuine spiritual activity within the soul, which is also the case in *Religious Affections*. In short, much of the Puritan assurance theology which Timothy Edwards had taught was adopted by Jonathan.

Fourth, the "Personal Narrative," within its relative brevity, paints a portrait of an authentic conversion and assurance experience by an orderly rehearsal of the means of grace. For some of the changes that he experiences, he confesses that he cannot account for the means. Yet for other changes, he cites the power of Scripture, the confirmation of his father, and the inward experiences and insights into spiritual realities. Conclusively, Edwards associates a variety of means and evidences as relevant pieces in the final assessment of his own spiritual state. This multi-pronged approach to reasoning through the issue of assurance presents itself again in *Religious Affections*.[29]

The Occasion for Religious Affections

The extraordinary events which occurred first in the revival of 1734–35, and to a greater extent in the Great Awakening of 1740–42, have been the subject of extensive discussion and need not be re-

[29] Other interpretations of Edwards's conversion should be noted. Yarbrough and Adams see Edwards's conversion as primarily intellectual: "His conviction apparently did not occur in response to a sermon, biblical reading, or personal experience. It seems not like an 'experience' at all; he describes it as being intellectual, not emotional, in character." Stephen R. Yarbrough and John C. Adams, *Delightful Conviction: Jonathan Edwards and the Rhetoric of Conversion* (Westport, CT: Greenwood, 1993), 6. Marsden also sees Edwards's conversion as an intellectual "breakthrough," but conditioned by a psychological obstacle: "So long as Jonathan's God was substantially a projection of his father or of other human analogies, he could not believe. If God were simply a cosmic version of the greatest imaginable human, God would still be by human standards a capricious and unreasonable tyrant, the father whose love turned out to be petty control, harsh judgments, tenderness mixed with fits of anger, unyielding disciplines, and punishments." Marsden, *Jonathan Edwards*, 42–43.

hearsed here. The events of the Awakening—on the individual level, within the ecclesiastical domain, and on the broad American landscape—were so penetrating in their influence and so comprehensive in their scope that some interpretation was urgently required of the ecclesiastical authorities of the day. The joys of heaven and the fears of hell literally transformed the personal existence of a significant portion of the colonial population. Those who had not been personally affected by the spiritual message found themselves with no choice but to live and to work with those who had been personally affected. Historians of the American experience continue to marvel at the depth to which the Awakening has registered itself on the national conscience in the form of evangelicalism.[30]

Controversy Concerning the Authenticity of the Awakening

The fact that the revivals were attended by unusual, even inexplicable, forms of individual behavior occasioned a controversy as to whether or not the revival was an authentic work of God's Spirit. Unrestrained zeal and "enthusiasm," episodes of fainting and other bodily effects, and a growing distrust between the laity and the ecclesiastical establishment led to a polarization of the populace.

This polarization quickly manifested itself in a quasi-formalization of parties. The "Old Lights" rallied behind the leadership of the articulate Charles Chauncy, who maintained that the Christian faith had been greatly harmed by the superstition which the revivals had ushered in. The "New Lights" were convinced that the extreme outpouring of emotion and zeal was itself proof of the authenticity of the revivals.[31] The controversy was a matter of public

[30] For a brief but thoughtful analysis, see Sydney E. Ahlstrom, *A Religious History of the American People* (New Haven: Yale, 1972), 280–94. For an up-to-date assessment of the Awakening and its aftermath, see Mark A. Noll, *The Rise of Evangelicalism* (Downers Grove, IL: InterVarsity Press, 2003).

[31] See Murray, *Jonathan Edwards*, 203–29; Noll, *The Rise of Evangelicalism*, 129.

discourse by 1742; but by this time, Edwards had already gone public with his own interpretation of the revival.

Edwards's "Faithful Narrative"

Edwards's public comment on the revival began rather unintentionally. A letter in May of 1735 to Rev. Benjamin Coleman of Boston's Brattles Street Church conveyed a report of the revival in Northampton.[32] When Coleman replied with a request for a fuller account, Edwards produced a substantially expanded narrative by November of 1736. Coleman, inspired by the substance of what Edwards had provided, took the liberty to publish it apart from Edwards's knowledge as well as to forward its entirety to Isaac Watts and John Guyse in England. Watts and Guyse in turn proceeded to edit and to publish a London edition in 1737 under the title "A Faithful Narrative of the Surprising Work of God."[33] Though Edwards never intended the work to go public, its content clearly accounted for his own initial reservations as well as the incredulity of those who were critical of the revival. For readers of *Religious Affections*, "A Faithful Narrative" is the first of three important documents that supplies both historical and literary context. "A Faithful Narrative" displays Edwards's interest in interpreting a collective event by

[32] Jonathan Edwards, "Unpublished Letter of May 30, 1735," in *The Great Awakening*, ed. C. C. Goen, The Works of Jonathan Edwards, vol. 4 (New Haven: Yale, 1970), 99–110.

[33] Jonathan Edwards, "A Faithful Narrative of the Surprising Work of God," in *The Great Awakening*, ed. C. C. Goen, The Works of Jonathan Edwards, vol. 4 (New Haven: Yale, 1970). The liberties taken by Coleman presumed upon Edwards's consent. In fact, Coleman's publication introduced Edwards's work as an appendix to a work by his uncle, William Williams, without securing Edwards's permission, an indiscretion that became the occasion of a degree of family tension. Watts and Guyse not only published Edwards's work without permission, but took editorial liberties to such an extent that Edwards felt compelled to produce his own corrected edition in 1738 to set the record straight. See C. C. Goen, "Editor's Introduction," in *The Great Awakening*, ed. C. C. Goen, The Works of Jonathan Edwards, vol. 4 (New Haven: Yale, 1970), 32–46.

the analysis of individual experiences, his "empirical bent of his mind," and his appeal to "the new sense," all of which play a significant role in the argument advanced by *Religious Affections*.[34]

Edwards's "Distinguishing Marks"

The second of the three works leading up to *Religious Affections* is his "Distinguishing Marks of a Work of the Spirit of God." This work, originally prepared as an address for the Yale commencement of September 10, 1741, was intended to directly engage the controversy concerning the authenticity of the Awakening as is evident in its full title.[35] By September of 1741, much had changed since his 1737 composition of "A Faithful Narrative." A second revival was well under way, much greater in depth and scope than the first. Ministers sympathetic to Arminian principles and suspicious of events attending revivals were clearly in Edwards's mind in 1737; but by 1741, this group had coalesced with some distinction to become the "Old Lights." In addition, a radical element—the "New Lights"—had arisen from within the advocates of the Awakening, and the excesses of this element threatened to discredit the entire revival.[36]

In "Distinguishing Marks," the reader observes new elements which manifest themselves in *Religious Affections*. First, Edwards is compelled to address two opponents simultaneously by negotiating a middle course between two.[37] Second, Edwards introduces the idea of

[34] John E. Smith, "Editor's Introduction," in *The Works of Jonathan Edwards*, ed. Perry Miller, vol. 2, *Religious Affections* (New Haven: Yale, 1959), 5.

[35] The full title of the 1st (Boston) edition is "The Distinguishing Marks of a Work of the Spirit of God, Applied to That Uncommon Operation That Has Lately Appeared on the Minds of Many of the People of This Land: With a Particular Consideration of the Extraordinary Circumstances with Which This Work is Attended." Goen, "Editor's Introduction," WJE 4:53, 214.

[36] Ava Chamberlain, "Self-Deception as a Theological Problem in Jonathan Edwards's 'Treatise Concerning Religious Affections,'" *Church History* 63, 4 (December 1994): 541.

[37] Ibid., 541–42.

the "sign" in both positive and negative forms. By use of the positive signs, he nullifies the attempts of the Old Lights to discredit the revival; by use of the negative signs, he tempers the hasty accreditation of the revival on the part of the New Lights.[38] Third, Edwards follows the trajectory established in the "Faithful Narrative" by assessing the value of a corporate event by reducing it to a matter of the individual experience.[39]

Edwards's "Some Thoughts Concerning the Revival"

The third and final prelude to *Religious Affections* followed a year later. Intent on continuing his defense of the Awakening, Edwards writes "Some Thoughts Concerning the Present Revival" (1742) by addressing the revival in general terms rather than focusing on the authenticity of the individual conversion as he did in "Distinguishing Marks." In "Some Thoughts," Edwards introduces new elements for defending the revival, elements which will appear again in mature form in *Religious Affections*. First, Edwards approaches the topic of the revival in its general rather than individualized form. In this approach, he maintains that a general assessment of the revival requires the adoption of proper principles. Opponents of the revival, he argued, had drawn conclusions on the basis of unbiblical principles. As such, they were not only of an incorrect opinion but were standing as an obstruction to the work of God.

Second, Edwards takes the generalist's approach to defining the nature of true religion, which must demonstrate on a corporate level that which is known to be true on the individual level. Therefore, if the fruit of the Spirit is evident on the corporate level, it must speak as to the authenticity of the revival. Third, Edwards makes his first appeal for judging the authenticity of religion on the basis of affections. These three lines of thought make their first appearance in "Some Thoughts Concerning the Present Revival"; Edwards will use

[38] Smith, "Editor's Introduction," WJE 2:6–7.
[39] Chamberlain, "Self-Deception," 545.

these thoughts to launch his definitive defense of the revival in Part One of *Religious Affections*.[40]

Summary

The conversion theology of New England Puritanism is the theological context for Jonathan Edwards and his doctrine of assurance. These contextual pieces are vital to the exploration of Edward's use of theological method in his doctrine of assurance as expressed in *Religious Affections*. Working from the general to the specific, the reader can observe how the conversion of the soul served as the essential idea which propelled Puritanism and how that idea moved the Puritans to give such concentrated attention to the doctrine of assurance. The Puritans were also motivated to develop the doctrine of assurance in order to support the Reformers' doctrine of assurance, to address unresolved problems handed down from the Reformers, and to equip ministers for counseling those who were troubled with a lack of assurance.

The Puritan doctrine of assurance defined the nature of assurance as an experience independent from faith itself. Although some spoke of assurance in reference to certainty regarding the propositions of Scripture, the idea of Christian assurance solidified as a reference to individual certainty regarding one's own elect status. Assurance was not usually an all-or-nothing experience but normally attained by degree. The basis of assurance was a complex of factors involving the testimony of the Holy Spirit, the content of the Word of God, and the experience of sanctification. The Puritans applied this doctrine practically by use of the syllogism and by appeal to the experience of preparation.

Finally, the near historical context—Edwards's own story as well as the ecclesiastical and literary setting—is key to an informed reading of *Religious Affections*. With this spectrum of contextual elements in

[40] Smith, "Editor's Introduction," WJE 2:7–8.

view, several points of reference are now in place for a consideration of Edwards's thought and method.

3

The Question of Edwards's Theological Method

The question of Edwards's theological method has generated significant discussion for several decades. While efforts in this direction have produced little consensus, they have disclosed several challenges. These challenges include the importance of avoiding anachronism, the care required for proper contextualization, the problem of negotiating the variety of understandings for what constitutes *theological method*, and the broad scope of reference entailed in the expression *the theology of Jonathan Edwards*.

This chapter has three objectives: first, to review the difficulties which must be recognized; second, to provide evidence that indicates the entire enterprise of identifying Edwards's theological method is overextended; and third, to suggest an approach to Edwards's theological method that is decentralized and non-prescriptive.

The Challenge of Assessing Theological Method

Two potential problems present themselves upon an investigation of Edwards's theological method. First, as mentioned in chapter one, many have voiced the concern that anachronism has become a problem in the portrayal of Edwards's theology. As a result, efforts to represent Edwards's thought in general are countered with the objection that such generalization is insensitive to the development of his thought.[1]

Second, use of the term *theological method* in current discourse is in such a state of disarray that one is compelled to qualify the term before using it. While there is essential agreement that the term *theological method* refers to the rationale for "doing theology," there is little unanimity as to what the actual meaning and significance of theological method is. Even among evangelicals, who supposedly adhere to some theological common ground, considerable disagreement persists as to how theological method works—or ought to work.

Theologians have suggested a variety of approaches to theological method including models centered upon integration,[2] presupposition,[3] regulated matrix,[4] stratification with a central interpretive motif,[5] community relevance,[6] or the communicative act itself,[7] just to

[1] Rob Boss and Richard Hall, eds., "About JESociety." Jonathan Edwards Society, accessed June 24, 2011, http:// www.jesociety.org/about.

[2] Gordon R. Lewis and Bruce A. Demarest, *Integrative Theology* (Grand Rapids: Zondervan, 1996), 1:21–48. Lewis and Demarest call for a theological method which features the integration of informative sources with apologetic and practical implications.

[3] John M. Frame, *The Doctrine of the Knowledge of God* (Phillipsburg, NJ: Presbyterian and Reformed, 1987). Lewis and Demarest classify presuppositionalists (Cornelius Van Til, Rousas Rushdooney) with "deductive rationalists" (Gordon Clark, Carl Henry) on the basis that their respective methodologies share the same liabilities, particularly their ascription to some form of *a priori* reasoning. See Lewis and Demarest, *Integrative Theology*, 24–25.

[4] D. A. Carson, "Unity and Diversity in the New Testament: The Possibility of Systematic Theology," in *Scripture and Truth*, ed. D. A. Carson and John D. Woodbridge (Grand Rapids: Baker, 1983), 77–93.

[5] Millard Erickson, *Christian Theology*, 2nd ed. (Grand Rapids: Baker, 1998), 70–84; Michael Stallard, "A Proposal for Theological Method: Systematic Theology as Model Building," n.d., *Our Hope*, accessed November 4, 2011, http://faculty.bbc.edu/mstallard/wp-content/uploads/2009/09/Method2.pdf.

[6] Stanley J. Grenz and John R. Franke, *Beyond Foundationalism: Shaping Theology in a Postmodern Context* (Louisville: Westminster John Knox, 2001); Stanley J. Grenz, "Articulating the Christian Belief-Mosaic: Theological Method After the Demise of Foundationalism," in *Evangelical Futures: A*

mention a few. With such a diversity of opinion regarding the nature of theological method in general, it appears from the outset that there is little possibility of a fruitful discussion of Edwards's theological method in particular.

Yet these two challenges are not insurmountable. The challenge of anachronism can be resolved when consideration is given to the diachronic/synchronic issue in historical method. The challenge of defining *theological method* may, in some measure sufficient for understanding Edwards's method, be unraveled by addressing the equivocation in the use of the term.

Resolving the Problem of Anachronism

The problem of anachronism is a part of the larger discussion regarding the merits and demerits of diachronic and synchronic historiography.[8] Diachronic historical studies—studies of history throughout time (rather than within a particular time)—have been variously defined. Diachronic history has been described as the study of the *causal influence* of historical contexts occurring *prior* to the subject.[9] For example, historians assessing the attack on Pearl Harbor have

---

Conversation on Theological Method, ed. John G. Stackhouse (Grand Rapids: Baker, 2000), 107–36.

[7] Kevin J. Vanhoozer, *First Theology* (Downers Grove, IL: InterVarsity, 2002).

[8] Study in terms of *diachronics* and *synchronics* has its origins in the field of linguistics, and specifically in the early twentieth-century work of Ferdinand de Saussure. The diachronic/synchronic distinction has not only assumed a significant place in the study of linguistics but also in other disciplines including biblical, philosophical, political, and historical studies. See Ferdinand de Saussure, *Course in General Linguistics*, trans. Roy Harris (repr., Peru, IL: Open Court, 1983); Moisés Silva, *Biblical Words and Their Meaning*, rev. ed. (Grand Rapids: Zondervan, 1994), 34–38; David Holdcroft, *Saussure: Signs, Systems, and Arbitrariness* (Cambridge: Cambridge University, 1991); Tony Bennett, *Formalism and Marxism*, 3rd ed. (London: Routledge, 2003), 48–51; 56–60; Richard Karl Payne, *Re-Visioning "Kamakura" Buddhism* (Honolulu: University of Hawaii, 1998), 4.

[9] Payne, *Re-Visioning "Kamakura" Buddhism*, 4.

typically tried to interpret the event in terms of causes that precipitated it. A common interpretation is that the events of December 7, 1941 were set into motion by a series of other prior events beginning with the American possession of Manila in 1898. The fault attributed to this form of diachronics is failure to account for contemporaneous contexts influencing this historical subject such as the social, political, economic, and philosophical forces in play at the same time as the subject. Diachronic historiography has also been portrayed as the study of the development of a special historical subject throughout time. An example of this kind of historiography is the history of baseball in America, which typically is presented as a microcosm of America's economic and social problems throughout the 20th century. The liability of this form of diachronic study is the tendency of historians to impose an interpretive framework (such as a central interpretive motif) to bring unity to the interpretation, resulting in distortion.[10]

Synchronic historiography, on the other hand, appears to have a stable definition among historians. Synchronic study is generally understood as historical study based on the complex matrix of contexts contemporaneous with the historical subject.[11] The benefit of this approach is that historical studies which focus on contemporaneous contexts are thoroughly contextualized and—when combined with the results of other synchronic studies—are better suited to demonstrate progression, development, and causation in historical conclusions.[12] Yet synchronic studies are not without potential

[10] James E. Bradley and Richard A. Muller, *Church History: An Introduction to Research, Reference Works, and Methods* (Grand Rapids: Eerdmans, 1995), 29.

[11] Penelope J. Corfield, *The Time and Shape of History* (New Haven: Yale, 2007), xv.; Bradley and Muller, *Church History*, 31–32; Payne, *Re-Visioning "Kamakura" Buddhism*, 4.

[12] For an excellent example of historiography which compares multiple synchronic studies for the purpose of demonstrating progression of thought, see Stephen J. Stein, "Eschatology," in *The Princeton Companion to Jonathan Edwards*, ed. Sang Hyun Lee (Princeton, NJ: Princeton University, 2005),

liability. Synchronic studies may become so focused on influences at the time of the subject that they marginalize the influence the past had on the subject. As a result, this approach may also yield conclusions which are only partially contextualized.

The entire diachronic/synchronic discussion is pertinent, for it relates to the concern of anachronism regarding the study of Jonathan Edwards. Anachronistic historiography entails an historical presentation which collapses evidence from various periods of time and handles such evidence without distinction as if the evidence represented one point in time. The consequence of the anachronistic handling of evidence is the potential for historical conclusions that are oversimplified or distorted. It is this concern that lies behind comments such as the one offered by Stephen Stein: "McDermott's . . . study presents a[n] . . . account of Edwards's public theology, citing texts from early years side by side with those of the mature theologian with little or no recognition of the changing context."[13]

It is possible to respond to the problem of anachronism by insisting that the problem has been overstated by the citation of isolated instances. Stein's concern regarding McDermott may be a case in point: McDermott is accomplished in the field and highly regarded by the guild; his work and peer reviews are a sufficient testimony to his characteristic care in handling Edwards's corpus.[14]

226–42.

[13] Stephen J. Stein, "Review of *One Holy and Happy Society: The Public Theology of Jonathan Edwards* by Gerald R. McDermott," *The William and Mary Quarterly* 51, 1 (January 1994): 144. In this critique, Stein cites McDermott for giving a "synchronic" history. Stein's use of "synchronic" here is in the fallacious sense, and refers to the collapsing of several temporal elements by treating them without distinction, as though they were all informed by the same temporal context and thus effectually synchronizing them.

[14] McDermott's work gives ample evidence of being sensitive to temporal distinctions and contexts. For examples, his *Jonathan Edwards Confronts the Gods: Christian Theology, Enlightenment Religion, and Non-Christian Faiths* (Oxford: Oxford University, 2000), along with his joint work with Michael McClymond, *The Theology of Jonathan Edwards* (Oxford: Oxford University,

Nevertheless, historical anachronism is a real problem and presents a genuine threat to reliable conclusions. For this reason, the best response to anachronism is to consciously adopt both a diachronic and synchronic approach to historiography. By employing both approaches simultaneously, we are able to recognize that both actually depend upon one another to supply the most complete contextual picture. Corfield puts this point succinctly:

> To historians, it is axiomatic that the synchronic is always in the diachronic—in that every short-term moment contributes to a much longer term. And the converse is also true. The diachronic is always in the synchronic—in that long term frameworks always inform the passing moment as well. . . . Together, these different diachronic/synchronic perspectives combine to allow a full view of time, not just as it seems at any split second but also as it operates when the split seconds accumulate massively and inexorably to become millennia.[15]

The best response, then, to the problem of anachronism is the deliberate use of both diachronic and synchronic contexts. For this reason, this study of Edwards's theology endeavors to engage both types of contexts.

Resolving the Equivocation in the Definition of Theological Method

The diversity of opinion regarding theological method should not be regarded as something that precludes a productive discussion on the subject. From the outset, if the category of the method which is in view is stated, a discussion on method can be productive. One approach to theological method conceives of method as doing theology with a view toward a desired outcome. This approach to method has the end in view; it is *prescriptive in nature* and therefore is concerned with how theological statements are warranted in terms of the

2012); see, for example, 77–88.

[15] Corfield, *Time and the Shape of History*, xv.

desired end. As a result, those who discuss method from this vantage point are primarily concerned with *what the method ought to be*. This approach is typical for theologies designed to meet a particular political or sociological agenda.[16] As a consequence, this approach to theological method is a discussion regarding particular means and ends in theology, not a discussion about how theology in general actually works.

However, another approach to theological method exists as one that endeavors to understand theology with a view toward its justification. This approach to method has the starting point in view: it is *descriptive in nature*. Its concern focuses on how theological statements are warranted in terms of a governing principle. Consequently, those who discuss method from this perspective seem to be most concerned with showing how method *inherently functions*, provided that all theological conclusions maintain a given relationship with each of their respective data sources. Whereas the primary goal of prescriptive theological method is to express theology in terms of relevance and applicability, the primary goal of descriptive theological method is to express theology in terms of coherence and certainty. A discussion on theological method that recognizes this categorical watershed enters the conversation with an advance view of the landscape.[17]

[16] See, for example, George A. Lindbeck, *The Nature of Doctrine: Religion and Theology in a Postliberal Age* (Philadelphia: Westminster, 1984); D. F. Pilario, *Back to the Rough Grounds of Praxis* (Leuven, Belgium: Leuven University, 2005); Anselm Kyongsuk Min, *Dialectic of Salvation: Issues in Theology of Liberation* (Albany, NY: State University of New York, 1989); John B. Cobb, *Process Theology as Political Theology* (Philadelphia: Westminster, 1982).

[17] This dichotomy suggests that the fundamental divide occurs along philosophical lines precipitated by the postmodern turn. However, this is a generalization and should not be taken to suggest that modern approaches do not advocate one method over another or that postmodern approaches are in no way descriptive. In some respects, this dichotomy corresponds to the "correlational/anti-correlational" methodological divide described by David Tracy in "An Uneasy Alliance Reconceived: Catholic Theological Method,

The Interpretation of Edwards's Theological Method

An impressive array of scholarship has taken up residence under the banner of "the theology of Jonathan Edwards." The scope of reference for this expression is so broad as to encompass practically any thought or any way of thinking that Edwards might have had. And this is not without justification, for Edwards hardly wrote anything without reference to God in mind. The problem posed by this situation is that "the theology of Jonathan Edwards" is interchangeably used with reference to Edwards's view of a particular biblical subject, Edwards's metaphysical view of reality, Edwards's view of God in general, Edwards's view of some particular subject within God's creation, or the manner in which Edwards formulated any of these views.[18] The purpose of this section is to survey a variety of interpretations and to consider whether or not any of these approaches is reliable.

A Survey of Interpretations of Edwards's Theological Method

It is beyond the purpose of this chapter to provide a thorough overview of opinion on the theological method of Edwards. However, a brief survey of some of the latest and most highly regarded scholars in the field illustrates the variety of opinion concerning Edwards's method and illuminates some common interpretive threads that are worthy of analysis.

Modernity, and Postmodernity," *Theological Studies* 50, 3 (September 1989): 548–70.

[18] Although the term *theological method* has not been in vogue among scholars who analyze the works of Edwards, a number of studies should be classified under this rubric. These studies set out to define what particular feature controls Edwards's theology, and what interpretive key the reader should employ to understand it. The objective of these studies is to discover the essential element in Edwards's theology that brings comprehension, coherence, and purpose to his theological corpus. Therefore, in spite of the absence of the expression *theological method* in most of the studies regarding Edwards's theology, it is appropriate to consider these studies as investigations into his theological method.

William Wainwright proposes that all of Edwards's theology is a philosophical theology ordered around the twin themes of God's sovereignty and the beauty of God's holiness. From these two themes flow a theology driven by metaphysics, value theory (ethics and aesthetics), and epistemology. According to Wainwright, Edwards intended to unite these two themes in what would have been his definitive theological work, *A History of the Work of Redemption.*[19]

Gerald McDermott agrees that Edwards's theology is philosophical in nature but maintains that its distinctive is its apologetical character against deism: "Edwards considered deism to be Christianity's most formidable opponent, and . . . the better part of his theological project was a direct or indirect response to it."[20] In *Jonathan Edwards Confronts the Gods*, McDermott sees Edwards's method as the utilization of four particular tools: reason, revelation, his own revision of *prisca theologia*, and typology.[21] By crafting his theology with these four tools, Edwards was able to leverage the philosophical trends of the day to the advantage of the Christian faith and in opposition to forms of unbelief.

E. Brooks Holifield joins other scholars in the assessment that Edwards was a philosophical theologian but believes that this aspect of his theology has been overstated at the expense of his biblical priorities.[22] Holifield agrees with McDermott that the occasion for

[19] William J. Wainwright, "Jonathan Edwards," *Stanford Encyclopedia of Religion*, ed. Edward N. Zalta, August 2009, Metaphysics Research Lab, Center for the Study of Languages and Information, Stanford University, accessed October 26, 2011, http://plato.stanford.edu/archives/fall2009/entries/edwards.

[20] Gerald R. McDermott, *Jonathan Edwards Confronts the Gods*, 7.

[21] According to McDermott, Edwards's use of *prisca theologia* asserted that all religions possessed remnants of truth passed down from Adam through the post-deluvian fathers and into the various ancient ethnic groups by oral tradition. Edwards's use of typology had its grounding in the Reformed doctrine of general revelation; Edwards saw all of creation as symbolically pointing to God in some manner. See McDermott, *Jonathan Edwards Confronts the Gods*, chapters 5 and 6 respectively.

[22] E. Brooks Holifield, "Edwards as Theologian," in *The Cambridge Com-*

much of Edwards's work was the threat of deism and that Edwards employed—in addition to an array of metaphysical arguments—the combination of revelation, reason, *prisca theologia*, and typology of which McDermott takes note. Yet Holifield believes that the occasion and the apologetic tools were bound together by a central unifying theme—excellency. Holifield makes his case beginning with Edwards's 1723 paper on "The Mind," in which Edwards asserts, "There has nothing been more without a definition than excellency, although it be what we are more concerned with than anything else whatsoever. Yea, we are concerned with nothing else."[23] From here Holifield makes a compelling case that Edwards saw in Scripture and in nature a metaphysical reality in which excellency, harmony, beauty, symmetry, and the like constituted not simply the character of God but the very ontological ground of all reality. Since all reality consisted of both Creator and creation, this theme explained not only God but all that God created for his own ends.[24]

Conrad Cherry's treatment of Edwards's theology is considered a classic and has remained in print since its debut in 1966.[25] In this work, Cherry challenged the secularized interpretation which Perry Miller had established as the prevailing view in the academy at that time. Cherry's interpretation maintains that Edwards's theology was primarily informed by the Bible and his Reformed/Puritan heritage and oriented to serve a soteriological agenda. As such, Cherry's work stands in marked contrast to those interpretations which view Ed-

---

panion to Jonathan Edwards, ed. Stephen J. Stein (New York: Cambridge University, 2007), 145.

[23] Jonathan Edwards, "The Mind," in *Scientific and Philosophical Writings*, ed. Wallace E. Anderson, The Works of Jonathan Edwards, vol. 6 (New Haven: Yale, 1980), 332.

[24] Holifield, "Edwards as Theologian," 144–59; E. Brooks Holifield, *Theology in America* (New Haven: Yale, 2003), 102–26.

[25] Conrad Cherry, *The Theology of Jonathan Edwards: A Reappraisal* (Bloomington, IN: Indiana University, 1966).

wards's theological method as one controlled by epistemological, aesthetic, ethical, or typological themes.[26]

Sang Hyun Lee, in his *Philosophical Theology of Jonathan Edwards*, introduced an entirely new approach to interpreting Edwards.[27] Lee argues that the textual evidence in Edwards's corpus points to "a dispositional ontology, which underlies his reconception of the divine being, [and] is the clue to the originality and unity of Edwards' philosophical theology as a whole." This means that Lee sees "his category of disposition as the interpretive key" to "the dynamic character of the central aspects of Edwards' thought."[28] According to Lee, Edwards dispensed with older philosophical categories, adopted the new Enlightenment models of Newton and Locke, and recast his ontological outlook in terms of *dispositions* or *habits*. Lee shapes this interpretation in such a way that Edwards understands all reality—including God—in dynamic terms. As a consequence, he sees Edwards as a forerunner of contemporary process theologians.[29]

[26] Stephen J. Stein, "Foreword," in *The Theology of Jonathan Edwards: A Reappraisal* (Bloomington, IN: Indiana University, 1990), ix–xvi; Michael J. McClymond, *Encounters with God: An Approach to the Theology of Jonathan Edwards* (New York: Oxford University, 1998), 4.

[27] Sang Hyun Lee, *The Philosophical Theology of Jonathan Edwards* (Princeton, NJ: Princeton University, 1988), 3–14.

[28] Ibid., 4.

[29] Stephen R. Holmes, "Does Jonathan Edwards Use a Dispositional Ontology? A Response to Sang Hyun Lee," in *Jonathan Edwards: Philosophical Theologian*, ed. Paul Helm and Oliver D. Crisp (Burlington, VT: Ashgate, 2003), 99–100. Holmes explains that, in Lee's view, "Edwards rejected the old scholastic account of ontology which divided the being of things into substance and form," and instead saw all existence, first God himself, and then his creation, in terms of habit, law, or disposition. Lee, in arguing that Edwards saw all reality in terms of disposition rather than attribute, conceives Edwards as a progenitor of process theology. John Bombaro, in his recent analysis of Lee's proposition, agrees that Edwards indeed framed his theology in terms of disposition, but not exclusively so, and not at the expense of his rigid Calvinism. In addition to Holmes, see Lee, *The Philosophical Theology of Jonathan Edwards*, 6; John J. Bombaro, *Jonathan Edwards's Vision of Reality: The Relationship of God to the World, Redemptive History, and the Reprobate*,

Stephen Holmes contests Lee's proposition. Although noting that Lee's argument is meticulous and coherent, he dismisses it on the simple charge that it is decontextualized. Holmes argues that Lee's portrayal of Edwards reduces him to a defector of Reformed orthodoxy, but the historical evidence simply bears out the opposite.[30] Holmes believes that a contextually informed interpretation of Edwards should locate theological method in some theme that is theocentric. For this reason, Holmes commends McClymond's interpretation as superior to Lee's and others situated in philosophical categories. Holmes himself suggests that Edwards employed the theme of God's self-glorification as the unifying element in his theology.[31]

Norman Fiering's analysis of Edwards endeavors to capture Edwards's thought in terms of the moral philosophy prevalent in the 18th century.[32] By intersecting Edwards's reasoning with that of Nicholas Malebranche, Fiering attempts to show that Edwards

---

Princeton Theological Monograph Series (Eugene, OR: Pickwick, 2011), ix–x, 1–23; Douglas A. Sweeney, "Sweeney's Booknotes: Jonathan Edwards's Vision of Reality," *JEC Blog* January 11, 2012, Jonathan Edwards Center at TEDS, accessed March 28, 2012, http://jecteds.org/blog/2012/01/11/sweeneys-booknotes-jonathan-edwardss-vision-of-reality.

[30] Holmes, "Response to Lee," 99–110. Holmes concludes with an appeal to the same line of argument employed by Murray—that of authorial intent. In other words, a sound historiographical interpretive method must account for the intent of the author in such a way that there is ample reason to believe the author himself would accept the interpretation. In Holmes's concluding words, he states the following: "So, I suggest that one of the main reasons Lee offers for Edwards' supposed departure from the tradition is simply mistaken—and Edwards would have known it was mistaken." "Response to Lee," 110.

[31] Stephen R. Holmes, God *of Grace and God of Glory: An Account of the Theology of Jonathan Edwards* (Grand Rapids: Eerdmans, 2000). Holmes's commendation (see p. 22) of McClymond's argument that Edwards proceeded with a "theocentric motif" is in reference to McClymond's *Encounters with God*, 28–30.

[32] Norman Fiering, *Jonathan Edwards' Moral Thought and Its British Context* (Chapel Hill, NC: University of North Carolina, 1981).

oriented his thought around metaphysics in order to demonstrate that the true locus of morality was in Christianity. Fiering's interpretation, however, was shown to be liable to the same shortcoming as other philosophically oriented interpretations: "Although very insightful, Fiering's attempt to isolate Edwards's ethical reasoning from his larger theological agenda is ultimately unsuccessful. . . . Fiering artificially delimits the discussion of morality within Edwards's thought."[33]

Although the authors and positions surveyed are a fraction of those proposing theological interpretations of Edwards, they represent some of the latest and most highly regarded in the field.[34] This being the case, a profitable analysis is possible. This analysis will endeavor to address two questions regarding theological method which emerge from this survey. First, should Edwards's theological method be regarded as primarily philosophical in its character? Second, should Edwards's theological method be understood in terms of a central interpretive motif? The answers to these two questions will inform the

[33] Stein, "Foreword," xiv.

[34] Other interpretations are also noteworthy. John E. Smith suggests that "the whole of his thought might be viewed as one magnificent answer to the question, *What is true religion*?" William Danaher and Amy Plantinga Pauw propose an interpretive approach grounded in Edwards's trinitarianism. Stephen Nichols agrees with Michael McClymond when he maintains that, in spite of the variety of conflicting opinions, "there is an identifiable center to the thought of Jonathan Edwards. The elusive interpretive tool does exist. . . . The key to understanding Edwards is to understand him as an apologist." See John E. Smith, "Editor's Introduction," in *The Works of Jonathan Edwards*, ed. Perry Miller, vol. 2, *Religious Affections* (New Haven: Yale, 1959), 2; William J. Danaher, *The Trinitarian Ethics of Jonathan Edwards*, Columbia Series in Reformed Theology (Louisville: Westminster John Knox, 2004); Amy Plantinga Pauw, *The Supreme Harmony of All: The Trinitarian Theology of Jonathan Edwards* (Grand Rapids: Eerdmans, 2002); Stephen J. Nichols, *An Absolute Sort of Certainty* (Phillipsburg, NJ: P&R Publishing, 2003), 18; McClymond, *Encounters With God*, 80–112. It is interesting to note that both Nichols and Holmes invoke McClymond's *Encounters With God* to support their respective interpretations.

way in which Edwards's theological method is understood and applied to this study of *Religious Affections*.

The Inadequacy of Philosophical Interpretations

As is evident in the survey of interpretations, some are disposed to understand Edwards as primarily a philosopher and his theology as being driven by philosophical interests. This is understandable; his careful attention to metaphysics, epistemology, aesthetics, and ethics suggests that this is indeed the case. Yet this perspective of Edwards's method gives an inadequate account of Edwards's biblical interest; this perspective also disqualifies *prima facie* any notion of Christian historiography.

An Inadequate Account of Edwards's Biblical Interest. Holifield explains why he believes it is a mistake to portray Edwards as a philosophical theologian:

> While some have read Edwards chiefly as a metaphysical theologian, framing his thoughts through his engagement with John Locke, Nicholas Malebranche, the Cambridge Platonists, or the British moralists, others, like his disciple Samuel Hopkins, emphasized that he "studied the Bible more than all other books" and that he depended heavily on such works of biblical criticism as Matthew Poole's *Synopsis Criticorum* (1669–76) and Matthew Henry's *Exposition of the Old and New Testaments* (1708–10). Spurred partly by the Deist controversies, he devoted substantial energy to the topics of inspiration, the scope of the canon, the authorship of biblical texts, the historicity of biblical reports, and the biblical depictions of the end times. His works abounded in biblical allusions and proof texts.[35]

[35] Holifield, "Edwards as Theologian," 145.

If Holifield's assessment of the situation is correct, then those who read Edwards from a philosophical perspective do so by pushing the biblical interest of Edwards into the background. The result is a perspective of Edwards's theological method that is distorted. McClymond concurs with Holifield on this point, and suggests that academic specialization has had a hand in this conclusion:

> Much of recent scholarship on Edwards tends toward secularizing and naturalizing interpretations of his ideas. Thus Edwards's Christian sermonizing becomes rhetorical theory, while his reflections on the beauty of God translate into general aesthetics, and his typological worldview becomes semiotics. . . . The recent, cutting-edge research tends to be highly specialized, with the result that Edwards the theologian remains separate from Edwards the historian, the typologist, the spiritual seeker, the preacher, the pastor, the revivalist, and the metaphysician.[36]

The marginalization of Edwards's biblical interest may simply be the oversight of overly focused specialization. However, Stephen Holmes believes there is more to the situation. He suggests that a single, long-standing enigma is behind much of the effort to make sense of the philosophical side of Edwards:

> Edwards was a Puritan pastor, preaching for revival, defending Calvinism, and understanding the events of the world around him in thoroughly theological terms. For the last century and a half, this has been the chief riddle concerning Edwards: how could someone of undoubted genius, clearly alert to the implications of the new science and the new philosophy that were to launch the Enlightenment, remain wedded to

[36] McClymond, *Encounters with God*, 4.

> such an outmoded system of thought and, indeed, way of life?[37]

Even with no consensus in response to this question, a number of scholars who interpret Edwards through a philosophical grid have found common ground. The question of how Edwards joined his philosophical thinking to his Biblical Calvinism remains for them a point of dispute, but the fact that he did so is, in the view of many, a tragedy.

An Unjustified Disqualification of Christian Historiography. Murray explains the idea of "Edwards as tragedy" in the opening pages of his biography. He begins by reminding his readers about a time when all parties—both those who embraced Edwards and those who did not—agreed that Edwards was first and foremost a biblically-informed Christian Calvinist. But the twentieth century introduced a critical school of interpretation; by mid-century, Henry Parkes, Ola Winslow, and Perry Miller had recast Jonathan Edwards as a great American tragedy. According to this view, the tragedy of Edwards is the story of how his obsolete Reformed orthodoxy prevented him from realizing his intellectual potential and instead led him to impose his harmful religious ideas on generations of Americans to come. This new perspective brought Jonathan Edwards out of the academic "basement" and promoted him to a respectable subject of inquiry. One could now pursue the study of Edwards for intellectual purposes without being soiled by his religion.[38]

Murray offers a straightforward but compelling analysis of this tragedy motif, which is the perspective in the background of many critical interpretations. Murray's examination of the tragedy reduces the matter to one of the world view of the historian: when an anti-supernaturalist world view functions as the ground of the interpretive

[37] Holmes, *God of Grace*, 16.

[38] Murray, *Jonathan Edwards*, xx–xxvii; Paul Helm and Oliver D. Crisp, "Introduction," in *Jonathan Edwards: Philosophical Theologian*, ed. Paul Helm and Oliver D. Crisp (Burlington, VT: Ashgate, 2003), x.

process, a Christian supernaturalist world view is consequently and automatically regarded as a liability. Based on these terms, it is no wonder that Edwards's life and thought should be regarded as a failure. But there is no evidence that Jonathan Edwards considered his Christian principles an error or his life lived under them as a monumental mistake. Therefore, the "tragedy motif" paints a portrait of Edwards which Edwards himself would not have recognized.

According to Murray, such a distortion is irresponsible historiography. Murray correctly observes that something is amiss when Edwards's own viewpoints are disqualified from participating in the interpretation of Edwards. Murray's objection also points to the larger question of Christian historiography. When Murray proposed a Christian interpretation of Edwards, many within the Edwards guild promptly disqualified his work as legitimate history, dismissing it as hagiography. Murray's version of Edwards simply contained too much praise and too little critique. Murray's personal commitments were too much in line with the Calvinist tradition to afford the degree of objectivity necessary for a reliable biography of Edwards.[39]

[39] See Stephen J. Stein, "Review of *Jonathan Edwards: A New Biography* by Iain H. Murray," *Church History* 59, 4 (December 1990): 564–65; Allen C. Guelzo, "Review of *Jonathan Edwards: A New Biography* by Iain H. Murray," *Fides et Historia* 21 (June 1989): 81–83; M. X. Lesser, *Reading Jonathan Edwards: An Annotated Bibliography in Three Parts, 1729–2005* (Grand Rapids: Eerdmans), 325. Somewhat less critical is Kenneth Minkema in "Jonathan Edwards in the Twentieth Century," *Journal of the Evangelical Theological Society* 47, 4 (December 2004): 679. Marsden is respectful but distant, referring to Murray's work as "well researched and nicely done" but "intended ultimately as hagiography." George M. Marsden, "The Quest for the Historical Edwards: The Challenge of Biography," in *Jonathan Edwards at Home and Abroad: Historical Memories, Cultural Movements, Global Horizons*, ed. David W. Kling and Douglas A. Sweeney (Columbia, SC: University of South Carolina, 2003), 3. Allen C. Guelzo complains in his 1989 review that "Murray's Edwards is not so much a biography as it is a hagiography, calling to mind not Jonathan Edwards of Northampton but Martin Lloyd-Jones of Westminster Chapel." Yet in 2005, two years after the release of Marsden's biography, Guelzo appears to have reversed his opinion, and goes so far as to say that Murray's interpretation "may have caught far

Furthermore and noteworthy, this line of reasoning constitutes a disqualification of Murray's world view: since Murray was not sufficiently critical of Edwards and since Murray is of the same tradition as Edwards, we should conclude that Murray's Calvinist/Christian world view rendered him either unwilling or unable to write a reliable historical account of Edwards.[40] This line of reasoning suggests reliable Christian historiography is not possible if the subject and the object are of the same Christian tradition. In other words, it seems that a Christian historian cannot possibly bring the requisite objectivity to the historical task. The Christian historian is a captive to predispositions and inevitably distorts the account through the selection and the interpretation of historical data in light of the Christian world view.

The problem with this objection to a Christian historian is evident: it implies that the discrediting implies that credible historiog-

---

more accurately than his fellow biographers the Edwards whom Edwards himself would be most likely to recognize." Compare his "Review of *Jonathan Edwards: A New Biography* by Iain H. Murray," *Fides et Historia* 21 (June 1989): 81, with his "Unpalatable to Modern Sensibilities," *Books and Culture*, September-October 2005, accessed November 28, 2011, http://www.booksandculture.com/articles/ 2005/sepoct/7.16.html.

[40] Recent trends suggest that Murray may yet be vindicated. Although several scholars dismissed Murray as a religious commentator, references to his biography continued to surface in the research and bibliographies of scholarly work throughout the 1980s and 1990s; to this day his *Jonathan Edwards: A New Biography* retains a significant place of regard in spite of the publication of Marsden's definitive biography in 2003. Though Murray's portrayal of Edwards is still regarded by most scholars as too glossy, his call for a Christian/Calvinist version of Edwards seems to have found new life so that significant players in the academic community now endorse this general outlook on Edwards. Though quite diverse in many respects, Murray, Marsden, Holmes, Cherry, McClymond, Guelzo, and Holifield appear to present a united front on the issue of Edwards's fundamental commitment to biblical Calvinism. This group affirms in general terms that the post- Miller schools of interpretation have overplayed the significance of Edwards as a philosopher and that Edwards must first be taken as a Biblically-informed, religiously-motivated Calvinist and secondarily as a philosopher.

raphy reduces the concept of objectivity to neutrality. If the notion of neutral objectivity marks the criterion for reliable historiography, the openly Christian scholar is self-disqualified. But other considerations suggest that, on two counts, the objectivity question is not a reliable criterion for sound historiography.[41] First, such a governing principle would of necessity intrude upon all scholarship that carries a transparent point of view. Indeed, little evidence is at hand indicating the academy is disposed to censure all scholarship that falls short of dispassionate neutrality. Such a principle would disqualify African-American historians who interpret the history of southern slavery, the Civil Rights movement, and M. L. King; Jewish scholars would be deemed incapable of objectively documenting the Holocaust; Japanese historians researching the bombing of Hiroshima and Nagasaki would be dismissed by respected publishers; academics who endorse the platform of the Democratic party would be regarded as incapable of writing a credible biography of Franklin D. Roosevelt or John F. Kennedy. In cases such as these, personal identity, experience, association, and affinity are widely regarded as assets to the historian's credibility, rather than liabilities. Nevertheless, in the minds of many, an evangelical Calvinist such as Murray appears too sympathetic to the outlook of Edwards to provide a reliable account.

Second, the idea of the "neutral historian" is suspect at best. If objectivity is truly necessary for neutrality and if neutrality is necessary for credibility, an epistemological position is being taken that most of the academy has already vacated.[42] The notion of neutral inquiry was

[41] Edwards addressed the question of the objectivity of history as a means for authenticating the reliability of the Bible in Part Three, Section Five, of *Religious Affections*. Edwards argues that the discipline of the historian is one of subjectivity and probability; the primary sources must simply be accepted on their own terms. See Jonathan Edwards, *A Treatise Concerning Religious Affections*, ed. John E. Smith, The Works of Jonathan Edwards, vol. 2 (New Haven: Yale, 1959), 303.

[42] The fallacy of neutrality as the means to objectivity has been competently addressed in Paul R. Noble, *The Canonical Approach: A Critical Reconstruction of the Hermeneutics of Brevard S. Childs* (New York: Brill, 1995), 240–89;

thoroughly refuted in the second half of the twentieth century. Kuhn's landmark work, still in publication, is an iconic representation for the convincing demonstration that lines of inquiry are conditioned, including science—the one discipline which had been thought to be immune from the forces of bias.[43] Postmodernity gained traction in the second half of the twentieth century, building credibility by its convincing critique of the fallacy of neutrality.

This reaction has led some to conclude that objectivity of any kind is not possible—particularly epistemic certainty—and those who pursue it do so in ignorance. Those advancing arguments of this sort seem unaware of their reliance upon the objective use of the laws of language and logic. Indeed, these must be assumed in any effort to debunk the notion of objectivity.

If objectivity is indeed attainable apart from neutrality, then the neutrality objection is groundless; therefore, Christian historians can indeed write objective history. The integrity of the academy is not beyond question when the Christian scholar, and only the Christian scholar, is disqualified on account of personal bias. In short, the objection to Christian historiography—in general, and with respect to the interpretation of Edwards—reduces to an objection to the Christian world view and should be addressed as such.[44]

Carl R. Trueman, *Histories and Fallacies: The Problems Faced in the Writing of History* (Wheaton: Crossway, 2010), 25–68; Thomas L. Haskell, *Objectivity is not Neutrality* (Baltimore: Johns Hopkins, 1998). The legitimacy of Christian historiography (or Christian scholarship in general) in a postmodern context has been convincingly argued from various perspectives, including Bradley and Muller, *Church History*, 1–62; George M. Marsden, *The Outrageous Idea of Christian Scholarship* (New York: Oxford, 1997); Mark A. Noll, "Traditional Christianity and the Possibility of Historical Knowledge," *Christian Scholars Review* 19, 4 (June 1990): 388–406.

[43] Thomas S. Kuhn, *The Structure of Scientific Revolutions* (Chicago: University of Chicago, 1962).

[44] In this vein, Ronald Nash explores the plausibility problems attending rigid forms of objectivism on one side and relativism on the other. Nash recommends a "soft objectivism," which ascribes to a method that examines one's own governing presuppositions and a conclusion that is considered

The Inadequacy of Central Interpretive Motif Interpretations

In this survey of interpreters of Edwards, a common belief that his theology was controlled by a single central interpretive motif emerges. However, these beliefs have proven to be elusive, typically giving way to charges of reductionism and decontextualization.

The Problem of Reductionism. The effort to understand Edwards's theological method in terms of a central interpretive motif may prove to be altogether untenable. The pursuit has not produced any result upon which scholars have found substantial agreement. The growing variety of proposed controlling themes is being seen by some as the greatest piece of evidence against the very notion that such a controlling theme even exists:

> Douglas Elwood stresses "immediacy," Roland Delattre accents "beauty and sensibility," Norman Fiering emphasizes "moral philosophy," Sang Lee examines "dispositional ontology," and Stephen Daniel speaks in terms of "semiotics." All these authors have produced substantial studies that enrich our general understanding of Edwards. . . . It is unlikely that any one approach can claim ultimate priority over all others.[45]

---

reliable and sufficient, though not absolute or unquestionable. At the end of the day, the world view bias of the historian is conditioning the appropriation and employment of historical data. However, this need not lead to relativism. The subjectivity that the historian brings to the table on account of his/her world view may be offset by the process of testing, assessing, and correction. Nash maintains that those who ascribe to anti-naturalistic world views and who disqualify Christian interpretations of history on such grounds, "should reexamine the extent to which their naturalistic presuppositions control the way they handle their data." Ronald H. Nash, *Christian Faith and Understanding* (Dallas: Probe Ministries, 1984), 77–92; quotation from p. 92.

[45] McClymond, *Encounters with God*, 28. Authors and their views referred to in this quotation are, respectively, Douglas Elwood, *The Philosophical Theology of Jonathan Edwards* (New York: Columbia, 1960); Roland A. Delattre, *Beauty and Sensibility in the Thought of Jonathan Edwards* (New Haven: Yale, 1968); Fiering, *Jonathan Edwards' Moral Thought and Its British Context*; Lee, *The Philosophical Theology of Jonathan Edwards*; Stephen Hartley

The reason for this impasse seems to lie in the nature of the enterprise itself: each proposal, in the effort to identify a central interpretive motif, runs aground on the charge of reductionism. Critics see proposals for a central interpretive motif as leaning on evidence that is selected and edited to support the proposal. Evidence not conducive to the proposal is ignored or reshaped in ways that appear to serve the interest of the proposal. To be sure, the discovery of a single, simple, interpretive key would be a master-stroke. However, the long line of proposals for a central motif has been countered by a steady stream of rebuttals, each of which cites textual or contextual evidence to the contrary.[46]

A few scholars have conceded the short-sightedness of trying to reduce Edwards's theological method to a single interpretive element. McClymond, who himself suggests an interpretive motif of "theocentrism," admits the following:

> A scrutiny of the secondary literature should induce skepticism with regard to isolating and identifying such a fundamental motif or its equivalent. Past claims to having discovered one have not been accepted or assimilated into the ongoing scholarship on Edwards. Instead each new researcher has gone on with his or her own focus while neglecting the others.[47]

Daniel, *The Philosophy of Jonathan Edwards: A Study in Divine Semiotics* (Bloomington, IN: Indiana University, 1994).

[46] For examples, see the rebuttal of Conrad Cherry in William S. Morris, "Review of *The Theology of Jonathan Edwards: A Reappraisal*," *Church History* 36, 3 (September 1967): 332–33; the rebuttal of Perry Miller and Norman Fiering by Stephen Stein in "Foreword," in Cherry, *The Theology of Jonathan Edwards*, ix–xvi; the rebuttal of Sang Lee in Stephen R. Holmes, "Does Jonathan Edwards Use a Dispositional Ontology? A Response to Sang Hyun Lee," in *Jonathan Edwards: Philosophical Theologian*, ed. Paul Helm and Oliver D. Crisp (Burlington, VT: Ashgate, 2003), 99–110.

[47] McClymond, *Encounters with God*, 28.

Cherry maintains that "motif research" is valuable only inasmuch as it supplies "a window through which we may observe other aspects of his thought."[48] However, for Cherry, any idea of a controlling or central motif is untenable.[49]

The Problem of Decontextualization. Reductionism is not the only problem plaguing attempts to identify a central interpretive motif. Some scholars have come to disapprove of certain liberties taken by their colleagues. The practice of crafting interpretive schemes with little or no regard for contextual issues is the point of dispute; it seems that some in the scholarly community have simply gone too far in their revision of Edwards by insisting that his

> "Unpalatable" words must become a code that modern hearers can decipher and discover to be a friendly and relevant message for modern sensibilities. This is what goes into a great deal of modern scholarship on Edwards, whose authors hope devoutly that their recalcitrant subject can be made to yield to neo-orthodoxy, postmodernism, semiotics, and other modern intellectual dividends.[50]

These remarks, offered by Allen Guelzo in response to Philip Gura's recent biography, culminate in the charge that Gura's interpretation of Edwards is marred by "an act of extraordinary historical violence."[51]

[48] Cherry, *The Theology of Jonathan Edwards*, 7.

[49] Ibid.

[50] Guelzo, "Unpalatable to Modern Sensibilities." A recent example of this approach to Edwards is Studebaker's comparative analysis of the trinitarianism of Jonathan Edwards and David Coffey, intended as a catalyst to stimulate evangelicals to redemptive inclusivism and ecumenical dialogue. Steven M. Studebaker, *The Trinitarian Vision of Jonathan Edwards and David Coffey* (Amherst, NY: Cambria, 2011).

[51] Ibid.; Philip F. Gura, *Jonathan Edwards: America's Evangelical* (New York: Hill and Wang, 2005).

The "historical violence" Guelzo speaks of is decontextualization. McClymond recognizes the problem and considers it to be regrettable but believes there is some merit in the practice:

> To some extent it is perfectly acceptable to interpret Edwards in terms of the currently regnant academic disciplines, with political scientists, historians, philosophers, literary critics, and other specialists all viewing his writings through different lenses. Decontextualizing and detheologizing Edwards's ideas may be a help in understanding the individual segments of the corpus.[52]

McClymond's remarks amount to a generous concession to his colleagues, and his optimism is shared by others.[53] Nevertheless, given the extent to which the charge of decontextualization derails productive study, F. R. Ankersmit's assessment of the decontextualization in historical studies is more realistic: "This domain of the timeless presupposes contextualization and historicization, for without contextualization there is no decontextualization and thus no historical experience."[54]

The fact remains that most historians of Jonathan Edwards critique their colleagues on the basis of whether or not they have adequately contextualized their study. Much of the debate between historians of Edwards centers on issues concerning an inadequate handling of contextual issues. In a fairly recent exchange between significant scholars, Stephen Holmes dismisses Sang Hyun Lee's

[52] McClymond, *Encounters with God*, 4.

[53] Decontextualization has long been considered an inappropriate practice for historians, but a divergence of opinion exists as to whether or not recontextualization ("Texts or artifacts placed in any context other than their original") has a legitimate place in historiography. See Jennifer Fredale deWinter, "The Rhetorics of Context: An Ethics of Belonging" (Ph.D. diss., University of Arizona, 2008), 65–69.

[54] F. R. Ankersmit, *Sublime Historical Experience* (Palo Alto, CA: Stanford University, 2005), 156.

theory of "dispositional ontology" on the basis that the theory is not properly contextualized.[55] A host of other studies are similarly basing their critiques on the need for increased attention to contextualization.[56] Contextualization is considered to be of such importance that some commentators are making the point in the titles of their works such as Stephen Stein's *Jonathan Edwards's Writings: Text, Context, Interpretation* and Norman Fiering's *Jonathan Edwards' Moral Thought and Its British Context*.[57]

If the central interpretive motif is beset with the liabilities of oversimplification and decontextualization, is there another approach by which the reader can ascertain Edwards's methodology? If we conclude that the answer to this question is "no," we essentially affirm that Edwards was not methodical in his thought and that he reasoned in an arbitrary fashion or at least without a genuine point of reference. The reader of scholarship on Edwards is hard-pressed to find someone who suggests an absence of methodology on Edwards's part. If we conclude the answer is "yes," then some alternative must be proposed which points to the fundamental principle that brought order and coherence to Edwards's thought.

[55] Holmes, "Response to Lee," 99–110.

[56] For examples, see Stein, "Foreword," in Cherry, *The Theology of Jonathan Edwards*, xi.; Marc M. Arkin, "The Great Awakener: A Review of *Jonathan Edwards* by John E. Smith," *The New Criterion* May 1993, accessed October 27, 2011, http://www. newcriterion.com/articles.cfm/The-great-awakener - 4763; Avihu Zakai, *Jonathan Edwards's Philosophy of History: The Reenchantment of the World in the Age of Enlightenment* (Princeton, NJ: Princeton University, 2009), 282–83; Douglas L. Winiarski, "Seeking Synthesis in Edwards Scholarship," *The William and Mary Quarterly* 61, 1 (January 2004): 137–40; 147–48; Emile Cailliet, "Review of *Puritan Sage, Collected Writings of Jonathan Edwards* by Vergilius Ferm," *The New England Quarterly* 27, 1 (March 1954): 125–27.

[57] Stephen J. Stein, ed., *Jonathan Edwards's Writings: Text, Context, Interpretation* (Bloomington, IN: Indiana University, 1996); Norman Fiering, *Jonathan Edwards' Moral Thought and Its British Context* (Chapel Hill, NC: University of North Carolina, 1981).

The Inadequacy of a Categorical Systematic Theology Approach

One alternative that has been proposed is a recommendation that the reader interpret Edwards in terms of the traditional categories systematic theology. Such an approach must concede from the outset the fact that Edwards himself did not systematize his own theology or express it in categories. This approach, advocated by John Gerstner in *The Rational Biblical Theology of Jonathan Edwards*, applies the traditional categories of systematic theology to the Edwards corpus.[58] The advantage of this model is that it operates on the presupposition that Edwards himself clearly embraced: the unity, infallibility, and coherence of God and His written revelation in the form of the Biblical canon. By adopting the traditional categories of systematic theology, the model works in the same patterns of thought that were employed by sources most prized by Edwards.[59]

Yet the liabilities of this approach outweigh the merits. The systematic theology approach invites anachronistic conclusions: systematic categories make little provision for explaining change or development of thought over the course of time. Furthermore, the systematic

[58] John H. Gerstner, *The Rational Biblical Theology of Jonathan Edwards*, 3 Vols. (Powhatan, VA: Berea, 1993).

[59] Peter van Mastricht and Francis Turretin were especially valued by Edwards. In a letter to Joseph Bellamy, Edwards mentions Mastricht and Turretin "are both excellent." He especially valued Mastricht, noting his superior balance in presentation: "But take Mastricht for divinity in general, doctrine, practice, and controversy; or as an universal system of divinity; and it is much better than Turretin or any other book in the world, excepting the Bible, in my opinion." Jonathan Edwards, "Letter to the Reverend Joseph Bellamy, January 15, 1747," in *Letters and Personal Writings*, ed. George S. Claghorn, *The Works of Jonathan Edwards*, vol. 16 (New Haven: Yale, 1998), 217. Edwards's high opinion of Mastricht seems to have continued to the end of his life. Upon his acceptance of the presidency at Princeton, Edwards apparently selected his most valuable books to accompany him on the journey. Among these 57 books (which have remained to this day in Princeton's custody) is Edwards's personal copy of Mastricht's *Theoretico-Practica Theologia*. See Paul Ramsey, "Appendix IV: Infused Virtues in Edwardsean and Calvinistic Context," in *Ethical Writings*, ed. Paul Ramsey, The Works of Jonathan Edwards, vol. 8 (New Haven: Yale, 1989), 744n4.

approach seems to be an imposition upon Edwards. It is one thing to observe the ways in which Edwards manifested coherence, confirming the methodical character of his work; it is quite another to demonstrate that a particular approach was the device that he intentionally utilized to govern his theology and to achieve its coherence. Gerstner's systematic theology approach explains the former, but not the latter. Although this approach does not impose a central interpretive motif upon the interpretation of Edwards, Gerstner's interpretation is geared more to addressing Edwards's conclusions than his method *per se*.

Edwards's Theological Method as a Regulated Matrix

The last fifty years of scholarship on Edwards has generated a series of controversies, one of which debates the question of whether Edwards should be taken as an early modernist or a conservative Calvinist. This dispute was, in general terms, a running feud between the views of Perry Miller and Conrad Cherry; but by the end of the 20th century, Cherry had clearly prevailed.[60] Consequently, some are now conceding what evangelical scholars have long maintained—that Edwards was, first and foremost, a man of the Bible. McClymond and McDermott join Minkema in this assessment, noting that the result is that the secular "historicists" and the evangelical "theologizers" have found a remarkable degree of common ground.[61]

Evangelical Approaches to Theological Method

If Edwards was indeed such a man, his view of the Bible and theology has implications for how his theological method should be understood. Whether or not Edwards was an evangelical is immaterial

[60] Michael J. McClymond and Gerald R. McDermott, *The Theology of Jonathan Edwards* (Oxford: Oxford University, 2012), 641–45.

[61] McClymond and McDermott, *The Theology of Jonathan Edwards*, 647–48; Kenneth P. Minkema, "Jonathan Edwards in the Twentieth Century," 676–78.

in the final analysis; the fact that his biblical and theological outlook shares so much in common with traditional evangelicalism suggests that his method of doing theology also has much in common with evangelical approaches to doing theology.[62] For this reason, an overview of some late versions of evangelical theological method can serve as a useful point of reference for assessing Edwards's theological method.

A Stratified Approach. Some evangelical theologians have argued that theological method should be a descriptive, rather than a prescriptive, exercise. Whereas agenda-driven theologies have prescribed how theology should be done in order to achieve a particular sociological or political ideal, many conservatives have recommended that all theology be considered in terms of describing its use of sources. Millard Erickson calls for a multi-step theological method which collates and analyzes both biblical and non-biblical sources before stratifying them according to their relative importance.[63] Gregory Thornbury's prolegomena for Daniel Akin's *Theology for the Church* commends Erickson's stratification as an exemplary approach to theological method.[64]

Erickson's influence is evident in Mike Stallard's "A Proposal for Theological Method," which views theology as a task that integrates all data from all possible sources regarding God and the universe into

[62] The assumption here is that Edwards may legitimately be taken as a foundational figure for the evangelical movement as maintained by Mark Noll in *The Rise of Evangelicalism* (Downers Grove, IL: InterVarsity, 2003). John Stackhouse calls evangelicals to retain evangelical distinctives within their theological method and appeals to the evangelical tradition as marked by key historical figures, Jonathan Edwards being one among them. John G. Stackhouse, "Evangelical Theology Should Be Evangelical," in *Evangelical Futures: A Conversation on Theological Method*, ed. John G. Stackhouse (Grand Rapids: Baker, 2000), 40–41, 52, 56.

[63] Millard J. Erickson, *Christian Theology*, 2nd ed. (Grand Rapids: Baker, 1998), 70–84.

[64] Gregory Alan Thornbury, "Prolegomena: Introduction to the Task of Theology," in *A Theology for the Church*, ed. Daniel L. Akin (Nashville: Broadman and Holman, 2007), 63–64.

a coherent whole.[65] Stallard affirms that special revelation, Holy Spirit illumination, reason, experience, empirical data, historical data, mathematics, philosophy, linguistics, psychology, sociology, law, politics, and data generated by other disciplines all have a seat at the table.[66]

However, in order to achieve coherence, one source must inevitably function in a role that validates the others and arbitrates the relative value of their contributions.[67] In reference to this controlling source, remaining sources stratify in order of their respective value, revealing a process by which a theologian constructs a theology by an ordered stratification of contributing sources, all of which rest on the foundation of the controlling source. As Biblical conservatives, Erickson, Thornbury, and Stallard maintain that the Scriptures maintain this validating role.[68]

[65] Stallard, "A Proposal for Theological Method."

[66] Ibid., 9–13.

[67] For Stallard, validation entails the demonstration of consistency, coherence, comprehensiveness, and congruity. Stallard, "A Proposal for Theological Method," 16. See also Millard J. Erickson, *The Word Became Flesh* (Grand Rapids: Baker, 1991), 523–24; Erickson, *Christian Theology*, 148–49; Frederick Ferré, *Language, Logic, and God* (New York: Harper, 1961), 162–63.

[68] It should be noted that Erickson maintains that an important feature of a well-written systematic theology is an intentionally crafted central interpretive motif. According to Erickson, this thematic feature supplies the kind of unity needed in such a work; indeed, "it could be argued that any theology which has coherence has an integrating motif." But Erickson's proposition is burdened by qualifications. Erickson recommends that the employment of a central interpretive motif be a conscious exercise but allows for the unconscious formulation of it and appeals to theologians of the past who were renowned for particular theological themes. Erickson admits that the use of a central interpretive motif may be neither central nor unifying when he says that "sometimes there may be more than one motif and that these might even be somewhat contradictory in nature." Erickson, *Christian Theology*, 81. Erickson's lack of clarity on this point is evident in the interaction of Lewis and Demarest, who mistake Erickson's idea of a central interpretive motif as the central message of the Bible, rather than what Erickson apparently intends, which is the unifying emphasis of the theologian. See Lewis and

An Integrative Approach. Similar to the stratified approach is the recommendation of an integrative approach by Gordon Lewis and Bruce Demarest. This model recommends the same kind of source utilization as the stratified approach but calls for a more explicit method of relating the various sources to one another:

> Integrative theology utilizes a distinctive verificational method of decision making as it defines a major topic, surveys influential alternative answers in the church, amasses relevant biblical data in their chronological development, formulates a comprehensive conclusion, defends it against competing alternatives, and exhibits its relevance for life and ministry.[69]

This verificational method consists of six steps, which involve (1) identification of the problem in a subject of study; (2) consultation with historical treatments of the problem; (3) acquisition of data from relevant exegetical studies; (4) formulation of a non-contradictory conclusion based upon the data; (5) employment of the conclusion in apologetic situations; and (6) employment of the conclusion in the church.[70]

Although the stratification approach does not articulate the verification sequence in the same terms as Lewis and Demerest, the content presented in Erickson's method does not differ significantly from the content within the verification sequence recommended by Lewis and Demarest with the exception of the final two applicational elements. Furthermore, the integrative method follows the stratification method by establishing basic criteria for verification.[71] The integrative approach has been adopted recently by other evangelicals

---

Demarest, *Integrative Theology*, 26.

[69] Lewis and Demarest, *Integrative Theology*, 25.

[70] Ibid., 26.

[71] Lewis and Demarest present three: "logical noncontradiction, empirical adequacy, and existential viability." Lewis and Demarest, *Integrative Theology*, 25.

who find this approach to be helpful in describing the task of doing theology.[72]

A Regulated Matrix Approach. D. A. Carson presents a model of theological method that reflects some of the features of the stratified *and* integrative approaches. Carson agrees that systematic theology is a multidisciplinary task but takes a different view on the function and participation of the disciplines. First, Carson's approach is epistemologically self-conscious, advocating a "chastened foundationalism" that endeavors to avoid the unwarranted confidence which proceeded from modern notions of hermeneutics and epistemology. Second, Carson sees the task of theology as a discipline in the more narrow sense that concerns special revelation. Consequently, the disciplines which inform systematic theology are restricted to exegesis, Biblical theology, and historical theology. Third, Carson is silent on the subject of a central interpretive motif, and apparently, he does not see this as a necessary feature for a credible theological method.

Additionally, Carson believes that the relationship between the disciplines in the theological task has been misunderstood. The relationship is not linear as suggested by the stratification approach. Such a linear relationship correctly identifies a foundational and controlling source, but it fails to account for the complexity of the influence that each source exchanges with the other. Neither is the relationship circular: although the hermeneutical circle acknowledges the role of presuppositions, it fails to account for an epistemological frame of reference.[73] Rather than linear or circular, Carson maintains

[72] Wayne Grudem, *Systematic Theology* (Grand Rapids: Zondervan, 1994), 22; Larry D. Pettegrew, *The New Covenant Ministry of the Holy Spirit*, 2nd ed. (Grand Rapids: Kregel, 2001), 20–22.

[73] The term *hermeneutical circle* is intended here to refer to the general principle in hermeneutics which observes that interpretation and understanding relate to one another in a relationship of mutual reference. The implication which has been inferred by some is that this sort of circularity reduces language to a solipsism. However, not all are agreed that the hermeneutic circle necessarily reduces language to absurdity. See Piet Van de Craen, "Hermeneutics," in *Philosophical Perspectives for Pragmatics*, ed. Marina Sbisá,

that the theological disciplines (exegesis, biblical theology, historical theology, and systematic theology, along with applicational and experiential elements) relate to one another in an interdependent, regulated matrix and that the exegesis of Scripture assumes the role of regulation.[74] This approach recognizes that theological method must account for the limitations of the human theologian, the gap between the biblical author and the biblical reader, the distinction between exhaustive and reliable knowledge, and the complexity of what "authorial intent" entails.[75]

Jan-Ola Östman, and Jef Verschueren (Philadelphia: John Benjamins, 2011), 127; Shaun Gallagher, *Hermeneutics and Education* (Albany, NY: State University of New York, 1992), 58–61. In order to emphasize the belief that the hermeneutical circle is not logically vicious, leading to relativism, the term *hermeneutical spiral* has been adopted by some, most notably Grant Osborne. Carson recommends several epistemological models, all of which express the view that "it is possible and reasonable to speak of finite human beings knowing some things truly, even if nothing exhaustively or omnisciently." Carson includes among these the "fusion of horizons," the "asymptotic approach," and Osborne's "hermeneutical spiral." Andrew Naselli, who served as Carson's research assistant, classifies Carson's view of theological method as compatible with these epistemological models. See D. A. Carson, *Becoming Conversant with the Emerging Church* (Grand Rapids: Zondervan, 2005), 116 (quote above), 116–24; Grant R. Osborne, *The Hermeneutical Spiral*, rev. ed. (Downers Grove, IL: InterVarsity Press, 2006); Andrew David Naselli, "D. A. Carson's Theological Method," *Scottish Bulletin of Evangelical Theology* 29, 2 (Autumn 2011): 249–72.

[74] The term *regulated matrix* has been adopted by this study to refer to the approach to theological method which views the sources of theology in an interconnected relationship to one another with one of those sources exercising epistemic control.

[75] D. A. Carson, "The Role of Exegesis in Systematic Theology," in *Doing Theology in Today's World*, ed. John D. Woodbridge and Thomas E. McComiskey (Grand Rapids: Zondervan, 1991), 39–76; D. A. Carson, "Unity and Diversity in the New Testament: The Possibility of Systematic Theology," in *Scripture and Truth*, ed. D. A. Carson and John D. Woodbridge (Grand Rapids: Baker, 1983), 77–93; Naselli, "D. A. Carson's Theological Method," 249–72.

The Value of Assessing Edwards in Terms of a Regulated Matrix

Rather than understanding Edwards's theological method as being driven by philosophical concerns, central interpretive motifs, or systematic categories, it is preferable to consider his method in the terms of the regulated matrix suggested by Carson. This approach is recommended for two key reasons: epistemological value and historical value.

The Epistemological Value of a Regulated Matrix. The regulated matrix is recommended because it is essentially an epistemological model for theological method. Because this approach concerns itself with knowing *how* conclusions are derived from data, *it is explanatory rather than prescriptive.* The regulated matrix explains how the relationship between theological sources leads to theological conclusions; it does not prescribe how the theologian should do theology; rather, it explains how he does (or did) his theology. Since the model is descriptive of the theological process as it relates to the theological sources employed, it is an excellent model for viewing how theology was done in the past. The most valuable part of this descriptive process is its epistemological component, the feature of the theological method that functions as the governing epistemological authority. Since the regulated matrix approach clarifies this foundational element, it avoids the problems normally associated with postmodern relativism.

The regulated matrix is also valuable because its approach to epistemology is not insensitive to the problems associated with narrow foundationalism. The regulated matrix, working from an epistemological platform of "chastened foundationalism," gives a more satisfying account of the way in which presuppositions and perspectives are accounted for within theological method. One might object that such considerations are the product of the postmodern critique, so any use of them for the assessment of an 18th century theologian is an anachronism. But such is not the case; Edwards himself gives ample evidence of being sensitive to the role of presuppositions and their significance in drawing theological conclusions.[76] Because the regulated matrix model is descriptive rather than prescriptive and because it is sensitive to the concerns of both foundationalism and non-foundationalism, the regulated matrix model is an approach that is epistemologically appropriate.

The Historical Value of a Regulated Matrix. Not only is the regulated matrix epistemologically appropriate, but it is also historically appropriate. The regulated matrix accommodates the evangelical tradition inasmuch as it consciously recognizes the fact that all forms of theology ultimately proceed from some governing idea. The value here is that the historical evidence clearly points to the fact that Edwards and evangelicals share the same epistemological starting point: God's self-revelation in Scripture. Reality can be comprehended only to the degree that God serves as the point of reference. As Mardsen observes, "The key to Edwards' thought is that everything is related because everything is related to God."[77] In Marsden's simple but profound observation, he suggests that Edwards is best understood in terms of what this study proposes, namely, a regulated matrix: all things are related to one another but are comprehended only in reference to an authoritative source.

As observed earlier, some historians object to the notion of interpreting Edwards in evangelical terms, citing the fallacy of anachronism. This objection assumes that the potential for fallacy must result in a fallacy. However, this is an unwarranted assumption, which is itself a fallacy. Progenitors of movements are usually found to be different than the movements they instigated, but that fact does not mean there is no essential relationship between the individual and the tradition he/she was instrumental in launching. Responsible historiography can account for the differences between the founders of movements and the outcomes of movements while at the same time

[76] See chapter 6 and the discussion concerning the self-authentication of Scripture.

[77] George M. Marsden, *Jonathan Edwards: A Life* (New Haven: Yale, 2003), 460.

acknowledging the essential and genetic relationship that exists between the two.

In addition to the question of anachronism, one might also question the appropriateness of the regulated matrix by suggesting that it introduces bias into the assessment, "stacking the deck" in favor of an evangelical interpretation. This concern is unwarranted. The regulated matrix describes only what source self-evidently governs a theological method; it is not inherently evangelical in functional terms. The method imposes no alien criterion upon Edwards. If, in the final analysis, the Scriptures are taken to function as the governing element in Edwards's theology, sufficient primary source documentation demonstrates that Edwards himself had such a governing element in mind.

Summary

This study recommends a regulated matrix approach to investigating the way in which Edwards formulated his doctrine of assurance in *Religious Affections*. This approach is preferable because of its capabilities in epistemological terms. While the stratification and integrative models acknowledge the supremacy of Scripture, they suggest a linear order of logic which does not account as well for the complexity of communication among the sources of theology. Since the regulated matrix is regulated by an epistemological authority, this approach retains the foundational character which Edwards's own work assumed.

Although evangelicals employ a regulated matrix with the Bible in mind as the controlling authority, the matrix model itself is not controlling; it simply describes a process that naturally occurs with respect to other world views and their respective governing authorities. The model clearly portrays how a theologian handles sources and the way in which source treatment reveals which sources are controlling and which are supporting. This in turn reveals the theologian's basis for bringing unity, order, and coherence to theological conclusions. This approach to theological method is less ambitious as it does not lead to a single interpretive key to an author's theological corpus. Yet the conclusions are more sustainable as they are less vulnerable to reductionism, decontextualization, and anachronism. The regulated matrix is also appropriate in historical terms, facilitating a study of Edwards's theology which recognizes his priorities and accounts for his contexts, consequently leading toward conclusions which Edwards himself would recognize.

Finally, the regulated matrix is not a novel approach. Rather, its basic synthetic character is in keeping with opinion of scholars who, like Cherry and McClymond, maintain that motif studies supply pieces of the whole of Edwards's thought, rather than controlling explanations. If Cherry and McClymond are correct, then Edwards's theological method, and our comprehension of it, must be synthetic in its character. This is precisely what Norman Fiering has in mind when he refers to Edwards's work as "system building" and the "intertwining" of various disciplines and interests.[78] The regulated matrix, then, harmonizes with the multi-source synthesis that Cherry, McClymond, and Fiering suggest is most appropriate for interpreting Edwards's theology.

In order to demonstrate that the regulated matrix is indeed a preferable approach to reading Edwards, *Marks of Saving Grace* seeks to apply this approach to *A Treatise Concerning Religious Affections*, doing so with a view toward his theology of Christian assurance. This procedure first entails an examination of the sources employed by the treatise, all of which are enveloped in three categories: philosophical, historical, and biblical. These three source types are examined respectively in the next three chapters. Afterward, on the basis of these three chapters *Marks of Saving Grace* endeavors to synthesize Edwards's theology of assurance as expressed in *Religious Affections*. Finally,

[78] Fiering, *Jonathan Edwards' Moral Thought and Its British Context*, 49–51. Christopher Morgan adopts this point of Fiering's thought in his development of Edwards's theological method in *Edwards and the Doctrine of Hell* (Fearn, Scotland: Christian Focus, 2004), 114.

Marks of Saving Grace concludes with the consideration of three implications which may be drawn from the application of Edwards's theological method to his doctrine of assurance in *Religious Affections*.

4

The Illustrative Power of Metaphysics and Epistemology in *Religious Affections*

Perry Miller's groundbreaking work opened the door to the philosophical side of Jonathan Edwards. Miller's study recast Edwards as a philosopher who arrived on the American scene with impeccable talent and timing. Though much of Miller's original thesis has long since been discarded, the academy has adopted his view that Edwards's philosophy left an indelible mark on the American psyche. It is beyond the scope of this book to summarize, much less analyze, the variety of philosophical interpretations of Edwards which have been proposed. Similarly, it is not possible to investigate the question of which philosophers were most influential in Edwards's thought or to what extent he incorporated the principles of the Enlightenment into his own theology. These worthy subjects are adequately addressed in a number of studies.[1]

[1] Miller proposed that Locke was the key to understanding Edwards and proceeded to interpret Edwards's corpus in light of this hypothesis. The consequence was a naturalized, secularized portrait of Edwards. Conrad Cherry's work was the first to mount a serious challenge to Miller, and significant studies by Wallace Anderson and Norman Fiering demonstrated that Miller's hypothesis, though creative and stimulating, was an overstatement. See Perry Miller, *Jonathan Edwards* (New York: William Sloan, 1949), 52–68; Conrad Cherry, *The Theology of Jonathan Edwards: A Reappraisal* (Bloomington, IN: Indiana University, 1966), 15–30; Wallace E. Anderson, "Editor's Introduction," in *Scientific and Philosophical Writings*, ed. Wallace E. Anderson, The Works of Jonathan Edwards, vol. 6 (New Haven: Yale,

With few exceptions, the study of Edwards's philosophy has been an enterprise conducted by the academy and for the academy. The sheer volume and complexity of Edwards's thought has occasioned a surge of publishing, the volume of which, according to Lucas, "outpaces several third-world countries."[2] The vast majority of this academic publishing concerns the philosophical thought of Edwards. Many of these studies are diachronic in their approach, systematizing individual philosophical themes as they occur throughout his corpus. Others are synchronic, comparing Edwards's philosophical themes with the same or similar themes appearing in the influential philosophical works of the day. Unfortunately, the value of this approach is often limited by the frequent practice of lifting philosophical discussions out of the biblical/theological context in which they occur.[3]

1980), 24–27, 33–34; Michael J. McClymond, *Encounters with God: An Approach to the Theology of Jonathan Edwards* (New York: Oxford University, 1998), 11–14. Norman Fiering argues convincingly that Edwards was more significantly influenced by Malebranche than Locke in "The Rationalist Foundations of Jonathan Edwards's Metaphysics," in *Jonathan Edwards and the American Experience*, ed. Nathan O. Hatch and Harry S. Stout (Oxford: Oxford University, 1988), 73–101. The Locke/Malebranche question is discussed further by Paul Copan in "Jonathan Edwards' Philosophical Influences: Lockean or Malebranchean?" *Journal of the Evangelical Theological Society* 44 (March 2001): 107–24.

[2] Sean Michael Lucas, "Jonathan Edwards Between Church and Academy: A Bibliographic Essay," in *The Legacy of Jonathan Edwards*, ed. Sean Michael Lucas, D. G. Hart, and Stephen J. Nichols (Grand Rapids: Baker, 2003), 235.

[3] See, for example, Leon Chai, *Jonathan Edwards and the Limits of Enlightenment Philosophy* (Oxford: Oxford University, 1998). Lucas contrasts Chai's approach with interpretations by Alvin Plantinga and Stephen Nichols, who agree that Edwards's epistemology must be taken within the larger context of Edwards's appraisal of biblical revelation. See Lucas, "Jonathan Edwards Between Church and Academy," 236, 242–43; Alvin Plantinga, *Warranted Christian Belief* (New York: Oxford University, 2000); Stephen J. Nichols, *An Absolute Sort of Certainty* (Phillipsburg, NJ: P&R Publishing, 2003).

Religious Affections at times takes sudden, almost awkward, excursions into metaphysics and epistemology in order to secure a point of clarity, a degree of persuasion, or an extended audience for the theological message. As such, *Religious Affections* gives adequate evidence that Edwards viewed philosophical categories as necessary components to a compelling theological argument. The objective of this chapter is to examine Edwards's use of these categories and the way in which they functioned within the larger matrix of his theological method. Furthermore, this chapter seeks to understand how his use of philosophical categories informed his doctrine of assurance.

The Role of Metaphysics in the Theological Method of *Religious Affections*

Edwards employs two metaphysical discussions to advance the argument of *Religious Affections*. These two discussions concern the nature of the affections and the concept of the "simple idea" as proposed by John Locke. Each of these is employed intentionally to sustain a particular point. The purpose of this section is to examine how these two elements were employed as philosophical sources within the matrix of his larger theological method.

The Nature of the Affections

Edwards opens *Religious Affections* with an introductory exposition of 1 Peter 1:8 for the purpose of establishing, in the customary form, the doctrinal proposition that "true religion, in great part, consists in holy affections."[4] Upon introducing this proposition,

[4] Jonathan Edwards, *A Treatise Concerning Religious Affections*, ed. John E. Smith, The Works of Jonathan Edwards, vol. 2 (New Haven: Yale, 1959), 95. The form that Edwards adopts for Part One adheres closely to the standard form of the Puritan sermon, which typically launched with the exposition of a single text, proceeded to a statement of doctrine accompanied by a series of justifications and explanations, and concluded with applications and practical exhortations. See Babette May Levy, *Preaching in the First Half Century of New England History*, ed. Matthew Spinka and Robert Hastings

Edwards does not immediately move to elaborate upon it or to justify it. Rather, he takes a strategic detour at this very early stage of the treatise to consider the question of what "affections" are in the first place. The answer that Edwards supplies, however, is not biblical, but metaphysical. Edwards answers the question by utilizing a four-fold metaphysical argument. This argument includes a definition of *affections* in terms of faculty, a discussion concerning the relation of affections to the body, a juxtaposition of affections to "passions," and an explanation of the relationship of affections to activity. Within this discussion, Edwards signals his intent to utilize philosophical considerations in the formation of his theologically-driven argument.[5]

The Affections in Terms of Faculty. Edwards's first argument for the definition of affections is to explain how they relate to the immaterial aspect of the human being. Edwards maintains that God created the soul with only two faculties, perception (understanding) and will (inclination). The affections, Edwards goes on to argue, are not a separate faculty, but rather the "more vigorous and sensible exercises" of the will.[6]

The location of the affections within the will is significant to the larger argument for three reasons. First, by locating the affections within the will, Edwards could deflect the charge that the outpouring of affections which characterized the Awakening was evidence of irrational enthusiasm. If the essential unity of the affections and the will could be established, then the appropriateness of affections in

---

Nichols, Studies in Church History, vol. 6 (Hartford, CT: American Society of Church History, 1945), 88–95.

[5] Edwards, *Religious Affections*, WJE 2:96–101.

[6] Ibid., 96–97. It should be observed that Edwards is not utilizing the idea of "faculty" in the classic Platonic sense, but rather in keeping with Enlightenment discourse. Locke and Melbranche disputed the traditional notion that faculties were entities unto themselves and insisted that they were merely capacities of the mind. See William J. Danaher, *The Trinitarian Ethics of Jonathan Edwards*, Columbia Series in Reformed Theology (Louisville: Westminster John Knox, 2004), 120–24. However, Edwards did object to the Greek division of the faculties, a point discussed later in this chapter.

religion could not be easily dismissed. Second, the placing of the affections within the will buttressed standard Reformed doctrine, which taught that outward expressions were merely the "fruit" which was evidence of the essential nature of the individual. By maintaining the unity of the affections and the will, the genuineness of affections could be reasonably confirmed by other expressions of the will. These confirming evidences could serve as signs to distinguish truly gracious affections.

Third, as McClymond and Nichols have explained in detail, Edwards's theology was quite often apologetic in character and clearly so in *Religious Affections*. As such, Edwards frequently and deliberately shifts into the philosophical realm in order to establish common ground with the New England intelligentsia. For the sake of the argument of *Religious Affections*, it was not necessary to define the nature of the affections vis-à-vis the will so early in the discussion. However, by placing this metaphysical discussion in the introductory remarks, he secures an apologetic goal by engaging the interest of the academic audience. It does not appear that Edwards's interest in securing this demographic was to marginalize the laity, but rather to directly confront those whom he deemed most influential in the effort to oppose the revival. If Edwards could gain a foothold within Boston's clerical and academic elite, then opposition to the revival could be stymied at its source.[7]

[7] The plethora of editions printed between the publication of the original (1746) and that of Edward Hickman (1829) suggests that many shared the opinion that the original version of *Religious Affections* was too difficult a read for the general public. Smith, noting the editorial freedoms evident in these subsequent editions, remarks that "for some unexplained reason almost everyone who had anything to do with the reprinting of *Affections* fell into the same pattern of thinking; the work is very important as an evangelical tract; it ought to be read by everyone; it is too subtle for the average reader; it must be rewritten." John Wesley, for one, opined that Edwards's metaphysical arguments rendered *Religious Affections* unsuitable—even detrimental—to the laity: "He heaps together so many curious, subtle, metaphysical distinctions, as are sufficient to puzzle the brain, and confound the intellects, of all the plain men and women in the universe, and to make them doubt of, if not

The Affections in Relation to the Body. Edwards's argument for the unity of the affections and the will is paired with a second metaphysical argument: the "laws of the union of soul and body." Edwards asserts that a "law" exists which unifies the soul (or mind) and the body so that the two exist in a relationship in which the state of one inevitably affects the state of the other. Since the affections are properly associated with the mind, the reader is led by Edwards to the conclusion that the state of affections will manifest itself bodily and that the state of the body will manifest itself in the affections.[8]

Edwards does not give an explicit explanation of the connection between the physical and the mental, but his affirmation that both aspects shared a mutual influence was in keeping with the accepted psychological theories of the day. Much of this theory of mutual influence traded on the Cartesian notion of "animal spirits," a particular property of the blood which could influence the nerves by means of the brain's pineal gland. Edwards's frequent reference to "animal spirits" refers to this theory, and Edwards's educated audience was well-informed on the theory and its implications.[9]

Edwards does not develop the implications of this point until later in the work. Nevertheless, for the well-read among his readers, the import of this point was immediately obvious. The extraordinary outward displays—such as the widespread faintings, weepings, shouting, visions, and so forth—were very much at the center of the controversy concerning the authenticity of the Awakening.[10] By establishing a metaphysical union between the body and the affections, Edwards effectively ensures that whatever opinion is formed of

wholly deny, all the work which God had wrought in their souls." John E. Smith, "Editor's Introduction," WJE 2:78; John Wesley, *The Works of the Rev. John Wesley*, vol. 14 (London: Wesleyan Conference, 1872), 270.

[8] Edwards, *Religious Affections*, WJE 2:98.

[9] Ann Taves, *Fits, Trances, and Visions: Experiencing Religion and Explaining Experience from Wesley to James* (Princeton, NJ: Princeton University, 1999), 27–28.

[10] For a thoughtful assessment of experiential phenomena during the Great Awakening, see Taves, *Fits, Trances, and Visions*, 13–75.

the affections will also apply to the bodily expressions. If affections can be demonstrated to have legitimate place in the Christian religion, so can their bodily expressions. And if bodily expressions are legitimized, the opposition to the revival is deprived of one of its chief objections.

The Affections Distinguished from Passions. The third argument for the definition of affections immediately follows the first two. In a brief paragraph, Edwards qualifies his definition of affections. Observing the fact that many used the terms affections and passions interchangeably, Edwards calls for a distinction to be made between the two. Whereas affections should be understood as a general reference to "all vigorous lively actings of the will or inclination," passions are to be understood as a particular subset of these, distinct on account that they are "more sudden, and whose effects on animal spirits are more violent, and the mind more overpowered, and less in its own command."[11]

By making this observation, Edwards accomplishes two goals with one stroke. First, Edwards identifies his own position with respected scholarly opinion on the matter, employing a line of thought similar to that expressed by Francis Hutcheson in 1728:

> When the word *Passion* is imagined to denote any thing different from the *Affections*, it includes, beside the *Desire* or *Aversion*, beside the *calm Joy* upon apprehended Possession of Good, or *Sorrow* from the Loss of it, or from impending Evil, "a *confused Sensation* either of Pleasure or Pain, occasioned by some violent bodily Motions, which keeps the Mind much employed upon the present Affair, to the exclusion of every thing else, and prolongs or strengthens the Affection sometimes to such a degree, as to prevent all *deliberate Reasoning* about our Conduct."[12]

[11] Edwards, *Religious Affections*, WJE 2:98.

[12] Francis Hutcheson, *An Essay on the Nature and Conduct of the Passions and Affections, with Illustrations on the Moral Sense*, ed. Aaron Garrett, Natural

By aligning his ideas with those in respectable academic discourse, Edwards introduces a compelling element, one likely to engage the attention of the cultural elite. Second, he also signals Charles Chauncy and the Old Lights that the charge of "enthusiasm"— which traded freely with the currency of the "passions"—is about to come under closer scrutiny. As opponents of the revival, they frequently claimed that the common and public display of "passions" was sufficient evidence that the revival was fraudulent.[13] Edwards responds

---

Law and Enlightenment Classics (1728; repr., Indianapolis: Liberty Fund, 2002), 30–31; italics his. The quotation within the quotation is undocumented by Hutcheson; the majority of quotations within this work are undocumented, and this was in keeping with the literary standard of the day. David Hume likewise used unacknowledged sources: "In accordance with the customs and genre constraints of the period, Hume often obliquely points to a source or a type of source, while omitting the name of the source and giving no hint of how to trace it." See Tom L. Beauchamp, "Introduction," in *The Works of David Hume*, ed. Tom L. Beauchamp (Oxford: Oxford University, 1998), xxii. Two additional observations should be made with respect to Francis Hutcheson and this text. First, Hutcheson points to Malebranche's *Recherche de la Verité* for further reference concerning his thought regarding sensation; however, the editor suggests that Malebranche's *Elucidation* is more directly responsible for Hutcheson's thought. As mentioned previously, Malebranche's influence on Edwards has been well-documented. Second, the fact that Edwards agrees with Hutcheson on this one point should not lead the reader to anticipate a general agreement between Edwards and Hutcheson. To draw this conclusion is tempting; Marsden observes that "Edwards' language and categories sounded a lot like Hutcheson's because the two had worked within the same wider eighteenth-century discourse." Hutcheson, however, maintained that all humanity possessed a divine moral capacity "sufficient to lead them . . . to a life of virtue for which they were also promised eternal rewards." This, of course, was a view squarely opposed to traditional Westminster theology and its teachings concerning total depravity and inability. See George M. Marsden, *Jonathan Edwards: A Life* (New Haven: Yale, 2003), 465–66.

[13] Chauncy supplied the most articulate expression of this sentiment in his *Seasonable Thoughts on the State of Religion in New-England* (1743). His conflation of the affections and passions is evident: "Reasonable Beings are not to be guided by Passion or Affection, though the Object of it should be

by insisting that a distinction should be observed between "affections" and "passions." The adoption of this metaphysical distinction is preparatory for the position he is about to recommend: that a distinction must be made between those inward impulses that are motivated by the Spirit and those which are not.

The Affections in Relation to Actions. The fourth metaphysical component concerns the manner in which affections relate to actions. Although this discussion in *Religious Affections* appears in Section Two of Part One, it should be considered as an extension of the introductory metaphysical section since its purpose in the argument is to sustain the same proposition as the first three. Edwards defines the relation of affections to actions in terms of the human constitution:

> The Author of the human nature has not only given affections to men, but has made 'em very much the spring of men's actions. As the affections do not only necessarily belong to the human nature, but are a very great part of it; so (inasmuch as by regeneration, persons are renewed in the whole man, and sanctified throughout) holy affections do not only necessarily belong to true religion, but are a very great part of that. And as true religion is of a practical nature, and God has so constituted the human nature, that the affections are very much the spring of men's actions, this also shows, that true religion must consist very much in the affections.[14]

The essential point Edwards makes in the paragraph is the observation that God created the human constitution to operate in such a

---

GOD, and the Things of another World." "The plain truth is, an enlightened Mind, and not raised Affections, ought always to be the Guide of those who call themselves Men; and this, in the Affairs of Religion, as well as other Things." Charles Chauncy, *Seasonable Thoughts on the State of Religion in New England* (Boston: Samuel Eliot, 1743), 324, 326–27. See also Marsden, *Jonathan Edwards*, 280–83; Edward M. Griffin, *Old Brick: Charles Chauncy of Boston, 1705–1787* (Minneapolis: University of Minnesota, 1980), 74–84.

[14] Edwards, *Religious Affections*, WJE 2:100–101.

way that affections maintain a causal relationship with behavior. The result is a proposition that, when joined with the previous three, forms a sustainable metaphysical understanding of the human affections. With this final point in place, Edwards can reasonably argue that affections are an undeniable component of human existence and unified with the mind/will. Consequently, any attempt by his opponents to discredit the revival on account of "affections" must bear the burden of giving a better account of human existence.[15]

The Significance of the Nature of the Affections for Edwards's Theological Method. The opening lines of Section Two in *Religious Affections* are positioned after the first three metaphysical arguments but prior to the fourth. These lines are noteworthy, for they indicate the significance of the metaphysical ideas to the theological method of the work:

> What has been said of the nature of the affections, makes this evident, and may be sufficient, without adding anything further, to put this matter out of doubt: for who will deny that true religion consists, in a great measure, in vigorous and lively actings of the inclination and will of the soul, or the fervent exercises of the heart.
>
> That religion which God requires, and will accept, does not consist in weak, dull and lifeless wouldings, raising us but a little above a state of indifference: God, in his Word, greatly insists upon it, that we be in good earnest, fervent in spirit, and our hearts vigorously engaged in religion: "Be ye fervent in spirit, serving the Lord" (Rom. 12:11). "And now Israel, what doth the Lord thy God require of thee, but to fear the Lord thy God, to walk in all his ways, and to love him, and to serve the Lord thy God, with all thy heart, and with all thy soul?" (Deut. 10:12). And ch. 6:4–5, "Hear, O Israel; the

[15] Ibid., 2:101.

> Lord our God is one Lord; and thou shalt love the Lord thy God, with all thy heart, and with all thy soul, and with all thy might." 'Tis such a fervent, vigorous engagedness of the heart in religion, that is the fruit of a real circumcision of the heart, or true regeneration, and that has the promises of life; "And the Lord thy God will circumcise thine heart, and the heart of thy seed, to love the Lord thy God, with all thy heart, and with all thy soul, that thou mayest live" (Deut. 30:6).[16]

This section of text is significant for two reasons. First, it indicates that Edwards intends for the metaphysical arguments ("what has been said of the nature of the affections") to dovetail directly into other theological sources—in this case, biblical material—to sustain a single proposition. This evidence clearly supports a view of Edwards's theological method as that of a matrix, a coordinated synthesis of different source types communicating with one another for the purpose of producing a single theological message.

Second, this text is significant in that it indicates *how* Edwards intends for the metaphysical elements to function in relation to the other sources. The first three arguments (unity of the affections and will, unity of the soul and body, distinction of affections and passions) are intended to preempt early objections to the doctrinal proposition that "true religion . . . consists in holy affections." By using metaphysical arguments to "put this matter out of doubt," Edwards anticipates and outflanks those objections most likely to arise from intellectuals well-informed on current metaphysical discourse.[17] When considered in the context of the preceding and succeeding paragraphs as well as the historical context, metaphysical arguments evidently serve a defensive role. Consequently, we should conclude that Edwards does

[16] Ibid., 2:99. Note that "wouldings" is updated to read "wishes" in the Hickman edition. Jonathan Edwards, *A Treatise Concerning Religious Affections*, ed. Edward Hickman, in The Works of Jonathan Edwards, vol. 1 (1834; repr., Edinburgh: Banner of Truth, 2003), 237.

[17] Edwards, *Religious Affections*, WJE 2:99.

not view these metaphysical points as the ground of his own position, but rather as a necessary concession to readers who would be more inclined to ground their own opinion in sound metaphysics. Edwards has already grounded his proposition in the text of 1 Peter 1:8, rendering the metaphysical points which follow to a supporting role.

The "Simple Idea"

Not only does Edwards employ a metaphysical argument for the definition of *affections*, but he also makes use of metaphysics to assist in the definition of the biblical idea of the operation of the Spirit in regeneration. In Part Three of *Religious Affections*, Edwards presents twelve indicators "showing what are distinguishing signs of truly gracious and holy affections."[18] The first sign is that "affections that are truly spiritual and gracious, do arise from those influences and operations on the heart, which are spiritual, supernatural, and divine."[19] Edwards justifies this sign with a multi-pronged argument, one point of which rehearses the standard Calvinist dichotomy between the fleshly nature of the unregenerate and the spiritual nature of the regenerate.

Edwards's Use of Locke's "Simple Idea." At this juncture, the item which Edwards focuses upon is the unique nature of the regenerated person, and he abruptly turns to metaphysics to underscore the theological point:

> For doubtless if God by his mighty power produces something that is new, not only in degree and circumstances, but in its whole nature, and that which could be produced by no exalting, varying or compounding of what was there before, or by adding anything of the like kind; I say, if God produces something thus new in a mind, that is a perceiving, thinking, conscious thing; then doubtless something entirely new is felt,

[18] Ibid., 2:192.
[19] Ibid., 2:197.

> or perceived, or thought; or, which is the same thing, there is some new sensation or perception of the mind, which is entirely of a new sort, and which could be produced by no exalting, varying or compounding of that kind of perceptions or sensations which the mind had before; or there is what some metaphysicians call a new simple idea.[20]

Edwards makes reference to the "simple idea" only once in *Religious Affections*, but the reference has generated significant interest within the academic community. The notion of a "simple idea" was a category advanced by John Locke as a component in his larger epistemological scheme. Locke, in his *Essay Concerning Human Understanding*, proposed that all knowledge was constituted of "simple ideas" and "complex ideas," with the former being foundational for the latter. According to Locke, "simple ideas" were ideas which were not produced actively by the mind, but came passively to the mind by means of the senses.[21] Just as Locke worked with this ontological concept in order to advance his version of empiricism, so Edwards, by way of analogy, borrows Locke's term to advance his own epistemological case for the spiritual "new sense."

Interpretations of Edwards's Use of Locke's "Simple Idea." This single reference to the "simple idea" has been the occasion of considerable discussion. Garry Williams observes that this section within *Religious Affections* "is often said to be his most revealingly Lockean text at this point."[22] Perry Miller leveraged this text to support his

[20] Ibid., 2:205.

[21] John Locke, *An Essay Concerning Human Understanding*, ed. Kenneth P. Winkler (1689; repr., Indianapolis: Hackett, 1996), 40–55, 66–69, 115–20; R. S. Woolhouse, *Locke: A Biography* (Cambridge: Cambridge University, 2007), 99–100; Perry Miller, *Errand Into the Wilderness* (New York: Harper Collins, 1956), 168–73; Michael J. McClymond, *Encounters with God: An Approach to the Theology of Jonathan Edwards* (New York: Oxford University, 1998), 11.

[22] Garry J. Williams, "Enlightenment Epistemology and Eighteenth-Century Evangelical Doctrines of Assurance," in *The Advent of Evangelical-*

assertion that Edwards was essentially a follower of Locke, a position which became the focal point of extended debate in the mid-twentieth century and which received renewed momentum in Bebbington's *Evangelicalism in Modern Britain*.[23] Williams maintains that Edwards can in no wise be interpreted as Lockean, especially at this juncture in *Religious Affections*; Edwards simply did not use the technical terms to advance Locke's individual issues. Instead, Edwards uses Locke's language and concepts to advance his own ideas.[24] Williams points to Brad Walton's study for a superior accounting of the data and agrees with Walton's conclusion on the matter: "On the rare occasion he uses a Lockean technical term, such as 'simple idea,' he does so metaphorically, in an un-Lockean sense, for the purposes of illustration by analogy."[25]

The Significance of the "Simple Idea" for Edwards's Theological Method. In short, Edwards borrows Locke's concept of the "simple idea" to advance a theological idea: regeneration entails the work of the Spirit; since the Spirit's nature is unique, so is the nature of his work. When this unique work of the Spirit comes to the mind of the regenerated individual, it does so in a manner analogous to Locke's "simple idea." Just as Locke's "simple idea" is passively received by the senses without the influence of the mind, so for Edwards the work of the Spirit in regeneration exists apart from the human mind and only comes to the mind as it is apprehended by a spiritual sense.

The significance of this concept is that the metaphysical point is used in an analogical manner: It illustrates to readers acquainted with

---

ism, ed. Michael A. G. Haykin and Kenneth J. Stewart (Downers Grove, IL: InterVarsity, 2008), 357.

[23] Miller, *Jonathan Edwards*, 186–87; Miller, *Errand Into the Wilderness*, 169–81; McClymond, *Encounters with God*, 11–14; David W. Bebbington, *Evangelicalism in Modern Britain: A History from the 1730's to the 1980's* (London: Unwin Hyman, 1989), 47–55.

[24] Williams, "Enlightenment Epistemology," 356–61.

[25] Brad Walton, *Jonathan Edwards, Religious Affections, and the Puritan Analysis of True Piety, Spiritual Sensations, and Heart Religion* (Lewiston, NY: Edwin Mellen, 2002), 218.

Locke the biblical teaching concerning the uniqueness of the regenerating work of the Spirit. Since the function of the "simple idea" is illustrative, it maintains a communicative relationship with another theological source (that which is being illustrated: scripture), pointing again to a theological method involving a matrix of sources. Furthermore, Edwards modifies the notion of the "simple idea" from Locke's original design to suit a biblically-informed agenda; this points to a theological method which is governed by Scripture as its authoritative theological source.

The Role of Epistemology in the Theological Method of *Religious Affections*

Consideration of the "simple idea" supplies a convenient opportunity to shift the focus of the study to Edwards's epistemology since he used the "simple idea" to advance his larger discussion of "the new sense," a line of thought that trades in the epistemological categories of the day. Interestingly, Edwards appeals to epistemology to launch Part Three of *Religious Affections*, much in the same manner that he used the language of metaphysics to begin Part One. In Part One, Edwards offered a metaphysical argument to establish the nature of the affections; in Part Three, Edwards offers an epistemological argument to establish a rational basis for discerning spiritual realities. Herein, two significant epistemological elements present themselves, the first being the question of perception and the second concerning the role of presupposition. An examination of each of these will reveal the contribution of epistemological categories to the theological agenda of *Religious Affections*.

Religious Affections is rather unbalanced in its structure; Part One takes the first nine percent of the text and Part Two the next eighteen percent. Part Three consumes the remaining seventy-three percent of the text. Whatever might be deduced from this disparity, the reader is justified in concluding that Edwards was primarily interested in the substance of Part Three. The title for Part Three is stated simply:

"Shewing What Are Distinguishing Signs of Truly Gracious Affections."[26] The agenda of the section is discernment, and the business of discernment inevitably involves criteria for knowledge and other matters pertaining to epistemology. For this reason, Edwards opens up this final and most important section with an argument involving the issue of perception with regard to discernment.

The Problem of Perception

Since discernment is a key theme in *Religious Affections*, Edwards is compelled to discuss the questions of how and why people perceive things incorrectly. People may perceive objects incorrectly on account of being impeded as he explains in his "Object and Eye" discussion. Perception can also function on incorrect principles, leading to self-deception.

The agenda for Part Three in *Religious Affections* is a series of twelve signs for discerning authentic Christian affections. These signs, or marks of saving grace, are the focal point of the work. In short, Edwards maintains that true religious affections (1) arise on account of the Spirit of God; (2) love God rather than self; (3) delight in God's nature and character; (4) entail a new spiritual sense; (5) involve a certainty of divine things; (6) are marked by humility; (7) are attended by conversion, or a change of nature; (8) display a spirit of love, meekness, forgiveness, and mercy; (9) express tenderness toward the things of God; (10) display their various virtues with relative balance; (11) reveal a desire for increased holiness; and (12) manifest themselves in biblical and obedient behavior.

The Problem of Object and Eye. However, before he introduces these signs, Edwards begins by inserting two qualifications concerning their value. First, he observes that the Scripture supplies "rules" for knowing the nature of Christian affections but that these rules are intended only for personal introspection and not for knowing the spiritual state of others. Second, he observes that the signs will not be

[26] Edwards, *Religious Affections*, WJE 2:191.

helpful to Christians "who are very low in grace, or are such as have much departed from God, and are fallen into a dead, carnal, unchristian frame."[27] The reason for this second point comes in the form of an epistemological explanation.

Perception of spiritual realities will likely be impeded by spiritual deficiencies. If a Christian is "low in grace," he/she will likely suffer from either a "defect in the object" or a "defect in the eye." By a "defect in the object," Edwards refers to what the Christian is observing spiritually within. In the physical realm, if an object is small or undeveloped, it is difficult to identify. Similarly, says Edwards, the Christian may have a perception problem concerning the authenticity of one's own profession because the spiritual object being observed (one's own spirituality) is "defective," i.e., too small to see clearly or too immature in its development to identify positively. The ability to clearly perceive one's own spiritual state may also be compromised by the "defect of the eye." That is, just as a physical eye that is not functioning properly may impede perception of the material world, so a Christian in a "dead, carnal frame" lacks the spiritual sensory capacity to clearly view internal spiritual realities.[28]

Edwards appears once again to be borrowing from Locke. Locke, in his *Essay Concerning Understanding*, parses the relationship between the physical eye and external material objects and how sensation of these objects results in knowledge. Yet he admits to an internal capacity for obtaining knowledge of immaterial things and suggests that this capacity is analogous to the way in which the body senses the material world. This capacity is an internal sense of immaterial realities.[29]

Interpreters of Edwards have mused over the significance of Edwards's use of Locke on this point. Leon Chai is convinced that

[27] Ibid., 2:193.

[28] Ibid., 2:194–95.

[29] Locke, *An Essay Concerning Human Understanding*, 34. For Locke, the primary immaterial reality was the reality of spirit or a "thing capable of thinking"; 119. See also 123–24, 140–43.

Edwards uses Locke to establish a degree of certainty not possible with a simple appeal to Scripture.[30] Chai acknowledges that Edwards claims to be "far from undertaking to give such signs of gracious affections, as shall be sufficient to enable any certainly to distinguish true affections from false in others."[31] Yet he concludes that Edwards is disingenuous because "his interest in the question seems undeniable . . . . The issue of objective verification . . . receives . . . the most extensive treatment." Since Edwards is "attempting to assimilate true religious experiences to external sensations or perceptions . . . [he] manifestly hopes to press the case for objectivity to its limit."[32]

The fact that Edwards is leaning on Locke is undeniable as is Edwards's quest for achieving objective knowledge. But is Chai correct to assert that Edwards uses Locke in order to achieve a degree of certainty not otherwise obtainable by the use of Scripture? Such a claim can be the case only if the context demonstrates that Edwards uses Locke to ground an argument for the acquisition of knowledge. A careful reading of the key sections in which Edwards appeals to Locke (object/eye; new sense) indicates that such is not the case. Chai is able to sustain his conclusion only by assessing Edwards's use of Locke out of context. Consequently, Chai fails to adequately account for the use of Locke in relation to the biblical sources and theological ideas operating within the same argument.[33]

A review of Edwards's use of the "object/eye" distinction *in context* shows that such is the case. The discussion is clearly intended to explain the preceding theological assertion that a Christian "low in grace" will have a problem perceiving his/her own spiritual condition. Therefore, the entire purpose of invoking Locke in this case is to

[30] Chai, *Jonathan Edwards and the Limits of Enlightenment Philosophy*, 25.

[31] Edwards, *Religious Affections*, WJE 2:193.

[32] Chai, *Jonathan Edwards and the Limits of Enlightenment Philosophy*, 26.

[33] See Chai's chapter "Religious Affections" in *Jonathan Edwards and the Limits of Enlightenment Philosophy*, 22–35. While Chai skillfully intersects the relevant sections of *Affections* with Locke, he gives almost no attention to the bulk of biblical and theological material which frames the use of the Lockean concepts.

argue for *a less objective certainty*, not a more objective certainty. Furthermore, the nature of the explanation is not to establish the ground of the assertion but the manner in which the assertion is manifest. For the "object/eye" discussion, the theological assertion is restated, this time with grounding support from biblical texts. Subsequently, two conclusions can be drawn: first, the *purpose* of the "object/eye" discussion is to *qualify* the degree of certainty one can expect from the signs; second, the *function* of the "object/eye" discussion is *illustrative*, not foundational. In view of these considerations, it seems unreasonable to conclude with Chai that Edwards employed Lockean categories to achieve a greater degree of objectivity than what could be obtained from the Scriptures.

The Problem of Self-Deception. The "object/eye" discussion, as a perception problem, stands alongside another problem of perception in *Religious Affections*: the problem of self-deception. In fact, the problem of self-deception is alluded to from the very opening words of *Religious Affections*. Edwards observes in the preface that "it would be endless to reckon up the variety of opinions, in this point, that divide the Christian world; making manifest the truth of that of our Saviour, 'Strait is the gate, and narrow is the way, that leads to life, and few there be that find it.'"[34]

Edwards borrows from Thomas Shepard's *Parable of the Ten Virgins* in order to confront the problem of self-deception in terms of "hypocrisy." Shepard distinguished between "legal" and "evangelical" hypocrites, and Edwards borrows these categories to assist in his description of self-deception.[35] As Ava Chamberlain observes in her insightful study, the hypocrisy in view with Shepard and Edwards is not the sort by which a person misrepresents himself to others, but rather to himself.[36] According to Edwards, "legal" hypocrites were

[34] Edwards, *Religious Affections*, WJE 2:84.

[35] Thomas Shepard, *The Parable of the Ten Virgins* (1659; repr., Orlando: Soli Deo Gloria, 1990), 191.

[36] Ava Chamberlain, "Self-Deception as a Theological Problem in Jonathan Edwards's 'Treatise Concerning Religious Affections'," *Church History*

Arminian in their doctrine of justification and "deceived with their outward morality and external religion."[37] "Evangelical" hypocrisy, on the other hand, was of a far more dangerous and deceptive sort. The New Lights were boasting of certain assurance of salvation based on visions and revelations, impressions and experience. Convinced that no other evidence was relevant, the New Lights "despise[d] all argument and inquiry" to the contrary.[38] Their confidence was "like the confidence of some mad men, who think they are kings: they will maintain it against all manner of reason and evidence."[39]

In Edwards's estimation, the self-deception of the New Lights was based on grounding of assurance in a combination of false doctrine and the euphoria of the conversion experience. It involved, as Chamberlain quips, "a policy of selective attention" by which these professing converts rehearsed the details of their experiences while ignoring questions concerning motives and behavior.[40] Edwards believed that the misuse of bible doctrines had a hand in "establish[ing] this delusion and the false confidence of the hypocrites." The doctrine of "Christians living by faith, not by sight" and "their giving glory to God, by trusting him in the dark" were misconstrued to justify a wholesale discounting of other biblical truths.[41]

Edwards objects to the doctrinal formulations of the New Lights because they used Scriptures, such as Hebrews 11 (which elevated faith over sight), out of context. These texts, argues Edwards, address the error of preferring what can be seen physically in the material world over the promise of God. These texts cannot be used to describe spiritual sight; the biblical author did not intend that "sight" in the text be spiritualized.[42] The result is a doctrinal deviation that

---

63, 4 (December 1994): 543.

[37] Edwards, *Religious Affections*, WJE 2:173.

[38] Ibid., 2:174.

[39] Ibid.

[40] Chamberlain, "Self-Deception," 549; Edwards, *Religious Affections*, WJE 2:174.

[41] Edwards, *Religious Affections*, WJE 2:175.

[42] Ibid.

violates other biblical texts describing the nature of spiritual perception:

> But this doctrine, as it is understood by many, is that Christians ought firmly to believe and trust in Christ, without spiritual sight or light, and although they are in a dark dead frame, and, for the present, have no spiritual experiences or discoveries. And it is truly the duty of those who are thus in darkness, to come out of darkness into light, and believe. But that they should confidently believe and trust, while they yet remain without spiritual light or sight, is an antiscriptural and absurd doctrine.[43]

The correct response, says Edwards, is faith by sight—sight of Christ: "The Scripture is ignorant of any such faith in Christ of the operation of God, that is not founded in a spiritual sight of Christ."[44] From this point forward, Edwards makes an extended case for spiritual perception by means of spiritual sight and light. Without spiritual light in the soul and sight of Christ, faith will not lay hold of Christ as its object but will instead lay hold of itself, having faith in faith.[45]

Although this entire discussion does not speak in overt epistemological terms, good reasons demand consideration in this discussion as part of Edwards's epistemology. First, the subject matter is self-deception, a point which introduced elements of justification of knowledge. The dispute between Edwards and the New Lights concerns a correct basis for justifying the knowledge of salvation. Second, the response is crafted in terms of perception, especially "sight" and "light." The relationship between perception and knowledge was of great interest to Edwards's philosophically-oriented audience.

[43] Ibid.
[44] Ibid.
[45] Ibid., 2:176–78.

Edwards knew this. Readers of Locke could hardly have missed the similarities. By making much of "sight" and "light" to describe inward realities, he was—in addition to using biblical terminology—quite likely alluding to Locke's *Essay Concerning Human Understanding*. Committed to empiricism, Locke was given to defining metaphysical perception in terms that were analogous to physical perception. Additionally, in his *Essay*, Locke regularly described perception in the metaphysical realm as comparable to sight in the physical realm.[46] The need for "light" to "see" was for Locke the best way to describe the perception of internal matters—the same point that Edwards makes with the same terms.

The Significance of Perception Problems for Edwards's Theological Method. The significance of this discussion for Edwards's theological method can be summarized as follows. First, although Edwards was likely alluding to Locke, it was only to borrow his categories, not his conclusions. The inward "light" of which Locke spoke reason whereas the light of which Edwards spoke is the knowledge of Christ. Once again, just as in the case of the "object/eye" discussion, Edwards's use of an epistemological category functions in a supporting role. Second, Edwards interfaces this discussion on perception with both historical and biblical sources. Thomas Shepard's two types of hypocrites supplies the occasion for explaining self-deception in terms of spiritual perception. Afterward, the ideas of "sight" and "light" are defined

[46] Philip Vogt, *John Locke and the Rhetoric of Modernity* (Lanham, MD: Lexington, 2008), 110–14. Vogt substantiates his observations by citing texts from Locke's *Reasonableness of Christianity*, *A Letter Concerning Toleration*, and *An Essay Concerning Human Understanding*. See John Locke, *The Works of John Locke*, vol. 6, *The Reasonableness of Christianity* (1695; repr., London: Rivington, 1824), 133; Locke, *An Essay Concerning Humane Understanding*, 154; John Locke, *A Letter Concerning Toleration*, ed. James H. Tully (1689; repr., Indianapolis: Hackett, 1983), 27–28. The later transcendentalists would reject the attempt on Locke's part to draw this analogy, citing it as internally inconsistent with his own empiricist principles. See Orestes A. Brownson, "Norton's Evidence," in *The Transcendentalists: An Anthology*, ed. Perry Miller (Boston: Harvard University, 1950), 207–8.

by theological categories and biblical proof-texts. With philosophical ideas, historical theology, and biblical material all in play, this section of Edwards's text in *Religious Affections* demonstrates an exchange of all three major source types in order to make the single theological assertion for the necessity of spiritual sight. This is further evidence for a matrix-like function of Edwards's theological method.

"The New Sense"

Though Edwards made much of the problems of spiritual perception, his intent was not to cast doubt on the possibility of spiritual knowledge but to direct attention to the authentic means of obtaining that knowledge. This means was "the new sense" which comes to every believer at the point of conversion. Prior to assessing its significance, it will be helpful to review its historical context as well as to survey interpretive approaches to this idea.

"The New Sense" Prior to Religious Affections. Although Edwards gave his most complete treatment of the "new sense" in *Religious Affections*, he had circulated the idea in earlier works. In his earliest published work, "A Faithful Narrative," Edwards describes conversion experiences in Northampton in such terms:

> The converting influences of God's Spirit very commonly bring an extraordinary conviction of the reality and certainty of the great things of religion. They have that sight and taste of the divinity and divine excellency of the things of the Gospel . . . and very often speak of their sense of the excellency of the way of salvation by free and sovereign grace. . . . They appear to have a new sense of things, new apprehensions and view of God, and the great things of the Gospel. They have a new sense of the truth of them. . . .[47]

[47] Jonathan Edwards, "A Faithful Narrative of the Surprising Work of God," in *The Great Awakening*, ed. C. C. Goen, The Works of Jonathan Edwards, vol. 4 (New Haven: Yale, 1970), 125–26.

In "Some Thoughts Concerning the Revival," he speaks again of conversion bringing "a new sense":

> When these persons are extraordinarily affected with a new sense, and recent discovery they have received of the greatness and excellency of the divine Being, the certainty and infinite importance of eternal things, the preciousness of souls, and the dreadful danger and madness of mankind, together with a great sense of God's distinguishing kindness and love to them; no wonder that now they think they must exert themselves, and do something extraordinary for the honor of God . . .[48]
>
> The disposition that was then felt was, on the contrary, to prefer others to self, and to hope that they saw more of God and loved him better; though before, under smaller discoveries and feebler exercises of divine affection, there had been felt a disposition to censure and condemn others. And another thing that was felt at that time, was a very great sense of the importance of moral social duties, and how great a part of religion lay in them: there was such a new sense and conviction of this, beyond what had been before, that it seemed to be as it were a clear discovery then made to the soul. But in general, there has been a very great increase of a sense of these two things, as divine views and divine love have increased.[49]

These early published expressions raise an important question: Was Edwards thinking of this "new sense" in perceptual terms, analogous to philosophical discourses on perception, this early in his writing career? McClymond argues that the answer to this question is

[48] Jonathan Edwards, "Some Thoughts Concerning the Revival," in *The Great Awakening*, ed. C. C. Goen, The Works of Jonathan Edwards, vol. 4 (New Haven: Yale, 1970), 321–22.

[49] Ibid., 4:335–36.

"yes," pointing to Edwards's early personal writings, beginning with "Miscellany aa. FAITH":

> There may undoubtedly be such a thing as is called the testimony of faith, and a sort of certainty of faith that is different from reason, that is, different from discourse by a chain of arguments, a certainty that is given by the Holy Spirit; and yet such a belief may be altogether agreeable to reason, agreeable to the exactest rules of philosophy. Such ideas of religion may be in the mind, as a man may feel divinity in them, and so may know they are from God, know that religion is of divine original, that is, is divine truth. Yea, this faith may be to the degree of certainty, for he may certainly intuitively see God and feel him in those ideas; that is, he may certainly see that notion he has of God in them. The notion of God, or idea I have of him, is that complex idea of such power, holiness, purity, majesty, love, excellency, beauty, loveliness, and ten thousand other things. Now when a man is certain he sees those things, he is certain he sees that which he calls divine. . . . Now no man can deny but that such an idea of religion may possibly be wrought by the Holy Spirit. 'Tis not unphilosophical to think so.[50]

[50] Jonathan Edwards, "Miscellany aa. FAITH," in *The "Miscellanies" a–500*, ed. Thomas A. Schafer, The Works of Jonathan Edwards, vol. 13 (New Haven: Yale, 1994), 177–78. Through a patient analysis of biographical entries, paper and ink types, and orthography, Schafer establishes April of 1723 as the date for the composition of this miscellany. See Thomas A. Schafer, "Editor's Introduction," in *The "Miscellanies" a–500*, ed. Thomas A. Schafer, The Works of Jonathan Edwards, vol. 13 (New Haven: Yale, 1994), 75–80, 92. Given such an early date, Schafer concludes that "these words furnish the earliest evidence in the 'Miscellanies' of JE's acquaintance with the thought of John Locke." See Edwards, "Miscellany aa. FAITH," 177n9. For McClymond's analysis, see his *Encounters With God*, 16–17.

Mark Valeri observes that Edwards continues to develop this epistemological idea of spiritual sensation throughout the 1730s as is evident in miscellanies 489, 540, 628, and 630.[51] His maturing thought on the spiritual sense is also evident in his 1733 sermon "A Divine and Supernatural Light," in which he speaks of a spiritual sense in the same perceptual terms as were in vogue with both the leading empiricists (John Locke) and moralists (Francis Hutcheson) of the day.[52]

"The New Sense" in Religious Affections. Consequently, the idea of the "new sense" as expressed in *Religious Affections* is the product of seasoned thought. In Section One of Part Three in *Religious Affections*, Edwards argues for the supernatural character of truly spiritual affections since they are the product of the Holy Spirit. Since they are supernatural, they do not originate from or act in response to any natural principle within man. The inward principle is of a truly different sort (the appeal to the "simple idea"). Edwards then proceeds to explain this principle:

> [It] is a new inward perception or sensation of their minds, entirely different in its nature and kind, from anything that ever their minds were the subjects of before they were sanctified. . . . If grace be . . . an entirely new kind of principle. . . [,] then the exercises of it are also entirely a new kind of exer-

[51] Mark Valeri, "Preface to the Period," in *Sermons and Discourses: 1730–1733*, ed. Mark Valeri, The Works of Jonathan Edwards, vol. 17 (New Haven: Yale, 1999), 40. See Edwards, "Miscellany 489. FAITH, OR SPIRTUAL KNOWLEDGE" in *The "Miscellanies" a–500*, 533; see also "Miscellany 540. SPIRITUAL UNDERSTANDING," "Miscellany 628. SPIRITUAL KNOWLEDGE. FAITH," and "Miscellany 630. SPIRITUAL KNOWLEDGE. FAITH," in Jonathan Edwards, *The "Miscellanies" 501–832*, ed. Ava Chamberlain, The Works of Jonathan Edwards, vol. 18 (New Haven: Yale, 2000), 88–89; 156–58.

[52] Jonathan Edwards, "A Divine and Supernatural Light," in *Sermons and Discourses: 1730–1733*, ed. Mark Valeri, The Works of Jonathan Edwards, vol. 17 (New Haven: Yale, 1999), 407–26; Valeri, "Preface to the Period," WJE 17:41–42.

> cises. And if there be in the soul a new sort of exercises . . . then it follows that the mind has an entirely new kind of perception or sensation; and here is, as it were, a new spiritual sense that the mind has, or a principle of new kind of perception or spiritual sensation, which is in its whole nature different from any former kinds of sensation of the mind, as tasting is diverse from any of the other senses; and something is perceived by a true saint, in the exercise of this new sense of mind, in spiritual and divine things, as entirely diverse from anything that is perceived in them, by natural men, as the sweet taste of honey is diverse from the ideas men get of honey by only looking on it, and feeling of it. . . . Hence the work of the Spirit of God in regeneration is often in Scripture compared to the giving a new sense, giving eyes to see, and ears to hear, unstopping the ears of the deaf, and opening the eyes of them that were born blind, and turning from darkness unto light. And because this spiritual sense is immensely the most noble and excellent, and that without which all other principles of perception, and all our faculties are useless and vain; therefore the giving this new sense, with the blessed fruits and effects of it in the soul, is compared to a raising the dead, and to a new creation.[53]

The point of invoking the "new sense" is to explain the nature and the true source of holy affections:

> From what has been said it follows, that all spiritual and gracious affections are attended with, and do arise from some apprehension, idea or sensation of mind, which is in its whole nature different, yea exceeding different from all that is or can be in the mind of a natural man; and which the natural man discerns nothing of, and has no manner of idea of (agreeable

[53] Edwards, *Religious Affections*, WJE 2:205–6.

> to 1 Cor. 2:14), and conceives of no more than a man without the sense of tasting can conceive of the sweet taste of honey, or a man without the sense of hearing can conceive of the melody of a tune, or a man born blind can have a notion of the beauty of the rainbow.[54]

Part Three of *Religious Affections* will return to the "new sense" in order to develop the third sign for distinguishing authentic Christian affections.

Interpretive Approaches to "The New Sense." The idea of the "new sense" has been a point of special intrigue and debate. Perry Miller sees the idea as proof-positive that Edwards was Lockean to the core.[55] David Bebbington sees Edwards adjusting Locke to suit his immaterial theological agenda in a manner similar to Francis Hutcheson, who adapted Locke's empiricism to serve his immaterial moral philosophy.[56] Doug Sweeney and Brandon Winthrow object to Bebbington's analysis, arguing that it amounts to the claim that Edwards attempted to correct Locke.[57] Norman Fiering argues that

[54] Ibid., 2:207–8.

[55] Miller, *Errand Into the Wilderness*, 179.

[56] Bebbington, *Evangelicalism in Modern Britain*, 48.

[57] Douglas A. Sweeney and Brandon G. Winthrow, "Jonathan Edwards: Continuator or Pioneer of Evangelical History?" in *The Advent of Evangelicalism*, ed. Michael A. G. Haykin and Kenneth J. Stewart (Downers Grove, IL: InterVarsity, 2008), 286–87. A careful reading of Bebbington's presentation does not give sufficient evidence that he (Bebbington) holds the view that Edwards endeavored to "correct" Locke. Instead, he compares Edwards to Hutcheson, who was among others who "while accepting his [Locke's] axiom that knowledge comes from experience . . . set about explaining what human beings do know in terms that modified Locke's analysis." The modification that Bebbington speaks of, however, is not so much a correction as it is an adaptation: "Edwards's teaching in moral philosophy, logic, and metaphysics differs from Locke's. Yet it remains true that the debt to Locke in certain specific fields was substantial. And there is a palpably Enlightenment tone about Edwards's form of expression. Although he is prepared to describe the soul's awareness of God in traditional theological language as a spiritual infusion or in phraseology derived from the Platonic tradition as

Edwards employed only Locke's language, but adopted nothing from his empiricism.[58] Robert Brown counters Fiering's pessimism with the observation that "Locke did not deny the possibility of an illuminated knowledge, and in fact he explicitly allowed for it."[59] Brown takes a mediating position between an Edwards who was saturated with Locke (Miller) and an Edwards who hardly knew Locke (Fiering). Sweeney and Winthrow agree with Brown's assessment, concluding that Edwards's "new sense" is a case of "plunder[ing] the Egyptians while remaining guarded against Enlightenment extremes."[60]

The debate surrounding the interpretation of the "new sense" concerns more than the extent to which Locke is lurking in the background of Edwards's thought; it concerns the question of "whether the spiritual sense should be seen as basically continuous with, and integral to, the sphere of everyday sense experience, or as

---

illumination, he is generally eager to translate the older idiom into up-to-date terminology. . . . Because philosophical discourse in his day was shaped so largely by Locke, Edwards invariably speaks as his disciple. For Locke, knowledge derived from the senses is certain. Edwards was simply extending the range of senses available to a human being when he put the capacity to embrace the gospel in that category." Bebbington, *Evangelicalism in Modern Britain*, 48. It seems, then, that Bebbington's position is not incompatible with that of Sweeney, Winthrow, and Brown.

[58] Norman Fiering, *Jonathan Edwards' Moral Thought and Its British Context* (Chapel Hill, NC: University of North Carolina, 1981), 37, 125.

[59] Robert E. Brown, *Jonathan Edwards and the Bible* (Bloomington, IN: Indiana University, 2002), 38. Sweeney and Winthrow acknowledge Brown on this point. Brown, however, does not cite or source a particular text, so Sweeney and Winthrow supplement this deficiency by citing the following text from Locke to substantiate the point: "In what I have said I am far from denying, that GOD can, and doth sometimes enlighten Mens Minds in the apprehending of certain Truths, or excite them to Good Actions by the immediate influence and assistance of the Holy Spirit, without any extraordinary Signs accompanying it. But in such Cases too we have Reason and the Scripture, unerring Rules to know whether it be from GOD or no." John Locke, *An Essay Concerning Human Understanding*, ed. J. A. St. John, The Works of John Locke, vol. 2 (London: George Bell and Sons, 1877), 321. See also Sweeney and Winthrow, "Jonathan Edwards," 287.

[60] Sweeney and Winthrow, "Jonathan Edwards," 288.

discontinuous with ordinary perception, and thus distinct and separate from it."[61] A discontinuous interpretation of the "new sense" sees Edwards explaining it as a purely spiritual sense intended only for the perception of spiritual objects. This interpretation appeals to Edwards's identification of "the new sense" as a "simple idea," making it distinctly unrelated to the other five senses. Such an interpretation appears to be agreeable to the classic Puritan conviction that only those having spiritual life have spiritual sight.[62] A continuous interpretation suggests a more secular approach, seeing "the new sense" as simply a new perspective of viewing the material world.[63] McClymond diplomatically suggests the debate is needless because evidence supports a "both/and" approach.[64]

[61] McClymond, *Encounters With God*, 9.

[62] Paul Helm, "John Locke and Jonathan Edwards: A Reconsideration," *Journal of History and Philosophy* 7 (1969): 51–61.

[63] Examples include Miller, *Errand Into the Wilderness*, 167–83; John E. Smith, "Religious Affections and the 'Sense of the Heart'," in *The Princeton Companion to Jonathan Edwards*, ed. Sang Hyun Lee (Princeton, NJ: Princeton University, 2005), 103–14.

[64] McClymond, *Encounters With God*, 9–10. McClymond concisely summarizes the difference between the two perspectives, the first being "a way of looking at certain things," and the second being "a certain way of looking at everything." McClymond's argument appears to be convincing simply because Edwards gives ample evidence for viewing everything—both spiritual realities and earthly realities—as ultimately spiritual realities. The fact that Edwards sees all creation as typological manifestations of spiritual realities supports this view. Additionally, McClymond points out that Edwards's apologetic motive compelled him to explain God's truth in terms relevant to both the spiritual and material world. Although McClymond's argument is compelling from a contextual point of view, the textual data clearly favors Helm's interpretation. In texts which Edwards refers to the "new sense" in reference to the object of sensation, Edwards is consistent in portraying the object of the new sense as belonging to the realm of spiritual realities. Edwards affirms this explicitly: "I have already shown what that new spiritual sense is, which the saints have given them in regeneration, and what is the object of it. I have shown that the immediate object of it is the supreme beauty and excellency of the nature of divine things, as they are in themselves. And this is agreeable to the Scripture: the Apostle very plainly teaches that the great thing discovered

The Significance of "The New Sense" for Edwards's Theological Method. An expositional approach to interpreting "the new sense" is to be preferred as it keeps the interpretation in context. "The new sense" is clearly and intentionally defined in Section One of Part Three in *Religious Affections.* Section One begins with an explicit appeal to New Testament theology on the meaning of the idea contained in the term spiritual. Afterward, Edwards transitions with an appeal to systematic theology, delineating the doctrine of the indwelling work of the Holy Spirit in the believer and supplementing his case with a battery of proof-texts. From these two arguments, Edwards establishes two points: first, that the work of the Holy Spirit

---

by spiritual light, and understood by spiritual knowledge, is the glory of divine things, 'But if our gospel be hid, it is hid to them that are lost; in whom the God of this world hath blinded the minds of them that believe not, lest the light of the glorious gospel of Christ, who is the image of God, should shine unto them' (2 Corinthians 4:3–4), together with: 'For God who commanded the light to shine out of darkness, hath shined in our hearts, to give the light of the knowledge of the glory of God in the face of Jesus Christ' (ver. 6): and ch. 3:18 preceding: 'But we all, with open face, beholding as in a glass, the glory of the Lord, are changed into the same image, from glory to glory, even as by the Spirit of the Lord.' And it must needs be so, for as has been before observed, the Scripture often teaches that all true religion summarily consists in the love of divine things." Edwards, *Religious Affections*, WJE 2:271. For a sample of the many texts implying that the object of the "new sense" is purely spiritual, see also Jonathan Edwards, "A Faithful Narrative," WJE 4:208; Jonathan Edwards, "Some Thoughts Concerning the Revival," WJE 4:321; Jonathan Edwards, *The Life of David Brainerd*, ed. Norman Pettit, The Works of Jonathan Edwards, vol. 7 (New Haven: Yale, 1985), 506; Jonathan Edwards, "Images of Divine Things," in *Typological Writings*, ed. Wallace E. Anderson, The Works of Jonathan Edwards, vol. 11 (New Haven: Yale, 1993), 122–23; Jonathan Edwards, "Personal Narrative," in *Letters and Personal Writings*, ed. George S. Claghorn, The Works of Jonathan Edwards, vol. 16 (New Haven: Yale, 1998), 792; Jonathan Edwards, "Born Again," in *Sermons and Discourses: 1730–1733*, ed. Mark Valeri, The Works of Jonathan Edwards, vol. 17 (New Haven: Yale, 1999), 188; Jonathan Edwards, "Entry 782. IDEAS. SENSE OF THE HEART. SPIRITUAL KNOWLEDGE OR CONVICTION. FAITH," in *The "Miscellanies" 501–832*, ed. Ava Chamberlain, The Works of Jonathan Edwards, vol. 18 (New Haven: Yale, 2000), 464–66.

in conversion is of a supernatural kind, entirely different from what is known in the natural sphere; and second, that the consequence of this work is that the believer has a new capacity, a capacity which corresponds to its supernatural Source, and which is suited to sense supernatural realities.[65]

All of this is established *prior to* the invocation of "the simple idea" and "the new sense." The "new sense" was established on the ground of biblical theology, systematic theology, and individual biblical texts. The introduction of both philosophical concepts is subsequent to the establishment of the two points which are being made; there is no alternative but to conclude that they function in a supporting role. The phraseology introducing them also suggests that these play a supporting role: "There is what some metaphysicians call a new simple idea."[66] Such language, after the establishment of the two points, is clearly a concession to a segment of his audience who might not be as fully informed on the current metaphysical discourse as others. Edwards does not wish to leave them behind as he reframes the two points already established in terms that correspond with Locke's categories. In short, Edwards is employing the epistemological category of "the new sense" to illustrate his point, not substantiate it.

Wayne Proudfoot concurs with this perspective, expressing concern that the significance of "the new sense" continues to be overplayed:

> The new sensation, and the analogy with the deliverances of the other senses, plays no epistemic role in Edwards's criteria for distinguishing genuine from spurious affections. Despite the fact that Perry Miller's characterization of Edwards as an

[65] Edwards, *Religious Affections*, WJE 2:198–205. The epistemological point stated here is summarized in a helpful manner by Paul Kjoss Helseth in *Right Reason and the Princeton Mind: An Unorthodox Proposal* (Phillipsburg, NJ: P&R Publishing, 2010), 18–19.

[66] Edwards, *Religious Affections*, WJE 2:205.

> enthusiastic Lockean has been discredited, the references to sense and taste continue to influence readers in ways that detract from the main argument of the book. . . . To discriminate genuine from spurious affections, Edwards turns away from the analogy with sense perception and toward the practice of moral appraisal.[67]

The value of Proudfoot's observation is in recognition not only of how "the new sense" functions in relation to the argument of the work as a whole but also of how it functions in the context that *follows* the exposition of "the new sense," a contextual element that is frequently ignored. The "moral appraisal" Proudfoot refers to is substantiated by biblical data. In other words, Proudfoot reminds the reader of what should be obvious: the discussion of "the new sense" is just an aside and should not be taken as more than that. It is flanked both before and after by the overwhelming weight of biblical grounding and content. "The new sense," then, serves only as an analogy to assist in comprehending theological points grounded in biblical data.

The Significance of Philosophical Categories for Edwards's Theology of Assurance

Edwards's use of metaphysical and epistemological concepts in *Religious Affections* is most intriguing as it presents a certain tension. If his work is read in both literary and historical contexts, no doubt Edwards views the Scriptures as his epistemological ground.[68] But if, in Edwards's mind, Scripture (and, more properly, God himself) serves as the foundation to all knowledge and if Scripture speaks authoritatively to metaphysical realities, why does Edwards go to

[67] Wayne Proudfoot, "Perception and Love in *Religions Affections*," in *Jonathan Edwards's Writings: Text, Context, Interpretation*, ed. Stephen J. Stein (Bloomington, IN: Indiana University, 1996), 122–23.

[68] This point will be developed in chapter 6.

Locke and the categories of the Enlightenment to discuss matters of knowledge and reality?

This question is all the more interesting when the subject of assurance is added to the equation. Consider for a moment the following premises: (1) assurance of salvation is the primary theological focus of *Religious Affections*; (2) assurance of salvation engages issues pertaining to the nature of things as they really exist (ontology, a subset of metaphysics); (3) assurance of salvation also pertains to understanding the proper objects and means of knowledge (epistemology); and (4) Christian assurance, as a subject of Christian theology, is properly situated within the domain of the Christian source of authority, the Bible. If these premises are valid, then the Biblical issue of assurance of salvation intersects with philosophical categories that were of special interest in 18th century Western thought. The purpose of this section is to assess the significance that Edwards assigns to the philosophical categories he employs in his doctrine of Christian assurance. The historical and rhetorical contexts of *Religious Affections* function as helpful guides for this task.

Philosophical Categories in Historical Context

If scholars of Edwards are agreed upon anything, then certainly Edwards stands as a transitional figure in the history of Western thought. The conversion of the West to Christianity planted Christian Theism as the ground of all knowledge and being for over a millennium. The coincidence of the Renaissance and the Reformation ushered in the age of the individual. The freedom of the individual to think and to worship apart from the approving eye of Christendom served as the threshold for an entirely new outlook on reality—the Enlightenment.[69]

[69] Avihu Zakai, "The Age of Enlightenment," in *The Cambridge Companion to Jonathan Edwards*, ed. Stephen J. Stein (Cambridge: Cambridge University, 2007), 80–81. For discussions concerning the relationship between Edwards and the Enlightenment, see (in addition to the remaining portion of Zakai's chapter) Mark A. Noll, *The Rise of Evangelicalism* (Down-

The Enlightenment introduced the age of human sufficiency. Edwards's brief appearance in history was at this juncture, so his awareness of the enormity of the moment was acute. The implications of rationalism and empiricism did not bode well for the perpetuity of the Christian world view. Edwards endeavored to pass on the Christian faith to the next generation, doing so in an intellectual context dismissive of the traditional Calvinist ideals which he cherished. Edwards was convinced that such a task demanded Christian dialogue that was relevant to the intellectual trends of the culture. His task, therefore, was apologetic, and careful assessments of his corpus substantiate the claim that much of Edwards's public work was apologetically motivated and crafted.[70]

In the mid 1740s, the subject which dominated public discourse was the recent revival along with the question as to what had really happened in New England between 1740 and 1742. The event had shaken New England to its core, to be sure. But whether or not it was the work of God's blessing or God's judgment was a point of dispute. Edwards was so bold in his affirmation of the revival in "Distinguishing Marks" (1741) and "Some Thoughts Concerning the Revival" (1742) that Charles Chauncy felt it necessary to respond to Edwards directly. Chauncy proceeded to make the case that the revival was

ers Grove, IL: InterVarsity, 2003); Sweeney and Winthrow, "Jonathan Edwards," 278–301; Bebbington, *Evangelicalism in Modern Britain*, 46–65; Chai, *Jonathan Edwards and the Limits of Enlightenment Philosophy*.

[70] The two leading pieces advocating the apologetic character of the work of Edwards are MyClymond's *Encounters With God* and Nichols' *An Absolute Sort of Certainty*. Other noteworthy discussions include K. Scott Oliphint, "Jonathan Edwards: Reformed Apologist," *Westminster Theological Journal* 57, 1 (Spring 1995): 165–86; K. Scott Oliphint, "Jonathan Edwards on Apologetics: Reason and the Noetic Effects of Sin," in *The Legacy of Jonathan Edwards*, ed. Sean Michael Lucas D. G. Hart, and Stephen J. Nichols (Grand Rapids: Baker, 2003), 131–46; George Marsden's chapter entitled "Challenging the Presumptions of the Age" in *Jonathan Edwards, A Life*, 459–71; Michael J. McClymond and Gerald R. McDermott's chapter on apologetics in *The Theology of Jonathan Edwards* (Oxford: Oxford University, 2012), 149–66.

more likely an act of God's judgment than it was an act of God's blessing.[71] Chauncy argued that the disorder in the colonies—manifest in personal revelations, itinerant preaching, disregard for ecclesiastical authorities, and public outbursts—could be best diagnosed in metaphysical terms. Chauncy appealed to the basic orderliness of God and his creation, insisting that the human constitution was so ordered in its faculties that the affections were subordinate to the intellect. To reverse that priority was an unholy reversal of God's design.[72]

In *Religious Affections*, Edwards is clearly sympathetic to some of Chauncy's sentiments. Edwards agreed that the disorderliness, doctrinal deviation, and disregard for the intellect were by no means the fruit of the Spirit. Edwards also agreed that the question of the authenticity of the revival reduced to the question of the authenticity of the individual conversion. And the authenticity of the individual conversion inevitably brought about a discussion of the individual constitution; but at this level, controversy ensued. Discussion of the human constitution usually made use of the philosophical category of "faculties." Faculty psychology had already been invoked to discredit the revival, but Edwards objected to this assertion:

> Some make philosophy instead of the Holy Scriptures their rule of judging of this work; particularly the philosophical notions they entertain of the nature of the soul, its faculties and affections. Some are ready to say, "There is but little sober, solid religion in this work; it is little else but flash and noise. Religion nowadays all runs out into transports and high flights of the passions and affections." In their philosophy, the affections of the soul are something diverse from the will, and not appertaining to the noblest part of the soul, but the

[71] Chauncy, *Seasonable Thoughts*, 329.

[72] Concerning the order of God and creation, see Ibid., 51–52, 108, 345, 366; concerning the subordination of the affections to the intellect, see Ibid., 111, 119, 309, 384, 422; see also Griffin, *Old Brick*, 79–84.

> meanest principles that it has, that belong to men as partaking of animal nature, and what he has in common with the brute creation, rather than anything whereby he is conformed to angels and pure spirits. And though they acknowledge that there is a good use may be made of the affections in religion, yet they suppose that the substantial part of religion don't consist in them, but that they are rather to be looked upon as something adventitious and accidental in Christianity.[73]

Chauncy replied to Edwards's objection with a stinging rebuttal:

> There is an evident Difference between using Philosophy as an Help in order to understand the Scripture, and the placing it in the room of Scripture. In the former Sense, I suppose this Gentleman will not deny, but Scripture and Philosophy may very well consist together. If no use might be made of Philosophy, in explaining the Scripture, how monstrous must our Conceptions of the infinite GOD be, while he is represented, according to the Letter of numberless texts, as having Eyes, and Ears, and Hands, and Feet. . . . We must be allowed the Exercise of our Reason, (which is but another Name for what is here meant by Philosophy) or we shall be liable to be wretchedly impos'd on by our Imaginations: Nor is there any Error, however extravagant, but we shall be in Danger of falling into it. If we give up our Understandings, how shall we be able to ascertain the Sense of any one Text of Scripture? What should hinder our running into all the Wilds of Delusion? But this Use of Philosophy, I conclude this Gentleman will not object against. If he does, I see not but he will be self-condemn'd; for he has himself, under this very

[73] Edwards, "Some Thoughts Concerning the Revival," WJE 4:296–97.

> Head, made use of more Philosophy . . . than anyone I know of.[74]

Chauncy goes on to complain that neither Edwards nor anyone else had produced a single example of anyone who had used philosophical categories in a way that had supplanted the authoritative role of Scripture.[75] Chauncy's deft dismissal of Edwards's philosophical objection cleared the way for his main theme: "The plain truth is, an enlightened Mind, and not raised Affections, ought always to be the Guide of those who call themselves Men; and this, in the Affairs of Religion, as well as other Things."[76]

Chauncy's response was part substance and part rhetoric. Chauncy knew that philosophical categories had a long history of use in the Christian church and that such categories had enabled the church, from the days of Nicea and Chalcedon, to articulate difficult theological ideas in terms that assisted human understanding. Chauncy's charge of possible hypocrisy is a red herring, for Edwards did not decry the use of philosophy, only its controlling exercise. Chauncy's complaint that Edwards could not supply a single instance ignores the substance of Edwards's original charge: Edwards objected to the practice of pitting the affections against the mind. This practice assumed the validity of classic Greek psychology of the faculties, which maintained that the mind and the affections are separate. This, Edwards claimed, was an assumption that contradicted the Scriptures, which described the mind and affections as being united.[77]

As a result of the exchange with Chauncy, Edwards did not change his mind on his view that the affections and mind were united; but he knew that in order to make the case, he would have to articulate it in both biblical and metaphysical terms, rather than simply complaining of the opposition's use of philosophy. For this reason,

[74] Chauncy, *Seasonable Thoughts*, 383–84.
[75] Ibid., 384–85.
[76] Ibid., 326–27.
[77] Marsden, *Jonathan Edwards*, 280–82.

Edwards's use of philosophy in *Religious Affections* is apologetic; it squarely meets the metaphysical and epistemological arguments with arguments in kind, employing the same categories to sustain a cautiously positive interpretation of the revival. By expressing his theology in terms that cohered with metaphysical and epistemological descriptions of the day, he was able to refute the position of the Old Lights without dismissing their concerns.[78] This apologetic posture was intended to enhance the receptivity of the message of *Religious Affections*, and in turn his doctrine of assurance, which was key to the message of the book.

Philosophical Categories in Rhetorical Context

Though not immediately apparent, the four philosophical components in *Religious Affections*—the unity of the mind and affections, the "simple idea," the "object/eye," and the "new sense"—have a bearing on Edwards's doctrine of assurance. The extent to which they register a contribution to this aspect of his theology is significant, but this philosophical contribution remains subordinate to the priority of biblical data.

Metaphysics and Assurance. The metaphysical argument concerning the nature of the affections is designed to overturn the notion that the affections are separate from and inferior to the mind; its design does so by demonstrating the rationale for the essential unity of the mind and the affections. If the readers of *Religious Affections* are persuaded that the affections are one with the mind, they will no longer look upon the affections as a faculty of lower order than the mind, a faculty which is essentially emotional in nature and not to be trusted. With trust in the affections restored, Edwards is able to proceed to what he believes is the biblical model. The former metaphysical concerns, which pitted affections against the mind, are no longer sustained in the discussion. The biblical model that Edwards is building toward is a series of signs which point to authentic Christian

[78] Griffin, *Old Brick*, 84–86.

faith, each of which is the evidence of holy affections, and each of which speaks implicitly or explicitly to the matter of assurance.

In short, the relationship between the authenticity of the revival, assurance, and metaphysics may be traced from the general propositions to the specific: (1) the authenticity of the revival depends on the authenticity of the individual conversion; (2) individual conversion must be measured by Scripture; (3) Scripture indicates that the knowledge of salvation (assurance) is sustained by particular forms of evidence; (4) the forms of evidence identified by Scripture entail the affections; and (5) the affections are portrayed by the Scripture to be one with the will, a reliable indicator of the heart. This final point is a metaphysical one, one which Edwards recognizes to be vital to the entire argument; to yield this final point would call into question the biblical conclusions concerning the marks of genuine salvation and the assurance which proceeds from those marks.

As noted earlier, Edwards's purpose in utilizing Locke's "simple idea" is to employ the metaphysical concept to draw an analogy to a biblical truth: the Spirit's work of regeneration is necessarily unique because the Spirit himself is unique. Therefore, this work of the Spirit must also come to the mind of the regenerated individual in a unique—or "simple"—manner. Just as Locke explains that a "simple idea" is one which is passively received by the senses, without the influence of the mind, so, says Edwards, the work of the Spirit in regeneration exists apart from the initiation of the human mind and only comes to the mind as it is "sensed" by a "spiritual sense."

The relationship between the doctrine of assurance and the "simple idea" is not direct, but indirect. The "simple idea" expresses the concept that some ideas are fundamentally not complex in that they are not influenced by other ideas. In this sense they are pure, unique, original, and self-sufficient. This concept of a lack of complexity is very useful to Edwards, for it has the power to illustrate the biblical truth that the work of the Spirit is distinct in its character. Consequently, the work of the Spirit can serve as a unique and reliable "mark," distinct from other works which can possibly be attributed to other sources. Edwards will proceed to argue that these "marks" of the Spirit are holy and gracious affections. Such marks are the basis for the assurance of the believer, and stand in accordance with the Westminster formulation, which appealed to "inward evidences" and "proper fruit" as reliable and objective markers for assurance.[79]

Epistemology and Assurance. Edwards's use of the "object/eye" distinction is intended to illustrate the theological assertion that a Christian "low in grace" will have a problem perceiving his/her own spiritual condition. Since the perception of one's own spiritual condition pertains to the issue of assurance, the connection between the philosophical point and the doctrine of assurance is rather direct. While the signs may be valid in their own right, a difference remains between their validity and usefulness. The signs, in order to supply useful objective evidence for assurance, must be able to be perceived. By speaking to the issue of perception, Edwards carefully observes a reality that has an immediate bearing for those seeking assurance: assurance requires not only the presence of evidence but also the ability of the soul to perceive it. The "object/eye" distinction is invoked not to authenticate this principle but to illustrate biblical teaching on assurance in terms of spiritual perception as in 2 Peter 1:5–11.[80]

[79] "The Westminster Confession of Faith," in *The Creeds of Christendom*, ed. Phillip Schaff, vol. 3, *The Evangelical Protestant Creeds* (repr., Grand Rapids: Baker, 2007), 638–39.

[80] Edwards uses the text from 2 Peter to emphasize the relationship between perception and assurance: "Giving all diligence to grow in grace, by adding to faith, virtue, etc., is the direction that the apostle Peter gives us, for making our calling and election sure, and having an entrance ministered to us abundantly, into Christ's everlasting kingdom; signifying to us, that without this, our eyes will be dim, and we shall be as men in the dark, that cannot plainly see things past or to come, either the forgiveness of our sins past, or our heavenly inheritance that is future, and far off (2 Peter 1:5–11). Therefore, though good rules to distinguish true grace from counterfeit, may tend to convince hypocrites, and be of great use to the saints, in many respects; and among other benefits, may be very useful to them to remove many needless scruples, and establish their hope; yet I am far from pretending to lay down

Faulty perception on account of self-deception has obvious implications for the doctrine of assurance. Self-deception serves as the foundation for false assurance. Those seeking true assurance, and finding it, would inevitably question whether or not their assurance was well-founded. Since self-deception is undetectable by the self, the danger posed by this threat was acute. Only a frame of reference outside of the self could discover its presence. The New Lights, with their propensity to authenticate salvation with criteria not firmly grounded in Scripture, were vulnerable to false notions of assurance. Self-deception had been a constant theme of warning in the Puritan version of assurance. Edwards, who retained much of the Puritan outlook on assurance, was intent on using the current discourse on sensory perception and knowledge and applying it to the assurance discussion.

Finally, the "new sense" draws on contemporaneous epistemology to illustrate two biblical truths: first, that the work of the Holy Spirit in conversion is of a supernatural kind, entirely different from what is known in the natural sphere; second, that the consequence of this work is that the believer has a new capacity which corresponds to its supernatural Source and which is suited to sense supernatural realities. If the reader concedes that Edwards is correct—that genuine conversion entails the creation of a "new sense" as a feature of regeneration—then the believer is, by virtue of his new birth, endowed with the capacity for assessing spiritual realities, including his/her own spiritual standing. Edwards will revisit the "new sense" when he makes his case for the third sign, that "those affections that are truly holy, are primarily founded on the loveliness of the moral excellency of divine things."[81] He employs the "new sense" to assist in the explanation:

---

any such rules, as shall be sufficient of themselves, without other means, to enable all true saints to see their good estate, or as supposing they should be the principal means of their satisfaction." Edwards, *Religious Affections*, WJE 2:196.

[81] Edwards, *Religious Affections*, WJE 2:253.

> Under the head of the first distinguishing characteristic of gracious affection, I observed that there is given to those that are regenerated, a new supernatural sense, that is as it were a certain divine spiritual taste, which is in its whole nature diverse from any former kinds of sensation of the mind, as tasting is diverse from any of the other five senses, and that something is perceived by a true saint in the exercise of this new sense of mind, in spiritual and divine things, as entirely different from anything that is perceived in them by natural men, as the sweet taste of honey is diverse from the ideas men get of honey by looking on it or feeling of it; now this that I have been speaking, viz. the beauty of holiness, is that thing in spiritual and divine things, which is perceived by this spiritual sense, that is so diverse from all that natural men perceive in them: this kind of beauty is the quality that is the immediate object of this spiritual sense: this is the sweetness that is the proper object of this spiritual taste. The Scripture often represents the beauty and sweetness of holiness as the grand object of a spiritual taste, and spiritual appetite.[82]

The relation between the "new sense" and assurance, then, is that which exists between the subject and the object of knowledge. The "new sense" pertains to the believer as subject of knowledge; the beauty of God is the object of knowledge. When the believer exercises the "new sense," the believer sees God in his glory, delights in God's glory; the act of delighting accrues evidence for assurance.

Summary

Religious Affections makes periodic and abrupt forays into philosophical categories. In the area of metaphysics, Edwards endeavors to establish a definition of the human constitution that uses the meta-

[82] Ibid., 2:259–60.

physical categories of 18th century dialogue to clarify biblical notions of the unity of the mind and affections. With the "simple idea," he attempts to illustrate the biblical concept of the unique character of the regenerating work of the Holy Spirit. Edwards's discussion of perception capitalizes on epistemological trends to illustrate biblical ideas of spiritual perception. And with "the new sense," Edwards correlates current conversation on the relationship between sense and knowledge with biblical concepts of the new creation that takes place at regeneration. In short, *Religious Affections* employs these philosophical categories, not as a ground for building his doctrine of assurance, nor for establishing the overall message of the work, but in order to explain biblical concepts in a persuasive manner to the academic constituency within his larger audience.[83] As such, *Religious Affections* gives adequate evidence that Edwards viewed philosophical categories as helpful but subordinate components to a compelling theological argument.

[83] "Edwards's metaphysical reasoning was never detached from his theological concepts and convictions. His God was never abstract, but the mighty 'I AM' who spoke in thunder and performed mighty acts. . . . Philosophical reasoning, for Edwards, was a means of affirming God's transcendent greatness and glory." McClymond and McDermott, *The Theology of Jonathan Edwards*, 115.

5

The Confirmation of History in *Religious Affections*

Historical sources entail the second category from which *Religious Affections* draws in order to make its argument. This chapter investigates Edwards's use of these sources by examining his earlier defenses of the revival, by considering the apologetic and polemic purposes behind the use of historical sources in *Religious Affections*, and by analyzing the individual usages and their significance for the doctrine of assurance. These three areas suggest that Edwards's theological method was one in which historical sources played a significant and supportive role in the formation of his doctrine of assurance in *Religious Affections*.

Edwards's Prior Use of Historical Sources in the Defense of the Revival

As previously mentioned, *Religious Affections* is the last and greatest of Edwards's three works in defense of the revival. "Distinguishing Marks of a Work of the Spirit of God" (1741) and "Some Thoughts Concerning the Revival" (1742) had already been offered up as justifications for the revival. Since the character and purpose of these two works corresponds in some measure with that of *Religious Affections*, a comparison of all three works promises to reveal a development in Edwards's use of historical sources.

Edwards's Use of Historical Sources in "Distinguishing Marks"

"Distinguishing Marks" makes minor use of historical components. On a few occasions, Edwards appeals to the history of the church as a benchmark for assessing the revival as well as the claims of those who are attempting to discredit it. In one instance, Edwards rejects the notion that God does not work through the influence of other people, citing both Scripture and church history:

> 'Tis agreeable to Scripture that persons should be influenced by one another's good example: the Scripture directs us to set good examples to that end . . . and also directs us to be influenced by the good examples that others set . . . . There never yet was a time of remarkable pouring out of the Spirit, and great revival of religion, but that example had a main hand; so it was in the time of the Reformation.[1]

Elsewhere in "Distinguishing Marks," Edwards observes that the opponents of the revival were quick to point to its excesses and errors and to conclude on this basis that the revival was not of God. He responds with an appeal to church history, noting that revivals are characteristically accompanied by apostasies:

> If we look into church history, we shall find no instance of great revival of religion, but what has been attended with many such things: instances of this nature in the apostles' days were innumerable, both of those that fell away into gross heresies, and also vile practices . . . So in the time of the Reformation from popery, how great was the number of those that for a while seemed to join with the Reformers, that fell away

[1] Jonathan Edwards, "Distinguishing Marks of a Work of the Spirit of God," in *The Great Awakening*, ed. C. C. Goen, The Works of Jonathan Edwards, vol. 4 (New Haven: Yale, 1970), 238–39.

> into the grossest and most absurd errors, and abominable practices.[2]

Even those who were esteemed as pillars of the faith, such as Calvin, were given to the worst of excess:

> In the days of Constantine the Great, the zeal of Christians against heathenism, ran out into a degree of persecution. So in that glorious revival of religion, in the time of the Reformation, zeal in many instances appeared in a very improper severity, and even a degree of persecution; yea, in some of the most eminent Reformers, as in the great Calvin in particular: and many in those days of the flourishing of vital religion, were guilty of severely censuring others that differed from them in opinion in some points of divinity.[3]

As a result, the Reformation itself suffered from the same reproach as the New England revival. Edwards concludes this unpalatable history by reminding readers of their Puritan forbears:

> So in England at the time when vital religion did much prevail in the days of King Charles I, the Interregnum, and Oliver Cromwell, such things as these abounded. And so in the beginning of New England, in her purest days, when vital piety flourished, such kind of things as these broke out. Therefore the Devil's sowing such tares is no proof that a true work of the Spirit of God is not gloriously carried on.[4]

These appeals to church history are indirect: they reveal past practice as evidence of past belief (in both positive and negative aspects) instead of appealing directly to past belief. In one case only

[2] Ibid., 4:244–45.
[3] Ibid., 4:243.
[4] Ibid., 4:246.

does "Distinguishing Marks" appeal directly to the doctrine of past authorities. In this instance, Edwards maintains that fainting and weeping were phenomena acknowledged by revered saints of both the distant and recent past:

> Besides those that are overcome with conviction and distress, I have seen many of late, that have had their bodily strength taken away with a sense of the glorious excellency of the Redeemer . . . . Many have been even overcome with pity to the souls of others, and longing for their salvation.
>
> And many other things I might mention in this extraordinary work, answering to every one of those marks that have been insisted on. So that if the Apostle John knew how to give signs of a work of the true spirit, this is such a work. . . . I had the happiness to be settled in that place two years with the venerable Stoddard; and was then acquainted with a number that, during that season, were wrought upon under his ministry, and have been intimately acquainted with the experiences of many others, that were wrought upon before under his ministry, in a manner agreeable to his doctrine, and the doctrine of all orthodox divines; and of late that work has been carried on there, with very much of these uncommon operations: but 'tis apparent to all to be the same work, not only that was wrought there six or seven years ago, but elder Christians there know it to be the same work that was carried on there, in their former pastor's days, though there be some new circumstances. And certainly we must throw by all the talk of conversion and Christian experience; and not only so, but we must throw by our Bibles, and give up revealed religion, if this be not in general the work of God.[5]

[5] Ibid., 4:267–68.

From these passages, Edwards makes an interesting but relatively insignificant use of history in his effort to support the revival through "Distinguishing Marks." Edwards sees a direct theological and practical lineage between authentic faith in his time in the form of the revival, the faith of the Puritan era, the faith of the Reformation era, and the apostolic faith. Yet he is content to employ the lesser form of historical support by employing historical example instead of the history of doctrine.

Edwards's Use of Historical Sources in "Some Thoughts Concerning the Revival"

"Some Thoughts Concerning the Revival" was published only one year after "Distinguishing Marks." "Some Thoughts," over three times the length of its predecessor, is therefore more thorough in several respects. As in the earlier work, Edwards continues to draw an identity between the revival and the Reformation:

> And 'tis worthy to be noted that America was discovered about the time of the Reformation, or but little before: which Reformation was the first thing that God did towards the glorious renovation of the world, after it had sunk into the depths of darkness and ruin under the great antichristian apostasy. So that as soon as this new world is (as it were) created, and stands forth in view, God presently goes about doing some great thing to make way for the introduction of the church's latter-day glory, that is to have its first seat in, and is to take its rise from that new world.[6]

In a similar comparison, Edwards observes that "persons that are influenced by an indiscreet zeal are always in too much haste; they are impatient of delays, and therefore are for jumping to the uppermost

[6] Jonathan Edwards, "Some Thoughts Concerning the Revival," in *The Great Awakening*, ed. C. C. Goen, The Works of Jonathan Edwards, vol. 4 (New Haven: Yale, 1970), 355–56.

step first, before they have taken the preceding steps; whereby they expose themselves to fall and break their bones."[7] This, he says, was precisely the problem of the Reformation, which was plagued by the zealous indiscretions of many Protestants.[8]

In addition to the example of the Reformation, Edwards enlists for support the weight of credible and trustworthy "divines." Sometimes a general reference to such revered theologians is sufficient for supporting a point.[9] In other cases, a particular historical figure proved to be more effective. The memory of Stoddard remained vivid in the minds of those who were older and who were situated in places of influence. For these, the name *Stoddard* represented a solid reference point in a time of confusion. The grandson of Stoddard could do no better than invoke his name in support of the revival. In one such appeal, Edwards sternly rebukes the New Light practice of evaluating the fervor of sermon delivery for the purpose of labeling ministers as converted or not along with the supposed duty of publicly censuring those ministers deemed unconverted:

> When the Spirit of God was wonderfully poured out in this place more than seven years ago, and near thirty souls in a week, take one with another, for five or six weeks together, were to appearance brought home to Christ, and all the town seemed to be alive and full of God, there was no such notion or humor prevailing here; when ministers preached here, as very many did at that time, young and old, our people did not go about to discern whether they were men of experience or not: they did not know that they must: Mr. Stoddard never brought 'em up in that way; it did not seem natural to 'em to go about anything of that nature, nor did any such thing enter into their hearts; but when any minister preached, the business of everyone was to listen and attend to what he said, and

[7] Ibid., 4:449.
[8] Ibid., 4:450.
[9] Ibid., 4:362, 393.

apply it to his own heart, and make the utmost improvement of it.[10]

The most significant use of historical sources in "Some Thoughts" is a full subsection dedicated to the use of historical argumentation in sustaining a conclusion regarding the revival. The agenda for Part One of "Some Thoughts" is to substantiate the claim that the revival is indeed a work of God.[11] In support of this, Part Two of "Some Thoughts" argues that the question is theological in nature and should be primarily informed by the Scriptures.[12] Edwards proceeds to expose three false criteria that have usurped the place of Scripture in determining the nature of the revival: philosophy (employed by the Old Lights), physical manifestations (employed by the New Lights), and *appeals to history* (employed to the greatest extent by the Old Lights). History, says Edwards, was being misused in two ways. First, historical precedent was being set up as the standard for genuine Christianity. On this principle, critics reasoned that the revival was only of God if its character was attested in the church of ages past.[13] Second, Edwards argued that it was a fallacious use of history to compare selective features of the revival with the character of heresies of the past. This practice, claimed Edwards, was unjustly reductionist.[14]

Most of Edwards's comment on history concerns the first of these two abuses of history. In an attempt to counter the suggestion that the New England revival was unlike anything in church history, Edwards proceeds to offer historical evidence that there was much in church history similar to the extraordinary events in New England. Edwards relates brief historical accounts of the conversion of Robert Bolton, the testimony of Catherine Brettergh, the account of Alexan-

[10] Ibid., 4:475.
[11] Ibid., 4:293.
[12] Ibid., 4:296.
[13] Ibid., 4:306–7
[14] Ibid., 4:313.

der Allyn of revivals in Scotland and England (penned by his father Timothy Edwards), the testimony of the revered John Flavel, the memoirs of Captain Roger Clap, and the verbal testimony of John Williams.[15]

Each of these sources was significant for two reasons. First, each could be verified, either because they were in print or because there were individuals who were alive who could testify to their authenticity. Timothy Edwards was still alive and ministering in East Windsor; John Williams had died in 1729, but the Williams family was one of the most famous in all of New England; so a host of relatives could easily attest the veracity of the claim. Furthermore, two men of the Williams family were uncles to Jonathan. Jonathan's mother, Esther Stoddard, was the second of the twelve Stoddard children. Esther's sister (sixth of the Stoddard children) Christian married William Williams Sr., and Esther's sister Hannah (twelfth of the Stoddard children) married William Williams Jr.[16]

The second point of significance is that several of these individuals were noteworthy in some unique way. The case of Robert Bolton was a bit of a sensation, given his high-profile opposition to Puritans before his conversion. Catherine Brettergh was widely known and "regarded as a model of Puritan piety and virtue." Flavel's works "had long been a staple of New England devotional literature."[17] Captain Roger Clap was a highly regarded statesman and military officer, having commanded Fort Independence from 1665 until his death in 1691. His memoirs were published in Boston in 1731.[18]

[15] Ibid., 4:307–13.

[16] For the significance of the Williams family and relevant genealogical data, see Iain H. Murray, *Jonathan Edwards: A New Biography* (Edinburgh: Banner of Truth Trust, 1987), 74, 78–81.

[17] For information on Robert Bolton, and quotations concerning Catherine Brettergh and John Flavel, see the editor's comments in Edwards's "Some Thoughts Concerning the Revival," WJE 4:307n7; 310n4; 312n5, respectively.

[18] William Richard Cutter, *New England Families, Genealogical and Memorial*, vol. 1 (New York: Lewis, 1913), 413; also Goen's comments in Ed-

Ironically, this extended appeal to history was part of his claim that history should not be a definitive criterion for assessing the revival. But Edwards, it seems, cannot resist the opportunity to appeal to history to support the revival. In other locations, Edwards will return to the voice of history to make his case, even if in passing:

> The weakness of human nature has always appeared in times of great revival of religion, by a disposition to run to extremes and get into confusion; and especially in these three things—enthusiasm, superstition, and intemperate zeal. So it appeared in the time of the Reformation, very remarkably; and also in the days of the apostles. . . . Many, as ecclesiastical history informs us, fell off into the most wild enthusiasm, and extravagant notions of spirituality.[19]

It appears, then, that Edwards attempts to minimize the role of history while himself making use of it when his sense of propriety permitted. Edwards's frequent forays into church history give the impression that he saw the revival to be in keeping with historic church orthodoxy. The opposition was not slow to seize upon this discrepancy.

Chauncy's Response in Seasonable Thoughts

Chauncy refused to concede that Edwards had made good use of history, much less that he had history on his side. He responded by carefully following up on Edwards's use of his sources. Chauncy found an inaccuracy, so he made the most of it. In the account of Robert Bolton, Edwards claimed that he was "awakened by the preaching of the famous Mr. Perkins," crediting Robert Fleming's *The Fulfilling of the Scripture* as the source for the account.[20] Chauncy's objection was sharp:

---

wards's "Some Thoughts Concerning the Revival," WJE 4:312n6.

[19] Edwards, "Some Thoughts Concerning the Revival," WJE 4:318–19.

[20] Ibid., 4:307.

> He [Edwards] has very much misunderstood his author [Fleming], in representing from him Mr. Perkins as the person, by whose preaching Mr. Bolton was subjected to terrors that threw him to the ground; for it is not so much as insinuated in the *Fulfilling of Scripture*, either that Mr. Perkins was the instrument of Mr. Bolton's terrors, or that he was ever thrown into them at the time of preaching.[21]

Chauncy excoriated Edwards for the way in which he had misused the source. The reason for which Edwards inferred the influence of Perkins upon Bolton is unclear, but for Chauncy, the reason was irrelevant.[22] Edwards had mishandled the data, and Chauncy was intent on bringing that fact front and center.[23] The implication of Chauncy's charge was clear: If Edwards could not be trusted to handle his sources carefully, could the rest of his work be trusted?

Beyond discrediting Edwards, there was more at stake in the critique of the Bolton account. Edwards, by crediting the conversion to

[21] Charles Chauncy, *Seasonable Thoughts on the State of Religion in New England* (Boston: Samuel Eliot, 1743), 81–82.

[22] Fleming's brief account of Bolton's conversion, which was the occasion of Edwards's remarks and Chauncy's objection, reads as follows: "A second instance I shall offer is, the remarkable conversion of worthy Mr. Bolton, a choice minister in the church of England, in whose life this is recorded, that being eminently prophane, an horrid swearer, and much accustomed to mock at holiness, and those who most shined therein, and particularly that excellent man of God Mr. Perkins, then preacher in Cambridge, whom he much undervalued for his plainness in preaching the truths of God, yea, was near the length of Popery; but on the Lord's gracious appearance to him, was put to have other thoughts, with a very remarable [*sic*] change upon him, though with that terrour, that as he said himself, the Lord seemed to run upon him, like a giant, throwing him to the ground, and with such a terrifying discovery of sin, caused him to roar in anguish, and oft rise in the night on that account, which continued for diverse months . . . but at last a blessed sunshine broke up, and shone bright." Robert Fleming, *The Fulfilling of the Scripture* (London: Sprint, Ward, Ford, and Oswald, 1726), 103–04.

[23] See Goen's comments in Edwards's "Some Thoughts Concerning the Revival," WJE 4:307–8n7.

the ministry of William Perkins, had in fact laid claim to the ministry of Perkins as further support for the revival. Chauncy would have none of this misconception. Perkins's "works were more highly esteemed by New England Puritans than those of any other modern theologian, excepting Perkins's pupil, William Ames."[24] In *Seasonable Thoughts*, Chauncy cites Perkins in his own defense—and not only Perkins, but a host of unimpeachable Reformed and Puritan sources including John Calvin, William Gurnall, Richard Baxter, John Flavel, the *Westminster Confession*, Thomas Shepard, Increase Mather, and—for "spice"—Robert Bolton.[25] The message from Chauncy was clear: history testified to the cause of the Old Lights, not the cause of Edwards or the revival.

For three years, there was no convincing response to *Seasonable Thoughts*. Chauncy appeared to have had the last word, so he seemed to be the clear victor in the debate.[26] If Chauncy took Edwards's silence as a concession, he was mistaken. It was during this silence that Edwards amassed an overwhelming arsenal of philosophical, historical, and biblical sources for the construction of an irrefutable response: *A Treatise Concerning Religious Affections* (1746). Chauncy never attempted a refutation of *Religious Affections*; his *Seasonable Thoughts* faded into obscurity while *Religious Affections* became recognized as the definitive defense of the revival, a landmark for an incipient American evangelicalism, and one of the most significant pieces in the history of ecclesiastical literature.[27]

[24] Samuel Elliot Morison, *The Founding of Harvard College* (Boston: Harvard University, 1935), 95.

[25] For examples, see Chauncy, *Seasonable Thoughts*; regarding Perkins, 237; regarding John Calvin, 276, 338–39, 343, 360; regarding William Gurnall, 227–28; regarding Richard Baxter, 237–39, 259–63, 281; regarding John Flavel, 221–23, 231–36, 276–78, 291–93; regarding the *Westminster Confession*, 273; regarding Thomas Shepard, 1–2, 116, 131–32, 289–91; regarding Increase Mather, 299; regarding Robert Bolton, 236–37.

[26] Perry Miller, *Jonathan Edwards* (New York: William Sloan, 1949), 176–77.

[27] Although Chauncy and Edwards never engaged in debate after *Religious*

Edwards's Use of Historical Sources in Religious Affections

Although Puritanism had become outmoded by the time of Edwards, the crisis of the revivals moved both Chauncy and Edwards to find justification in the Puritans. For Chauncy, the claim to orthodoxy was verifiable in history. Edwards's prolific use of history in *Religious Affections* suggests that he agreed with this sentiment and understood that the general populace was of the same opinion. However, Edwards's use of history indicates that his purpose was more than apologetic; Edwards's stylistic elements in general and his use of Thomas Shepard in particular suggests that he intended to extract a degree of polemic value from the historical sources as well.

Edwards's Apologetic Use of Historical Sources

When John E. Smith prepared the introduction to the critical edition of *Religious Affections* in 1959, he lamented that "there has almost been a complete silence, in commentary touching the *Affec-*

Affections, Edwards's three protégés—Jonathan Edwards, Jr., Samuel Hopkins, and Joseph Bellamy—confronted Chauncy in public discourse after Edwards's death. Chauncy went to his grave convinced that Edwards was an enthusiast but evidently regarded him highly for his intellectual talent as evidenced in a piece of correspondence penned in 1768. According to Griffin, "In answering Ezra Stiles's request for his estimate of the greatest men in American history, he included Edwards and ranked him well above his famous grandfather, Solomon Stoddard. 'I suppose this Mr. Stoddard to have been a gentleman of very considerable powers, though not so great as some have imagined. Mr. EDWARDS, his grandson was much the greatest man. I have read all Mr. Stoddard's writings, but was never able to see in them that strength of genius some have attributed to him.'" Griffin, *Old Brick*, 197n74. Origin of quotation is Charles Chauncy, "A Sketch of Eminent Men in New England. In a Letter from the Rev. Dr. Chauncy to Dr. Stiles, May 6, 1768," in *Collections of the Massachusetts Historical Society, Vol. X* (Boston: Massachusetts Historical Society, 1809), 157. See also Griffin, *Old Brick*, 126–27, 169; Miller, *Jonathan Edwards*, 177; Michael A. G. Haykin, "Evangelicalism and the Enlightenment: A Reassessment," in *The Advent of Evangelicalism*, ed. Michael A. G. Haykin and Kenneth J. Stewart (Downers Grove, IL: InterVarsity, 2008), 57.

tions, about the theologians and scholars Edwards had read."[28] Beyond noting the obvious fact that Shepard represents the majority share of the historical source work in *Religious Affections*, most commentators have preferred to explore the philosophical sources rather than the historical ones. In spite of the lack of interest on the part of most scholars, the evidence of the volume and the content of the historical sources points to the conclusion that Edwards regarded the historical sources as more significant to his argument than the philosophical ones.

Source Distribution within the Structure for Apologetic Purposes. Smith, in his "Introduction," provides a convenient survey of the scholars that Edwards cites. Thomas Shepard, Solomon Stoddard, John Flavel, John Preston, William Perkins, William Ames, John Owen, Richard Sibbes, Anthony Burgess, and Samuel Rutherford were Puritan theologians of repute. John and Theophilus Gale were non-conformist scholars, educated at Cambridge and Oxford respectively. The Continentals John Calvin, Martin Luther, and François Turretin were prized by the Puritans for their Reformed stance and skillful systematization. Jeremiah Jones of Wales and Philip Doddridge of England were 18th century nonconformists that Edwards considered valuable sources for his agenda.[29]

An analysis of these sources by section and frequency points to Edwards's intended emphasis. Part One of *Religious Affections* refers to no individual authors though it makes a passing reference on two occasions to the general opinion of the past "divines" and one to the general opinion of the populace in former times.[30] Part Two of *Religious Affections* appeals to Shepard seven times, Stoddard thirteen

[28] John E. Smith, "Editor's Introduction," in *The Works of Jonathan Edwards*, ed. Perry Miller, vol. 2, *Religious Affections* (New Haven: Yale, 1959), 52.

[29] Ibid., 2:52–73.

[30] Jonathan Edwards, *A Treatise Concerning Religious Affections*, ed. John E. Smith, The Works of Jonathan Edwards, vol. 2 (New Haven: Yale, 1959), 111, 118, 121–22 respectively.

times, Flavel nine times, and once each to Perkins and Ames, for a total of thirty-one uses of historical sources in Part Two. Part Three of *Religious Affections* escalates to seventy-four separate citations of historical sources: from Shepard, thirty-seven; Stoddard, six; Flavel, ten; Preston, five; and Calvin, three. Two citations each are made from Owen and Ames; one each from Smith, Doddridge, Sibbes, Gale, Burgess, Rutherford, Luther, Turretin, and Jones.[31]

The most obvious feature in the statistical analysis contained in Appendix 1 is the disproportionate use of historical sources in Part Three. This comes as no surprise, given that the volume of text itself is also disproportionately distributed along similar lines.[32] The reader is led by this imbalance to conclude that the essence of the message has been reserved for the finale.

Other structural features point in the same direction. The proposition around which Part One is organized is clearly introductory in character. Part Two is developed to support a negative proposition, designed to create unresolved tension. Therefore, the structure points to the expectation of a solution in Part Three. Consequently, the disproportionate size of Part Three is due in part to the burden of developing a resolution and in part to the mass of historical data assembled in support of that resolution.

The Debate with Chauncy. The sheer volume of references to historical sources makes sense given the context of his debate with Chauncy. Certainly, Chauncy's *Seasonable Thoughts* had made two things clear to Edwards. First, the debate concerning the authenticity of the revival entailed one's understanding of authentic Christianity in general, and both sides were agreed that the stamp of authenticity included the approval of the Puritan and the Reformed fathers. In order to secure a favorable hearing from all parties in the New England churches, the demonstration of historical continuity was indis-

[31] See Appendix 1.

[32] Part One constitutes 9% of the text; Part Two, 18%; Part Three, 73%. The use of historical sources roughly corresponds: Part One employs 0% of the historical sources; Part Two, 29%; Part Three, 71%.

pensable. Second, documentation of historical sources would be scrutinized in detail; inaccuracies and liberties in historical citation would be scandalized.[33] Justifiably, Edwards makes a significant, thorough, and rigorous application of historical theology in *Religious Affections*.

The nature of the exchange between Edwards and Chauncy, combined with the overwhelming use of historical sources, strongly suggests that Edwards's motivation for escalating the historical argument was, in part, apologetic. Edwards had originally argued in "Some Thoughts" that neither history nor philosophy should have a defining hand in forming conclusions, but rather Scripture. And Chauncy agreed in *Seasonable Thoughts* that Scripture should have the definitive role. Yet neither could resist the urge to claim the mantle of history; each subscribed to the maxim that history and orthodoxy walked hand-in-hand. Edwards refrained from using *ideas* in history to support his cause in "Some Thoughts," but instead, he confined himself to historical anecdotes. Why he restricted himself in this way is unknown, but this may have been Edwards's attempt to prevent history from becoming a major feature of the debate. In any case, Chauncy escalated the use of history by using the thought of past theologians—historical theology—rather than mere anecdotes.

By appealing to historical theology, Chauncy had taken the debate into a new territory. Edwards had no choice but to respond. Silence would have been taken as a concession that the New England revival was incompatible with trusted interpretations of orthodoxy. Edwards's response would require him to move beyond historical anecdotes to historical theology. And he would have to use historical

[33] Edwards's heightened attention to documentation should be qualified. Due to the general scarcity of books, citation standards of the day permitted periphrastic representations if the substance of the original statement remained intact. Such liberties were considered acceptable and do not fall into the same category as that for which Chauncy faulted Edwards, which involved an error in content. Accordingly, Edwards rarely quotes verbatim. See Smith, "Editor's Introduction," WJE 2:81.

sources in such a persuasive manner, and with such overwhelming volume, that no doubt could possibly remain as to which position was truly orthodox. Given the context of the exchange between Chauncy and Edwards, clearly Edwards's use of historical theology was in some measure apologetic in nature.

Edwards's Polemic Use of Historical Sources

Although it seems certain that Edwards intended to establish continuity with the orthodoxy of the past, the manner in which he used his sources indicates that his purpose was not only apologetic, but polemic as well. Edwards argued for the legitimacy of the revival by making a case for the nature of authentic conversion. The measure of authentic revival was not to be determined by the question of the external experiences of the individual, but rather by the evidences of each person's conversion of heart. In order to strengthen his case, Edwards makes a persuasive appeal to venerated voices of the past. The manner in which he employs his historical sources suggests his polemic intent. Evidence for this intent is seen in his general stylistic approach as well as in his special use of Thomas Shepard.

General Stylistic Elements for Polemic Purposes. A number of general stylistic features point to Edwards's polemic intent in the use of historical sources. First, Edwards prefers to place nearly all quotations of historical sources within footnotes to buttress the argument to which they refer. By relegating quotations to footnotes, Edwards clearly intends to keep his own argument front and center. To this end, Edwards generally does not interact with his sources but simply employs them to bolster his own positions. He does not engage in analysis or critique with his source; he simply integrates the content of the quotation seamlessly into his own agenda.[34] He makes his case in lawyer-like fashion, stating his position, calling witnesses to the stand, comparing the testimony of the witness to the written authority of the

[34] Smith, "Editor's Introduction," WJE 2:52.

law, as it were, and closing the argument with an urgent appeal for justice.

Second, the distribution of historical sources is heavily weighted in the support of Part Three, which sets forth the affirmative case for *Religious Affections*. The persuasive effect of this strategy is two-fold: (1) it helps to present the work in such a way that the message of the book is not so much defensive as it is offensive, not so much a treatise of negation as it is one of affirmation. The approach is more winsome than the defensive conservationist tone adopted by Chauncy in *Seasonable Thoughts*. In addition, (2) this approach of source usage presents the argument in such a way that the reader encounters increasing levels of historical support as the argument develops. The effect is increasing degrees of persuasion as the argument moves toward its climax.

Third of the stylistic features, Edwards uses a careful selectivity of the content for his own purposes, a practice which Smith views with a cynical eye:

> When he dipped into a work he invariably knew exactly what he wanted, and often had to ignore some passages and stress others in order to achieve his purpose. He learned from others only insofar as he was willing to be taught, only insofar as he could see their contribution to the elaboration and defense of his own position.[35]

Brad Walton also observes Edwards's selectivity and suggests that some patterns might be discernable with respect to the topic of discussion and whether or not the source was Puritan. Yet Walton declines to speculate what intent might have dictated these patterns.[36] Elsewhere Walton argues that Edwards departs from Shepard on

[35] Ibid., 2:81.

[36] Brad Walton, *Jonathan Edwards, Religious Affections, and the Puritan Analysis of True Piety, Spiritual Sensations, and Heart Religion* (Lewiston, NY: Edwin Mellen, 2002), 137–38.

preparation, noting that the first section of Shepard's *Sincere Convert* is a rather thorough exposition on preparation. The implication here is that Edwards was highly selective with Shepard since Edwards goes so far as to cite from *Sincere Convert* to downplay preparation. Given that Edwards simply objected to the activity of the Spirit ensuring a rigid order and method of preparation, and not to preparation *per se*, it is more likely that Edwards simply took Shepard to be a less rigid preparationist, with sentiments on conversion most in keeping with Scripture.[37] This is further evidenced in the fact that Edward makes three uses of Shepard for the purpose of deregulating the stricter versions of preparationism.[38] The most striking example of Edwards's selectivity is in his use of Shepard's *Parable of the Ten Virgins*. Whereas Shepard confronts false professors while comforting weak believers, Edwards adopts most of the former and little of the latter. This disparity seems explainable, given circumstances attending the revival and Edwards's purpose in *Religious Affections*.[39]

Fourth in reference to stylistic features, Edwards is not reluctant to cite extended quotations. Quotations of paragraph-length are frequent; and in some cases, a single quotation extends to several paragraphs. The extensive quotations are partly responsible for the inflated size of the third part of the work. Yet the long citations achieve an added value, in three ways: (1) simple citations of source and page number merely reflect that the idea in the text has support in the source. Consequently, simple citations are not entirely persuasive; the reader is left to wonder how strong the level of support is from the source being cited. However, with extended quotations, the reader is able to independently determine the significance of the sources. Furthermore, (2) the long citations also enable Edwards to pre-empt

[37] Ibid., 92–93; Edwards, *Religious Affections*, WJE 2:162–63.

[38] See Appendix 2.

[39] William K. B. Stoever, "The Godly Will's Discerning: Shepard, Edwards, and the Identification of True Godliness," in *Jonathan Edwards's Writings: Text, Context, Interpretation*, ed. Stephen J. Stein (Bloomington, IN: Indiana University, 1996), 93–94.

the possibility that Chauncy will question his use of sources since the extended quotations empower the reader to independently assess the degree to which Edwards is legitimately leaning on the source. Finally, (3) the extended quotations permit the sources to actually articulate the point on Edwards's behalf. By inserting the lengthy paragraphs of historically-revered figures, Edwards unleashes the persuasive skills of voices from the past, allowing them to multiply the force of his own argument.

Special Use of Thomas Shepard for Polemic Purposes. Perhaps the most obvious aspect of the use of historical sources in *Religious Affections* is the unusual amount of support derived from the work of Thomas Shepard, particularly his *Parable of the Ten Virgins*. Stoever's study on the relationship between Shepard and Edwards is most helpful on this subject. Although Edwards never gives any indication why he utilized Shepard to such a great degree, Stoever points to a number of contextual pieces that might provide an explanation. First, Shepard's style was pastoral rather than systematic. Shepard's objective of bringing his readers to the place of conviction was very much in keeping with Edwards's goal of challenging the views of his readers, particularly the New Lights and their presumptuous confidence based on experience. Shepards's pastoral content and tone was such that Edwards was able to frequently dovetail his work seamlessly into the argument of *Religious Affections*.[40]

Second, Shepard was also a figure that was identifiable with the Antinomian crisis of the mid-17th century. The predicament attended religious nonconformity on both sides of the Atlantic, so the social and religious fallout was a reminder to all parties of the consequences of undisciplined religion. The Antinomians were a paradox; they were non-conformists who refused to conform to their fellow non-conformists. They presented a unique challenge which entailed "a cluster of interrelated errors," including direct forms of revelation, unorthodox views of the work of the Spirit, direct and absolute forms

[40] Ibid., 87.

of assurance, and a dismissal of the relationship between sanctification and justification.[41] Furthermore, the Antinomians threatened ecclesiastical and societal order with their rebellion against the established system of recognizing clergy. Perhaps in no instance was this threat more evident than in the case of the followers of Anne Hutchinson, who escalated tensions by dispensing with traditional convictions concerning male authority.[42]

Shepard ministered on both sides of the Atlantic in the midst of this crisis and was a prominent figure among the 17th century clergy who opposed Antinomianism. Edwards's use of Shepard effectively imported not only his ideas but his context, which recalled to the mind of his 18th century readers a striking parallel between the kind of unorthodoxy in Shepard's day and that which had now taken root among the New Lights. Therefore, the extended use of Shepard seems to have been intended to remind his readers of lessons to be learned from the not-too-distant past.[43]

Finally, it appears that Edwards's personal spiritual journey motivated him to use Shepard on the subject of conversion. William Stoever's careful comparison of *Miscellanies* 4, 43, 45, 123, 201, 239, and 397 with Edwards's "Catalogue" of reading, Shepard's *Theses Sabbaticae* (1649), and Shepard's *Parable of the Ten Virgins* suggests two relevant points. First, Edwards began reading Shepard in earnest

[41] Theodore Dwight Bozeman, *The Precisionist Strain: Disciplinarian Religion and Antinomian Backlash in Puritanism to 1638* (Chapel Hill, NC: University of North Carolina, 2004), 317. While Bozeman recognizes the lines the Puritans drew in the exclusion of the Antinomians, he complains that their religious perspective warped their capacity to represent the historical situation accurately: "By framing narratives to serve their own designs, colonial Puritans left a checkered legacy for historical research. They forged a record spotty in coverage, laced with resentment yet smugly triumphal and adjusted to preconceptions of heresy. Their sharply dualistic understanding of truth and error encouraged exaggeration of heterodox belief; it led them to minimize variations and ambiguities." Bozeman, *The Precisionist Strain*, 315.

[42] Ibid., 317–20.

[43] Stoever, "The Godly Will's Discerning," 87.

by the year 1723; second, Edwards was heavily influenced by Shepard on the subject of "spiritual understanding."[44] The significance of this becomes apparent when Edwards's biography is brought into the picture. Edwards began his journal on December 18, 1722, with a lament concerning his lack of assurance, a theme which recurs throughout the journal for the duration of his consistent use of that journal, a period which lasted until the summer of 1725.[45] Therefore, the period of life in which Edwards labored for assurance, 1722–25, coincides with that time in which he immersed himself in the work of Shepard. Shepard played a significant role in assisting Edwards in his own quest for assurance, and it seems most reasonable to conclude that Edwards incorporated the same elements of Shepard which had been instrumental in his own assurance to his doctrine of assurance in *Religious Affections*.[46]

[44] Ibid., 97n4.

[45] Edwards made regular use of his journal between December 18, 1722 and June 6, 1725. In the fall of 1725, Edwards was incapacitated by a severe illness, after which time he made only seven additional entries into his journal: one in 1725, one in 1726, one in 1734, and three in 1735. From the silence in his journal after the illness it appears that Edwards's anxiety began to subside. By the spring of 1726, Edwards was preaching again. In the summer of 1726, Edwards had returned to New Haven, which doubtless included the renewal of his friendship with Sarah Pierpont, whom he would marry the following summer. In August of 1726, Edwards was invited by Stoddard to join him in serving the Northampton congregation. These events indicate that Edwards was gradually obtaining assurance from the winter of 1725 until the fall of 1726, when he took to his journal again on September 26 after ten months of silence: "'Tis just about three years, that I have been for the most part in a low, sunk estate and condition, miserably senseless to what I used to be, about spiritual things. 'Twas three years ago, the week before commencement; just about the same time this year, I began to be somewhat as I used to be." Jonathan Edwards, "Diary," in *Letters and Personal Writings*, ed. George S. Claghorn, The Works of Jonathan Edwards, vol. 16 (New Haven: Yale, 1998), 788; Kenneth P. Minkema, "A Chronology of Edwards' Life and Writings," The Jonathan Edwards Center, accessed April 5, 2016, http://edwards.yale.edu/research/ chronology.

[46] It appears that Edwards continued to read and to digest the work of Shepard for many years to come. Shepard's extended influence in the thought

The Significance of Historical Sources for the Doctrine of Assurance in *Religious Affections*

An analysis of each historical source in its context indicates that these sources play a subordinate but influential role for the doctrine of assurance as Edwards presents it in *Religious Affections*. Each citation of an historical source, without exception, advances an argument which locates its primary justification in a Scriptural element. Furthermore, nearly every historical citation is set in a footnote rather than the text. Although the Scriptural elements vary between proof-texting, allusions, general statements of biblical theology, and references to Scripture in general, in each case the historical source substantiates the point that is grounded (either in the preceding or following text) by a Scriptural element.[47]

The influence of the historical sources on the doctrine of assurance is evident upon an examination of each citation in context. Each citation is designed to sustain a particular theological proposition, and each proposition is carefully positioned by Edwards to advance a larger theological topic or theme. By tracing each historical citation first to its immediate theological proposition and then to its larger theological theme, the significance of these sources for the doctrine of assurance becomes apparent. Each of the theological themes

---

of Edwards resurfaces between the two revivals. In the years 1737–38, Edwards delivered two sermon series which appear to borrow from Shepard's thought on self-examination, the task of distinguishing between true conversion and self-deception and marks of authentic salvation. The first series (in ten parts), launched on November of 1737 and continued intermittently until March of 1738, is a treatment of Matthew 25:1–12 (the parable of the ten virgins). The second series, in fourteen parts, is an exposition of 1 Corinthians 13 entitled "Charity and Its Fruits." See Stoever, "The Godly Will's Discerning," 89; M. X. Lesser, "Appendix B: Dated Sermons, January 1734–December 1738," in *Sermons and Discourses: 1734–1738*, ed. M. X. Lesser, The Works of Jonathan Edwards, vol. 19 (New Haven: Yale, 2001), 808–10.

[47] See Appendices 2, 3, 4, and 5, "scripture" column.

proves to be, without exception, a direct corollary of the doctrine of assurance.[48]

The analyses contained in Appendices 2, 3, 4, and 5 delineate the 105 historical citations as being oriented around thirteen theological themes. Given Edwards's description of the "eye" and the "object," not surprisingly Edwards directs each of the thirteen themes to either the subject or the object of spiritual perception.

Theological Themes Concerning the Subject of Spiritual Perception

Five of the thirteen themes concern the subject (as opposed to the object) of spiritual perception. The first of these five is the theme of *preparation*. The doctrine of preparation, in Edwards's view, was a significant trouble spot in the doctrine of assurance; its unbiblical standards were capable of bringing false assurance to some and preventing true assurance for others. Edwards employed Shepard, Stoddard, and Perkins to help to provide a corrective to this obstacle of biblical assurance.[49]

The subject or theme of *self-deception*, which concerns the capacity of the soul to discern one's own spiritual state, is a strong theme throughout the work, so Edwards calls upon several sources to speak to the many ways in which hypocrites obtain a false assurance through self-deception.[50] The theme of *spiritual sight*, famously illustrated by Edwards's appeal to metaphysics, is actually addressed more directly by the use of historical sources. The significance of this subject is evident because the capacity for spiritual perception is prerequisite for perceiving one's own salvation.[51] The *witness of the Spirit* is a staple

[48] See Appendices 2, 3, 4, and 5; refer to column titled "theological theme."

[49] See Appendices 2, 3, and 5.

[50] Self-deception is addressed by Shepard's *Parable* and *Sound Believer*, Stoddard's *Guide to Christ* and *Treatise Concerning Conversion*, Flavel's *Touchstone of Sincerity*, *Husbandry Spiritualized*, and *Works*, and Ames's *Conscience*. See Appendices 2, 3, 4, and 5.

[51] Spiritual sight employs Shepard's *Parable*, Stoddard's *Treatise Concerning*

theme for the doctrine of assurance, and Edwards is quick to point out that the Reformed and Puritan fathers would never have countenanced a version of the Spirit's testimony as immediate as that of the New Lights.[52] The New Lights advocated a view of the Spirit's witness essentially equivalent to special revelation; the consequence of such a revelatory work was that sanctification no longer had a voice in attesting to the reality of conversion. The Puritan tradition which Edwards invoked spoke otherwise, insisting that the witness of the Spirit brought the capacity to see one's own standing in the faith. Yet such an understanding was providential, not miraculous, and employed the powers of reason rather than revelation.[53]

The fifth and final theological theme which underscores spiritual perception is the theme of *discernment*. The Reformers and Puritans made much of the depravity of the human heart as well as the powerful activity of Satan; the combination of the two resulted in a recipe for self-deception that was formidable. For this reason, much of the assurance theology was defensive in nature, dedicated to taking every measure to prevent the false assurance that would lead to the horror described in Matthew 7:21–23. Conclusively, the theme of *discernment* dominated the conversion literature of the Puritans; and Edwards leaned on this theme, not only for a defensive measure, but as the justification of the signs by which true saints could positively identify themselves with confidence. Although the theme of discernment has much in common with that of self-deception, the latter focuses on drawing distinctions and making comparisons in order to unmask the false and to embrace the true.[54] These five theological

---

Conversion, Calvin's *Institutes*, Burgess's *Doctrine of Original Sin*, Turretin's *Institutio Theologiae Elencticae*, and Rutherford's *Survey of the Spirit of Antichrist*.

[52] This discussion also envelops that of the "seal of the Spirit"; see Edwards, *Religious Affections*, WJE 2:233–37.

[53] Edwards cites Shepard's *Parable* and *Sound Believer*, Stoddard's *Treatise Concerning Conversion*, and Flavel's *Meditations* to support his view of the witness of the Spirit. See Appendices 2, 3, and 4.

[54] On the subject of discernment, Edwards quotes from Shepard's *Parable*;

themes—*preparation*, *self-deception*, *spiritual sight*, *the witness of the Spirit*, and *discernment*—contribute to the aspect of assurance which concerns the capacity of a person to perceive spiritual realities.

Theological Themes Concerning the Object of Spiritual Perception

The remaining eight themes speak concerning the object of spiritual perception—in other words, that which the subject is able to see. The Spirit grants the true convert the capacity to see. The primary object that the converted person sees with this new perception is the glory, beauty, and excellency of the person of Christ himself. Such sight leads to affections for him and all that he values. Additionally, the converted soul perceives the work of the Spirit, and this includes the work he does within the very person who has been empowered to see spiritual realities. It would seem that simply possessing the capacity to see spiritual realities would be enough to erase all doubts concerning salvation, but the effect of inner depravity and the temptation of Satan are able to create doubt.

The theme of *holy affections*, is, as the reader would expect, prominent in *Religious Affections*.[55] Edwards uses historical sources to attest to the nature of false affections and that natural affections are no proof of salvation.[56] The theme of *perseverance*, a benchmark of

---

Stoddard's *Treatise Concerning Conversion*, *Appeal to the Learned*, and "The Way to Know Sincerity and Hypocrisy"; Flavel's *Husbandry Spiritualized*, *Works*, *Preparation for Suffering*, and *Discourse*; and Smith's "Discovery of the Shortness and Vanity of a Pharisaic Righteousness." See Appendices, 2, 3, 4, and 5.

[55] Not only does Edwards teach that holy affections are an object of spiritual perception but also that they *cause* spiritual perception: "Gracious affections are from those influences that are supernatural. From hence it follows, that in those gracious exercises and affections which are wrought in the minds of the saints, through the saving influences of the Spirit of God, there is a new inward perception." Edwards, *Religious Affections*, WJE 2:205. Later in the same discussion, Edwards affirms that holy affections are also an *effect* of spiritual perception. Ibid., 207–8.

[56] On the subject of "holy affections," Edwards utilizes Shepard's *Parable*;

Puritan soteriology, is reaffirmed as a testament to true conversion. Shepard observes the negative aspects, affirming the biblical teaching that false professors fall away, return to sin, forsake Christ, and become apostate. Stoddard exalts the positive, noting that obedience in difficult circumstances is evidence of authentic conversion.[57] In a similar vein, perseverance in the midst of trials is held as sign that distinguishes genuine converts from hypocrites.[58]

The remaining objects of spiritual perception are traditional virtues associated with the believer's quest to be conformed to the character of Christ. These virtues could be observed in the life of an authentic believer; their absence raised legitimate questions regarding the authenticity of one's own profession. *Love for God* marks those who are truly converted, giving true believers assurance, for it distinguishes them from those who are driven by self-love. Love for God and love for Christ is the priority of God's people. This love for God is the first and most fundamental experience of those who are given spiritual perception.[59] A host of voices are invoked to distinguish *true humility* from the false impersonations of it. The note of urgency on this theme suggests Edwards believed that humility was perhaps the virtue most misunderstood by the church; such a misunderstanding was likely to lead many into notions of false assurance.[60] Additional virtues, or the remaining objective themes, marking the life of a true believer are *gentleness*,[61] *desire for growth*,[62] *holy living*,[63] and the

---

Stoddard's *Guide to Christ* and *Treatise Concerning Conversion*; and Flavel's *Touchstone of Sincerity*. See Appendices 2, 3, and 4.

[57] Shepard's *Parable* and *Sincere Convert* are employed as is Stoddard's "Sincerity and Hypocrisy." See Appendices 2 and 3.

[58] On the subject of trials, Edwards uses Shepard's *Parable*, Flavel's *Touchstone of Sincerity*, and Sibbes's *Bruised Reed*. See Appendices 2, 4, and 5.

[59] Edwards cites Shepard's *Parable* and Owen's *Pneumatologia* in support. See Appendices 2 and 5.

[60] Sources included Shepard's *Parable* and *Sound Believer*, Calvin's *Institutes*, Ames's *Conscience*, Gale's *Court of the Gentiles*, and Luther's *Ominum Operum*.

[61] "Gentleness" is addressed by Shepard in *Parable*. See Appendix 2.

[62] "Desire for growth" is supported by Shepard in *Parable*. See Appendix 2.

general possession of all *virtues held in balance* with one another.[64] For Edwards, each of these virtues stood as objective evidence. The Spirit presented this evidence to the believer; so the believer, whose heart had been granted spiritual sight, responded with grateful assurance.

Summary

In "Some Thoughts Concerning the Revival," Edwards had sought to downplay the role of historical theology in the debate over the authenticity of the revival. Chauncy, however, insisted that orthodoxy and historicity walked hand in hand. Consequently, Edwards chose to respond with an overwhelming testimony of historical sources in favor of his interpretation of the revival. His use of historical sources was carefully managed so as to advance his argument without serving as the ground for it. He ensured that historical sources maintained their subordinate role by relegating them to the footnotes and employing Scripture in the text for the ground of each point. An analysis of each historical usage confirms that Scriptural content controlled each discussion for which a historical source was employed. A further analysis of each historical usage shows that a series of theological themes were supported, themes which maintained the standard course of Puritan assurance theology while avoiding the unbiblical strictures of preparationism.

---

[63] "Holy living" is attested to by Shepard in *Parable* and *Sound Believer*, Stoddard in "Sincerity and Hypocrisy," Preston in *The Onely Love*, and Doddridge in "The Scripture Doctrine of Salvation." See Appendices 2, 3, and 5.

[64] The idea of the "balance of virtues" is spoken of by Shepard in both *Parable* and *Sound Believer*, Flavel in *Meditations* and *Touchstone*, Preston in *The Onely Love*, Ames in *Conscience*, and Owen in *Pneumatologia*. See Appendices, 2, 4, and 5.

6

The Supremacy of Scripture in *Religious Affections*

In chapters four and five, an investigation of the philosophical and historical sources in *Religious Affections* confirmed that each interacts with Scripture in a subordinate manner. The purpose of this chapter is to investigate in detail the approach *Religious Affections* takes toward Scripture as well as the use it makes of Scripture, confirming the proposal that Scripture is in fact the governing source in the theological method of the treatise. Additionally, this chapter will explore the direct relationship that *Religious Affections* draws between the Scriptures and the doctrine of assurance.

Edwards's View of Scripture in *Religious Affections*

The great interest of *Religious Affections* is *authenticity*. Edwards's objective in *Religious Affections* is to argue in favor of the authenticity of the revival by means of defining authentic conversion. Yet such reasoning would be considered presumptuous unless it found firm footing in the *ground* of authenticity. All parties in the debate agreed in principle that Scripture was that ground. Therefore, in order to arbitrate between the competing opinions of the revival and true conversion, Edwards calls all parties to consider the broad range of relevant Biblical content. Both the Old Lights and the New Lights gave verbal assent to the orthodoxy of Biblical authority; both parties also made extended appeals to Scripture to justify their respective positions on the questions of the revival and individual conversion. Yet little consensus prevailed between the two, and Edwards was of the opinion that both parties were in error. Convinced that the errors within both camps proceeded from a deficient view of Scripture, Edwards revisits the doctrine of Scripture in *Religious Affections*.

The Sufficiency of Scripture

Nearly all Christians in New England would have publicly professed a high view of Scripture, but Edwards challenges the self-satisfaction of rank-and-file church goers in *Religious Affections*. It is one thing, says Edwards, to profess a high view of Scripture; it is quite another to reconcile that profession with one's belief and behavior. Edwards raised concerns of this sort throughout the work, indicating that he viewed the sufficiency of Scripture as a matter relevant to a number of subjects.

From the very outset of his work, Edwards notes that failure to attend to the sufficiency of Scripture is at the root of spiritual misconceptions. In his early argument for the proper place of affections, he asserts that "the holy Scriptures do everywhere place religion very much in the affections; such as fear, hope, love, hatred, desire, joy, sorrow, gratitude, compassion and zeal."[1] Then, in an address to the immovable Old Lights, those who followed Chauncy's distrust of the affections, Edwards escalates the confrontation by challenging their view of Scripture:

> I have mentioned but a few texts, out of an innumerable multitude, all over the Scripture, which place religion very much in the affections. But what has been observed, may be sufficient to show that they who would deny that much of true religion lies in the affections, and maintain the contrary, must throw away what we have been wont to own for our Bible,

[1] Jonathan Edwards, *A Treatise Concerning Religious Affections*, ed. John E. Smith, The Works of Jonathan Edwards, vol. 2 (New Haven: Yale, 1959), 102.

> and get some other rule, by which to judge of the nature of religion.[2]

The New Lights were no less vulnerable to this charge; their religious experiences had become the dominant source for drawing theological conclusions, a point Edwards was quick to expose. Those who were "disposed to be abundant in the talking of things of religion" had become

> Captivated into a confident and undoubting persuasion that they are savingly wrought upon, if they are not only free and abundant, but very affectionate and earnest in their talk. But this is the fruit of but little judgment, a scanty and short experience; as events do abundantly show: and is a mistake, persons often run into, through their trusting to their own wisdom and discerning, and making their own notions their rule, instead of the Holy Scripture. Though the Scripture be full of rules, both how we should judge of our own state, and also how we should be conducted in our opinion of others; yet we have nowhere any rule, by which to judge ourselves or others to be in a good estate, from any such effect: for this is but the religion of the mouth and of the tongue, and what is in the Scripture represented by the leaves of a tree, which though the tree ought not to be without them, yet are nowhere given as an evidence of the goodness of the tree.[3]

For Edwards, the doctrine of the sufficiency of Scripture required that believers adopt theological beliefs and Christian practices that were in submission to that principle. Anything less was a facade, a deceptive fabrication which served the purposes of the evil one.

[2] Ibid., 2:106.
[3] Ibid., 2:136.

The Essential Clarity of Scripture

Whereas Edwards addresses the sufficiency of Scripture explicitly, he addresses the clarity of Scripture implicitly, but with effect. Throughout the course of the entire treatise, Edwards consistently appeals to the essential clarity of Scripture to sustain particular arguments. The reader may observe this appeal to the "plain" reading of Scripture from the very outset of *Religious Affections*. In the preface, Edwards observes that the church in the present time is a mix of true believers and hypocrites: "yet, 'tis evident, that there will come a time of much greater purity in the church of God, than has been in ages past; it is plain by those texts of Scripture, Isaiah 52:1."[4]

Such appeals to the self-evident meaning of Scripture are a staple of the work. In response to the critics of the revival who disparaged zealous devotion to "reading, praying, singing, hearing sermons, and the like," Edwards simply replies, "'Tis plain from the Scripture that it is the tendency of true grace to cause persons very much to delight in such religious exercises."[5] Similarly, when opponents of the revival cited the loss of physical control as proof that the revival was not of God, Edwards notes that Scripture chronicles physical responses to the perception of eternal realities: "I would farther observe, that 'tis plain the Scripture often makes use of bodily effects, to express the strength of holy and spiritual affections, such as trembling, groaning, being sick, crying out, panting, and fainting."[6] And to the same critics

[4] Ibid., 2:86.

[5] Ibid., 2:163.

[6] Ibid., 2:135. Edwards sustains this claim with thirteen proof-texts in corresponding footnotes. This statement appears to be a response to Chauncy. Chauncy (in *Seasonable Thoughts*) had complained how Edwards had treated this subject in "Some Thoughts." Edwards had argued that the sufficiency of Scripture was compromised by the New Lights, who leaned on bodily effects as evidence for the authenticity of the revival. Chauncy complained that Edwards qualified this point, rather than fully prosecuting it against the New Lights. In Chauncy's view, the bodily signs could in no way be construed as positive evidence for the revival. See Jonathan Edwards, "Some Thoughts Concerning the Revival," in *The Great Awakening*, ed. C. C. Goen, The Works of Jonathan Edwards, vol. 4 (New Haven: Yale, 1970),

who questioned the place of the affections in spiritual life, Edwards is bold to assert the following:

> 'Tis very plain in some places, in the texts themselves, that by hardness of heart is meant a heart void of affection. . . . Now therefore since it is so plain, that by a hard heart, in Scripture, is meant a heart destitute of pious affections, and since also the Scriptures do so frequently place the sin and corruption of the heart in hardness of heart; it is evident, that the grace and holiness of the heart, on the contrary, must, in a great measure, consist in its having pious affections.[7]

Edwards continues his appeal to the plain reading of Scripture in his confrontation of the New Lights. Making his case for a theologically-governed view of the work of the Spirit, he insists that "'tis very plain, that the seal of the Spirit is the same thing with the earnest of the Spirit, by 2 Corinthians 1:22."[8] Moving to themes of holiness as the proper evidence of conversion, Edwards continues his appeal to the clarity of the biblical text:

> The Apostle says . . . we have received the more ingenuous noble spirit of children, a spirit of love, which naturally disposes us to go to God, as children to a father, and behave towards God as children. And this is the evidence or witness which the Spirit of God gives us that we are children. This is the plain sense of the Apostle . . . . And the same thing is evident from all the context: 'tis plain the Apostle speaks of the Spirit, over and over again, as dwelling in the hearts of the

---

Charles Chauncy, *Seasonable Thoughts on the State of Religion in New England* (Boston: Samuel Eliot, 1743), 385–86; Ann Taves, *Fits, Trances, and Visions: Experiencing Religion and Explaining Experience from Wesley to James* (Princeton, NJ: Princeton University, 1999), 21–23.

[7] Edwards, *Religious Affections*, WJE 2:118.

[8] Ibid., 2:235.

> saints, as a gracious principle, set in opposition to the flesh or corruption.[9]

To sustain the assertion that "a spiritual conviction of the divinity and reality of the things exhibited in the gospel . . . arises from a spiritual understanding of those things," he refers back to the battery of texts previously discussed and summarizes that on this subject "the Scripture is very plain and express."[10] As for the sign of conversion "that all true saints are of a loving, benevolent and beneficent temper," he asserts that "the Scripture is very plain and abundant."[11] Other signs are similarly derived from the plain reading of Scripture: "The Scripture is as plain as it is possible it should be, that none are true saints, but those whose true character it is, that they are of a disposition to pity and relieve their fellow creatures, that are poor, indigent and afflicted."[12] Elsewhere Edwards reasserts the motif of obedience as an obvious message in the Bible: "Obedience, good works, good fruit, are to be taken . . . as a sure evidence to our own consciences of a true principle of grace . . . . This is the intent of the Scripture, not only does the nature and reason of the thing show, but it is plain by the Scripture itself."[13]

At this point it is important to view Edwards's "plain" reading of Scripture within the larger context of his exegetical method. Edwards's approach to Scripture was by no means exclusively literal. In general terms, his approach to hermeneutics was in keeping with the Puritan ideal, which presupposed a literal meaning unless ample evidence dictated that the author intended otherwise. On account of this principle, Edwards frequently appealed to the "plain" reading of Scripture. Nevertheless, Edwards saw a place for spiritual readings, maintaining that it was also God's way to communicate by way of

[9] Ibid., 2:238.
[10] Ibid., 2:297.
[11] Ibid., 2:354.
[12] Ibid., 2:355.
[13] Ibid., 2:424.

types or signs.[14] God's signs were found not only in Scripture but also in the created order, given by the Creator so that "beings give glory to God because they express God."[15] Consequently, interpretation by way of allegory and typology was both appropriate and necessary, though such interpretive work required considerable discretion.[16]

Investigation into Edwards's use of Scripture is a comparatively recent area of study. Concentrated focus on his use of types is a part of this effort.[17] The extent to which Edwards sustains his thought on typology remains a point of debate, but there is a general consensus among scholars that typology is a major aspect of his larger exegetical method.[18] Indeed, for some, Edwards's typology is "a discipline

[14] Michael J. McClymond and Gerald R. McDermott, *The Theology of Jonathan Edwards* (Oxford: Oxford University, 2012), 177–80. For a convenient and current analysis of Edwards's use of typology, see Chapter 8 of this volume, "Typology: Scripture, Nature, and All of Reality,"116–29.

[15] McClymond and McDermott, *The Theology of Jonathan Edwards*, 116.

[16] Douglas A. Sweeney, *Jonathan Edwards and the Ministry of the Word* (Downers Grove, IL: InterVarsity Press, 2009), 95–106.

[17] Significant contributions include Robert E. Brown, *Jonathan Edwards and the Bible* (Bloomington: University of Indiana, 2002); Robert E. Brown, "The Bible," in *The Princeton Companion to Jonathan Edwards*, ed. Sang Hyun Lee (Princeton, NJ: Princeton University, 2005); Douglas A. Sweeney, "Longing for More and More of It? The Strange Career of Jonathan Edwards's Exegetical Exertions," in *Jonathan Edwards at 300: Essays on the Tercentenary of His Birth*, ed. Harry S. Stout, Kenneth P. Minkema and Caleb D. J. Maskell (Lanham, MD: University Press of America, 2005); Sweeney, *Jonathan Edwards and the Ministry of the Word*; Sweeney, "Jonathan Edwards, the Harmony of Scripture, and Canonical Exegesis." *Trinity Journal*, 34(2013): 171–207; McClymond and McDermott, "Chapter 11, Biblical Exegesis," in *The Theology of Jonathan Edwards*, 167–80; Stephen J. Stein, "Jonathan Edwards and the Rainbow: Biblical Exegesis and Poetic Imagination," *The New England Quarterly* 47, 3 (September 1974): 440–56; Stephen J. Stein, "The Quest for Spiritual Sense: The Biblical Hermeneutics of Jonathan Edwards," *Harvard Theological Review* 70, 1 (January 1977): 99–113; Stephen J. Stein, "The Spirit and the Word: Jonathan Edwards and Scriptural Exegesis" in *Jonathan Edwards and the American Experience*, ed. Nathan O. Hatch and Harry S. Stout (Oxford: Oxford University, 1988), 118–30.

[18] Though there is a general consensus that Edwards made use of both

identified so often with his treatment of the Bible that it serves as a synecdoche for all his exegesis."[19] It is beyond the scope of this book to probe the bearing of typology on the overall corpus of Edwards's work and thought.[20] Nevertheless, at this juncture, one unusual feature in *Religious Affections* must be observed: Edwards makes an evident effort to avoid typological interpretations. Of the over thirteen hundred Biblical texts referred to in *Religious Affections*, Edwards makes a clear reference to types in only seven instances, and none of these seven are called upon as the ground of an argument.[21]

The significant point here for the reader of *Religious Affections* is that Edwards elects to make his appeal to the "plain" reading of Scripture rather than figurative or typological interpretations. The motivation for this approach seems to be clear: the "plain" meaning of Scripture was sufficiently clear to all parties in the dispute. The only

---

literal and typological interpretive approaches to interpretation, there appears to be some variance of opinion regarding the degree to which Edwards depended upon one or the other. Sweeney is convinced that Edwards "majored in the literal sense," whereas McClymond and McDermott are persuaded that Edwards "tilted toward an affirmation of scripture's fecundity rather than its perspicuity." See Sweeney, *Jonathan Edwards and the Ministry of the Word*, 101–2; McClymond and McDermott, *The Theology of Jonathan Edwards*, 178.

[19] Sweeney, "Jonathan Edwards, the Harmony of Scripture, and Canonical Exegesis," 195.

[20] For a convenient and current survey of Edwards's use of typology, see McClymond and McDermott, "Chapter 8, Typology: Scripture, Nature, and All of Reality," in *The Theology of Jonathan Edwards*, 116–29; Sweeney, "Jonathan Edwards, the Harmony of Scripture, and Canonical Exegesis," 195–205; and Janice Knight, "Typology," in *The Princeton Companion to Jonathan Edwards*, ed. Sang Hyun Lee (Princeton, NJ: Princeton University, 2005), 190–209.

[21] See Edwards, *Religious Affections*, WJE 2:153 for Joseph as a type of Christ; 2:201 for oil as a type of the Holy Spirit; 2:349 for Noah's dove as a type of a true saint; 2:360 for Naaman as a type of the renewed soul; 2:362 for Rebecca as a type of the bride of Christ; 2:400 for the golden lampstand as a type of the church; 2:401 for the temple as a type of the church. For an accounting of the citations of biblical references in *Religious Affections*, see Appendix 6.

way for Edwards to arbitrate among all positions—his own included—was to appeal to the sort of Scriptural interpretation which all parties were obliged to recognize.

This "plain" reading of Scripture is evident in his challenge of the Old Lights and the New Lights—both of which claimed Scriptural warrant for their respective positions. He did this by obligating all parties to observe the meaning of Scripture texts as intended by the author. Edwards stressed this point when confronting the New Lights, who maintained that suggestions to the mind, when accompanied by a text of Scripture, were in fact the instruction of the Holy Spirit—a true "spiritual understanding" of the biblical text. Edwards deconstructs this notion:

> Spiritually enlightening the eyes to understand the Scripture, is to open the eyes, "Open thou mine eyes, that I may behold wondrous things out of thy law" (Ps. 119:18); which argues that the reason why the same was not seen in the Scripture before, was that the eyes were shut; which would not be the case, if the meaning that is now understood was not there before, but is now newly added to the Scripture, by the manner of the Scripture's coming to my mind. This making a new meaning to the Scripture, is the same thing as making a new Scripture: it is properly adding to the Word; which is threatened with so dreadful a curse.[22]

The problem behind this thought of making new meaning, says Edwards, is in the assumption that a different kind of understanding entails a different kind of meaning. Nothing of the sort occurs: "Spiritually to understand the Scripture, is rightly to understand what is in the Scripture, and what was in it before it was understood: 'tis to understand rightly, what used to be contained in the meaning of it;

[22] Edwards, *Religious Affections*, WJE 2:280.

and not the making a new meaning."[23] Edwards explains that a true "spiritual understanding," is

> To have the eyes of the mind opened, to behold the wonderful spiritual excellency of the glorious things contained in the true meaning of it, and that always were contained in it, ever since it was written; to behold the amiable and bright manifestations of the divine perfections, and of the excellency and sufficiency of Christ, and the excellency and suitableness of the way of salvation by Christ, and the spiritual glory of the precepts and promises of the Scripture, etc. Which things are, and always were in the Bible, and would have been seen before, if it had not been for blindness, without having any new sense added by the words being sent by God to a particular person, and spoken anew to him, with a new meaning.[24]

The key to the plain interpretation of Scripture is context. For example, when Edwards explains that the term *spiritual* refers not to a person's immaterial nature but what is produced by the Holy Spirit, he appeals to interpretation based on context:

> Thus Christians are called spiritual persons, because they are born of the Spirit, and because of the indwelling and holy influences of the Spirit of God in them. And things are called spiritual as related to the Spirit of God; 1 Corinthians 2:13–14, "Which things also we speak, not in the words which man's wisdom teacheth, but which the Holy Ghost teacheth, comparing spiritual things with spiritual. But the natural man receiveth not the things of the Spirit of God." Here the Apostle himself expressly signifies, that by spiritual things, he means the things of the Spirit of God, and things which the

[23] Ibid.

[24] Ibid., 2:281.

> Holy Ghost teacheth. The same is yet more abundantly apparent by viewing the whole context.[25]

Similarly, concerning the doctrine of the witness of the Spirit, Edwards invokes context:

> It appears that the witness of the Spirit the Apostle speaks of, is far from being any whisper, or immediate suggestion or revelation; but that gracious holy effect of the Spirit of God in the hearts of the saints, the disposition and temper of children, appearing in sweet childlike love to God, which casts out fear, or a spirit of a slave. And the same thing is evident from all the context: 'tis plain the Apostle speaks of the Spirit, over and over again, as dwelling in the hearts of the saints, as a gracious principle, set in opposition to the flesh or corruption: and so he does in the words that immediately introduce this passage we are upon [Romans 8:14–16], ver. 13: "For if ye live after the flesh, ye shall die; but if ye, through the Spirit do mortify the deeds of the flesh, ye shall live."[26]

Again, regarding this doctrine, Edwards repeats appeals to context:

> And when the Apostle speaks of the witness of the Spirit, in Romans 8:15–17; he has a more immediate respect to what the Christians experienced, in their exercises of love to God, in suffering persecution; as is plain by the context. . . . It is more especially plain by the verse immediately following.[27]

[25] Ibid., 2:198–99.

[26] Ibid., 2:238.

[27] Ibid., 2:454. Two other appeals to context are contained in the same paragraph. See also an appeal to context in the exposition of several verses in 1 John, 439; Edwards's explanations of Romans 8:20 and Jeremiah 3 appear in two successive pieces of correspondence to Thomas Gillespie. For these see Jonathan Edwards, "Letter to Thomas Gillespie, September 4, 1747" and "Letter to Thomas Gillespie, April 2, 1750," in *A Treatise Concerning*

Edwards suggests that even the refusal to accept a plain meaning may be a case of willful ignorance. Referring to Paul's teaching on the affections, Edwards says, "Now if anyone can consider these accounts given in the Scripture of this great Apostle, and which he gives of himself, and yet not see that his religion consisted much in affection, must have a strange faculty of managing his eyes, to shut out the light which shines most full in his face."[28]

In short, Edwards regularly resorts to the duty of his readers to study the Scripture in its plain sense, the sense intended by the author as evidenced by the context of the text.[29] This appeal to the clarity of Scripture in addition to the previously mentioned appeal to the sufficiency of Scripture enables Edwards to attach his argument to biblical authority in a way that is distinct from his opponents.

The Self-Authentication of Scripture

For Edwards, the subject of biblical authority was immediately relevant to the character of a true believer. In Section Three of

---

Religious Affections, ed. John E. Smith, The Works of Jonathan Edwards, vol. 2 (New Haven: Yale, 1959), 483, 510 (respectively).

[28] Edwards, *Religious Affections*, WJE *2*:111.

[29] Edwards's most penetrating comment on the legitimacy and necessity of a "plain" reading of Scripture *as a norm* is located in his conclusion of *Original Sin*. Edwards responds to the notion proposed by leading intellectuals that much of the writings of Paul were incomprehensible to "vulgar Christians, or indeed the herd of common divines, such as the Westminster Assembly, etc." According to this opinion, no one, from the outset of the Reformation until the day of Edwards, had understood Paul properly, until Edwards's time: "But . . . there is risen up, now at length in this happy age of light and liberty, a set of men, of a more free and generous turn of mind, a more inquisitive genius, and better discernment. By such insinuations, they seek advantage to their cause; and thus the most unreasonable and extravagant interpretations of Scripture are palliated and recommended." Interestingly, Edwards also appeals to the clarity of Scripture in his conclusion to *Freedom of the Will*. See Jonathan Edwards, *The Great Christian Doctrine of Original Sin Defended*, ed. Clyde A. Holbrook, The Works of Jonathan Edwards, vol. 3 (New Haven: Yale, 1970), 435; Jonathan Edwards, *Freedom of the Will*, ed. Paul Ramsey, The Works of Jonathan Edwards, vol. 1 (New Haven: Yale, 1957), 439.

Religious Affections, the fifth sign of "truly gracious affections [is that they] are attended with a reasonable and spiritual judgment, of the reality and certainty of divine things."[30] Such a proposition was an affront to the Enlightened mind, which regarded notions of "reality and certainty" as subject to verification by human reason. Although Edwards had outflanked this objection in Section One of Part Three with his introduction of "the new sense," he revisits the subject to explain that genuine believers possess

> a spiritual conviction of the divinity and reality of the things exhibited in the gospel, which arises from a spiritual understanding of those things; I have shown already what that is, viz. a sense and taste of the divine, supreme and holy excellency and beauty of those things. So that then is the mind spiritually convinced of the divinity and truth of the great things of the gospel, when that conviction arises, either directly or remotely, from such a sense or view of their divine excellency and glory as is there exhibited. This clearly follows from things that have been already said; and for this the Scripture is very plain and express.[31]

In Section Five of *Religious Affections*, Edwards observes that many "have no thorough and effectual conviction" of the truth of the gospel. Some are superficially persuaded by subjective impressions; others simply concede by way of intellectual acquiescence. Time and trial show these to be like Judas and like the seed sown on the stony ground, who fail to persevere.[32] However, for those who by "a view of this divine glory" have received the new sense and gracious affections, there is a divine capacity to *reasonably* be convinced of the truth of Scripture:

[30] Edwards, *Religious Affections*, WJE 2:291.
[31] Ibid., 2:297.
[32] Ibid., 2:294–96.

> He that has his judgment thus directly convinced and assured of the divinity of the things of the gospel, by a clear view of their divine glory, has a reasonable conviction; his belief and assurance is altogether agreeable to reason; because the divine glory and beauty of divine things is in itself, real evidence of their divinity, and the most direct and strong evidence. . . . They therefore that see the stamp of this glory in divine things, they see divinity in them, they see God in them, and so see 'em to be divine; because they see that in them wherein the truest idea of divinity does consist. Thus a soul may have a kind of intuitive knowledge of the divinity of the things exhibited in the gospel; not that he judges the doctrines of the gospel to be from God, without any argument or deduction at all; but it is without any long chain of arguments; the argument is but one, and the evidence direct; the mind ascends to the truth of the gospel but by one step, and that is its divine glory.[33]

The regenerated soul, then, has the capacity to perceive without doubt the character of divine things, and among these divine things is the written Word. Historical evidences may produce a certain level of persuasion in favor of the veracity of Scripture, but all evidential arguments can approach only degrees of probability, not certainty. The supernatural sense is able to detect the supernatural character of the Scriptures including the supernatural character of the God who stands behind His covenant.[34] Because God's character is one and the same with the character of the written Word,[35] the Scriptures have authority on par with God, so the Scriptures are self-authenticating:

[33] Ibid., 2:298–99.

[34] Ibid., 2:298–305.

[35] "As the beauty of the divine nature does primarily consist in God's holiness, so does the beauty of all divine things. . . . Herein consists the excellency of the Word of God, that it is so holy." Ibid., 2:258.

> The gospel of the blessed God don't go abroad a-begging for its evidence, so much as some think; it has its highest and most proper evidence in itself. Though great use may be made of external arguments, they are not to be neglected, but highly prized and valued; for they may be greatly serviceable to awaken unbelievers, and bring them to serious consideration, and to confirm the faith of true saints: yea they may be in some respects subservient to the begetting of a saving faith in men.[36]

Having considered the express thought of Edwards in *Religious Affections* regarding the sufficiency, clarity, and self-authenticating authority of Scripture, certainly, as a matter of principle, neither philosophical nor historical considerations had a governing role in the argument of the work. However, to demonstrate that this was borne out in practice requires an examination of how Edwards employed Scripture in *Religious Affections*.

Edwards's Use of Scripture in *Religious Affections*

In order for Edwards's case to prevail over the opinions of both the Old Lights and the New Lights, Edwards needed to demonstrate that his position was correct because it was *biblically* correct. Edwards's primary audience was the clergy of New England, a body of men who would measure his argument first and foremost on the grounds of biblical fidelity. It comes as no surprise, then, that the reader of *Religious Affections* is inundated with Scripture. Edwards

[36] Ibid., 2:307. For helpful assessments of Edwards's view of the self-authenticity of Scripture, see Michael J. McClymond, *Encounters with God: An Approach to the Theology of Jonathan Edwards* (New York: Oxford University, 1998), 97, and Stephen J. Nichols, *An Absolute Sort of Certainty* (Phillipsburg, NJ: P&R Publishing, 2003), 131–41. For a penetrating analysis of how the self-authentication of Scripture and the certainty of belief cohere, especially in the thought of Calvin and Owen, see Paul Helm, *The Varieties of Belief* (repr., London: Routledge, 2002), 101–17.

employs Scripture indirectly in the form of allusion, reference to Scripture in general and theological generalizations. He uses Scripture directly in the form of exegesis and proof-texting.

Edwards's Indirect Use of Scripture

As Robert Brown has aptly observed, "*Religious Affections* (1746) offers, in effect, one long exposition of Scripture; biblical references pepper it throughout."[37] The "biblical references" which Edwards uses are not only direct citations of Scripture, but he also uses countless allusions to biblical themes, characters, and phrases, all of which Edwards's audience would have immediately recognized. In fact, the weaving of biblical allusions throughout the work gives *Religious Affections* a thoroughly biblical flavor and generates the sense that the work is thoroughly biblical as though it were almost "one long exposition of Scripture."

The Use of Biblical Allusion. A few examples illustrate his seamless use of allusion. Alluding to Elijah on Mount Carmel in 1 Kings 18, Edwards says, "All those who are truly gracious persons have a solid, full, thorough and effectual conviction of the truth . . . . They no longer halt between two opinions; the great doctrines of the gospel cease to be any longer doubtful things."[38] Alluding to the Parable of the Soils in Matthew 13, Edwards remarks that hypocrites "are not attended with a thorough conviction of the mind, they are not at all to be depended on; however great a show and noise they make, 'tis like the blaze of tow, or crackling of thorns, or like the forward flourishing blade on stony ground, that has no root, nor deepness of earth to maintain its life."[39]

Some allusions are quite unmistakable such as the example given to illustrate partial repentance: "He that forsakes other sins, but saves his leading sin, the iniquity he is chiefly inclined to; is like Saul, when

[37] Brown, "The Bible," 89.

[38] Edwards, *Religious Affections*, WJE 2:291.

[39] Ibid., 2:294; Edwards also uses the "stony-ground" allusion on numerous other occasions. See 2:85, 145, 165, 217, 278, 390, 393, 406, 432.

sent against God's enemies the Amalekites, with a strict charge to save none of them alive, but utterly to destroy them, small and great; who utterly destroyed inferior people, but saved the king, the chief of 'em all, alive."[40] The book of Proverbs was especially familiar to the readers of both the clergy and the laity; easily, Edwards integrated ideas and phrases from this well-known section of Scripture seamlessly into the course of a discussion: "The high affections of many seem to be so soon come to nothing, and some who seemed to be mightily raised and swallowed with joy and zeal, for a while, seem to have returned like the dog to his vomit: hence religious affections in general are grown out of credit, with great numbers, as though true religion did not at all consist in them."[41] Since the Bible dominated the literary currency of the English-speaking world in the 18th century, allusions such as these effectively contacted the mental framework of every New Englander.[42]

The Use of Scripture in General. In keeping with his belief in the unity and authority of Scripture, Edwards frequently sustains an argument by appealing to "the Scriptures." Like the appeal to biblical allusion, this indirect appeal to the Scriptures in general was woven seamlessly into his discourse. Edwards uses generalized expressions such as "commonly given . . . in Scripture," "often spoken of in the Scripture," "all over the Scripture," "according to the Scripture representation," "the Scripture itself abounds," "the promises of

[40] Ibid., 2:342.

[41] Ibid., 2:119.

[42] For an interesting comment on Edwards's "addiction" to allusion, see Edwin Cady's analysis of Edwards's sermon "Sinners in the Hands of an Angry God." Edwin H. Cady, "The Artistry of Jonathan Edwards," *The New England Quarterly* 22, 1 (March 1949): 65. Kimnach notes that "Edwards' most impressive use of the Scripture is in the very fabric or verbal contexture of his sermons. The average Edwards sermon contains many images, metaphors, aphorisms, and seemingly prosaic phrases from the Bible." Wilson H. Kimnach, "General Introduction, Chapter IV: Literary Theory and Practice," in *Sermons and Discourses: 1720–1723*, ed. Wilson H. Kimnach, The Works of Jonathan Edwards, vol. 10 (New Haven: Yale, 1992), 210.

Scripture," "the Scripture speaks," and "the Scripture often represents."[43] Edwards makes nearly 400 general references to Scripture with the terms the *Scriptures*, *the Bible*, and *the Word of God*. Most of these uses are employed for the purpose of serving as the basis for a theological idea.[44]

The Use of Theological Generalization. In addition to appealing to biblical allusion and the Scriptures in general, Edwards expressed another form of biblical appeal in terms of theological generalization. In other words, themes from the traditional categories of systematic theology were cited in support for particular points. Themes such as *heaven*, *the person and work of the Holy Spirit*, *the character and deeds of Satan*, *the heart of man*, *the person and work of Christ*, *salvation*, *faith*, and *assurance* are all referred to in general.[45] These theological themes are not conclusions being argued for but mature biblical ideas, derived implicitly from Scripture, for supporting a particular point in the treatise. Similarly, Edwards utilizes themes of biblical theology such as the theology of David, Paul, John, and the entirety of the Old Testament narrative.[46] These general biblical evidences—appeals to Scripture in general along with appeals to theology in general—were convenient and effective ways to substantiate a point. They were convenient because they did not require elaboration, and they were effective because they made the most of the biblical literacy (and

[43] Edwards, *Religious Affections*, WJE 2:103 (first two expressions), 106, 113, 212, 224, 232, 260.

[44] Statistic is based on data provided by the Jonathan Edwards Center, www.edwards.yale.edu.

[45] For examples, see the following in Edwards, *Religious Affections*, WJE 2: for heaven, 113, 242; for the person and work of the Holy Spirit, 138, 141, 146, 156, 158; for the character and deeds of Satan, 144, 146, 156, 158, 172; for the heart of man, 145; for the person and work of Christ, 112; for salvation, 152, 161–63; for faith, 176–78; for assurance, 178–81. On one occasion Edwards refers to "scripture principles" as evidence; see 160.

[46] Some of these are supplemented with proof-texts, so they are explicitly supported from Scripture. For examples, see the following in Edwards, *Religious Affections*, WJE 2: for David 108–9, 167–68; for Paul, 109–11, 168–69; for John, 111–12; for the Old Testament narrative, 167.

tradition) of his readers by employing theological ideas that were commonly accepted as factual.

Edwards's Direct Use of Scripture

Scholarly comment on the subject of Edwards's exegesis is diverse, describing his exegesis in terms of his high view of Scripture, his Enlightenment context, his analogical and typological hermeneutics and the literary outcomes of his exegetical efforts. In terms of exegetical method, the bulk of the discussion appears to be set on the subject of his hermeneutics, with a particular interest in his non-literal usages.[47] Most commentators speak of Edwards's exegesis in a broad sense as a general reference to invoking the Bible to support an argument, including the use of proof-texts. This perspective on "exegesis" permits McClymond and McDermott to assert that "biblical exegesis is an integral part of such published works as *Religious Affections*, *Original Sin*, *End of Creation*, *Miscellanies*, and other writings."[48] Douglas Sweeney's recent work brings new clarity to the subject, demonstrating that Edwards employed not one method, but several distinct methods of exegesis.[49] For the sake of this discussion, Edwards's direct use of Scripture is divided into two categories: exegesis and proof-texting.

The Use of Biblical Exegesis. If exegesis were taken to refer to "the obtaining of the meaning of a passage by drawing the meaning out from rather than reading it into the text,"[50] it is difficult to characterize exegesis as "an integral part" of *Religious Affections*. When Edwards cites a text in the work, he rarely endeavors to do more than summa-

[47] See McClymond and McDermott, *The Theology of Jonathan Edwards*, 167–80; Stein, "The Spirit and the Word" 118–28; Douglas A. Sweeney, *Jonathan Edwards and the Ministry of the Word*, 83–106.

[48] McClymond and McDermott, *The Theology of Jonathan Edwards*, 167.

[49] Douglas A. Sweeney, *Edwards the Exegete: Biblical Interpretation and Anglo-Protestant Culture on the Edge of the Enlightenment* (New York: Oxford University, 2016), x.

[50] Millard Erickson, "Exegesis," in *Concise Dictionary of Christian Theology* (Grand Rapids: Baker, 1994), 53.

rize it, cite its illustrative value, or restate its essential propositional message. Only in a small percentage of cases does Edwards take a text and pause to explicate its meaning, in either a literal or allegorical sense, by such exegetical methods as lexical study, phrase-level analysis, literary context, historical context, typological analysis, or justification of allegory.

Exegetical treatments in *Religious Affections* are brief. The lengthiest exegetical discussion—and that which is most significant to the work—is his treatment of 1 Peter 1:8, which appears in the opening lines of Part One of *Religious Affections*. Edwards's nine-paragraph exegesis of this text is based on the preceding literary context and consists of a phrase-by-phrase analysis; Edwards positions this exegesis to prepare the reader for the main doctrinal proposition of the treatise.[51] No other exegetical discussion appears in Part One. A typical exegetical treatment appears in Part Two, Section Four, in which Edwards gives a brief, one-paragraph exegetical explanation from Ephesians 1:18–19, elaborating on the relationship between the ideas of "knowing" and "power" as expressed in this text.[52]

A number of other comments are exegetical in nature; they make an appeal to the original language to substantiate the interpretation. Edwards makes fleeting, single phrase references to the original language in the text on a handful of occasions. The following three examples illustrate the case:

> In Ephesians 6:24: "Grace be with all them that love the Lord Jesus Christ in sincerity." The last word, in the original, signifies "in incorruption"; which shews that the Apostle was sensible that there were many who had a kind of love to Christ, whose love was not pure and spiritual.[53]

[51] Edwards, *Religious Affections*, WJE 2:93–95.
[52] Ibid., 2:140–41.
[53] Ibid., 2:147.

> In James 3:17: "The wisdom that is from above, is first pure, then peaceable, gentle," etc., for this the Apostle opposes to natural wisdom, v. 15. "This wisdom descendeth not from above, but is earthly, sensual," the last word in the original is the same that is translated "natural," in 1 Corinthians 2:14.[54]
>
> In James 1:15: Grace is said to be made perfect or finished in its work or fruit, in the same manner as 'tis said of sin, "When lust hath conceived, it bringeth forth sin; and sin, when it is finished, bringeth forth death" (James 1:15). Here are three steps; first, sin in its principle or habit, in the being of lust in the heart; and nextly, here is its conceiving, consisting in the immanent exercises of it in the mind; and lastly, here is the fruit that was conceived actually brought forth, in the wicked work and practice. And this the Apostle calls the finishing or perfecting of sin: for the word in the original is the same that is translated "perfected" in those forementioned places. Now certainly if it be so, if grace be in this manner made perfect.[55]

While Edwards in a number of other places in *Religious Affections* makes similar brief exegetical arguments based on the original languages, that number is limited, and *Religious Affections* makes no use of an extended exegetical discussion based on the original languages.[56] Similarly, the reader will observe that only on occasion does Edwards appeal to the literary context of a passage to justify his interpretation.[57]

[54] Ibid., 2:200.

[55] Ibid., 2:435.

[56] See Edwards, *Religious Affections*, WJE 2:95, 107, 197, 256, 365, 420, 434 for additional references to the Greek text; see 148 and 186 for references to the Hebrew text. Compare the brevity of these with the extended exegetical discussions from the Hebrew text found in *Original Sin*. See Edwards, *Original Sin*, WJE 3:234–35; 242–44; 247; 326; 328–29.

[57] See Edwards, *Religious Affections*, WJE 2:199, 238, 439, 454.

The Use of Proof-Texting. The vast majority of direct Scriptural citations in *Religious Affections* are used as simple proof-texts.[58] Many proof-texts are cited with a summary of content, a word to enhance its illustrative or applicational value, or a comment to bring it into relation to the point being supported. In these cases, no exegesis is taking place, at least in the sense of bringing meaning out of the text by referring to some objective feature within the text or its context.

Scholars have been reluctant to comment upon Edwards's use of proof-texting. Social and cultural historians find Edwards's profuse citation of biblical references to be either annoying or of little interest. Evangelical scholars, as of late quite disenchanted with the practice of proof-texting, seem to be disappointed with Edwards on this score. For some, the extent to which Edwards was given to proof-texting is laborious and unnecessary.

Wilson Kimnach views Edwards's propensity to engage in elaborate proof-texting as something to be expected yet at the same time something new. According to Kimnach, the reader of Edwards should expect to see proof-texting since he followed in the Puritan pattern of substantiating doctrinal premises with Scriptural references "like so many pins securing the joints of a logical structure."[59] Yet the massive quantity of Scriptural references, which at times "cluster[ed] thickly about a point" suggests to Kimnach that Edwards was leveraging proof-texts in a way that transcended his forefathers: "When the density of biblical passages reaches a certain point one feels the presence of a new type of rhetorical argument, incantation."[60] Kimnach sees Edwards's "sheer accumulation of Scripture passages" as a "ritual invocation of the Word," unleashing the "raw quantitative power of massed Scriptural citations to substantiate his argument," escalating his credibility in the eyes of his audience.[61] John Carrick

[58] For a summary of Scripture citations in *Religious Affections*, see Appendix 6.

[59] Kimnach, "Literary Theory and Practice," WJE 10:209.

[60] Ibid., 10:209–10.

[61] Ibid., 10:210.

argues that the notion of "incantation" is a distortion of Edwards but concedes that Kimnach is justified in his observation that Edwards was excessive in his use of proof-texts.[62]

Three observations from Edwards's context help place his practice of proof-texting in perspective. First, Edwards was the product of a confessional culture, and a confessional culture expected proof-texting as the chief means of evidence that a given argument was biblical.[63] Second, in Edwards's day, the practice of proof-texting had not yet succumbed to the critique of decontextualization. Proof-texting was not perceived as the illegitimate practice of imposing confessional ideology upon the authorially intended meaning of a text. The Puritans viewed the Westminster Confession as the fruit of inductive labor and the proof-texts as the necessary evidence of that work. Without supplied proof-texts, all opinion was regarded nothing more than the arbitrary thought of the human mind.

Third, *Religious Affections* was presented as an alternative biblical interpretation of the revival and conversion. As such, it addressed both Old Lights and the New Lights on their own terms. In order to compete with two other views laying claim to biblical justification, Edwards assumed the burden of supplying a measure of biblical evidence that was clearly superior to that produced by the Old Lights and New Lights.[64]

[62] John Carrick, *The Preaching of Jonathan Edwards* (Edinburgh: Banner of Truth, 2008), 231–36.

[63] Allister E. McGrath, *Christianity's Dangerous Idea* (New York: Harper Collins, 2007), 103.

[64] Conrad Cherry defends Edwards's use of proof-texting in *Original Sin*, noting that producing this kind of evidence was necessary "for putting the question of sin in its proper context (redemption), and in order to meet Taylor on his own grounds. The title of Taylor's challenge is important: *The Scripture-Doctrine of Original Sin Proposed to Free and Candid Examination*. Taylor's objection of Calvinism purported to be a defense of the proper interpretation of Scripture." Conrad Cherry, *The Theology of Jonathan Edwards: A Reappraisal* (Bloomington, IN: Indiana University, 1966), 200–201.

Robert Brown agrees that the historical context is the key to properly assessing Edwards's use of proof-texting as part of his larger theological method:

> [The] integration of biblical references into his theological treatises ought to be expected from Edwards: it was, after all, the ground on which doctrine was contested in the eighteenth century. But it ought not for this reason be dismissed or overlooked as mere proof-texting. Rather, we need to examine more closely just how his biblical interpretation extended itself into this theoretical arguments, to consider the substantive contribution it made to the development of his thought. Recognition needs to be given to the fact that for Edwards, the content of the Bible served as a vital resource for his constructive theology, and not merely as a rhetorical referent. In the same way that contemporary theologians employ fiction, narrative, and other forms of literature in shaping the form and substance of their ideas, Edwards used biblical literature and narrative as the source of creative reflection, as an evocative influence. It was the "stuff" out of which his theology was made, without which it would have been inconceivable. More attention needs to be given, therefore, to the nuances in his use of scriptural texts in theological argument.[65]

In short, Edwards believed that extensive proof-texting was necessary for the theological and the apologetic task at hand. The theologically-informed culture of New England, which still viewed the practice as a summary of inductive work rather than the imposition of dogma upon biblical interpretation, expected proof-texting. In order to make a compelling, culturally relevant case that *Religious Affections*

[65] Brown, "The Bible," 89–90.

represented the opinion of the Bible, Edwards considered the abundant use of proof-texts both necessary and effective.[66]

The Significance of Biblical Sources for the Doctrine of Assurance

Edwards draws direct relationships between Scripture and assurance. His primary emphasis in this relationship is that Scripture serves as the measure, or the standard, by which assurance should be understood. Edwards also makes consistent reference to Scripture as a primary ground for assurance.[67]

Scripture as the Measure of Assurance

Edwards presents Scripture in such a way as to reassert the doctrine of assurance within the framework of the traditional Reformed/Puritan view, which affirmed the absolute authority and sufficiency of Scripture for all faith and practice. Because the Scriptures partook in the perfections of the Divine Author, the Scriptures were authoritative, sufficient, and internally coherent. For Edwards, the Scriptures were the sole standard for assessing what true assurance was and how it was obtained. Consequently, *Religious Affections* discusses Scripture in relation to signs, preparation, and perseverance.

Scripture and Signs. Edwards's clear intent was to bring Scripture front and center as the measure of assurance. This is evident in the basic structure of *Religious Affections.* The message of Part One is that, according to Scripture, "true religion, in great part, consists in holy affections."[68] Part Two discredits twelve non-Scriptural measures of assurance. Part Three delineates twelve Scriptural measures of genu-

[66] The significance and appropriateness of proof-texting for the theological task will be addressed in chapter 8.

[67] It should be noted that Edwards does not see Scripture as the sole ground of assurance but one part of a triad involving the Holy Spirit, Scripture, and sanctification. See the discussion entitled "The Basis of Assurance: The Spirit, the Word, and Sanctification" in chapter 7.

[68] Edwards, *Religious Affections*, WJE 2:95.

ine conversion. The unreliable "signs" of Part Two and the reliable "signs" of Part Three provide biblically-informed markers for discerning the authenticity of a Christian profession of conversion. By framing the treatise in these terms, Edwards identifies Scripture as the point of reference for assessing questions of conversion and assurance.

Edwards is convinced that Scripture supplies certain points of instruction for the purpose of enabling people to discern the difference between a true and a false convert. These marks of saving grace are uniform in that they describe objective characteristics that attend a genuine conversion. Since the biblical authors intended these characteristics to be recognized as signals of spiritual reality, Edwards refers to the biblical evidences of salvation as "signs."[69]

Much of the appeal to "signs" was directed to the New Lights, who cited the experience of having Scriptures come powerfully to the mind as proof of conversion. To them Edwards poses a simple question: "Where is any such rule to be found in the Bible, the great and only sure directory in things of this nature?"[70] The New Lights were particularly given to drawing rash conclusions regarding the certainty of their own salvation as well as the spiritual state of others. Such presumption was evidence of a low view of Scripture:

> 'Tis strange how hardly men are brought to be contented with the rules and directions Christ has given them, but they must needs go by other rules, of their own inventing, that seem to

[69] It is this feature of Edwards's thought that has arrested the attention of students of postmodern linguistic theory. Edwards's use of "signs" in *Religious Affections* as well as his view that all creation typifies spiritual realities suggests to some that Edwards was far ahead of his time, viewing reality in terms of communication rather than things. See Stephen H. Daniel's *The Philosophy of Jonathan Edwards: A Study in Divine Semiotics* as well as his "Postmodern Concepts of God and Edwards's Trinitarian Theology," in *Edwards in Our Time*, ed. Sang Hyun Lee and Allen C. Guelzo (Grand Rapids: Eerdmans, 1999); M. X. Lesser, *Reading Jonathan Edwards: An Annotated Bibliography in Three Parts, 1729–2005* (Grand Rapids: Eerdmans, 2008), 482.

[70] Edwards, *Religious Affections*, WJE *2*:143.

> them wiser and better. I know of no directions or counsels which Christ ever delivered more plainly, than the rules he has given us, to guide us in our judging of others' sincerity; viz. that we should judge of the tree chiefly by the fruit: but yet this won't do; but other ways are found out, which are imagined to be more distinguishing and certain. And woeful have been the mischievous consequences, of this arrogant setting up men's wisdom above the wisdom of Christ.[71]

For Edwards, the sign of all signs is perseverance in holiness. Perseverance is "chiefly insisted on in the Scripture, as a special note of the truth of grace, [and] is the continuance of professors in the practice of their duty, and being steadfast in an holy walk, through the various trials that they meet with."[72] Elsewhere Edwards remarks that "the Scripture plainly teaches that practice is the best evidence of the sincerity of professing Christians."[73] Assurance is again tied to perseverance when he affirms that "Christian practice, doing good works, or keeping Christ's commandments" is that which "the Scripture represents . . . as a sure sign to our own consciences, that we are real Christians."[74] Edwards concludes his thoughts on this subject with a warning to those who would minimize the point: "'Tis greatly to the hurt of religion, for persons to make light of, and insist little on, those things which the Scriptures insist most upon, as of the most importance in the evidence of our interest in Christ."[75]

Scripture and Preparation. The sufficiency of Scripture had other implications for assurance. Not only did it serve positively to identify the true marks of conversion, but it also negated other means of obtaining assurance, means not specified in Scripture. On this principle, Edwards subjected the Puritan doctrine of preparationism

[71] Ibid., 2:185.
[72] Ibid., 2:389.
[73] Ibid., 2:409.
[74] Ibid., 2:421.
[75] Ibid., 2:459.

to close scrutiny, reasoning from the sufficiency of Scripture that preparatory experiences could not serve as a basis for assurance:

> We don't find any legal convictions, or comforts following those legal convictions, in any certain method or order, ever once mentioned in the Scripture, as certain signs of grace . . . . We do find gracious operations and effects themselves, so mentioned, thousands of times. Which should be enough with Christians, who are willing to have the Word of God, rather than their own philosophy, and experiences, and conjectures, as their sufficient and sure guide in things of this nature.[76]

The preparatory steps had become so important that biblical marks of salvation had become marginalized in the minds of some holding the pastoral office:

> Ministers . . . have no warrant from Christ to encourage persons, that are of a contrary character and behavior, to think they are converted, because they tell a fair story of illuminations and discoveries. In so doing they would set up their own wisdom against Christ's, and judge without, and against that rule by which Christ has declared all men should know his disciples. Some persons place religion so much in certain transient illuminations and impressions (especially if they are in such a particular method and order) and so little in the spirit and temper persons are of, that they greatly deform religion, and form notions of Christianity quite different from what it is, as delineated in the Scriptures. The Scripture knows of no such true Christians, as of a sordid, selfish, cross and contentious spirit.[77]

[76] Ibid., 2:160. Edwards fully develops his thoughts on preparationism in 160–62.

[77] Ibid., 2:356.

Elsewhere he asserts the following:

> We don't find any legal convictions, or comforts following those legal convictions, in any certain method or order, ever once mentioned in the Scripture, as certain signs of grace, or things peculiar to the saints; although we do find gracious operations and effects themselves, so mentioned, thousands of times.[78]

Although preparatory signs as a basis for assurance were not to be found in Scripture, Scripture nevertheless pointed to signs of conversion, and these signs Edwards presented with all earnestness. And these signs, on several occasions, were directly linked to the believer's duty to observe the sufficiency of Scripture. For example, concerning the sign of humility, he says, "As we would therefore make the holy Scriptures our rule, in judging of the nature of true religion, and judging of our own religious qualifications and state; it concerns us greatly to look at this humiliation, as one of the most essential things pertaining to true Christianity."[79] The duty of assessing the reality of conversion by means of signs is nothing less than honoring the express intent of Scripture. It is the believer's duty, says Edwards, to make much of what the Scripture makes much of. To make little of what the Word emphasizes and to make much of minor points is "dangerous" and "tends to give us a monstrous idea of religion."[80]

Scripture as a Ground for Assurance

Edwards invested a considerable portion of his argument refuting the New Light notion that the promises of Scriptures, when they came to mind, were assuring words from the Holy Spirit that such a person belonged to God. Such a revelation was regarded by New Lights as self-evident and irrefutable, even in cases when faith and

[78] Ibid., 2:160.
[79] Ibid., 2:314.
[80] Ibid., 2:438.

repentance did not precede. For Edwards, this assumption was nothing short of bypassing the biblical conditions for salvation. But by refuting this idea, Edwards opened the question as to whether or not, and under what circumstances, the promises of Scripture could be appropriated for assurance and comfort.[81]

Saving faith is faith in Christ, and faith in Christ is faith in the promises of the Word. Therefore, faith in the promises of Christ is commanded:

> If persons pretend that they come to high attainments in religion, but have never yet arrived to the lesser attainments, 'tis a sign of a vain pretense. . . . Or if they pretend . . . that they are not afraid to venture their souls upon Christ, and commit their all to God, trusting to his bare word, and the faithfulness of his promises, for their eternal welfare; but at the same time, han't confidence enough in God, to dare to trust him with a little of their estates, bestowed to pious and charitable uses: I say, when it is thus with persons, their pretenses are manifestly vain.[82]

The promises of God, according to Edwards, are to be believed because God gave them for the purpose of serving as the objective ground for human certainty:

> 'Tis unreasonable to suppose, that God has provided for his people, no more than probable evidences of the truth of the gospel. He has with great care, abundantly provided, and given them, the most convincing, assuring, satisfying and manifold evidence of his faithfulness in the covenant of grace; and as David says, made a covenant, "ordered in all things, and sure." Therefore it is rational to suppose, that at the same time, he would not fail of ordering the matter so, that there

[81] Ibid., 2:143–45, 182, 218–26, 233n3.
[82] Ibid., 2:370.

> should not be wanting, as great, and clear evidence, that this is his covenant, and that these promises are his promises; or which is the same thing, that the Christian religion is true, and that the gospel is his Word. Otherwise in vain are those great assurances he has given of his faithfulness in his covenant, by confirming it with his oath, and so variously establishing it by seals and pledges. For the evidence that it is his covenant, is properly the foundation on which all the force and effect of those other assurances do stand. We may therefore undoubtedly suppose and conclude, that there is some sort of evidence which God has given, that this covenant, and these promises are his, beyond all mere probability; that there are some grounds of assurance of it held forth, which, if we are not blind to them, tend to give an higher persuasion, than any arguing from history, human tradition.[83]

Consequently, the promises are indeed intended as a ground of assurance. Referring again to 2 Samuel 23:5, Edwards says,

> The promises are most full, and very often repeated, and various ways exhibited . . . and God has confirmed his promises with an oath. And God's declared design in all this is, that the heirs of the promises might have an undoubting hope, and full joy, in an assurance of their future glory. "Wherein God willing, more abundantly to show to the heirs of promise, the immutability of his counsel, confirmed it by an oath; that by two immutable things, in which it was impossible for God to lie, we might have a strong consolation, who have fled for refuge, to lay hold on the hope set before us" (Heb. 6:17–18). But all this would be in vain, to any such purpose, as the saints' strong consolation, and hope of their obtaining future glory, if their interest in those sure promises in ordinary cases,

[83] Ibid., 2:304–5.

> was not attainable. For God's promises and oaths, let them be as sure as they will, can't give strong hope and comfort to any particular person, any further than he can know that those promises are made to him. And in vain is provision made in Jesus Christ, that believers might be perfect as pertaining to the conscience, as is signified (Heb. 9:9), if assurance of freedom from the guilt of sin is not attainable.[84]

These three texts are but a sample of the frequent reminders in *Religious Affections* that all people must come to God by faith; that faith must rest upon the promises contained in Scripture.[85]

Summary

In contrast to the supporting roles that philosophical and historical sources play, Scripture functions as the governing source for the theological method employed in *Religious Affections*. This governing is evident in those principles expressed in *Religious Affections* concerning the nature of Scripture, which include the sufficiency, clarity, and self-authenticity of the written Word. It is also evident in his practice of building theological arguments in *Religious Affections* on the ground of Scripture. His indirect uses of Scripture—allusion, appeal to Scripture in general, and theological generalization—give the work a tenor and tone that is thoroughly biblical. His direct uses of Scripture—biblical exegesis and proof-texting—fulfill the standard of objective authority in a manner recognized by the spectrum of his audience. By establishing Scripture as the governing element, the measure for obtaining assurance is biblically informed; post-conversion "signs" displace pre-conversion preparation as the measure by which assurance is verified.

[84] Ibid., 2:169.
[85] Ibid., 2:103, 168–69, 176, 281, 178, 417, 446, 459.

7

Edwards's Theology of Assurance in *Religious Affections*: A Synthesis

The preceding chapters have considered Edwards's historical context, key issues attending theological method, and his use of philosophical, historical, and biblical sources in *Religious Affections*. In order to establish a frame of reference for a final analysis and concluding thoughts, it will be beneficial to summarize Edwards's theology of assurance in *Religious Affections*. However, before proceeding, some qualification is necessary. First, it is important to respect the literary character of *Religious Affections* as well as what the historical context suggests the author's purpose was in its composition. Second, it must be acknowledged from the outset that *Religious Affections* is not a systematic theology of assurance cloaked in rhetorical form, nor was it ever intended to be a systematic presentation of the doctrine of assurance. To be sure, *Religious Affections* is Edwards's most complete expression on the subject of assurance; for that reason, a doctrinal synthesis can be valuable. But *Religious Affections* cannot be construed to be an exhaustive expression of his theology on the subject, neither should it be assumed that it represents his views before or after the time of writing. Third, it would be inappropriate to assume that Edwards's thought can be organized into a scheme that invariably reflects the image of the Reformed/Puritan tradition with which he is so closely associated.

Finally, the student of *Religious Affections* must acknowledge that Edwards had a high regard for systematics, evidenced in his expressed affinity for the Westminster Confession and the work of the "divines." If his *Miscellanies* may be taken as a reliable gauge of his thought over an extended period of time, it is no overstatement to assert that the categories of systematic theology were woven into the fabric of his thought. For this reason, it is possible to cautiously contextualize Edwards's theology of assurance as it arises from the text of *Religious Affections* with a selection of proof-texts which he employed in a manner reflective of theological categories that he himself would have acknowledged. With these qualifications in mind, it seems possible to synthesize his theology without overstatement or undue distortion.[1] This summary of his theology of assurance is based upon a series of assurance themes which are emphasized in *Religious Affections*.

The Nature of Assurance: Not of the Essence of Faith

The Puritans spoke of two kinds of certainty: certainty in the proposition of the gospel message and certainty in the proposition that the benefits of the gospel had been applied to oneself. Although the term *assurance* was used for a time to refer to both, the late Puritans reserved this term to refer to the latter. Edwards likewise spoke of the certainty of the gospel but reserved the expression of *assurance* to refer to the experiential certainty of one's own "good estate."

[1] It is important to recognize the potential for distortion, as McClymond and McDermott point out: "Edwards's soteriology was complex. . . . Scholars have sometimes misrepresented Edwards by focusing on only a few of the many themes contained in his theology. Particular sermons, notebook entries, or treatises offer only one piece of the puzzle. Interpreting one text in isolation from the rest results in a distorted presentation of his theology." Michael J. McClymond and Gerald R. McDermott, *The Theology of Jonathan Edwards* (Oxford: Oxford University, 2012), 372. For this reason, this theological synthesis is not intended to represent the whole of his theology. The value of this synthesis is to function as a part of the whole and not the whole itself.

The Nature of Assurance as Expressed in Religious Affections

Religious Affections supports the maintaining of the Westminster view that Christian assurance is not of the essence of faith itself.[2] Edwards addresses this subject in response to the aftermath of the revival in which it had become apparent that many professing believers had not genuinely perceived Christ as the object of their faith.[3] Although such professors characterized their faith as "faith in Christ," the evident carnality of their lives demonstrated that the holy character of Christ had never been apprehended and that such "faith in Christ" was really faith in their own faith.[4] These professors equated saving faith with the belief that their faith was saving. As a corollary, they also believed that doubting one's own salvation was doubting God's promises, which amounted to a lack of saving faith.[5]

Edwards vigorously opposed this doctrine as both unbiblical and nonsensical. Scripture plainly cast saving faith as the means by which people are saved: "Therefore it can't be the same thing, as believing that they are already in a good estate. To suppose that faith consists in persons believing that they are in a good estate, is in effect the same thing, as to suppose that faith consists in a person's believing that he has faith, or in believing that he believes."[6]

The Nature of Assurance as Clarified in the Gillespie Correspondence

Thomas Gillespie, in his now famous correspondence with Edwards regarding particular points expressed in *Religious Affections*, found the distinction between assurance and saving faith difficult to

[2] "The Westminster Confession of Faith," in *The Creeds of Christendom*, ed. Phillip Schaff, vol. 3, *The Evangelical Protestant Creeds* (repr., Grand Rapids: Baker, 2007), 638–39.

[3] Jonathan Edwards, *A Treatise Concerning Religious Affections*, ed. John E. Smith, The Works of Jonathan Edwards, vol. 2 (New Haven: Yale, 1959), 2:175.

[4] Ibid., 2:176.

[5] Ibid., 2:177.

[6] Ibid., 2:178.

accept.[7] Edwards replies to his concerns by offering the following explanation:

> Here, Sir, you seem to suppose that a person's doubting of his own good estate, is the proper opposite of faith, and . . . that doubting of one's own good estate and unbelief is the same thing, and so, that being confident of one's good estate and faith are the same thing. This I acknowledge I don't understand; I don't take faith, and a person's believing they have faith, to be the same thing. Nor do I take unbelief, or being without faith and doubting they have it, to be the same thing, but entirely different.[8]

Gillespie responded with a second letter to Edwards; and on this point, he indicated a substantive disagreement: for him, assurance was not categorically distinct from belief; nor was doubting substantively different from unbelief.[9] Edwards attempts in his second response to Gillespie to clarify the matter: "If by a man's believing that he is in a good estate, be meant no more than his believing that he does believe in Christ, does love God, etc., I think there is nothing of the nature of faith in it; because knowing it or believing it depends on our own immediate sensation or consciousness, and not on divine testimony."[10]

[7] Thomas Gillespie, "Letter to Jonathan Edwards, November 24, 1746," in *A Treatise Concerning Religious Affections*, ed. John E. Smith, The Works of Jonathan Edwards, vol. 2 (New Haven: Yale, 1959), 474.

[8] Jonathan Edwards, "Letter to Thomas Gillespie, September 4, 1747," in *A Treatise Concerning Religious Affections*, ed. John E. Smith, The Works of Jonathan Edwards, vol. 2 (New Haven: Yale, 1959), 480.

[9] Thomas Gillespie, "Letter to Jonathan Edwards, September 19, 1748," in *A Treatise Concerning Religious Affections*, ed. John E. Smith, The Works of Jonathan Edwards, vol. 2 (New Haven: Yale, 1959), 492.

[10] Jonathan Edwards, "Letter to Thomas Gillespie, April 2, 1750," in *A Treatise Concerning Religious Affections*, ed. John E. Smith, The Works of Jonathan Edwards, vol. 2 (New Haven: Yale, 1959), 502.

In this second letter to Gillespie, Edwards offers three reasons for viewing assurance and saving faith and as separate matters. For his first explanation, he refers to the classic assurance syllogism:

> Major: whoever believes shall be saved
> Minor: I believe
> Conclusion: therefore, I am saved

Edwards explains that the syllogism properly portrays the distinction between saving faith and assurance. The major premise is the gospel message, and the minor premise refers to the certainty that one owns the benefits of the gospel. The source of the major premise is Scripture; to doubt a biblical proposition is to doubt the Scripture, and the sin of unbelief is to doubt Scripture. The minor premise, however, is *not* stated in Scripture, being the product of the individual conscience. The conscience is not infallible, so no Scriptural principle morally obligates the soul to believe the dictates of the conscience. For this reason, says Edwards, doubting one's own salvation is not tantamount to unbelief in the message of the gospel.[11]

The second explanation concerns a problem of logic which develops when assurance is conceived to be of the essence of faith:

> That a believing that I am in a good estate, is no part or ingredient in the essence of saving faith, is evident by this, that the essence of saving faith, must be complete in me, before it can be true, that I am in a good estate. If I have not as yet acted faith, yea if there be anything wanting in me to make up the essence of saving faith, then I am not as yet in a state of salvation, and therefore can have no ground to believe that I am so. Anything that belongs to the essence of saving faith is prior, in the order of nature, to a man's being in a state of salvation, because it is saving faith that brings him into such a

[11] Ibid., 2:502–3.

> state. And therefore believing that he is in such a state cannot be one thing that is essential or necessary in order to his being in such a state; for that would imply a contradiction. It would be to suppose a man's believing that he is in a good estate to be prior, in the order of nature, to his being in a good estate. But a thing cannot be both prior and posterior, antecedent and consequent, with respect to the very same thing.[12]

A third reason faith is not of the essence of salvation involves an irony: the doubting of salvation may offer evidence that a person is a true believer. Edwards argues this point on the basis of four theological observations: (1) true believers, because of the humility instilled in them by conversion, have "a lively sense of how great a thing it is to appear before an infinitely holy, just and omniscient judge" whereas unbelievers are generally given to spiritual insensitivity;[13] (2) true believers, because of their humility, have a less confident opinion of their own capacity for discernment than unbelievers have;[14] (3) the devil is not interested in disturbing the hope of unbelievers but does all he can to bring despair to true believers. This point regarding the work of Satan is so significant to Edwards that he says, "There is perhaps no true Christian but what has had his hope assaulted by him";[15] and (4) true believers, because of their humility, see themselves as utterly sinful, so much so, that "it often appears a very mysterious thing, that any grace can be consistent with such corruption, or should be in such a heart." On the other hand, the unbeliever takes his sin and "covers it all over," so "the hypocrite looks clean and bright in his own eyes."[16]

Therefore, (1) since assurance concerns believing the message of the conscience, (2) since it is impossible to posit assurance as both

[12] Ibid., 2:504–5.
[13] Edwards, *Religious Affections*, WJE 2:172.
[14] Ibid.
[15] Ibid.
[16] Ibid., 2:172–73.

cause and effect (or the cause of itself), and (3) since there are sound theological reasons for a true believer to be overcome by doubt, the notion of assurance being of the essence of faith is both illogical and unbiblical.[17]

The Basis of Assurance: The Spirit, the Word, and Sanctification

Religious Affections gives strong evidence that Edwards embraced the traditional Puritan view that the basis of assurance was formed by a union of the active Spirit, the objective Word, and subjective sanctification. These three worked in concert to attest the truth of one's spiritual state to the conscience.

The Witness of the Spirit

For Edwards, the "witness of the Spirit" is not to be understood as a direct communication to the believer that he or she is truly converted.[18] Some of the New Lights had taken the term *witness* as evidence that the Spirit engaged in secret verbal communication to the individual. Edwards rebuts the view, citing several biblical passages which speak of a "witness" as the presentation of evidence rather than a verbal assertion. The witness of the Spirit, then, is to be taken

[17] The logic assumes that the salvation being spoken of here is a state of justification. Earlier in *Religious Affections* Edwards affirmed this understanding of salvation: "Men that are saved are in two exceeding different states, first a state of condemnation, and then in a state of justification and blessedness." Ibid., 2:152.

[18] Ibid., 2:173, 212, 222, 229–31. In order to support the disconnect between regeneration and immediate communication from God, Edwards appeals to Gen. 20:6–7 (God's communication to Abimelech), Gen. 31:24 and Ps. 105:15 (God's communication to Laban). Edwards then cites 1 Cor. 13:2 to support the assertion that, if a truly saved person were to receive a communication from God by immediate suggestion, this would be of no unique character but would be of the same kind of communication as the gift of prophecy. Ibid., 2:229.

as the evidence the Spirit presents, not an assertion that he makes.[19] The witness of the Spirit is also spoken of in the Scripture as the "seal of the Spirit," which is a

> holy stamp, or impressed image, exhibiting clear evidence to the conscience, that the subject of it is the child of God, is the very thing which in Scripture is called the seal of the Spirit, and the witness, or evidence of the Spirit. And this image enstamped by the Spirit on God's children's hearts, is his own image: that is the evidence by which they are known to be God's children, that they have the image of their Father stamped upon their hearts by the spirit of adoption.[20]

This seal, this holy stamp, comes in the form of a "holy nature, being a communication of the divine nature and beauty." This kind of evidence, unlike direct impressions on the mind, is something that cannot be forged by Satan.[21]

The "witness of the Spirit" and the "seal of the Spirit" are one and the same with "the earnest of the Spirit."[22] The first-fruits of the Spirit, which the Spirit presents to the conscience as evidence of

[19] Ibid., 2:231–32.

[20] Ibid., 2:232.

[21] Ibid., 2:233.

[22] Edwards later equates "the firstfruits of the Spirit" in Rom. 8:22–23 with "the earnest of the Spirit" and "the seal of the Spirit." Ibid., 2:237. Edwards's equation of the witness of the Spirit, the seal of the Spirit, and the earnest of the Spirit is further evidence of Edwards's close ties to the Westminster standards: "This certainty is not a bare conjectural and probable persuasion, grounded upon a fallible hope; but an infallible assurance of faith, founded upon the divine truth of the promises of salvation, the inward evidence of those graces unto which these promises are made, the testimony of the Spirit of adoption witnessing with our spirits that we are the children of God: which Spirit is the earnest of our inheritance, whereby we are sealed unto the day of redemption." "The Westminster Confession of Faith," in *The Creeds of Christendom*, ed. Phillip Schaff, vol. 3, *The Evangelical Protestant Creeds* (repr., Grand Rapids: Baker, 2007), 638.

salvation, is also intended to serve as the down payment, "the token of the whole to be paid in due time."[23] Thus, the witness of the Spirit is part of the larger Trinitarian scheme: the Father gives the Son, the Son is both "purchaser and the price," and the Spirit is the benefit purchased for the elect, the "sum of all blessings of eternal life."[24]

The witness of the Spirit, then, is the work of the Spirit which he does upon the heart, particularly as a testimony to the conscience of the believer. The precise nature of this holy work is the creation of love in the heart. This love cries out to God in love, causing the believer to relate as a child to the heavenly Father. And it is this love which casts out the fear of judgment from God, bringing assurance.[25] For Edwards, the entire matter of assurance hinges on whether or not the heart is possessed by love or by fear:

> God has wisely ordained, that these two opposite principles of love and fear, should rise and fall, like the two opposite scales of a balance; when one rises, the other sinks. As light and darkness, necessarily and unavoidably succeed each other; if light prevails, so much does darkness cease, and no more; and if light decays, so much does darkness prevail; so it is in the heart of a child of God: if divine love decays and falls asleep, and lust prevails, the light and joy of hope goes out, and dark fear and doubting arises; and if on the contrary, divine love prevails, and comes into lively exercise, this brings in the brightness of hope, and drives away black lust, and fear with it. Love is the spirit of adoption, or the childlike principle; if that slumbers, men fall under fear, which is the spirit of bondage, or the servile principle: and so on the contrary. And

[23] Edwards, *Religious Affections*, WJE 2:236.

[24] Ibid. Edwards cites in support Luke 24:49; Acts 1:4; 2:38–39; Gal. 3:14; Eph. 1:13; John 14–16; and he asks readers to compare John 7:37–39 and John 4:14 with Rev. 21:6 and Rev. 22:1, 17. This string of references, and those that follow, are given in the same order as given by Edwards.

[25] Ibid., 2:237–38.

> if it be so, that love, or the spirit of adoption, be carried to a great height, it quite drives away all fear, and gives full assurance; agreeable to that of the Apostle, 1 John 4:18, "There is no fear in love, but perfect love casts out fear."[26]

The soul perceives such growing and maturing love as a sure evidence of a saving relationship with God. Romans 8:16, speaking of the Spirit bearing witness "with our spirit," does not describe the divine and human spirit bearing witness together in a joint exercise. Rather, the Spirit presents the evidence of holy love to the human "spirit," or the conscience. The human spirit, in response, "receives and declares this evidence for our rejoicing."[27]

The Testimony of Scripture

In addition to the Spirit, the Scriptures are taken to be a second basis of assurance. The role of the Scriptures in assurance, as presented in *Religious Affections*, provides objective ground for knowing the way in which God views the matter. Each believer must take care to possess assurance in such a way as to avoid Satan's deceptions, and only the Scriptures supply divine and reliable principles to this end. Such principles are to be taken as "rules" and "signs"; they are authoritative markers without which no reliable discernment is possible.[28]

In order for Scripture to function as a basis of assurance, it must be taken on its own terms, interpreted as the author intended.[29] Taking the Scripture in any other way negates the critical foundational role that God intends for it to play. Edwards exhorts his readers to distinguish between the message of Scripture as contained in the text

[26] Ibid., 2:179–80; see also 2:436.

[27] Ibid., 2:239. Edwards cites Rom. 8:16; Prov. 20:27; 2 Cor. 1:12; and 1 John 3:19–21 in support.

[28] Ibid., 2:136, 185.

[29] "Things be not to be learned from the Scripture any other way than they are taught be in the Scripture." Ibid., 2:268 (Edwards here cites Luke 24:32); see also 2:280, where Edwards argues that this is the implication to be drawn from Ps. 119:18.

and the experience of Scripture coming to mind.[30] The latter is not an authoritative ground for knowledge, but

> is wholly an uncertain and precarious determination . . . and therefore is a false and sandy foundation for faith; and accordingly that faith which is built upon it is false. The only certain foundation which any person has to believe that he is invited to partake of the blessings of the gospel, is that the Word of God declares that persons so qualified as he is, are invited, and God who declares it is true and cannot lie. If a sinner be once convinced of the veracity of God, and that the Scriptures are his Word, he'll need no more to convince and satisfy him that he is invited; for the Scriptures are full of invitations to sinners, to the chief of sinners, to come and partake of the benefits of the gospel: he won't want any new speaking of God to him, what he hath spoken already will be enough with him.[31]

This Scriptural foundation for assurance is critical, serving as the objective ground for knowing as well as a safeguard against a purely subjective assurance. For this reason, Edwards juxtaposes Scripture and experience, describing experience as the great deceiver in the wake of the revival. As Part Two of *Religious Affections* explains, experiences in and of themselves prove nothing; the danger is in promoting experiences, as the New Lights did, to the ground of knowledge, interpreting reality in light of them.[32] Some New Lights

[30] Edwards appears to see reliance upon experience as the common cause for the errors of the New Lights, the Old Lights, and the strict preparationists. He points to revelatory and bodily experiences as the seat of New Light errors; he points to the reaction to these experiences as well as empirical rationalism as the motivation for Old Light errors. Preparationism, in its excesses, was also built on the basis of observed experiences collected and analyzed by the Puritan clergy.

[31] Edwards, *Religious Affections*, WJE 2:223.

[32] Ibid., 2:135, 137, 143, 252.

were convinced that their own experiences were valid because they coincided with the Scriptures coming to mind. Edwards is quick to disqualify this thought, for they transform Scripture into but another experience, discounting its intended propositional purpose.[33]

New Lights were not the only ones who permitted experience to supplant Scripture as a ground for assurance. Many of the old-line Puritans, not the least of whom was his own father, strongly insisted on a particular order and type of pre-conversion experience as grounds for assurance. This, says Edwards, is simply another form of experiential authority.[34] Edwards equates such strict preparationism as a mistake on par with the Old Lights, who elevated philosophy, or the New Lights, who elevated experience.[35] In their own way, they set aside the Scripture as the controlling feature in their theological method:

> God has revealed no certain connection between salvation, and any qualifications in men, but only grace and its fruits. And therefore we don't find any legal convictions, or comforts following those legal convictions, in any certain method or order, ever once mentioned in the Scripture, as certain signs of grace, or things peculiar to the saints; although we do find

[33] Ibid., 2:143.

[34] Ibid., 2:159, 416, 419, 443.

[35] In an interesting turn of reasoning, Edwards appeals to experience to discount preparationism, which itself was an empirically derived doctrine: "Experience does greatly confirm, that persons seeming to have convictions and comforts following one another in such a method and order, as is frequently observable in true converts, is no certain sign of grace. I appeal to all those ministers in this land, who have had much occasion of dealing with souls, in the late extraordinary season, whether there han't been many who don't prove well, that have given a fair account of their experiences, and have seemed to be converted according to rule, i.e. with convictions and affections, succeeding distinctly and exactly, in that order and method, which has been ordinarily insisted on, as the order of the operations of the Spirit of God in conversion." Ibid., 2:160. In note 8 of this same page, Edwards cites Stoddard in support of this statement.

> gracious operations and effects themselves, so mentioned, thousands of times. Which should be enough with Christians, who are willing to have the Word of God, rather than their own philosophy, and experiences, and conjectures, as their sufficient and sure guide in things of this nature.[36]

Edwards realizes that this strong position against experience could be misunderstood. Sanctification, after all, is something experienced. Some who objected to the signs of sanctification said that self-examination for signs amounted to trusting in experience rather than the promises and character of Christ. Edwards responds by acknowledging that the evidence of sanctification can possibly be abused in such a way, in the act of looking to one's own good works in order to "make a righteousness of them."[37] But this misappropriation of good

[36] Ibid., 2:160.

[37] Ibid., 2:180. Elsewhere Edwards acknowledges that sanctification is a sort of experience, but that the experience of sanctification is categorically different, being sanctioned in Scripture, and not serving as an independent ground. In one instance, he describes experience as "the true saint's super-structure . . . [but] the hypocrite's foundation." Ibid., 2:251. (This language suggests that sanctification, in Edwards's mind, does *not* serve as a ground for assurance. However, in light of his other statements regarding sanctification, it is best to interpret this to mean that Edwards does not see sanctification as a ground with the same degree of ultimacy as Scripture and the Spirit, given that sanctification is dependent upon both. This interpretation is in keeping with Carson's helpful description of sanctification as a kind of "corroborating evidence," which the Puritans typically overemphasized. See D. A. Carson, "Reflections on Assurance," in *Still Sovereign: Contemporary Perspectives on Election, Foreknowledge, and Grace*, ed. Thomas R. Schreiner and Bruce A. Ware [Grand Rapids: Baker, 2000], 274.) In a similar vein, and with a note of sarcasm, Edwards cites Luke 6:44 to draw a sharp line between the experience of sanctification and common experience: "Christ nowhere says, Ye shall know the tree by its leaves or flowers, or ye shall know men by their talk, or ye shall know them by the good story they tell of their experiences, or ye shall know them by the manner and air of their speaking, and emphasis and pathos of expression, or by their speaking feelingly, or by making a very great show by abundance of talk, or by many tears and affectionate expressions, or by the affections ye feel in your hearts towards them: but by their

works "is a far different thing from a mere improving experiences as evidences of an interest in a glorious Redeemer."[38] For Edwards, Scripture is the true ground of assurance, but experience the false ground.[39] Authentic Christian experience does exist since "all Chris-

---

fruits shall ye know them." Edwards, *Religious Affections*, WJE 2:407.

[38] Ibid., 2:181. Later in the work, Edwards uses strong language to distinguish between experiences as a ground of assurance and the biblical use of sanctification experience as evidence: "There is no man living that is lifted up with a conceit of his own experiences and discoveries, and upon the account of them glisters in his own eyes, but what trusts in his experiences, and makes a righteousness of 'em . . . . Thus he trusts in what is inherent in him, to make him shine in God's sight, and recommend him to God: and with this encouragement he goes before God in prayer; and this makes him expect much from God; and this makes him think that Christ loves him, and that he is willing to clothe him with his righteousness; because he supposes that he is taken with his experiences and graces. And this is a high degree of living on his own righteousness; and such persons are in the high road to hell. Poor deluded wretches, who think they look so glistering in God's eyes, when they are a smoke in his nose, and are many of 'em more odious to him, than the most impure beast in Sodom, that makes no pretense to religion! To do as these do, is to live upon experiences, according to the true notion of it; and not to do as those, who only make use of spiritual experiences, as evidences of a state of grace, and in that way receive hope and comfort from 'em." Ibid., 2:318.

[39] Edwards's strong stance against experience is a consistent thread throughout the treatise. However, it should be observed that Edwards does not view experience itself as inherently untrustworthy, only its abuse as an independent ground, or manifestations of it which are not confirmed by Scripture. See Ibid., 2:450–51. Edwards's dim view of experience is evident in the way in which it is most frequently mentioned in *Religious Affections*, often being cited as the occasion for introducing a topic of discussion or singled out as a threat to sound theology. For examples, see Ibid., 2:138, 141, 143, 151–52, 156–57, 170–71, 173–75, 182–85, 187. Edwards cites 1 Sam. 16:7, Isa. 11:3 in support of his distrust of natural experience (2:181). Because Edwards views natural experience as a chief adversary to a proper understanding of assurance and the message of *Religious Affections*, it is not surprising that Edwards avoids the appeal to natural experience as a theological source. The only reliable spiritual experience is that which is perceived by the new sense, which is capable of a true sight of Christ, as seen in John 6:40 (2:175). It is for this reason that this study does not consider experience as an element

tian practice is properly experience."[40] But true Christian experience is not self-authenticating; the Scriptures authenticate experience, and the Scriptures in turn identify sanctified living as the experience that properly informs the conscience.[41]

The Role of Sanctification

Many who came to Edwards for counsel sought answers concerning the extent of assurance, how much assurance a Christian could expect to receive, or at what point in the Christian experience it could be expected. Many of the New Lights boasted of receiving total and instantaneous assurance at their conversion. Edwards questioned this assertion, so he explained why he believed the Scriptures taught otherwise.

For Edwards, the timing, the duration, and the degree of assurance experienced by a true believer is in keeping with his or her progress in sanctification. Sin in the life of the believer marks a reality that Edwards acknowledges in the opening lines of *Religious Affections*:

> 'Tis a mysterious thing, and what has puzzled and amazed many a good Christian, that there should be that which is so divine and precious, as the saving grace of God, and the new and divine nature, dwelling in the same heart, with so much corruption, hypocrisy and iniquity, in a particular saint. Yet neither of these, is more mysterious than real.[42]

---

employed in Edwards's theological method.

[40] Ibid., 2:451. Edward cites Jer. 22:15–16; 1 John 5:3; 2 John 6; Ps. 34:11; Hezekiah's deathbed prayer (unreferenced); the entirety of Psalm 119; Rom. 1:9; 2 Cor. 1:12; 4:13; 5:7, 14; 6:4–7; Gal. 2:20; Phil. 3:7–8; 1 Thess. 2:2, 8–10; and 2 Tim. 4:6–7 in support. Ibid., 2:451–52.

[41] Ibid., 2:450–51.

[42] Ibid., 2:85. Edwards indicates that the mixed nature within the true saint is analogous to the mixed nature of the true church, in which some are clean and some are not, citing Jer. 3:10; 4:3–4; the reception of John the Baptist in John 5:35; the departure of the multitude which followed Christ,

Conversion, though a distinct and radical work, does not eradicate the inward propensity and susceptibility to sin:

> Indeed allowances must be made for the natural temper: conversion don't entirely root out the natural temper: those sins which a man by his natural constitution was most inclined to before his conversion, he may be most apt to fall into still. But yet conversion will make a great alteration even with respect to these sins. Though grace, while imperfect, don't root out an evil natural temper; yet it is of great power and efficacy with respect to it, to correct it.[43]

The difficulty for Edwards was reconciling the reality of sin in the life of the believer with the reality that the believer was characterized by holiness. Edwards at times seems to be aware of this tension, acknowledging the possibility that the signs could be construed as calls to perfectionism. For this reason, he revisits the reality of sin in the believer as a way of applying a practical qualification to his signs. After impressing upon his readers the eighth sign of true conversion—that of a gentle, forgiving, "lamb-like, dove-like" spirit—Edwards qualifies the expectation: "None will understand me that true Christians have no remains of a contrary spirit, and can never, in any instances, be guilty of a behavior disagreeable to such a spirit."[44]

---

and the parable of the soils, Matt. 24:10–13; Gal. 3:1; 4:11, 15; Phil. 2:21; 3:18–19; and the entirety of 1 and 2 Corinthians. Ibid., 2:85–86.

[43] Ibid., 2:341. See also Ibid., 2:357, where Edwards admits for "allowances . . . for men's natural temper," but qualifies this by maintaining that the change in nature is yet of a fundamental sort and supports this by saying that "the Scripture represents the change wrought by gospel grace." Edwards's text for support is Isa. 11:6–9 and 65:25, along with Titus 3:3 and Col 3:7–8. Edwards again admits that such allowances be made at 2:449.

[44] Ibid., 2:356. With respect to the sign of a gentle spirit and its inconsistent presence in a true Christian, Murray relates a rare anecdote from the family life of Edwards's home: "The quick temper of Sarah, the eldest daughter, so persisted that, according to tradition, when her hand was asked in marriage by Elihu Parsons . . . Edwards 'plainly disclosed to him the

In the discussion of the twelfth sign, persevering holiness of life, Edwards calls for perseverance under trial as a true sign of conversion, but then offers the following qualification concerning the believer under trial: "True saints may be guilty of some kinds and degrees of backsliding, and may be foiled by particular temptations, and may fall into sin, yea great sins: but they can never fall away so, as to grow weary of religion, and the service of God, and habitually to dislike it and neglect it."[45]

Remaining sin is a reality for the believer, but not the dominant reality. The dominant reality of salvation is holiness, a deliverance from sin unto the likeness of Christ. Edwards reminds his readers of the doctrine of progressive sanctification by using Rutherford's quotation of Luther:

> Nothing is more pernicious to a believer, than that presumption, that he has already apprehended, and has no further need of seeking. Hence also many fall back, and pine away in spiritual security and slothfulness. . . . he is not a Christian, that is a Christian, that is, he that thinks himself a finished Christian, and is not sensible how he falls short. We reach after heaven, but are not in heaven. Woe to him that is wholly renewed that is, that thinks himself to be so. That man, without doubt, has never so much as begun to be renewed, nor did he ever taste what it is to be a Christian.[46]

Genuine believers are humbled by their own sinfulness, yet they are growing in grace:

---

unpleasant temper of his daughter.' 'But she has grace, I trust?' asked Parsons, to which Edwards replied, 'I hope she has, but grace can live where you cannot.'" Iain H. Murray, *Jonathan Edwards: A New Biography* (Edinburgh: Banner of Truth, 1987), 192; see also Perry Miller, *Jonathan Edwards* (New York: William Sloan, 1949), 202.

[45] Edwards, *Religious Affections*, WJE 2:390. In support, Edwards cites Gal. 6:9; Rom. 2:7; Heb. 10:36; Isa. 43:22; Mal. 1:13.

[46] Ibid., 2:322n1.

> The more grace they have, while in this state of imperfection, the more they see their imperfection and emptiness, and distance from what ought to be; and so the more do they see their need of grace; as I showed at large before, when speaking of the nature of evangelical humiliation. And besides grace, as long as it is imperfect, is of a growing nature, and in a growing state. And we see it to be so with all living things, that while they are in a state of imperfection, and in their growing state, their nature seeks after growth; and so much the more, as they are more healthy and prosperous. Therefore the cry of every true grace, is like that cry of true faith, "Lord I believe, help thou my unbelief" (Mark 9:24). And the greater spiritual discoveries and affections the true Christian has, the more does he become of an earnest beggar for grace, and spiritual food, that he may grow; and the more earnestly does he pursue after it, in the use of proper means and endeavors: for true and gracious longings after holiness, are no idle ineffectual desires.[47]

In light of this truth, it is a mistake to conclude that Edwards saw assurance as belonging to those who were practically perfect or belonging to some holy elite. In order for true Christians to be humbled by the greatness of their own sin, great sin had to be acknowledged as a reality in the life of a true believer. The fifth sign of holy affections is "evangelical humiliation," by which "the eminent saint, having such a conviction of the high degree in which he ought to love God, [sees] not only the littleness of his grace, but the greatness of his remaining corruption."[48]

Having made much of the importance of sanctification for assurance, Edwards anticipates an important objection: if the evidence of sanctification is necessary for a biblical assurance, does this mean that

[47] Ibid., 2:378.
[48] Ibid., 2:325.

new believers can have no legitimate basis for assurance? No, immediate assurance may come by other means, but such assurance will be temporary if not followed by the manifestation of spiritual fruit. Edwards illustrates the point by way of an analogy, comparing such a person to one who has been promised a treasure, but that person must be willing to leave all and journey through a difficult terrain in order to claim and to possess the treasure. Such a person may be confident that the promise is valid and that he is indeed willing to take the journey. But confidence in his own willingness will be short-lived unless the willingness is confirmed with action. In the same way, assurance will be short-lived if not supported by the evidence of holy behavior.[49]

The Relationship among the Spirit, the Word, and Sanctification

The Spirit, the Word, and sanctification each relate to one another in the acquisition of assurance. Together, they form the ground of the knowledge of personal salvation, for each attests in concert with one another to bring assurance to the conscience. In Edwards's theology, the Spirit of God is the actor, and the Word and sanctifica-

[49] Ibid., 2:443–44. Edwards justifies this principle with the following argument: "I think it to be abundantly manifest, that Christian practice is the most proper evidence of the gracious sincerity of professors, to themselves and others; and the chief of all the marks of grace, the sign of signs, and evidence of evidences, that which seals and crowns all other signs. I had rather have the testimony of my conscience, that I have such a saying of my supreme Judge on my side, as that, John 14:21, 'He that hath my commandments and keepeth them, he it is that loveth me'; than the judgment, and fullest approbation, of all the wise, sound and experienced divines, that have lived this thousand years, on the most exact and critical examination of my experiences, as to the manner of my conversion. Not that there are no other good evidences of a state of grace but this. There may be other exercises of grace, besides these efficient exercises, which the saints may have in contemplation, that may be very satisfying to them: but yet this is the chief and most proper evidence. There may be several good evidences that a tree is a fig tree; but the highest and most proper evidence of it, is that it actually bears figs." Ibid. 2:443.

tion are his instruments. Each sustains a relationship with the other in forming a unified ground of assurance for the believer. The "leading of the Spirit" is a two-part work by which he brings the Word to bear on the conscience. First, he works to instruct the conscience with the Word; second, he inclines the heart to respond in obedience.[50] This instruction, however, is more than cognitive comprehension; it entails a "spiritual taste" or the capacity of that "new sense." This capacity is given by the Spirit at the time of regeneration, and it enables the believer to perceive, to judge, and to discern spiritual realities for what they are.[51] In this way, the hearts of believers are now receptive to the Spirit. The Spirit then applies the Word to the hearts of believers, "enabling them to see their grace."[52] As a result, we witness the Spirit's uniting the Word and sanctification for a complete testimony to bring assurance to the conscience.[53]

[50] Ibid., 2:281.

[51] Ibid., 2:275–85.

[52] Ibid., 2:225.

[53] In Stoever's opinion, Edwards's view of the relationship among Spirit, Word, and sanctification is informed by Thomas Shepard. Stoever's exegesis of Shepard's *Parable of the Ten Virgins* portrays a theology of assurance in which the Spirit comforts the conscience "via the syllogism, in which 'the major is the Word, the minor experience, and the conclusion [is] the . . . Spirit's work.'" However, Edwards does not give any indication in *Religious Affections* of a syllogistic relationship of Spirit, Word, and sanctification. This silence suggests that Edwards had no such notion in mind when formulating his doctrine of assurance. Nevertheless, in spite of this silence, there is evidence to suggest that Stoever may be correct. First, Stoever proceeds on solid ground to appeal to Edwards's affinity for the assurance theology of Shepard in general; second, Edwards clarifies his theology of assurance in terms of the syllogism in his correspondence with Gillespie, in which Edwards refers to the major as the biblical proposition to believe the gospel and the minor as the profession of faith. Finally, the whole point of the assurance theology in *Religious Affections* is to vet what amounts to the minor premise—the validity of one's profession of faith by signs of holy affections. Only in this way could a reliable conclusion be determined. See William K. B. Stoever, "The Godly Will's Discerning: Shepard, Edwards, and the Identification of True Godliness," in *Jonathan Edwards's Writings: Text, Context, Interpretation*, ed. Stephen J. Stein (Bloomington, IN: Indiana

The Accessibility of Assurance: Attainable and Normative

For the many ministers who counseled their people in the aftermath of the Awakening, the question of obtaining assurance was a pressing one. Those experiencing the terror of being within a heartbeat of eternity without the assurance of heaven appealed to their pastors, seeking assurance with all possible urgency. The obtaining of assurance had been misunderstood in both extremes. Assurance was not a commodity to be obtained so easily as a commercial transaction, nor was it unattainable. The Scriptures presented the attainability of assurance in terms that were closely associated with the believer's sanctification.

The Loss of Assurance as the Consequence of Sin

The believer's experience with sin and sanctification are woven into the fabric of Edwards's theology of assurance. Assurance may come and go in degrees, and those degrees invariably correspond with one's experience of sanctification. The believer's failure under the struggle with sin is therefore the first cause of a loss of assurance. Though all saints have the principle of holiness within, the Christian life frequently becomes "mingled with so much corruption, which clouds and hides it, [making] it impossible for it certainly to be known."[54] For Christians ensnared in sin, "guilt lies on the conscience, which will bring fear, and so prevent the peace and joy of an assured hope."[55]

Since matters of sin and sanctification were integral to the extent to which a believer could enjoy assurance, Edwards believed it was possible for assurance to extend to a certain degree and for a certain period of time, only to collapse into fear in doubt at a later time: "A true assurance is not upheld, but by the soul being kept in a holy

---

University, 1996), 88–89; Thomas Shepard, *The Parable of the Ten Virgins* (1659; repr., Orlando: Soli Deo Gloria, 1990), 216; Edwards, "Letter to Thomas Gillespie, April 2, 1750," WJE 2:502–3.

[54] Edwards, *Religious Affections*, WJE 2:194.

[55] Ibid., 2:195.

frame, and grace maintained in lively exercise. If the actings of grace do much decay in the Christian, and he falls into a lifeless frame, he loses his assurance."[56] Some, like Gillespie, saw the doubting of salvation the doubting of God's promise to save in response to faith, evidencing a lack of faith in God's saving promises; Edwards saw doubting as biblical and appropriate; some *should* doubt their salvation, he says, when they are "under the prevalence of their lusts, and an unchristian spirit."[57]

The Gain of Assurance as the Normative Reward of Sanctification

Because a lack of sanctification was not an unusual experience, neither was the problem of doubting one's salvation. Nevertheless, a lack of assurance should not be construed as the intended norm of the Christian life. Edwards gives seven reasons assurance of salvation should be viewed as attainable and normal. First, giving knowledge of one's own salvation is God's general way of dealing with converts. In Section Eight of Part Two of *Religious Affections*, Edwards addresses the subject of preparationism, maintaining that "nothing can certainly be determined concerning the nature of the affections by this, that comforts and joys seem to follow awakenings and convictions of conscience, in a certain order."[58]

Though Edwards himself does not subscribe to the *particular* formulas of preparation prescribed by his Puritan forbears, he does acknowledge that Scripture supports the idea that conviction and sorrow precede blessing and joy. In order for this pattern to make sense, both halves of this equation must be *sensible*. That is, God intended for people to be fully aware of their sin to repent, to believe, to be fully aware of "Christ's sufficiency and God's mercy" on their behalf, and to rejoice, giving praise to God. Edwards reasons through

[56] Ibid., 2:174.
[57] Ibid., 2:179.
[58] Ibid., 2:151.

numerous examples in the canon, concluding that "God's manner" in conversion makes converts fully aware of these experiences.[59]

A second reason for assurance as a normative experience is an appeal to history. Denial of assurance as a normative experience was the established doctrine of the Roman church, vigorously opposed by the Reformers. The fact that this argument is made in passing gives the appearance of an attempt to create guilt by association. Logical fallacy or not, this argument highlights the enormity of the gulf between Protestants and Rome in Edwards's context. The doctrine of assurance was an integral part of the Protestant cause, and Edwards reminds readers that meddling with this doctrine had implications for entire scope of Reformed soteriology.[60]

The next several reasons necessitate a complete tour of the canon: the third reason focuses on the examples of the saints throughout the entire Old Testament Scriptures. All of those who walked in faith are portrayed by the Scriptures as coming to the knowledge that they were accepted by God.[61] The fourth reason for normative assurance is the teachings of Jesus and Paul. Jesus taught his disciples in such a way that they would be certain of his love for them, demonstrating a pattern with all who are his disciples. Paul also adopts this confidence into his doctrinal portrayal of salvation and assurance.[62]

The fifth reason for viewing assurance as normative is that assurance was the intended benefit of the covenant of grace. The message of the book of Hebrews confirms this reasoning:

[59] Ibid., 2:152–55. In this extended discussion, Edwards cites for support Deut. 8:2, 16; 32:36–37; Ex. 2:23; 5:19; Luke 8:43–44; Matt. 8:24–26; 15:22; 2 Cor. 1:8–10; Lev. 13:45; Jer. 3:23–25; 8:11; Gen. 15:12–13; 1 Kings 19; Dan. 10; Rev. 1; Luke 15; Ps. 72:6; Heb. 6:18; Isa. 32, as well as several biblical allusions.

[60] Ibid., 2:167.

[61] Ibid., 2:167–168. Edwards references the biblical examples of Noah, Abraham, Isaac, Jacob, Moses, Daniel, Hezekiah, and Job, citing specifically Job 19:25, the general content of the Psalter, and 2 Kings 20:3.

[62] Ibid., 2:168–69. Edwards mingles several allusions with citations of John 14–16; 15:11; 16:13, 33; Gal. 2:20; Phil. 1:21; 2 Tim. 1:8, 12.

> The nature of the covenant of grace, and God's declared ends in the appointment and constitution of things in that covenant, do plainly show it to be God's design to make ample provision for the saints having an assured hope of eternal life, while living here upon earth. For so are all things ordered and contrived in that covenant, that everything might be made sure on God's part. The covenant is ordered in all things, and sure . . .God's declared design in all this is, that the heirs of the promises might have an undoubting hope, and full joy, in an assurance of their future glory. "Wherein God willing, more abundantly to show to the heirs of promise, the immutability of his counsel, confirmed it by an oath; that by two immutable things, in which it was impossible for God to lie, we might have a strong consolation, who have fled for refuge, to lay hold on the hope set before us" (Heb. 6:17–18). But all this would be in vain, to any such purpose, as the saints' strong consolation, and hope of their obtaining future glory, if their interest in those sure promises in ordinary cases, was not attainable. For God's promises and oaths, let them be as sure as they will, can't give strong hope and comfort to any particular person, any further than he can know that those promises are made to him. And in vain is provision made in Jesus Christ, that believers might be perfect as pertaining to the conscience, as is signified, (Heb. 9:9), if assurance of freedom from the guilt of sin is not attainable.[63]

Sixth, assurance is normal and attainable because Christians are directed to pursue it by the means of sanctification, in keeping with the instruction given in 2 Peter 1:5–8. Paired with this command are texts from 1 and 2 Corinthians, which lead Edwards to conclude that it was, in the minds of the apostles, "unbecoming," the result of "blamable negligence," that for "Christians . . . not to know whether

[63] Ibid., 2:169.

Christ be in them or no."[64] Finally, assurance was attainable and normative "because the apostles tell us by what means Christians (and not only apostles and martyrs) were wont to know this."[65] With the message of 1 John as the primary basis, Edwards speaks of the work of the Spirit, obedience to God's commandments, and love for the brethren as examples of the means which God has established for the purpose of all Christians obtaining assurance of salvation.[66]

The Means of Assurance

Edwards emphasizes self-examination and action as means whereby believers may practically pursue their assurance. Edwards appears to assume, but does not emphasize, the ordinary means of grace as a means to assurance.

The Means of Self-Examination

For Edwards, self-examination is the primary means designed by God for obtaining assurance. This assertion harmonizes with the biblical ground of assurance, which is found in the work of the Spirit, the authority of the Word, and the evidence of sanctification. The Scripture sets the agenda so that self-examination does not proceed on arbitrary principles, but on objective marks. These objective marks serve as standards of comparison, or tests. The holy nature, with its new sense, loves God, all that he is, and all that he delights in.[67] Self-examination is necessary because not all affections are truly holy, and only holy affections give evidence of the new birth:

[64] Ibid.

[65] Ibid., 2:170.

[66] Ibid.

[67] Ibid., 2:260–62. Edwards cites for support John 4:32, 34; the entirety of Ps. 119; Ps. 119:127; 19:7–10; 97:12; 98:1; 99:2–3, 5, 8–9; Isa. 6:3; Rev. 4:8; 15:4; 1 Sam. 2:2.

> By this . . . all may try their affections . . . . Natural men have no sense of the goodness and excellency of holy things . . . but the saints, by the mighty power of God, have it discovered to them: they have that supernatural, most noble and divine sense given them, by which they perceive it: and it is this that captivates their hearts, and delights them above all things. . . . By this you may examine your love to God, and to Jesus Christ, and to the Word of God, and your joy in them, and also your love to the people of God, and your desires after heaven; whether they be from a supreme delight in this sort of beauty, without being primarily moved from your imagined interest in them, or expectations from 'em. There are many high affections, great seeming love and rapturous joys, which have nothing of this holy relish belonging to 'em.[68]

Speaking of the importance of signs, Edwards makes a special appeal to John's gospel and first epistle: "Not one of the apostles is so express in laying down signs of grace, for professors to try themselves by, as he; and in his signs, he insists on scarcely anything but a spirit of Christian love, and an agreeable practice."[69]

In spite of the biblical evidence for signs as the primary means for obtaining assurance, many resisted the use of signs. Many who professed to follow Christ resisted "the rules and directions Christ had given them," choosing instead to "go by other rules, of their own inventing, that seem to them wiser and better."[70] Edwards found this resistance to be both puzzling and troubling. At the foundation of these "other rules" was confidence in experience, such as passages of Scripture coming to mind, great emotion concerning spiritual things, fainting and other physical symptoms for which no other account could be given, great terrors followed by great joys, and other like experiences. Many in the aftermath of the Awakening esteemed these

[68] Ibid., 2:262.
[69] Ibid., 2:354.
[70] Ibid., 2:185.

of more value than the signs of Scripture. For Edwards, this deferral was nothing less than direct disobedience, a dark path which invited divine chastisement for believers and which unmasked false professors:

> And woeful have been the mischievous consequences, of this arrogant setting up men's wisdom above the wisdom of Christ. I believe many saints have gone much out of the way of Christ's word, in this respect: and some of them have been chastised with whips, and (I had almost said) scorpions, to bring them back again. But many things which have lately appeared, and do now appear, may convince, that ordinarily, those who have gone furthest this way, that have been most highly conceited of their faculty of discerning, and have appeared most forward, peremptorily and suddenly to determine the state of men's souls, have been hypocrites, who have known nothing of true religion.[71]

The Means of Action

In spite of Edwards's high priority on self-examination as the biblical means to assurance, he believed that self-examination was inappropriate under certain circumstances. Self-examination required a clear spiritual eye and a suitable spiritual object to behold. Sin can cloud the spiritual eye so that it cannot see clearly.[72] Similarly, sin caused the spiritual object—sanctification, or the evidence of a holy life—to shrink to such small proportions as to be too difficult to perceive.[73]

Therefore, when a Christian is in "a corrupt and carnal frame" there are "no signs that can be given [which] will actually satisfy a person in such a case."[74] The most thorough self-examination,

[71] Ibid., 2:185.
[72] Ibid., 2:195.
[73] Ibid., 2:194.
[74] Ibid., 2:195.

whether that of carefully reviewing the past, or attending to the counsel of pastors or books, will all be in vain, for "there is other work for them to do . . . the accursed thing is to be destroyed from their camp, and Achan to be slain, and till this be done they will be in trouble."[75] Once sin is forsaken, the next step is not reflection, but action:

> 'Tis not God's design that men should obtain assurance in any other way, than by mortifying corruption, and increasing in grace, and obtaining the lively exercises of it. And although self-examination be a duty of great use and importance, and by no means to be neglected; yet it is not the principal means, by which the saints do get satisfaction of their good estate. Assurance is not to be obtained so much by self-examination, as by action.[76]

It is important to recognize that Edwards is not involved in a self-contradiction on this subject because assurance requires the evidence of sanctification. Sanctification is the common thread in both the necessity of self-examination as well as the recommendation to abandon self-examination. Self-examination reveals the presence or absence of sanctification. If self-examination reveals little evidence of sanctification, the proper course of action is not to continue seeking for sanctification, but to begin pursuing it by an active engagement of holy living. By doing this, the evidence of sanctification will accrue, and in time, self-examination will be a fruitful exercise.[77]

[75] Ibid.

[76] Ibid. Edwards goes on to cite 1 Cor. 9:26 and 2 Peter 1:5–11, with explanatory comments, for support.

[77] In a similar vein of thought, Edwards recommended to Gillespie that depressed persons could best resist dark thoughts through the disciplined dedication to daily duties, both secular and sacred. Dedication to action deprived both the flesh and the devil of opportunity to feed depression and served as a practical way to express trust in God while awaiting his deliverance. See Edwards, "Letter to Thomas Gillespie, September 4, 1747," WJE

Ordinary Means of Grace

Surprisingly, Edwards says very little concerning ordinary means of grace. With respect to conversion, he views the ordinary means of grace as indispensable for leading the unregenerate to salvation:

> And it is true, that for any to expect to receive the saving influences of the Spirit of God, while they neglect a diligent improvement of the appointed means of grace, is unreasonable presumption. And to expect that the Spirit of God will savingly operate upon their minds, without the Spirit's making use of means, as subservient to the effect, is enthusiastical.[78]

Most of Edwards's comments on ordinary means, however, are directed toward their role in sanctification:

> If it be so, that true religion lies much in the affections, hence we may infer, that such means are to be desired, as have much of a tendency to move the affections. Such books, and such a way of preaching the Word, and administration of ordinances, and such a way of worshiping God in prayer, and singing praises, is much to be desired, as has a tendency deeply to affect the hearts of those who attend these means.[79]

Similarly, he says,

> The greater spiritual discoveries and affections the true Christian has, the more does he become of an earnest beggar for grace, and spiritual food, that he may grow; and the more earnestly does he pursue after it, in the use of proper means

---

2:482–83; Edwards, "Letter to Thomas Gillespie, April 2, 1750," WJE 2:511–12.

[78] Edwards, *Religious Affections*, WJE 2:138.

[79] Ibid., 2:121.

> and endeavors: for true and gracious longings after holiness, are no idle ineffectual desires.[80]

While Edwards regards seeking God, prayer, careful attendance to preaching and to the Word and the like as means of grace, these are also *evidences* of grace when the heart is fully engaged in these activities, particularly after comfort and assurance has been given. To neglect the means of grace after the soul has been quieted is a sign of hypocrisy, suggesting that one has come to Christ for his own comfort, rather than in a true embrace of Christ for his own sake:[81]

> Hence there is an end to many persons' earnestness in seeking, after they have once obtained that which they call their conversion: or at least, after they have had those high affections, that make them fully confident of it. Before, while they looked upon themselves as in a state of nature, they were engaged in seeking after God and Christ, and cried earnestly for grace, and strove in the use of means: but now they act as though they thought their work was done: they live upon their first work, or some high experiences that are past; and there is an end to their crying, and striving after God and grace.[82]

The significance of these texts is that none of the references to the ordinary means in *Religious Affections* are immediately directed to the problem of obtaining assurance even though Edwards sees the problem as instrumental to sanctification in general. This suggests that he views the problem of assurance as one that requires attention to *unique* means over and above (rather than in the place of) what is

[80] Ibid., 2:378.

[81] Ibid., 2:380–83. Edwards cites Ps. 24:6; 69:6, 32; 74:4; Luke 1:53; John 4:34; Isa. 33:6; 1 Tim. 6:6 in support.

[82] Ibid., 2:380.

normally required for the pursuit of sanctification. Those unique means are self-examination and action.

8

Theological Method and the Doctrine of Assurance in *Religious Affections*: An Appraisal and Appropriation

In November of 1746, Thomas Gillespie of Carnock, Scotland, penned a letter of response to *Religious Affections*. Though he sensed a certain impropriety of challenging the thought of one more mature than himself, he also perceived that Edwards was approachable as a person and that Edwards's motive in writing *Religious Affections* was to stimulate a theological reconsideration within each reader.[1] In such a spirit, this study presumes to engage the theological merits of *Religious Affections*. Historical theology often permits its participants to comment on the past without the burden of directly identifying with that on which they comment. Systematic theology, on the other hand, inevitably requires its participants to engage ideas and beliefs in an immediate, personal way. And with this interaction comes the liability that comes with expressing what is and what is not, what should be and what should not be.

[1] Thomas Gillespie, "Letter to Jonathan Edwards, November 24, 1746," in *A Treatise Concerning Religious Affections*, ed. John E. Smith, The Works of Jonathan Edwards, vol. 2 (New Haven: Yale, 1959), 470–77. For a convenient introduction to Thomas Gillespie and the circumstances attending the Gillespie/Edwards correspondence, see John E. Smith, "Introduction to Related Writings," in *The Works of Jonathan Edwards*, ed. Perry Miller, vol. 2, *Religious Affections* (New Haven: Yale, 1959), 465–69.

If the spirit and message of *Religious Affections* convey anything, certainly Edwards desired that every reader engage it in a direct comparison with his/her own personal theology. Edwards's subsequent dialogue with Thomas Gillespie regarding the theology of *Religious Affections* is compelling evidence that this is the case. Nothing would have disappointed him more than the thought that so many scholars would analyze its structure, literary devices, metaphysical constructs, and political influence as though it were merely a scientific exhibit. For this reason, a contemporary appropriation and an appraisal of Edwards's doctrine of assurance in *Religious Affections* becomes appropriate.

The objective of this section is to consider three issues which present themselves as a result of this study. The first concerns the idea of the practice of writing and of reading theology with a central interpretive motif in view. The second concerns the practice of proof-texting and the need for evangelical theologians to reconsider its ultimate necessity. The third concerns Edwards's view of the new creation and how reflection on this view might contribute to expressing a robust theology of assurance today.

Reconsidering the Central Interpretive Motif in the Task of Theology

Chapter three addressed the prevailing opinion that Edwards's body of work is somehow united by a central interpretive motif. Yet none of the proposals offered over the last several decades has been persuasive. The impasse, and the problems that have contributed to it, suggest that the expectations placed by some on the idea of a central interpretive motif have been somewhat optimistic. If this is the case, then it may be appropriate to reassess the place of the central interpretive motif within the larger task of theology.

A Review of the Central Interpretive Motif in the Appraisal of Edwards's Theology

The objective of chapter three was to discuss various views of Edwards's theological method and to recommend an approach referred to as a "regulated matrix." This discussion surveyed a considerable variety of approaches to interpreting Edwards. William Wainwright sees God's sovereignty and beautiful holiness as the definitive centers of Edwards's theology. McDermott and Nichols agree that Edwards's apologetic agenda unifies his writings. Holifield argues that the theme of excellency is the definitive element. Other proposals include the themes of soteriology, dispositional ontology, semiotics, God's self-glorification, moral philosophy, the nature of true religion, and trinitarianism. The variety here is also in the type of motif proposed: represented themes include agenda-driven themes (apologetics), metaphysical themes (ontology, aesthetics), hermeneutical themes (semiotics), and straightforward theological themes (soteriology, trinitarianism). Most of these have been proposed with the underlying belief that a central interpretive motif exists within his corpus.

To review and to summarize, chapter three continued with a consideration of the liabilities that have become apparent when trying to read Edwards in light of a central interpretive motif. The first liability is reductionism. Those texts of Edwards which support a particular motif are brought to the front and center of the discussion; those which do not are either molded to the theme or otherwise marginalized. Such is the typical complaint of one Edwards's scholar to another. The second liability is the problem of decontextualization. In order to substantiate claims to a central interpretive motif, texts from the works of Edwards are assembled as evidence. Yet many object to this practice, claiming that it tends toward the citation of texts out of context. Consequently, some scholars are questioning if the entire enterprise of locating a central interpretive motif is misguided.

An Assessment of the Use of the Central Interpretive Motif in the Task of Theology

This discussion has an interesting implication for theologians today. Millard Erickson strongly commends the idea of a central interpretive motif, insisting that "there is need for each theologian to formulate such a motif." This need is not only for the sake of effective communication and literary unity; Erickson maintains that the very legitimacy of one's theological presentation is at stake: "It could be argued that any theology which has coherence has an integrating motif."[2]

Not clear from the context is whether Erickson is referring to literary coherence or logical coherence. In either case, Erickson's proposition may be problematic. The claim that "any theology which has coherence has an integrating motif" suggests that a central interpretive motif exists in any work of theology, irrespective of the author's intent, whether implied or explicit. For this reason, Erickson is certain that we can confidently approach past works of theology—those which did not expressly identify a central interpretive motif such as those of Luther, Calvin, and others—and identify a central interpretive motif.[3] However, the case with Edwards illustrates that identifying the motif may not be so self-evident. It also illustrates that the adoption of a unifying motif may induce a distorted reading.

Erickson himself seems to be aware that the whole idea of a central interpretive motif is fragile. He concedes that (1) there may be more than one such motif in the same work, and that (2) such multiple motifs may be "somewhat contradictory in nature."[4] These two

[2] Millard J. Erickson, *Christian Theology*, 2nd ed. (Grand Rapids: Baker, 1998), 80–81; quotation is from 81.

[3] Ibid., 80.

[4] Ibid., 81. Erickson's lack of clarity on this point is evident in the interaction of Lewis and Demarest, who mistake Erickson's idea of a central interpretive motif as the central message of the Bible, rather than what Erickson apparently intends, which is the unifying emphasis of the theologian. See Gordon R. Lewis and Bruce A. Demarest, *Integrative Theology* (Grand Rapids: Zondervan, 1996), 1:26.

concessions seem to be counterproductive to the idea of unity, the purpose for which the motif exists in the first place. He also admits the central interpretive motif may be easily abused and taken as a determining principle for reading a theological corpus, the very phenomenon observed in the case of Edwards. In addition to these concessions, Erickson seems to be aware of the potential for reductionism. To avoid this problem, he recommends a broad theme to ensure it encompasses the whole. But broad themes are by nature generalizations, and generalizations do not provide significant leverage for crafting theology with any distinct character.[5]

It appears, then, that the literary virtues that come with a central interpretive motif come with a series of potential problems, and these pitfalls await both the writer and the reader. The liability does not seem so severe for the writer if we admit the plausibility of writing theology around a unifying theological theme while steering clear of the imposition of that theme upon the theological data. Nevertheless, for readers, the outlook seems less optimistic. With respect to theological works which do not expressly identify a central interpretive motif, it seems best, in light of the example provided by Edwards scholarship, for readers of theology to refrain from engaging in a quest for the hidden interpretive key.

Reconsidering the Use of Proof-Texting in the Task of Theology

Edwards's prolific use of proof-texting in *Religious Affections* is arresting to the sensibilities of the contemporary Bible student. This once venerated practice has fallen on hard times. Proof-texting is viewed as the preferred tool of the fundamentalists, who appealed to the masses with popular-level arguments to refute the proponents of higher criticism.[6] It was not long after the advent of fundamentalism

[5] Erickson, *Christian Theology*, 81–82.

[6] Kenneth J. Archer, *A Pentecostal Hermeneutic for the Twenty-First Century: Spirit, Scripture, and Community* (New York: T & T Clark, 2004), 46–48;

that the practice of proof-texting marked biblical conservatives as anti-intellectual.[7] The method itself is problematic; by all appearances it "assumes a uniform propositional revelation spread evenly throughout the Scripture: one verse, one vote," decontextualizing the text in the process.[8] Proof-texting also tends toward an unjust "textual positivism" and toward an insensitivity to literary types that ignores the fact that proposition is but one of many functions that language can serve.[9]

To complicate matters, these abuses can give birth to others. Proof-texting can easily become an imposition of a theological grid upon the biblical text, the effort to find verses to substantiate theological premises already in place.[10] Because the practice of proof-texting is used most frequently by those who believe in the absolute authority and inerrancy of the Bible, proof-texting has become a symbol of authoritarian theology. Those who view the Bible in such a totalizing way miss "what it means to be a human being" since they form their theology without participating in a meaningful conversation with psychology and sociology.[11] The most common objection to proof-texting is the practice of "taking of verses out of context in support of

---

Richard Lints, *The Fabric of Theology: A Prolegomenon to Evangelical Theology* (Grand Rapids: Eerdmans, 1993), 22–23; 183n93.

[7] Daniel J. Treier, *Introducing Theological Interpretation of Scripture: Recovering Christian Practice* (Grand Rapids: Baker, 2008), 23–24; Lints, *The Fabric of Theology*, 69.

[8] Kevin J. Vanhoozer, *The Drama of Doctrine: A Canonical-Linguistic Approach to Christian Theology* (Louisville: Westminster John Knox, 2005), 271; Graham A. Cole, "Doctrine of God," in *Dictionary for Theological Interpretation of the Bible*, ed. Kevin J. Vanhoozer (Grand Rapids: Baker, 2005), 262.

[9] Vanhoozer, *The Drama of Doctrine*, 271.

[10] Ben Witherington, *The Problem with Evangelical Theology: Testing the Exegetical Foundations of Calvinism, Dispensationalism, and Wesleyanism* (Waco, TX: Baylor University, 2005), 4–5.

[11] Clark M. Williamson, "The Human Question," in *Essentials of Christian Theology*, ed. William C. Placher (Louisville: Westminster John Knox, 2003), 168.

a theological or pastoral point."[12] Above all, there is the common *faux pas* of those systematic theologians who are busy "stringing together verses that seem to pertain to an issue without regard for the larger complex of ideas operating in the biblical passages."[13]

Proof-Texting and the Protestant Cause

The entire dispute over the matter of proof-texting is somewhat of a dilemma for evangelicals. Evangelicals, who claim to be the proper heirs of the Reformation, are by definition the guardians of a theological tradition substantiated by proof-texts. The heart of Protestantism was its protest against the established church, and much of the protest concerned the sole authority of Scripture, along with the right and ability of the individual to interpret it.[14] As the Protestants set themselves to the task of interpreting texts, they perceived that there was more than one way to preserve the fruits of their labor.[15] One way was to record the fruits of exegesis in the form of running commentary; another was to represent their exegetical work in themes that represented the entire canon. Calvin's example of

[12] Buist M. Fanning, "Theological Analysis: Building Biblical Theology," in *Interpreting the New Testament Text: Introduction to the Art and Science of Exegesis*, ed. Darrel L. Bock and Buist M. Fanning (Wheaton, IL: Crossway, 2006), 285.

[13] Ibid. See similar sentiments expressed by N. T. Wright, *The New Testament and the People of God*, Christian Origins and the People of God, vol. 1 (Minneapolis: Fortress, 1992), 138.

[14] This is not to suggest that proof-texting is a Protestant phenomenon. For comment on the practice of proof-texting in the early church, see Stephen K. Ray, *Upon This Rock: St. Peter and the Primacy of Rome in Scripture and the Early Church* (San Francisco: Ignatius, 1999), 183n70; 232n186; Jason Byassee, *Praise Seeking Understanding: Reading the Psalms with Augustine* (Grand Rapids: Eerdmans, 2007), 78n60; James L. Kugel and Rowan A. Greer, *Early Biblical Interpretation*, ed. Wayne A. Meeks, Library of Early Christianity (Louisville: Westminster John Knox, 1986), 192.

[15] Wayne E. Ward, "New Testament Theology: Retrospect and Prospect," *Review and Expositor* 78, 2 (Spring 1981): 156–57.

engaging in both exegetical and thematic work famously displayed the symbiotic necessity of both.[16]

The confessionalism that emerged from the Reformation witnessed a gradual shift from an inductive emphasis on Scripture to a deductive one. McGrath explains the role of proof-texting in this phenomenon:

> Given the central role of the Bible for Protestantism . . . the Bible tended to be read through the prism of "confessions"—statements of faith that frequently influenced, and sometimes determined, how certain passages of the Bible were to be interpreted. This shift was a combining factor to the rise of "proof-texting": citing isolated, decontextualized verses of the Bible in support of often controversial confessional positions. Paradoxically, this development actually lessened the influence of the Bible within Protestantism, in that biblical statements were accommodated to existing doctrinal frameworks rather than being allowed to determine them, and even to challenge them.[17]

The framers of the Protestant confessions, of course, did not see the proof-texts in this way. For them, the framing was the fruit of hard exegetical labor. In the interest of preserving the exegetical labors, proof-texting served as a convenient tool to accomplish two things. First, the "proof-texts functioned as shorthand references" representing the results of exegesis, interpretation in light of the exegesis, and implications for the larger body of truth.[18] Referring to

[16] R. Michael Allen and Scott R. Swain, "In Defense of Proof-Texting," *Journal of the Evangelical Theological Society* 54, 3 (September 2001): 600–602, 604.

[17] Allister E. McGrath, *Christianity's Dangerous Idea* (New York: Harper Collins, 2007), 103.

[18] Allen and Swain, "In Defense of Proof-Texting," 602.

the work of Aquinas and Calvin as examples, Allen and Swain prudently observe,

> For these theologians, proof texts did not subvert exegetical care—they symbolized and represented its necessity. Understanding the way in which doctrines develop out of and beyond explicit statements in biblical texts is crucial for grasping the kind of claim behind made when one gives a proof text: it does not necessarily suggest that the doctrine as stated can be found there, but it does claim that the doctrine is rooted there in principle, when viewed in its larger canonical lens and when its implications are fully teased out.[19]

Second, proof-texting permitted ecclesiastical communities to communicate efficiently; interpretations of texts that were mutually agreed upon could be cited in a public forum without explanation. This benefit, in addition to its function as exegetical shorthand, meant that proof-texting was both persuasive and efficient. The potential of this tool proved to be powerful; but whether or not the tool was constructive or destructive depended upon the skill and the responsibility of the user.[20]

Subsequently, the liabilities of proof-texting became apparent. With the privilege of the convenience of shorthand came the responsibility of periodically confirming the exegetical rational which linked reference to conclusion. When theological packages, along with their biblical proofs, were handed down from one generation to the next, it was incumbent upon the second generation to understand the exegetical basis for the theological system, not merely the system itself. Additionally, theologians found that positions could easily be fortified with proof-texts; proof-texts conveyed the impression that a legitimate relationship existed between text and proposition, and due

[19] Ibid., 602–3.

[20] John M. Frame, *The Doctrine of the Knowledge of God* (Phillipsburg, NJ: Presbyterian and Reformed, 1987), 197.

diligence had been given to exegesis prior to the textual appeal. Because the method was so vulnerable to abuse and because so much abuse actually occurred, the practice of proof-texting eventually became synonymous with the irresponsible and the abusive use of Scripture to reinforce one's dogmatic agenda.

A Qualified Case for Proof-Texting

With these concerns in mind, it is helpful to reflect on Edwards's use of proof-texting as well as its current counterpart in contemporary evangelicalism to consider its appropriateness in light of the current critique. The contention of this study is that proof-texting is both legitimate and necessary, given the following rationale and qualifications. First, it is important to recognize that *the term* proof-texting *is used with equivocation*. In some instances, proof-texting refers to the general practice of citing a biblical reference in support of a theological idea. In other instances, proof-texting refers to the abusive practice of citing biblical references in support of a theological point apart from responsible exegesis.[21] A third use combines the elements of the first two so that *proof-texting* refers to belief that every citation of a biblical text is *de facto* fallacious.[22] A fourth use of the term *proof-*

[21] Evangelicals recognize these two uses and distinguish between legitimacy of the former and the fallacy of the latter. Carson, in his *Gagging of God*, distinguishes "cheap proof-texting" from legitimate appeals to Scripture, and gives a fine example of the latter in a five point theological summary on the subject of the love of God. See D. A. Carson, *The Gagging of God* (Grand Rapids: Zondervan, 1996), 162, 239–40.

[22] This view proceeds from the presupposition that inerrancy is an untenable doctrine and the cause of the bankruptcy of fundamentalism. See Timothy P. Weber, "The Two-Edged Sword: The Fundamentalist Use of the Bible," in *The Bible in America: Essays in Cultural History*, ed. Nathan O. Hatch and Mark A. Noll (New York: Oxford, 1982), 101–17. Though Weber views fundamentalist proof-texting as scandalous, he acknowledges, in his tracing of the career of William Newton Clarke (1840–1912), that the higher critics during the fundamentalist/modernist controversy had no substantive alternative to offer the church. The only logical alternative to proof-texting was an incomprehensible Bible, which perhaps might one day

texting is somewhat less formal, a sort of code language for marginalizing a disapproved hermeneutic.[23] With this last use in view, Allen and Swain remind readers that, before hastily dismissing the use of biblical references by a theological perspective which is not our own, a moment of pause would be both prudent and gracious: "We should be willing to consider whether or not a particular usage of a text might make more sense to us if we considered the underlying hermeneutical rationale and the broader exegetical context which determined the particular usage." In this consideration, we would "not commit the fallacy of confusing method of citation with a hermeneutical procedure."[24] Doriani's caution is also appropriate: "It is all too easy to toss

---

be unraveled by the collective genius of the academy. Until that time, liberals like Clarke had nothing to commend to their parishioners except the advice that "they should follow their best Christian instincts." Ibid., 107–8.

[23] A case in point is highlighted by Gary Dorrien, who observes that Warfield, Hodge, and the Princetonians dismissed the early dispensationalists such as Darby, Torrey, and Scofield, as semi-literate exegetes who "persuaded impressionable readers that scripture scholarship consisted of mostly categorization and proof-texting." Yet "Warfield was anxious to explain why this method was not to be confused with Princeton-style scientific exegesis." When Charles Hodge cited texts, he was legitimately "gathering and classifying facts" whereas the textual classifications of dispensationalists were judged to be largely corrupted by decontextualization. The real issue, however, was not the inadequate educational stature of the early dispensationalists, nor their receptivity by the masses. The real issue was the hermeneutical protest lodged by the early dispensationalists, who argued that contextual evidence supported the application of a literal hermeneutic in places traditionally not so interpreted by conservatives. The Princetonians, and all within their tradition—from Calvin and Edwards to Warfield and Hodge—had no objection to proof-texting *per se* so long as the hermeneutic in the background was the correct one. See Gary J. Dorrien, *The Remaking of Evangelical Theology* (Louisville: Westminster John Knox, 1998), 31–32; Ernest R. Sandeen, *The Roots of Fundamentalism: British and American Millenarianism, 1800–1930* (Chicago: University of Chicago, 1970), 13, 66–68, 107–12.

[24] Allen and Swain, "In Defense of Proof-Texting," 598.

the accusation of 'proof texting' on what may be the fruit of painstaking exegesis."[25]

Second, *proof-texting can be both legitimate and useful within given boundaries.* Proof-texting can be both sensible and useful when the term is used as "simply a Scripture reference that is intended to show the basis for a particular theological assertion." Nothing in this understanding of the term *proof-texting* points to a practice that is inherently fallacious.[26] The alternative, forbidding the use of proof-texting, would suppress the expression of any theological statement that was not accompanied by an exegetical treatment, in turn forcing theology into a cumbersome form. Additionally, if proof-texting is disqualified as a legitimate practice, one must explain how it can remain legitimate for the biblical authors, who also practiced it.[27] For those within a community of faith who accept the unity of the canon, the authority of Scripture, and a basic hermeneutical outlook, proof-texting can serve as a convenient tool for referring to ideas proceeding from the biblical text. Above all, the legitimate use of proof-texting requires the theologian to assume responsibility for contextually-informed exegesis of the text which justifies the citation of a passage.

Third, the attempt by some to dismiss the practice of proof-texting while retaining the mantle of biblical authority has resulted in awkward posturing. In one interesting example, Paul Hedges endeavors to escape the charge of proof-texting by simply citing additional texts to support the point in question; this tactic is neither subtle nor convincing.[28] More typical is the appeal to biblical "trajectories." Doriani observes that those who would exchange proof-texting for trajectories have only entangled themselves in an a priori fallacy:

[25] Daniel M. Doriani, "A Redemptive-Historical Model," in *Four Views on Moving Beyond the Bible to Theology*, ed. Stanley N. Gundry (Grand Rapids: Zondervan, 2009), 96.

[26] Frame, *Doctrine of the Knowledge of God*, 197.

[27] Ibid.

[28] Paul Hedges, *Controversies in Interreligious Dialogue and the Theology of Religions* (London: SCM, 2010), 138.

> Tracing the trajectory of Scripture is judged superior to swapping proof texts, which, everyone knows, is no way to read the Bible. But opposition to proof texting is hardly adventurous. Indeed, the appeal to trajectories over proof texting looks like an attempt at victory by definition: we follow the progress of ideas; you grab ideas out of context to "prove" what you already believe.[29]

Finally, *proof-texting is ultimately necessary for theological language that claims to be derived from Scripture*. Proof-texts ensure expressions of theology that are transparent and accountable. Theology which claims to be biblically derived but fails to provide accompanying proof-texts unjustly presumes upon the indulgence of the reader. Such was the case with the Westminster Confession, which the House of Commons agreed to ratify only on condition that the Assembly supply the addition of proof-texts.[30] The case illustrates the dilemma that evangelicals face today. If evangelical scholars continue to cite Scriptural texts as foundational for their beliefs, they will surely continue to incur the charge of anti-intellectualism; if they do not, the charge of arbitrariness is certain to present itself.[31]

Considering the alternative to proof-texting helps put the matter into perspective. What would happen to evangelical theology if proof-texting were abandoned? The result would be theological expressions which claim to be biblically governed with no means of confirmation available to the audience. The theological product might be biblical, or it might not be. The audience is simply requested (or required) to accept the theological conclusion at face value. Distinguishing this kind of practice from any other form of ideological totalitarianism proves difficult. Proof-texting empowers the reader and holds theo-

[29] Doriani, "A Redemptive-Historical Model," 96.

[30] Benjamin Breckinridge Warfield, *The Printing of the Westminster Confession* (Philadelphia: MacCalla & Co., 1901), 607–11.

[31] For example, see Harriet A. Harris, *Evangelicalism and Fundamentalism* (repr., Oxford: Oxford University, 2008), 145–47, 168–72, 273–74, 317.

logical authorities accountable for their claims. Whatever guilt may be charged to those who abused the practice of citing Scripture, we must at the very least admit that they had the courtesy to disclose their evidence. In short, the use of bad textual evidence is just that—the use of bad evidence. But the refusal to disclose evidence is worse, suggesting the use of theology for a totalizing agenda.

For these reasons, the evangelical academy can do better than to demonize the practice of proof-texting. The abuses have received due attention. Critiques within the evangelical community suggest a willingness to admit that the real problem is not the citations of texts *per se* but the lack of sound exegesis frequently represented by those citations. Therefore, given the correction of this error, the evangelical community has reason to believe that Scriptural citations have credibility; the practice of hastily charging those who hold differing views with ignorance and textual abuse is neither necessary nor productive. In summary, those who wish to express theology in terms of the biblical text seem to have no option but to make reference to it at some point. This ultimate necessity leads to the conclusion that "all truly Christian theology must depend on proof-texting."[32]

Proof-Texting in Religious Affections

In light of these arguments, the question remains as to whether or not Edwards made good use of proof-texting in *Religious Affections*. The answer to this question is more elusive than appears at first glance. First, such an assessment would seem to require an examina-

[32] Kenneth S. Kantzer, "A Systematic Biblical Dogmatics: What is It and How is It to Be Done?" in *Doing Theology in Today's World*, ed. John D. Woodbridge and Thomas E. McComiskey (Grand Rapids: Zondervan, 1991), 487n47. The aforementioned sources by Allen and Swain, Frame, and Doriani concur with this perspective. Even Stan Grenz and John Franke, who urge theologians to move "beyond foundationalism" in their theological method, concede that "appealing to individual texts in reaching theological conclusions is, of course, crucial." Stanley J. Grenz and John R. Franke, *Beyond Foundationalism: Shaping Theology in a Postmodern Context* (Louisville: Westminster John Knox, 2001), 89.

tion of each of the over one thousand proof-texts in the treatise. Second, the answer to this question is complicated by the fact that the value of a proof-text is also bound up in the purpose for its citation. The purposes can range from illustration to doctrinal grounding. If the purpose of the proof-text is not recognized, its intended value will be missed. Third, the ever-present temptation remains to form a judgment regarding a proof-text which reduces to an opinion on Edwards's hermeneutic. Proof-texting is a reflection of one's own hermeneutic, not another's. Therefore, it is important not to confuse the propriety of Edwards's proof-texting with that of his hermeneutic.

It is beyond the scope of this book to carefully assess each of the Scriptural citations in *Religious Affections*. Yet, with the above qualifications in view, a sample of Edwards's proof-texting can serve as the basis for a preliminary analysis. A pivotal section in *Religious Affections* for the doctrine of assurance is his larger treatment of the witness of the Spirit.[33] In this section, Edwards makes a substantial use of proof-texting.

Upon introducing the problem of people embracing the notion of an immediate witness of the Spirit, he asserts that the experience of an immediate impression—even if that impression is from God—does not prove anything regarding one's own spiritual standing. In support, Edwards cites the examples of Abimelech and Laban, who received warnings concerning Abraham and Jacob, accompanied by citations of Genesis 20:6–7; 31:24; and Psalm 105:15. All three texts are clearly intended to serve illustratively. As a result, these proof-texts stand in proper relation to the point being made.[34]

Edwards continues by arguing that the nature of an immediate suggestion has no necessary connection to its source. Therefore, if an immediate suggestion comes from God, it is still no more than "a common influence of God's Spirit, as the gift of prophecy, and all

[33] Jonathan Edwards, *A Treatise Concerning Religious Affections*, ed. John E. Smith, The Works of Jonathan Edwards, vol. 2 (New Haven: Yale, 1959), 229–39.

[34] Ibid., 2:229.

revelation by immediate suggestion."[35] Consequently, such a suggestion to the mind is by no means to be regarded as a "higher kind" of knowledge. To support this point, Edwards cites 1 Corinthians 13:2. However, nothing in this text speaks to the question of the nature of prophecy in comparison to a natural impression that is not from God. This use of proof-texting is intended to substantiate the validity of an assertion, but the text invoked does not adequately supply the content to underwrite the assertion.[36]

Edwards then transitions toward a definition of the witness of the Spirit: "That which is called the witness of the Spirit (Rom. 8), is elsewhere in the New Testament called the seal of the Spirit (2 Cor. 1:22, Eph. 1:13 and Eph. 4:13)."[37] Here Edwards's intent for the role of the proof-texts is unclear. If his intent is to point the reader to texts in which the seal of the Spirit is discussed, then the first two are valid; but there seems to be no rationale for Ephesians 4:13. Conversely, if Edwards's intent is to justify the assertion that the witness of the Spirit is viewed by Paul as synonymous with the seal of the Spirit, then the use is not compelling; no data in these texts support that equation.

Edwards continues to elaborate on the seal of the Spirit:

> The seal of the Spirit is a kind of effect of the Spirit of God on the heart, which natural men, while such, are so far from a capacity of being the subjects of, that they can have no manner of notion or idea of it; agreeable to Revelation 2:17, "To him that over-cometh, will I give to eat of the hidden manna; and I will give him a white stone, and in the stone a new name written, which no man knoweth, saving he that receiveth it." There is all reason to suppose that what is here

[35] Ibid.
[36] Ibid.
[37] Ibid., 2:231.

> spoken of, is the same mark, evidence, or blessed token of special favor, which is elsewhere called the seal of the Spirit.[38]

The key term here is *agreeable*, which indicates that Edwards's intent is not to justify the assertion but to illustrate it by way of an analogy. The seal of the Spirit entails an outcome that is exclusively intimate between God and the saint, which distinguishes him from the unbeliever, much in the same way described by the reward of Revelation 2:17. This use is not problematic, given its clear intent as an analogy.

Edwards then goes on to argue that the witness of the Spirit is not an immediate suggestion to the mind but the presentation of evidence to the conscience of the believer. This, he argues, is evident in

> the manner in which the word "witness," or "testimony" is often used in the New Testament; where such terms often signify, not only a mere declaring and asserting a thing to be true, but holding forth evidence from whence a thing may be argued and proved to be true. Thus (Heb. 2:4), God is said to bear witness, with signs and wonders, and diverse miracles, and gifts of the Holy Ghost. Now these miracles, here spoken of, are called God's witness, not because they are of the nature of assertions, but evidences and proofs. So: "Long time therefore, abode they speaking boldly in the Lord; which gave testimony unto the word of his grace; and granted signs and wonders to be done by their hands" (Acts 14:3). And: "But I have greater witness than that of John; for the works which the Father hath given me to finish, the same works that I do, bear witness of me, that the Father hath sent me" (John 5:36). Again, "The works that I do in my Father's name, they bear witness of me" (ch. 10:25). So the water and the blood are

[38] Ibid.

> said to bear witness (1 John 5:8), not that they spake or asserted anything, but they were proofs and evidences.[39]

Edwards is careful not to overstate his case; he introduces his assertion with the claim that the term is "often used," and he clearly substantiates that assertion with evidence showing that the term *witness* or *testimony* is in fact used to refer to the presentation of evidence. Edwards continues with an illustrative use of Scriptural citations (Rev. 7:3; Ezek. 9:4; Song 9:6) to explain how the idea of a "seal," like the idea of "witness," entails the presentation of some kind of evidence. Afterward, he associates the idea of "seal" with that of "earnest," so that "witness of the Spirit," the "seal of the Spirit," and the "earnest of the Spirit" are considered to be one and the same. For support, Edwards cites 2 Corinthians 1:22 and Ephesians 1:13–14, texts which in fact associate the terms *seal* and *earnest.*

These are but a sample of the texts from this section on the "witness of the Spirit," but they sufficiently demonstrate that Edwards makes use of proof-texts in a variety of ways. The question of the legitimacy of Edwards's proof-texting depends on the expectations of the reader. A case in point can be seen in his use of Song of Solomon: "Therefore when Christ says to his spouse, 'Set me as a seal upon thine heart, as a seal upon thine arm' (Cant. 8:6); it is as much as to say, 'Let my name and image remain impressed there.'"[40] Many will dismiss this as an illegitimate proof-text on account of the hermeneutical conclusion that the message of the book was never intended to speak of either Christ or the church. This use, however, is not a proof-texting problem *per se* if (1) the use is seen in view of its intent to illustrate, in this case, how a custom in the ancient near east communicated ownership and identity and if (2) proof-texting as a practice is simply understood to be shorthand for an interpretive

[39] Ibid., 2:231–32.
[40] Ibid., 2:232.

conclusion.[41] If the reader of Edwards is willing to concede these two allowances—proof-texting in view of its intended purpose and proof-texting as an accurate expression of one's hermeneutic—then the reader will conclude that (within this brief sample, at least) Edwards generally, though not always, makes a compelling use of proof-texts.

Reconsidering Assurance Theology in Terms of the Believer's New Nature

Edwards's emphasis on the signs of authentic religious affections points to the importance of a sanctified life in his theology of assurance. As previously discussed, Edwards made allowance for the presence of sin and the absence of grace in the lives of true believers. In fact, one of the primary evidences of salvation is the humiliation of the believer as that believer encounters the enormity of remaining corruption. Such horror and sorrow over one's own sin is presumably authentic because the enormity of the sin is not imaginary. For Edwards, the holiness of the believer is genuine; so also is the believer's sin. But Edwards made little effort to reconcile the two as they consisted in the nature of the believer. This unaccounted coexistence of sin and holiness within the nature of the believer is perhaps the least compelling aspect of his theology of assurance in *Religious Affections*.[42]

Edwards's Portrayal of the Change Attending the New Creation

Edwards's reputation was not as a minister who comforted troubled souls, but rather one who troubled comfortable souls. His gospel emphasized the "narrow gate," a point that many found offensive.

[41] Even if a "correct" hermeneutic is considered to be a benchmark for defining what a proof-text is, it should be recalled that both Edwards and his audience accepted a figurative interpretation of Song of Solomon, and did not regard such a citation as illegitimate.

[42] In an effort to accurately represent Edwards's tone on this issue, this section will employ extended citations.

Three years after Edwards published *Religious Affections*, he published *An Humble Inquiry*, an apologetic for his view that only those who could give evidence to regeneration should be admitted to church membership.[43] Thus, in the prime of his ministry, Edwards marked his theology with narrow views of salvation and church membership. Ephraim Williams, a distant relative, branded Edwards as "a very great bigot, for he would not admit any person into heaven, but those that agreed fully to his sentiments, a doctrine deeply tinged with that of the Romish church."[44]

Religious Affections may well have contributed to this perception. Although Edwards admitted that true saints were also true sinners, reconciling this admission with his view of the "new creation" proves difficult. Edwards consistently describes the new creation in terms that are radical and comprehensive:

> But doubtless there are some hypocrites, that have only false affections, who will think they are able to stand this trial; and will readily say, that they desire not to rest satisfied with past attainments, but to be pressing forward, they do desire more, they long after God and Christ, and desire more holiness, and do seek it. But the truth is, their desires are not properly the desires of appetite after holiness, for its own sake, or for the moral excellency and holy sweetness that is in it; but only for by-ends. They long after clearer discoveries, that they may be better satisfied about the state of their souls; or because in

[43] Jonathan Edwards, "An Humble Inquiry Into the Rules of the Word of God, Concerning the Qualifications Requisite to a Complete Standing and Full Communion in the Visible Christian Church," in *Ecclesiastical Writings*, ed. David D. Hall, The Works of Jonathan Edwards, vol. 12 (New Haven: Yale, 1994).

[44] Jonathan Edwards, "Ephraim Williams to Jonathan Ashley, May 2, 1751," in *Correspondence by, to, and About Edwards and His Family*, The Works of Jonathan Edwards Online, vol. 32 (New Haven: Jonathan Edwards Center at Yale University, 2008), accessed February 18, 2012, www.edwards.yale.edu.

> great discoveries, self is gratified, in being made so much of by God, and so exalted above others, they long to taste the love of God (as they call it) more than to have more love to God. Or, it may be, they have a kind of forced, fancied or made longings; because they think they must long for more grace, otherwise it will be a dark sign upon them. But such things as these are far different from the natural, and as it were necessary appetite and thirsting of the new man, after God and holiness. There is an inward burning desire that a saint has after holiness, as natural to the new creature, as vital heat is to the body. There is a holy breathing and panting after the Spirit of God, to increase holiness, as natural to a holy nature, as breathing is to a living body.[45]

The radical nature of the new creation entails a radical life change; conversely, a lack of change indicates that there is no new creation within. In order to establish the tenor with which Edwards handles this subject, it is worthwhile to consider a number of texts. Each illustrates the strong emphasis he places on the remarkable and radical character of the changed life:

> There are many apprehensions and ideas which some have, that they call divine discoveries, which are affecting, but not convincing. Though for a little while, they may seem to be more persuaded of the truth of the things of religion, than they used to be, and may yield a forward assent, like many of Christ's hearers, who believed for a while; yet they have no thorough and effectual conviction; nor is there any great abiding change in them . . . . They are not men who live under the influence and power of a realizing conviction of the infinite and eternal things which the gospel reveals: if they were, it would be impossible for 'em to live as they do. Because their

[45] Edwards, *Religious Affections*, WJE 2:382–83.

affections are not attended with a thorough conviction of the mind, they are not at all to be depended on; however great a show and noise they make, 'tis like the blaze of tow, or crackling of thorns, or like the forward flourishing blade on stony ground, that has no root, nor deepness of earth to maintain its life.[46]

The Scripture representations of conversion do strongly imply and signify a change of nature: such as being born again; becoming new creatures; rising from the dead; being renewed in the spirit of the mind; dying to sin, and living to righteousness; putting off the old man, and putting on the new man; a being ingrafted into a new stock; a having a divine seed implanted in the heart; a being made partakers of the divine nature, etc.

Therefore if there be no great and remarkable, abiding change in persons, that think they have experienced a work of conversion, vain are all their imaginations and pretenses, however they have been affected.[47]

Conversion (if we may give any credit to the Scripture) is a great and universal change of the man, turning him from sin to God. A man may be restrained from sin, before he is converted; but when he is converted, he is not only restrained from sin, his very heart and nature is turned from it, unto holiness: so that thenceforward he becomes a holy person, and an enemy to sin. If therefore, after a person's high affections, at his supposed first conversion, it comes to that in a little time, that there is no very sensible, or remarkable alteration in him, as to those bad qualities, and evil habits, which before

[46] Ibid., 2:293–94.
[47] Ibid., 2:340.

were visible in him, and he is ordinarily under the prevalence of the same kind of dispositions that he used to be, and the same things seem to belong to his character, he appears as selfish, carnal, as stupid, and perverse, as unchristian, and unsavory as ever; it is greater evidence against him, than the brightest story of experiences that ever was told, is for him. For in Christ Jesus neither circumcision, nor uncircumcision, neither high profession, nor low profession, neither a fair story, nor a broken one, avails anything; but a new creature. If there be a very great alteration visible in a person for a while; if it ben't abiding, but he afterwards returns, in a stated manner to be much as he used to be; it appears to be no change of nature. For nature is an abiding thing. A swine that is of a filthy nature may be washed; but the swinish nature remains. And a dove that is of a cleanly nature may be defiled, but its cleanly nature remains.[48]

They that are truly converted are new men, new creatures; new, not only within, but without; they are sanctified throughout, in spirit, soul, and body; old things are passed away, all things are become new; they have new hearts, and new eyes, new ears, new tongues, new hands, new feet; i.e., a new conversation and practice; and they walk in newness of life, and continue to do so to the end of life.[49]

Without a change of nature, men's practice will not be thoroughly changed. Till the tree be made good, the fruit will not be good. Men don't gather grapes of thorns, nor figs of thistles. The swine may be washed, and appear clean for a little while, but yet, without a change of nature, he will still wallow in the mire. Nature is a more powerful principle of action,

[48] Ibid., 2:340–41.
[49] Ibid., 2:391.

than anything that opposes it: though it may be violently restrained for a while, it will finally overcome that which restrains it: 'tis like the stream of a river, it may be stopped a while with a dam, but if nothing be done to dry the fountain, it won't be stopped always; it will have a course, either in its old channel, or a new one. Nature is a thing more constant and permanent, than any of those things that are the foundation of carnal men's reformation and righteousness. When a natural man denies his lust, and lives a strict, religious life, and seems humble, painful and earnest in religion, 'tis not natural, 'tis all a force against nature; as when a stone is violently thrown upwards; but that force will be gradually spent; yet nature will remain in its full strength, and so prevails again, and the stone returns downwards. As long as corrupt nature is not mortified, but the principle left whole in a man, 'tis a vain thing to expect that it should not govern. But if the old nature be indeed mortified, and a new and heavenly nature infused; then may it well be expected, that men will walk in newness of life, and continue to do so to the end of their days.[50]

The tendency of grace in the heart to holy practice, is very direct, and the connection most natural close and necessary. True grace is not an unactive thing; there is nothing in heaven or earth of a more active nature; for 'tis life itself, and the most active kind of life, even spiritual and divine life. 'Tis no barren thing; there is nothing in the universe that in its nature has a greater tendency to fruit. Godliness in the heart has as direct a relation to practice, as a fountain has to a stream, or as the luminous nature of the sun has to beams sent forth, or as life has to breathing, or the beating of the pulse, or any other vital act; or as a habit or principle of action has to ac-

[50] Ibid., 2:395–96.

> tion: for 'tis the very nature and notion of grace, that 'tis a principle of holy action or practice. Regeneration, which is that work of God in which grace is infused, has a direct relation to practice; for 'tis the very end of it, with a view to which the whole work is wrought: all is calculated and framed, in this mighty and manifold change wrought in the soul.[51]

Edwards's final sign of a true believer is universal obedience. Obedience in all things, small and great, persevering at all times and under all circumstances, is the mark of a true Christian. Hypocrites are known by small sins, hidden sins, sins of commission, or sins that are "respectable" rather than heinous. Universal obedience is not merely the avoiding of sin, but the positive obedience of Christlikeness in every respect. Universal obedience is earnest, zealous, striving, running, pressing, laborious, and determined in its perseverance. Hypocritical professors of faith, on the other hand, are not characterized by these things.[52]

In short, Edwards's message of the new creation describes a radical change of nature, characterized by a love and holiness that pervades every area of thought and life. These assertions are so strong that they appear to make no allowance for sin in the life of the believer. Edwards did not subscribe to this extreme, and it appears that he was concerned that such statements would be taken in this way by his readers. In order to compensate for any misunderstanding, he frequently qualified his strong statements, conceding that true saints could have issues with sin in their lives. The new spiritual sense, Edwards admits, is experienced in a "very imperfect degree" at the time of new birth and requires time to mature.[53] When Edwards asserts that "a man may be restrained from sin, before he is converted; but when he is converted, he is not only restrained from sin, his very

[51] Ibid., 2:398.
[52] Ibid., 2:376–88.
[53] Ibid., 2:275.

heart and nature is turned from it, unto holiness,"[54] he quickly qualifies:

> Indeed allowances must be made for the natural temper: conversion don't entirely root out the natural temper: those sins which a man by his natural constitution was most inclined to before his conversion, he may be most apt to fall into still. But yet conversion will make a great alteration even with respect to these sins. Though grace, while imperfect, don't root out an evil natural temper; yet it is of great power and efficacy with respect to it, to correct it. The change that is wrought in conversion, is an universal change: grace changes a man with respect to whatever is sinful in him: the old man is put off and the new man put on: they are sanctified throughout: and the man becomes a new creature: old things are passed away, and all things are become new: all sin is mortified; constitution sins, as well as others. If a man before his conversion, was by his natural constitution, especially inclined to lasciviousness, or drunkenness, or maliciousness; converting grace will make a great alteration in him, with respect to these evil dispositions; so that however he may be still most in danger of these sins, yet they shall no longer have dominion over him; nor will they any more be properly his character.[55]

The difficulty here is that conversion is portrayed as a turning of the "nature" but that somehow the "nature" is distinguished from the "natural temper" so that the former is changed; but the latter is admittedly not "rooted out" but remains in the form of "evil dispositions." These dispositions clearly remain so that he remains in danger of these sins, but these sins will no longer dominate. Yet earlier in the same discussion he speaks of such dispositions as evidence against his

[54] Ibid., 2:341.
[55] Ibid., 2:341–42.

profession that he was ever a new creature in the first place.[56] It appears to the reader here that Edwards is attempting to communicate that sin can remain in the believer, but he is at the same time conveying that the presence of sin within the professor testifies against his/her profession.

Later in *Religious Affections*, Edwards makes a similar concession. While insisting that true believers have a "lamblike, dovelike spirit," of gentleness and humility, he says

> 'Tis true that allowances must be made for men's natural temper with regard to these things, as well as others. But not such allowances, as to allow men, that once were wolves and serpents, to be now converted, without any remarkable change in the spirit of their mind. The change made by true conversion, is wont to be most remarkable and sensible, with respect to that which before was the wickedness the person was most notoriously guilty of. Grace has as great a tendency to restrain and mortify such sins, as are contrary to the spirit that has been spoken of, as it has to mortify drunkenness or lasciviousness.[57]

This text again speaks of "allowances," and clearly such allowances are limited, for the change must still be "remarkable." Although there is no language in this paragraph that appears contradictory, it introduces ambiguity: it remains to the reader to determine what kind and how much of an allowance is to be made before a true conversion is questioned.

Edwards also concedes that allowances must be made for believers sinning under temptation:

> True saints may be guilty of some kinds and degrees of backsliding, and may be foiled by particular temptations, and may

[56] Ibid., 2:341.
[57] Ibid., 2:357.

> fall into sin, yea great sins: but they can never fall away so, as to grow weary of religion, and the service of God, and habitually to dislike it and neglect it; either on its own account, or on account of the difficulties that attend it: as is evident by Galatians 6:9, Romans 2:7, Hebrews 10:36, Isaiah 43:22, Malachi 1:13. They can never backslide, so as to continue no longer in a way of universal obedience; or so, that it shall cease to be their manner to observe all the rules of Christianity, and do all duties required, even the most difficult, and in the most difficult circumstances.[58]

In this case, Edwards calls the reader to distinguish between backsliding of one sort and another, noting that the true believer will return to the path of righteousness and of perseverance. But the "kinds" and "degrees" which apparently serve to distinguish the true believer from the false are not delineated, so the reader is again left with the task of appropriating an ambiguous principle.

Edwards's lack of clarity on this point prompted Thomas Gillespie to bring up the matter in his correspondence. Edwards had cited Stoddard to affirm that even one path of disobedience showed a person to be a hypocrite, regardless if great temptation is involved. Gillespie thought this to be an overstatement:

> I well remember the singularly judicious Dr. Owen somewhere says to this effect, "Prevalence of a particular sin over a person for a considerable time shows him to be no saint, except when under the power of a strong temptation." I would suppose such texts as Isaiah 64:6; Psalms 65:3, etc. warranted the Doctor to assert as he did. It is, I own, no small difficulty to steer the middle course betwixt affording hypocrites ground unwarrantably to presume on the one hand, and wounding the Lord's dear children on the other; and all the little

[58] Ibid., 2:390.

knowledge of the Scriptures I would hope the Lord has given me, makes me think Mr. Shepherd, good and great man as he was, verged not a little to the last extreme, with whom, if I mistake not, Mr. Stoddard symbolizes in the above assertion; for such as I have mentioned I apprehend is the drift and tendency of Mr. Shepherd's principles. In some instances, daily experience and observation confirms me still more, we should be very cautious and modest when asserting on that head, and should take care to go no farther in the matter than we have plain Scripture to bear us out.[59]

Appraisal and Appropriation

Gillespie's remarks are a helpful point of reference for assessing Edwards. In these remarks, Gillespie correctly places his finger on the tension produced by such strong statements for perseverance. The effort on Edwards's part to shake hypocrites from their false security appears to come at a price. First, as Gillespie observes, Edwards's use of Shepard and Stoddard undermines the security of false professors, but such overstatement also tends to a "wounding of the Lord's dear children" in the process. Gillespie's pastoral experience taught him that words intended for hardened hearts were felt keenly by tender consciences.[60]

Second, Edwards admits a considerable degree of ambiguity in accounting for the discrepancy between the radical convert and the convert who still sins. Some of this may simply be a traditional acceptance of the tension which the Westminster Assembly allowed in its doctrine of perseverance.[61] Edwards's theology of sin in the

[59] Thomas Gillespie, "Letter to Jonathan Edwards, November 24, 1746," in *A Treatise Concerning Religious Affections*, ed. John E. Smith, The Works of Jonathan Edwards, vol. 2 (New Haven: Yale, 1959), 475. The reference to "Mr. Shepherd" here refers to Thomas Shepard.

[60] Ibid.

[61] "The Westminster Confession of Faith," in *The Creeds of Christendom*, ed. Phillip Schaff, vol. 3, *The Evangelical Protestant Creeds* (repr., Grand Rapids: Baker, 2007), 637.

believer allows for some sin—limited in degree, kind, and duration—but these limits are not clearly defined or justified. This ambiguity, in combination with the high ideals of genuine conversion, heightens the tension between the claim that the convert is a thoroughly new creature and the claim that the convert remains a sinner. With the increase in tension is an increase in anxiety among professors of faith with the desire to know how to distinguish between the sin of a hypocrite and the sin of a saint. Ambiguous references to degree, kind, and duration of sin seem arbitrary without some point of reference. For this reason, Gillespie's caution is well taken:

> The consideration, that indwelling sin sometimes certainly gets such ascendant, that the new creature is, for the time the Lord sees meet, as fire burned under ashes, undiscerned and inactive, lays foundation, in my humble apprehension, for saying somewhat stronger on that point, than I would choose to utter in public teaching, and how long a saint may have been in the case now hinted, I suppose it belongs not to us precisely to determine.[62]

A third reason Edwards's overstatements are not helpful is the lack of coherence it brings to his theological message. Statements which call for change in absolute terms seem to stand in contradiction to other statements as previously observed. Edwards, in concert with extensive quotations from Shepard, portrays those who seek Christ for comfort and for safety as self-serving hypocrites, rather than seeking Christ on account of his excellency.[63] To be sure, the context indicates that Edwards intends to stir up those who are self-satisfied and no longer earnest in their religion. But when Edwards characterizes the motives of safety and of comfort as self-serving and hypocritical, that

[62] Gillespie, "Letter of Jonathan Edwards, November 24, 1746," WJE 2:475.

[63] Edwards, *Religious Affections*, WJE 2:379–83.

characterization calls into question the biblical authors who called for repentance and for faith on the basis of consequences and of blessings.

While it is certainly possible to desire spiritual safety and comfort through a feigned profession of faith, the motivations themselves cannot be discredited as they are employed by Scripture. The Psalmist loves the Lord because of what God does for him (Psalm 116); the Scriptures commonly enjoin readers to come to Christ on account of their heavy labor, their spiritual hunger and thirst, the futility of losing one's own soul, the agonies of eternal punishment, and the glories of eternal life. The biblical authors, in making common recommendations of these motives, nowhere suggest that they also should be suspected as potential counterfeits of higher motives.[64]

Edwards's theology of assurance in *Religious Affections* is certainly driven by his zeal to confront the masses who had professed Christ during the Awakening but gave little or no biblical evidence of conversion. This reality helps explain his overstatement in many places. Nevertheless, his efforts to disturb the complacent led to a somewhat unbalanced expression of assurance in which two other doctrines—the holiness of the convert and the reality of sin in the believer—come into significant tension. With these considerations in mind, Edwards's theology of assurance in *Religious Affections* can translate into constructive reflection for evangelical theology. Evangelicals should work toward a theology of assurance that accomplishes the difficult task identified by Gillespie—"to steer the middle course betwixt affording hypocrites ground unwarrantably to presume on the one hand, and wounding the Lord's dear children on the other."

Three adjustments promise to assist in steering this narrow pass. First, evangelicals ought to heed Carson's counsel to resist oversimplified definitions of assurance and to adopt an approach to the doctrine

[64] For a discussion concerning the influence of Shepard in Edwards's thought on this point, see William K. B. Stoever, "The Godly Will's Discerning: Shepard, Edwards, and the Identification of True Godliness," in *Jonathan Edwards's Writings: Text, Context, Interpretation*, ed. Stephen J. Stein (Bloomington, IN: Indiana University, 1996), 87–89.

that carefully accounts for exegetical, theological, and pastoral realities.[65] Close attention to the exegesis of pertinent texts is the prerequisite foundation for any facet of theology that claims to represent the biblical message. Major biblical treatments on the subject of assurance such as 2 Peter 1, Romans 8, and the book of 1 John, must play the leading roles in defining the doctrine. Texts advancing other themes may on occasion have relevance to assurance, but their significance must be qualified in light of the message being advanced by the larger context.

Theological realities call for a doctrine of assurance which does not overlook tension within theological formulation. In the case of the doctrine of assurance, tension exists between God's promise to keep the saint secure and God's warning that only those who persevere will be saved. Tension also exists in the definition of a believer's nature, which the Scriptures describe as both holy and sinful. These tensions must be addressed without forcing resolutions that directly contradict other portions of Scripture.

Additionally, pastoral realities must inform the way in which assurance is approached. As Carson reminds his readers, not all forms of doubt are the same; pastoral counsel and teaching must account for various situations including those who doubt the gospel, those who see themselves as beyond forgiveness, those entrapped in sin, those in bondage to perfectionism, and those who are comfortably self-deceived. The whole counsel of God's Word on the subject of assurance must be proportionately applied with pastoral discernment.[66]

For a second adjustment, there are many valuable components from Edwards's theology in *Religious Affections* which should be conveyed into contemporary expressions of assurance. One component is the separation of assurance from the essence of saving faith. The nature of saving faith has its object in Christ's sufficient work,

[65] See D. A. Carson, "Reflections on Assurance," in *Still Sovereign: Contemporary Perspectives on Election, Foreknowledge, and Grace*, ed. Thomas R. Schreiner and Bruce A. Ware (Grand Rapids: Baker, 2000), 247–76.

[66] Ibid., 273–75.

not on itself; therefore believing in Christ is a separate matter from believing that one has truly been regenerated.[67] Furthermore, true assurance can be only a post-salvation experience whereas saving faith is prior to salvation. Consequently, assurance cannot be of the essence of saving faith. While assurance is both attainable and normative,[68] a true believer may doubt his/her salvation.[69]

Another valuable component is the three-fold basis for assurance in the written Word, the evidence of grace, and the testimony of the Spirit. The written Word carries the perfections and the authority of God himself and serves as the objective ground for knowing all things as they actually exist.[70] The promises of salvation and the conditions by which those promises are appropriated are therefore utterly reliable.[71] While the Word presents Christ as truthful to his promises, it portrays humanity as vulnerable to self-deception. The Word, therefore, places all under the duty to employ a second ground of knowledge: the evidence of sanctification. While many may profess to believe, the Word insists that only those who manifest the marks of sanctification—especially love, obedience, and doctrinal fidelity—are in fact true believers.[72] The third ground of assurance is the unique work of the Holy Spirit, who first indwells the believer,[73] then exerts a controlling influence in the believer,[74] putting sin to death in the believer,[75] leading the believer to a natural fulfillment of his/her

[67] John 5:24; 12:44; 20:31; Acts 16:31; Rom. 10; Heb. 11.

[68] 1 Cor. 2:12; Eph. 3:16–19; 2 Peter 1:10; 1 John 4:13; 5:13.

[69] Mark 9:24; 2 Peter 1:9–11; 1 John 3:18–20; 5:13.

[70] It is for this reason that objective ground is often presented in terms of the person of Christ rather than the written Word. The traditional evangelical view acknowledges no true dichotomy between Christ's character, Christ's works, and Christ's words. See John 5:24; 8:31; 12:48; 14:24; Rev. 3:8.

[71] Isa. 55; John 5:24; Acts 2:39; Rom. 10:5–13; 2 Cor. 1:18–20; 7:1; Titus 1:2; Heb. 6:12, 17–19; 1 John 2:25.

[72] See Matt. 7:21–23; 13:1–29, 36–43; Rom. 1:5, 16:26; Titus 2:12; Heb. 5:9, 12:4–17; James 2; 1 Peter 1:2; and the entirety of 1 John.

[73] Rom. 8:9b.

[74] Rom. 8:9a.

[75] Rom. 8:13.

obligation to holiness,[76] and to a natural disposition to love and trust God.[77] In this context, the Spirit testifies to the spirit of the believer. This suggests most convincingly that the Spirit does not communicate his testimony in some other immediate manner, but rather that the Spirit's testimony is in fact the evidence of sanctification appearing in the context immediately preceding Romans 8:16.

For a third adjustment, those who teach the doctrine of assurance should draw attention not only to true holiness in the believer, but they should also explain in biblical terms how the convert can be genuinely holy while at the same time genuinely sinful. Edwards acknowledges elements of both but does not develop an explanation for their coexistence within the believer. To be sure, this imbalance is due to the fact that *Religious Affections* is an occasional piece of theology, not a systematic one. Edwards makes much of the fruit of sanctification, not the means or process involved. A full and balanced presentation of assurance theology to the church will speak of sanctification in more than terms of its fruit but also in terms of its means and its process.

Such a presentation will include several aspects of sanctification. First, the true convert obtains a new nature,[78] but not a perfectly holy one. A principle of sin remains within which must be resisted and overcome for the duration of the believer's earthly pilgrimage.[79] Sanctification is progressive, meaning that the believer's holiness comes by a process, is experienced by degree, and is frequently mingled with sin.[80] A direct relationship exists between progress in sanctification and progress in assurance; so the two should be taught hand in hand.[81] Finally, since sanctification is prerequisite to assur-

[76] Rom. 8:14b, 12, 5.

[77] Rom. 8:15.

[78] 2 Peter 1:4.

[79] Rom. 6; 7; 8:13; Gal. 5:16, 17, 24; Col. 3:5; 1 John 1:8–10.

[80] 2 Cor. 3:18; 4:16–17; Eph. 4:13; Phil. 1:6; 2:12–13; 3:12–14; Col. 3:10; 2 Peter 1:3–4.

[81] 2 Peter 1:5–11; 1 John 3:16–20. Edwards touched on this in his intro-

ance, the ordinary means of sanctification such as the Word,[82] prayer,[83] and the church,[84] must be highlighted as the ordinary means to assurance. In this way, assurance and sanctification are properly integrated, contributing to a more coherent picture of biblical soteriology.

Summary

Edwards's theology of assurance in the *Religious Affections* emphasizes four points. First, he affirms that assurance is not of the essence of saving faith. Second, he describes the basis of assurance in traditional Reformed terms, consisting of the witness of the Spirit, the testimony of Scripture, and the sanctification of the believer. The Scripture objectively speaks to the work of Christ on the sinner's behalf as well as the reliable marks of a truly converted soul. The Spirit brings both the Scripture and the evidence of sanctification to the court of conscience and testifies to the conscience that the Scriptural marks of salvation are indeed the authentic marks of salvation. Third, Edwards teaches that assurance is both normal and attainable and that its gain and loss are directly in correspondence to one's state of sanctification. Finally, Edwards identifies self-examination and action as the primary means for obtaining assurance, assuming that the ordinary means of grace for sanctification are also to be employed.

In keeping with the spirit of theological dialogue expressed in the correspondence between Edwards and Gillespie, this book

---

ductory remarks to Part Three, noting that, for certain ones who lacked evidence of sanctification, the signs would be of no use. For such persons, "action," or progressing in sanctification, was the appropriate course of action. Edwards cites the passage from 2 Peter 1, and calls such "action" the "principle means" of assurance. This emphatic language is interesting since he gives no further attention to this subject in the treatise. Edwards, *Religious Affections*, WJE 2:195–96.

[82] Ps. 1; Ps. 19; John 17:17; Eph. 5:26; Heb. 4:12–13; James 1:23–25.

[83] Eph. 6:18; Phil. 4:6–7.

[84] 1 Cor. 12; Eph. 4:7–16.

concludes with an appraisal in three parts. First, the idea of central interpretive motif has been employed with unwarranted confidence. Several decades of scholarship has illustrated its tendency to decontextualize data and promote distorted conclusions. While theologians may intentionally express a central interpretive motif and craft a body of theology around it, the practice of seeking to discover unidentified central motifs is an enterprise which invites the same liabilities as seen in the case of Edwards's work.

Second, Edwards's prolific use of proof-texting highlights the proof-texting problem in evangelicalism. Evangelicalism, as a Bible-centered movement claiming the mantle of the Reformers, has come to develop a particular distaste for proof-texting. A long history of irresponsible citation of biblical references to support theological conclusions and embarrassing critiques from the academy has made the term *proof-texting* synonymous with *theological irresponsibility*. The ultimate solution, however, is to return to responsible scriptural citation, rather than to dispose of it altogether.

Finally, this study seeks to engage a theological gap in Edwards's theology of assurance as expressed in *Religious Affections*. While acknowledging that Edwards's expression was conditioned by the circumstances attending the Awakening, *Religious Affections* is his most comprehensive treatment on the subject of assurance and as such may properly be viewed as a substantial representation of the comprehensiveness and the coherence of his position. Edwards frequently portrays the nature of the new creation as fundamentally holy and does so in terms that seem nearly absolute. Yet at other times, he recognizes the inevitable sin in the believer and attaches this sin to the imperfect nature of his constitution as a convert. These two pictures do not appear to reconcile, and Edwards makes little effort to explain this discrepancy. Gillespie's critique recognizes that this approach properly challenges the complacent, but tends to also strike at the tender consciences of God's true children. Edwards did hold to a progressive sanctification, but he did not make much of this truth as a mediator for this tension. In light of Edwards's theology of assurance, this study recommends that the heirs of his theological tradition give closer attention to sanctification theology in discussions of assurance, and in so doing, explain the new creation in terms which clearly account for remaining sin in the true convert.

Conclusion

A Treatise Concerning Religious Affections is one of the most widely known and read of the works of Jonathan Edwards. Historians and philosophers view the work as a definitive piece at a critical moment in American history; theologians and pastors have long esteemed it as a reservoir of gospel truth. Though Edwards is widely appreciated by a diverse constituency, that diversity has manifested itself in an astonishing array of interpretations of Edwards's work and legacy. For some, Edwards is a tragedy, a man whose genius was led astray by his religion. For others, Edwards is the personification of oppressive religion, the progenitor of America's proclivity to a backward and intolerant Christianity. But for others still, Edwards remains a champion of the Christian faith, a faithful steward and defender of the principles of the Reformation.

As a result of competing interpretations of Edwards, *Religious Affections* has also been viewed from a variety of perspectives. The doctrine of assurance, as it appears in *Religious Affections*, has received little direct and sustained attention. The question of Edwards's theological method has been discussed at length, but no detailed connection has been drawn between Edwards's method and his doctrine of assurance in *Religious Affections*. *Marks of Saving Grace* seeks to fill this gap.

In order to situate Edwards's theology in its context, it is critical to account for the historical situation in which Edwards, the doctrine of assurance, and the composition of *Religious Affections* appears. English Puritanism, its American version in particular, constituted the political, religious, and cultural context for the New England colonies in the seventeenth century. Its ideal was the establishment of a holy state, a "city on a hill" testifying the gospel to the world. For American Puritans, the objective was to succeed in this enterprise, the same one in which their British brethren had failed. As the eighteenth century dawned, it became clear that the American Puritans would also fail in this endeavor. Nevertheless, the eighteenth century successors to the Puritans were committed in great measure to the maintenance of pure religion, even if the pure state were unattainable.

For Puritanism, authentic conversion was the crown jewel of pure religion. The adversary of authentic conversion was a false profession of faith and the self-deception which led to this error. The lack of piety in the lives of third and fourth generation Puritan congregations prompted ministers to address false professions with stinging indictments of hypocrisy and calls to true conversion. As a result, many were pressed with doubts regarding their own spiritual state, and assurance of salvation became a prominent subject for both pastors and the laity. The Puritans took the doctrine of assurance handed down by the Reformers and made careful adjustments, the most noteworthy being the affirmation that assurance is not of the essence of faith. The Puritans also affirmed an understanding of assurance which defined it as that which regarded the certainty of one's own election (rather than a certainty in the gospel promises), as that which was experienced and attained by degree, and as that which was grounded in the Word of God, the fruit of sanctification, and the testimony of the Spirit. These benchmarks were eventually articulated in the Westminster Confession.

However, between the Westminster Confession and the birth of Edwards, the Puritans developed an understanding of assurance which turned upon one's experience prior to conversion. In the estimation of many Puritan ministers, who carefully studied and recorded the circumstances attending "true conversions," a true convert would experience a particular sequence of events prior to conversion. The conclusion was drawn that only such professions as were attended by this kind of preparation should be considered authentic. Preparationism in details and prescriptive forms soon attained status as sound doctrine, and it was into this theological climate that Edwards entered the world.

As a young adult, Edwards was perplexed that he never experienced the preparatory steps insisted upon by his father. Plagued by his own inadequate experience and disturbed by the apparent lack of biblical support for this form of doctrine taught by so many holy men, Edwards committed himself to discover the real basis by which one could have assurance of salvation. As Edwards searched out the matter privately, he preached to his congregation publicly about true conversion. The revivals of the 1730s and 1740s and the evident mixture of truth and error within them revealed a pressing need to equip the churches with principles for discerning true conversion. Edwards addressed this need, first with his "Distinguishing Marks," then in greater depth with "Some Thoughts Concerning the Revival," and finally with his comprehensive *Religious Affections*.

In addition to considering the historical context, this study endeavored to set the stage for an examination of the text of *Religious Affections* by assessing the question of his theological method. The question is especially important, given that the perception of Edwards's method determines in large measure one's interpretation of his work. A number of scholars view his method as fundamentally driven by philosophical concerns. Such interpretations neglect Edwards's overwhelming interest in the Scriptures and unjustifiably discount any assessment of the data in terms of Edwards's own Christian perspective. The majority of interpretations propose that a single interpretive element, or central interpretive motif, is the key to the entire body of Edwards's writings. However, there is little agreement among scholars as to which of the numerous proposed motifs is actually the correct key to reading Edwards. A closer examination of such motifs suggests that the evidence for them is compromised by reductionism and decontextualization. A few scholars have suggested a systematic theology interpretation, an approach which avoids the problems associated with the first two, but which falls prey to anachronism and overgeneralization.

A preferred approach to Edwards is a less-restrictive, source-oriented approach. This approach simply focuses on accounting for all sources contributing to the formation of theological conclusions along with the relative influence of each. There are different varieties of this concept, but Carson's approach appears to give the best explanation for the relationship between the controlling source and other supporting sources. This approach, which this study refers to as a "regulated matrix," does not require a central interpretive motif, nor does it lead to one. Instead, it simply accounts for the exchange of various sources disciplines under the governing authority of a single source. When applied to the reading of Edwards, this approach avoids reductionism and decontextualization, giving it historical value as it permits Edwards to speak on his own terms. In epistemological terms, this approach assumes a foundational platform. At the same time, it acknowledges the role of presuppositions. In this way a regulated matrix avoids fallacies associated with hard foundationalism on one hand and relativism on the other.

With Edwards's historical context as the backdrop and a source-oriented view of Edwards's theological method as a strategy, this study proceeded to examine *Religious Affections* in terms of its three key sources: philosophy, history, and Scripture. Edwards's use of philosophical thought entertains both metaphysics and epistemology. Edwards employs his grasp of metaphysics to argue that the affections are in essential unity with the mind. He also argues that the regenerating work of the Holy Spirit is fundamentally unique, analogous to Locke's "simple idea," a subject of interest in 18th century metaphysical discourse. Edwards also employs epistemological concepts of the day, using empirical ideas regarding perception and sense to illustrate spiritual realities as seen in his "object/eye" discussion, his language for describing self-deception, and his assertion that the capacities of the new nature amount to a "new sense." While many scholars see Edwards's philosophical ideas exerting a controlling influence on his thought, a closer examination reveals that the opposite is in fact the case. Edwards employs philosophical categories to illustrate the nature of certain ideas derived from the Scriptures, doing so in a manner that engages the interest of the academic segment of his audience. Since the nature of the affections, the unique work of the Holy Spirit, and the act of spiritual perception function as important components for explaining the evidence and the knowledge of salvation, Edwards's use of philosophical categories assists his attempt to clarify these key issues, each of which pertains to his doctrine of assurance.

Edwards's second key source in *Religious Affections* is history. As seen in his earlier works, Edwards had no desire to defend the revival or to articulate his theology with historical sources. Nevertheless, his debate with Charles Chauncy made it clear that the public perceived orthodoxy and history to be inseparable. Therefore, a convincing defense of the revival had to account for both simultaneously. Persuaded of the necessity of employing historical sources, Edwards marshals an overwhelming body of historical evidence from venerated names in the Puritan tradition.

Also, Edwards carefully manages his sources to assure readers that he has no intent to prove his point through those texts; historical sources serve to illustrate that his point is in keeping with those individuals known and trusted for their orthodoxy. Edwards uses historical sources in both defensive and offensive roles, making a special use of Thomas Shepard. These historical sources consistently address themes concerning spiritual perception, which in turn support and promote Edwards's theology of assurance.

Religious Affections depends upon the source of Scripture as the most significant source both in terms of volume and in terms of controlling influence. This appraisal is not that of an evangelical seeking to recreate Edwards in his own image. Edwards clearly indicates that Scripture is sufficient, authoritative, essentially clear, and self-authenticating. Edwards bears out this conviction in his consistent employment of Scripture throughout the treatise. Edwards's indirect and subtle appeal to Scripture is a practical baseline throughout the work, manifesting itself in countless biblical allusions, appeals to Scripture in general, and theological generalizations. His direct use of Scripture is evident in occasional exegetical excursions and dominant in his use of Scriptural proof-texting. For Edwards, Scripture is the definitive measure for marking the path of assurance and the only reliable arbiter for so many conflicting opinions on the subject. Scripture establishes itself as trustworthy in its own promises, marking the path of true conversion by pointing to persevering holiness as the chief evidence of those who are regenerated.

The theology of assurance woven into *Religious Affections* is in many respects what would be expected by a student of Puritanism. Edwards follows Westminster when affirming that assurance is not of the essence of faith. This means that true Christians can indeed doubt their salvation; it also means that professors cannot be certain they are saved merely because they have a sense of assurance. Additionally, the Scripture identifies itself, the evidence of sanctification, and the testimony of the Spirt as the three-fold ground of assurance. The Word proclaims its own promises as trustworthy and the signs of sanctification as reliable. The Spirit points the conscience to the promises of the Word and to the marks of holiness which accompany conversion, convincing the conscience that the soul has received God's salvation. Furthermore, assurance is normative and accessible as the reward of sanctification, and the primary means to obtaining assurance is self-examination and holy action. Edwards's doctrine of assurance, as expressed in these broad themes, harmonizes consistently with the Westminster standards.

Furthermore, Edwards's theology of assurance in *Religious Affections* in light of his theological method suggests three conclusions for application. First, thc task of formulating theology around a central interpretive motif is accompanied with liabilities, and the effort to read historical theology in terms of an *unexpressed* central interpretive motif is likely to be counterproductive. Second, Edwards's prolific use of proof-texting raises an interesting issue for evangelicals, many of whom revere Edwards's theology but doubt the merit of citing

Scripture references in support of theological ideas. This study seeks to reaffirm the legitimacy of the practice by clarifying its intended function and by reasserting the constraints of exegetical responsibility. Finally, this study joins hands with those of former generations by reasserting the value of Edwards's theology of assurance for the church today. For the sake of transferring the value of Edwards's theology of assurance in *Religious Affections* into a systematic expression, this study commends an intentional integration of the marks of sanctification, which Edwards stressed so vigorously, with the doctrines of the new nature, the ordinary means of sanctification, and the progressive nature of sanctification.

Edwards's theology of assurance never was, nor intended to be, a topic of speculation. For him, and for those who read him receptively, no matter posed more urgency for each person than to obtain Christ's salvation and to possess an assurance of it. For Edwards, his doctrine found its full application in his dying moments as witnesses recorded his expectation to see Christ.[1] It was, for him, a full realization of Peter's words, in which his life of diligent devotion to Christ culminated in eternal joy:

> Applying all diligence, in your faith supply moral excellence, and in your moral excellence, knowledge; and in your knowledge, self-control, and in your self-control, perseverance, and in your perseverance, godliness; and in your godliness, brotherly kindness, and in your brotherly kindness, love. For if these qualities are yours and are increasing, they render you neither useless nor unfruitful in the true knowledge of our Lord Jesus Christ. For he who lacks these qualities is blind or short-sighted, having forgotten his purification from his former sins. Therefore, brethren, be all the more diligent to make certain about His calling and choosing you; for as long

[1] Iain H. Murray, *Jonathan Edwards: A New Biography* (Edinburgh: Banner of Truth, 1987), 441.

as you practice these things, you will never stumble; for in this way the entrance into the eternal kingdom of our Lord and Savior Jesus Christ will be abundantly supplied to you (2 Peter 1:5–11, NASB).

Appendix 1: Distribution of Historical Sources in *Religious Affections*

Historical Source	Part	Part	Part	Total
Thomas Shepard	0	7	37	44
Solomon Stoddard	0	13	6	19
John Flavel	0	9	10	19
John Preston	0	0	5	5
John Calvin	0	0	3	3
William Perkins	0	1	0	1
John Smith	0	0	1	1
Philip Doddridge	0	0	1	1
William Ames	0	1	2	3
John Owen	0	0	2	2
Richard Sibbes	0	0	1	1
Theophilus Gale	0	0	1	1
Anthony Burgess	0	0	1	1
Samuel Rutherford	0	0	1	1
Martin Luther	0	0	1	1
François Turretin	0	0	1	1
Jeremiah Jones	0	0	1	1
Total	0	31	74	105[1]

[1] Table data is based upon search results from the Jonathan Edwards Center at Yale University, www.edwards.yale.edu. In several cases, Edwards makes multiple references to the same work within the same footnote. In such cases, the multiple references are represented as a single reference. Other accountings, such as that of J. A. Albro (upon which Smith depends), do not specify the method of accounting but appear to treat such multiple references within the same note separately. See J. A. Albro, "Life of Thomas Shepard," in *The Sincere Convert and The Sound Believer*, reprint ed. (Morgan, PA.: Soli Deo Gloria, 1999), clxxxix; Smith, "Editor's Introduction," 54.

Appendix 2: Reference to Thomas Shepard in *Religious Affections*[1]

pt:pg[2]	Theological Proposition in Context	Scripture[3]	Source[4]	Theological Theme
2:137	the nature of false affections	P A	*Parable*	holy affections
2:156	assurance not based upon terrors	T	*Parable*	preparation
2:162	first experiences of conversion incomprehensible	P X	*Parable*	preparation

[1] Table data for Tables 2–5 is based upon search results from the Jonathan Edwards Center at Yale University, www.edwards.yale.edu. In some cases, Edwards makes multiple references to the same work within the same footnote. In such cases, the multiple references are represented as a single reference.

[2] Part of *Treatise* and page number (Yale Edition of *Religious Affections*) in which the citation occurs. The same applies to Tables 3, 4, and 5.

[3] This column refers to the type of Scriptural support which the historical sources interact with and support. Legend: P – proof-text support; T – theological support; A – support by allusion to Scripture; S – support by reference to Scripture in general. In some cases other source types occur with Scriptural sources: X– specific appeal to experience; M – metaphysics.

[4] Sources of Thomas Shepard are *The Parable of the Ten Virgins* (1659), published after his death in 1649 on the basis of a sermon series, *The Sound Believer* (1645), and *The Sincere Convert* (1643).

2:162	nature of Spiritual fruit, not method, is significant	P X	*Sound*	preparation
2:173	two sorts of hypocrites	T	*Parable*	self-deception
2:174	inward peace despite evil practice	T	*Parable*	self-deception
2:182	professors often fall away	T	*Parable*	perseverance
3:214	not all who have sight of Christ are saints	P A	*Parable*	spiritual sight
3:215	Satan can give a false sight of Christ	P A	*Parable*	spiritual sight
3:222	Scripture coming to mind no evidence of grace	T	*Parable*	self-deception
	all the promises of Scripture are equally applicable	T S	*Sound*	self-deception
3:226	3:224	T S	*Parable*	self-deception
3:233–34	the witness of the Spirit is not immediate	T S	*Parable*	witness of Spirit
3:234–35	the witness of the Spirit is not immediate	T P	*Sound*	witness of Spirit
3:237	the Spirit does not communicate immediately	T P	*Parable*	witness of Spirit
3:242	self-love cannot result in love for God	T P	*Parable*	love for God
3:246	priority of God's loveliness cf. God's love for people	T	*Parable*	love for God
3:259	love of Christ for Christ's own beauty and character	T P	*Parable*	love for God

3:266–67	true affections arise from spiritual sight	T P M	*Parable*	spiritual sight
3:275–76	affections not arising from a spiritual sense are in vain	T P S	*Parable*	spiritual sight
3:318–19	some ministers make a pretense of humility	T	*Parable*	true humility
3:320	some ministers make a pretense of humility	P	*Parable*	true humility
3:337–38	false affections attended by a spirit of self-sufficiency	T P	*Parable*	true humility
3:338	false affections attended by a spirit of self-sufficiency	T P	*Sound*	true humility
3:340	conversion "a great and remarkable, abiding change"	T P S	*Parable*	true conversion
3:341	conversion entails a permanently changed nature	T P S	*Parable*	true conversion
3:344	gracious affections not unsteady like natural emotions	P A	*Parable*	holy affections
3:352	false boldness of hypocrites is rooted in pride	T P	*Parable*	true gentleness
3:359	hypocrites seek to use Christ to cloak sin	T P	*Parable*	true gentleness
3:366–67	saints know both joy of salvation and sorrow for sin	T P A	*Sound*	balance of virtues

3:367	saints know both joy of salvation and sorrow for sin	T P A	*Parable*	balance of virtues
3:374	saints are given to both public and private worship	T P A	*Parable*	balance of virtues
3:376–77	holy affections unsatisfied with spiritual attainments	T P	*Parable*	desire for growth
3:380–81	holy affections unsatisfied with spiritual attainments	T P A S	*Parable*	desire for growth
3:391	a temporary change of life marks a false believer	T	*Parable*	perseverance
3:391	a false belief in salvation may precipitate apostasy	T P	*Parable*	perseverance
3:402	hypocrites will return to sin	T P	*Sincere*	perseverance
3:402–3	hypocrites will return to sin	T P	*Parable*	perseverance
3:406	hypocrites will forsake Christ	P A	*Parable*	perseverance
3:426	holy living is the primary evidence of salvation	T P	*Parable*	holy living
3:431	endurance under trial is a chief evidence of salvation	T P A	*Parable*	trials
3:433–34	endurance under trial is a chief evidence of salvation	T P A	*Parable*	trials
3:459	"nothing legal" in the good works of holy living	T P	*Sound*	holy living

Appendix 3: Reference to Solomon Stoddard in *Religious Affections*

pt:pg	Theological Proposition in Context	Scripture[1]	Source[2]	Theological Theme
2:131	great affections no proof of salvation	P	*Guide*	holy affections
2:145	great affections no proof of salvation	T	*Guide*	holy affections
2:147	great affections no proof of salvation	P	*Guide*	holy affections
2:150	delight in the saints no proof of salvation	T P	*Treatise*	holy affections
2:156	Satan's terrors are not like the Spirit's convictions	T	*Guide*	self-deception
2:158	Satan can counterfeit sensations of grace	T P	*Guide*	self-deception

[1] This column refers to the type of Scriptural support which the historical sources interact with. Legend: P – proof-text support; T – theological support; A – support by allusion to Scripture; S – support by reference to Scripture in general.

[2] Sources of Stoddard are *A Guide to Christ* (1714), the sermon entitled "The Way to Know Sincerity and Hypocrisy" (1719), *A Treatise Concerning Conversion* (1719), and *An Appeal to the Learned* (1709). See Smith, "Editor's Introduction," 2:58–60.

2:160	method and order of experiences no proof	S P	*Appeal*	preparation
2:162	on not knowing the time of one's own conversion	S	*Guide*	preparation
2:170	confidence no proof of salvation	P	*Way*	self-deception
2:177	faith that one is saved is not Biblical saving faith	S	*Treatise*	spiritual sight
2:181	Christians cannot determine for certain who is elect	T P	*Treatise*	discernment
2:181	Christians cannot determine for certain who is elect	T P	*Appeal*	discernment
2:196	assurance chiefly by obedience rather than signs	T P	*Sincerity*	discernment
3:222	Scripture coming to mind no evidence of grace	T	*Guide*	self-deception
3:226	the misuse of Scripture promises	S	*Treatise*	self-deception
3:230	the uniqueness of the witness of the Spirit	P	*Treatise*	witness of Spirit
3:384	the necessity of obedience	P	*Sincerity*	holy living
3:390	obedience in difficult circumstances	T P	*Sincerity*	perseverance
3:453	obedience is a part of authentic Christian experience	T A	*Sincerity*	holy living

Appendix 4: Reference to John Flavel in *Religious Affections*

pt:pg	Theological Proposition in Context	Script.[1]	Source[2]	Theological Theme
2:137	the nature of false affections	P	*Touchstone*	holy affections
2:170	confidence no proof of salvation	T P	*Touchstone*	self-deception
2:171	confidence no proof of salvation	T P	*Husbandry*	self-deception
2:171	confidence no proof of salvation	T P	*Works*	self-deception
2:181	Christians cannot determine for certain who is elect	P	*Husbandry*	discernment

[1] This column refers to the type of Scriptural support which the historical sources interact with. Legend: P – proof-text support; T – theological support; A – support by allusion to Scripture; S – support by reference to Scripture in general.

[2] Sources of John Flavel (1630–91) are *Preparation for Suffering* (1681), *The Whole Works of Mr. John Flavel, A Discourse of the Occasions, Causes, Nature, Rise, Growth, and Remedies of Mental Errors* (1691), Sacramental *Meditations* (1679), *Husbandry Spiritualized* (1669), and *The Touchstone of Sincerity* (1679). See Smith, "Introduction," 2:60–62.

2:181	Christians cannot determine for certain who is elect	P	*Works*	discernment
2:182	professors often fall away	T	*Touchstone*	perseverance
2:186	the difficulty of distinguishing tares from wheat	T P	*Husbandry*	discernment
2:186	the difficulty of distinguishing tares from wheat	T P	*Works*	discernment
3:213	the susceptibility of people to impressions	T	*Preparation*	discernment
3:213	the susceptibility of people to impressions	T S	*Works*	discernment
3:215	Satan able to suggest thoughts to people	T P	*Discourse*	discernment
3:215	Satan able to suggest thoughts to people	T P	*Works*	discernment
3:235	the witness of the Spirit is not immediate	T P	*Meditations*	witness of Spirit
3:366	saints balance joy with holy fear	T P	*Meditations*	balance of virtue
3:373	inconsistency a sign of unsound affections	T P	*Touchstone*	balance of virtue
3:374	saints are given to both public and private worship	T P	*Touchstone*	balance of virtue
3:375	the affections and sorrows of saints are more silent	P A	*Touchstone*	balance of virtue
3:433	endurance under trial is chief evidence of salvation	T P	*Touchstone*	trials

Appendix 5: Reference to Minor Historical Sources in *Religious Affections*

pt:pg	Source[1]	Theological Proposition in Context	Support[2]	Theological Theme
3:367	Preston	saints know both joy of salvation and sorrow for sin	T P	balance of virtues

[1] Sources include, respectively, John Preston, "Discourses on Paul's Conversion" in *Remains of That Reverend and Learned Divine John Preston* (1634); John Preston, *The Onely Love of the Chiefest of Ten Thousand* (1640); John Preston, *The Church's Carriage* (1638); John Calvin, *Institutes of the Christian Religion*; William Perkins, *A Treatise Tending unto a Declaration, Whether a Man Be in the Estate of Damnation, or in the Estate of Grace* (1595); John Smith "A Discovery of the Shortness and Vanity of a Pharisaic Righteousness" in *Select Discourses* (1660); Philip Doddridge, *Practical Discourses on Regeneration* and *The Scripture Doctrine of Salvation* (1742); William Ames, *Conscience with the Power and Cases Thereof* (1630); John Owen, *Pneumatologia or, A Discourse Concerning the Holy Spirit* (1674); Richard Sibbes, *The Bruised Reed and Smoking Flax* (1630); Theophilus Gale, *The Court of the Gentiles* (1671); Anthony Burgess, *The Doctrine of Original Sin* (1659); Samuel Rutherford, *A Survey of the Spiritual Antichrist* (1648); Martin Luther, *Ominum Operum* (1558) as cited in Rutherford's *Survey*; François Turretin, *Institutio Theologiae Elencticae* (1679–85); Jeremiah Jones, *A New and Full Method of Settling the Canonical Authority of the New Testament* (1726).

[2] This column refers to the type of Scriptural support which the historical sources interact with. Legend: P – proof-text support; T – theological support; A – support by allusion to Scripture; S – support by reference to Scripture in general. In some cases other source types occur with Scriptural sources: X– specific appeal to experience; M – metaphysics.

3:372	Preston	inconsistency a sign of unsound affections	T P	balance of virtues
3:399	Preston	God's grace produces holy living	T P	holy living
3:399 –40	Preston	God's grace produces holy living	T P	holy living
3:437	Preston	holy living is the primary mark of conversion	T P	holy living
3:278	Calvin	spiritual understanding from doctrinal knowledge	T S	spiritual sight
3:314	Calvin	a humble spirit submits to Scripture as final rule	T P	true humility
3:322	Calvin	a humble spirit does not have a high self-opinion	T P	true humility
2:157	Perkins	distinguishing between conviction and depres- sion	T M	preparation
3:217	Smith	natural imaginations can raise carnal affections	T M	discernment
3:423	Doddri dge	"determinations of the will are indeed ... actions"	T M	holy living
2:174	Ames	inward peace despite evil practice	T	self-deception
3:362	Ames	modesty in worship a sign of humility	P A	true humility
3:374	Ames	saints are given to both public and private worship	T P	balance of virtues
3:250	Owen	saints' first delight is God's own perfections	T	love for God
3:372	Owen	inconsistency a sign of unsound affections	T P	balance of virtues

3:433	Sibbes	endurance under trial is chief evidence of salvation	T P	trials
3:316	Gale	humility distinguishes believers from heathen	P S	true humility
3:289	Burgess	Satan tempts people by means of the imagination	T M	spiritual sight
3:287	Rutherford	Church history testifies to false experiences	A	spiritual sight
3:322	Luther	a humble spirit does not have a high self-opinion	T P	true humility
3:289	Turretin	Satan tempts people by means of the imagination	T M	spiritual sight
3:335	Jones[3]	true humility does not speak of itself	P	true humility

[3] In addition to the use of these historical sources, Edwards employs a reference work by Ephraim Chambers on two occasions, once to authenticate data concerning ancient near eastern artifacts, and the other to verify the semantic domain of the term *taste*. Ephraim Chambers, *Cyclopedia: or an Universal Dictionary of Arts and Sciences*, 2 vols. (London, 1728); Edwards, *Religious Affections*, WJE 2:233, 283. Additionally, he alludes to Petrus van Mastricht: “Humility is (as the great Mastricht expresses it) a kind of holy pusillanimity.” Edwards does not cite the source, but the editors of the Jonathan Edwards Center have located the loose quotation from van Mastricht’s *Theoretico-Practica Theologia* (1699). www.edwards.yale.edu.

Appendix 6: Citations of Biblical References in *Religious Affections*

Genesis	13
Exodus	25
Leviticus	2
Numbers	11
Deuteronomy	20
Joshua	1
Judges	9
Ruth	1
1 Samuel	14
2 Samuel	4
1 Kings	9
2 Kings	10
1 Chronicles	3
2 Chronicles	3
Ezra	2
Nehemiah	3
Esther	0
Job	37
Psalms	148
Proverbs	32
Ecclesiastes	3
Song of Solomon	15
Isaiah	54
Jeremiah	20

Lamentations	3
Ezekiel	21
Daniel	12
Hosea	8
Joel	1
Amos	0
Obadiah	0
Jonah	0
Micah	4
Nahum	0
Habakkuk	0
Zephaniah	0
Haggai	0
Zechariah	10
Malachi	4
TOTAL	502

Citations of Biblical References in *Religious Affections*

Book	Citations
Matthew	113
Mark	13
Luke	63
John	78
Acts	24
Romans	60
1 Corinthians	46
2 Corinthians	62
Galatians	33
Ephesians	27
Philippians	26
Colossians	19
1 Thessalonians	9
2 Thessalonians	2
1 Timothy	5
2 Timothy	13
Titus	8
Philemon	2
Hebrews	43
James	26
1 Peter	27
2 Peter	11
1 John	57
2 John	1
3 John	3
Jude	7
Revelation	33
TOTAL	811

Note: Data is based on search results provided by the Jonathan Edwards Center, www.edwards.yale.edu. The accounting of the citations is based upon the appearance of the name of the biblical book in the text of *Religious Affections*, including citations in footnotes. Strings of chapter/verse citations proceeding from the citation of an initial citation of the biblical book are accounted as a single biblical citation. References to a book in general (without chapter in verse) as a proof-text are included.

Bibliography

Abraham, William J. "Predestination and Assurance." In *The Grace of God, the Will of Man*, edited by Clark Pinnock. Grand Rapids: Academie, 1989.

Ahlstrom, Sydney E. *A Religious History of the American People*. New Haven: Yale, 1972.

Albro, J. A. "Life of Thomas Shepard." In *The Sincere Convert and The Sound Believer*. Reprint, Morgan, PA: Soli Deo Gloria, 1999.

Allen, R. Michael. *Reformed Theology*. New York: T&T Clark, 2010.

Allen, R. Michael, and Scott R. Swain. "In Defense of Proof-Texting." *Journal of the Evangelical Theological Society* 54, 3 (September 2001): 589–606.

Allison, Gregg R. *Historical Theology*. Grand Rapids: Zondervan, 2011.

Alston, William. *The Reliability of Sense Perception*. Ithaca, NY: Cornell, 1993.

Ames, William. *Conscience with the Power and Cases Thereof*. 1630. Reprint, London, 1639.

Anderson, Wallace E. "Editor's Introduction." In *Scientific and Philosophical Writings*, edited by Wallace E. Anderson. The Works of Jonathan Edwards, vol. 6. New Haven: Yale, 1980.

Ankersmit, F. R. *Sublime Historical Experience*. Palo Alto, CA: Stanford University, 2005.

Archer, Kenneth J. *A Pentecostal Hermeneutic for the Twenty-First Century: Spirit, Scripture, and Community*. New York: T & T Clark, 2004.

Arkin, Marc M. "The Great Awakener: A Review of *Jonathan Edwards* by John E. Smith." *The New Criterion*. May 1993. Accessed October 27, 2011. http://www.newcriterion.com/articles.cfm/The-great-awakener-4763

Atchison, Thomas F. "Towards Developing a Theology of Christian Assurance from 1 John with Reference to Jonathan Edwards." Ph. D. diss., Trinity Evangelical Divinity School, 2004.

Beaton, D. "'The Marrow of Modern Divinity' and the Marrow Controversy." *Princeton Theological Review* 4, 1 (January 1906): 317–38.

Beauchamp, Tom L. "Introduction." In *The Works of David Hume*, edited by Tom L. Beauchamp. Oxford: Oxford University, 1998.

Bebbington, David W. *The Dominance of Evangelicalism*. Downers Grove, IL: InterVarsity, 2005.

——. *Evangelicalism in Modern Britain: A History from the 1730's to the 1980's*. London: Unwin Hyman, 1989.

Beeke, Joel R. "The Assurance Debate: Six Key Questions." In *Drawn Into Controversie: Reformed Theological Diversity and Debates Within Seventeenth-Century British Puritanism*. Edited by Michael A. G. Haykin and Mark Jones. Göttingen, Germany: Vandenhoeck and Ruprecht, 2011.

——. "Does Assurance Belong to the Essence of Faith? Calvin and the Calvinists." *The Master's Seminary Journal* 5, 1 (Spring 1994): 43–71.

——. *The Quest for Full Assurance: The Legacy of Calvin and His Successors*. Edinburgh: Banner of Truth, 1999.

Beeke, Joel R, and Randall J. Pederson. *Meet the Puritans*. Grand Rapids: Reformation Heritage, 2006.

Bellamy, Joseph. *A Careful and Strict Examination of the Covenant*. New Haven: Thomas and Samuel Green, 1760.

Benedict, Philip. *Christ's Churches Purely Reformed: A Social History of Calvinism*. New Haven: Yale, 2002.

Bennett, Tony. *Formalism and Marxism*. 3rd ed. London: Routledge, 2003.

Bombaro, John J. *Jonathan Edwards's Vision of Reality: The Relationship of God to the World, Redemptive History, and the Reprobate*. Princeton Theological Monograph Series. Eugene, OR: Pickwick, 2011.

——. "Jonathan Edward's Vision of Salvation." *Westminster Theological Journal* 65 (2003): 45–68.

Boss, Rob and Richard Hall, eds. "About JESociety." Jonathan Edwards Society. Accessed June 24, 2011. http://www.jesociety.org/about.

Bozeman, Theodore Dwight. *The Precisionist Strain: Disciplinarian Religion and Antinomian Backlash in Puritanism to 1638*. Chapel Hill, NC: University of North Carolina, 2004.

Bradley, James E., and Richard A. Muller. *Church History: An Introduction to Research, Reference Works, and Methods*. Grand Rapids: Eerdmans, 1995.

Brand, David C. *Profile of the Last Puritan: Jonathan Edwards, Self-Love, and the Dawn of the Beatific*. Atlanta: Scholars Press, 1988.

Bremer, Francis J. *The Puritan Experiment: New England Society from Bradford to Edwards*. Rev. ed. Lebanon, NH: University Press of New England, 1995.

Brook, Benjamin. *The Lives of the Puritans*. 1813. Reprint, Morgan, PA: Soli Deo Gloria, 1994.

Brooks, Thomas. *The Complete Works of Thomas Brooks*. Edited by Alexander Balloch Grosart. Vol. 2. Edinburgh: James Nichol, 1866.

——. *Heaven on Earth: A Treatise on Christian Assurance*, 1654. Reprint, Edinburgh: Banner of Truth, 1982.

Broughton, David J. "Mortise and Tenon in God's Hand: The Epistemology of Jonathan Edwards." Unpublished paper.

Virginia Beach, VA: Virginia Beach Theological Seminary, August 2009.

Brown, Robert E. "The Bible." In *The Princeton Companion to Jonathan Edwards*, edited by Sang Hyun Lee. Princeton, NJ: Princeton University, 2005.

——. *Jonathan Edwards and the Bible*. Bloomington, IN: Indiana University, 2002.

Brownson, Orestes A. "Norton's Evidence." In *The Transcendentalists: An Anthology*, edited by Perry Miller. Boston: Harvard University, 1950.

Burgess, Anthony. *The Doctrine of Original Sin*. London: T. Underhill, 1659.

Byassee, Jason. *Praise Seeking Understanding: Reading the Psalms with Augustine*. Grand Rapids: Eerdmans, 2007.

Cady, Edwin H. "The Artistry of Jonathan Edwards." *The New England Quarterly* 22, 1 (March 1949): 61–72.

Cailliet, Emile. "Review of *Puritan Sage, Collected Writings of Jonathan Edwards* by Vergilius Ferm." *The New England Quarterly* 27, 1 (March 1954): 125–27.

Calvin, John. *Institutes of the Christian Religion*. 1559. Edited by John T. McNeill. Translated by Ford Lewis Battles. 2 vols. Reprint, Louisville: Westminster John Knox, 2006.

Carrick, John. *The Preaching of Jonathan Edwards*. Edinburgh: Banner of Truth, 2008.

Carson, D. A. *Becoming Conversant with the Emerging Church*. Grand Rapids: Zondervan, 2005.

——. *The Gagging of God*. Grand Rapids: Zondervan, 1996.

——. "Reflections on Assurance." In *Still Sovereign: Contemporary Perspectives on Election, Foreknowledge, and Grace*, edited by Thomas R. Schreiner and Bruce A. Ware. Grand Rapids: Baker, 2000.

——. "The Role of Exegesis in Systematic Theology." In *Doing Theology in Today's World*, edited by John D. Woodbridge and Thomas E. McComiskey. Grand Rapids: Zondervan, 1991.

——. "Unity and Diversity in the New Testament: The Possibility of Systematic Theology." In *Scripture and Truth*, edited by D. A. Carson and John D. Woodbridge. Grand Rapids: Baker, 1983.

Chai, Leon. *Jonathan Edwards and the Limits of Enlightenment Philosophy*. Oxford: Oxford University, 1998.

Chamberlain, Ava. "Bad Books and Bad Boys: The Transformation of Gender in Eighteenth-Century Northampton, Massachusetts." In *Jonathan Edwards at Home and Abroad: Historical Memories, Cultural Movements, Global Horizons*, edited by David W. Kling and Douglas A. Sweeney. Columbia, SC: University of South Carolina, 2003.

——. "Brides of Christ and Signs of Grace: Edwards's Sermon Series on the Parable of the Wise and Foolish Virgins." In *Jonathan Edwards's Writings: Text, Context, Interpretation*, edited by Stephen J. Stein. Bloomington, IN: Indiana University, 1996.

——. "Self-Deception as a Theological Problem in Jonathan Edwards's 'Treatise Concerning Religious Affections.'" *Church History* 63, 4 (December 1994): 541–56.

Chambers, Ephraim. *Cyclopedia: Or an Universal Dictionary of Arts and Sciences*, 2 vols. London: Rinsen, 1728.

Charnock, Stephen. *The Doctrine of Regeneration*. 1840. Reprint, Grand Rapids: Baker, 1980.

Chauncy, Charles. *Seasonable Thoughts on the State of Religion in New England*. Boston: Samuel Eliot, 1743.

——. "A Sketch of Eminent Men in New England. In a Letter from the Rev. Dr. Chauncy to Dr. Stiles, May 6, 1768." In *Collections of the Massachusetts Historical Society, Vol. X*. Boston: Massachusetts Historical Society, 1809.

Cherry, Conrad. *The Theology of Jonathan Edwards: A Reappraisal*. Bloomington, IN: Indiana University, 1966.

Claghorn, George S. "Introduction to Personal Writings." In *Letters and Personal Writings*, edited by George S. Claghorn.

The Works of Jonathan Edwards, vol. 16. New Haven: Yale, 1998.

——. "Transcribing a Difficult Hand: Collecting and Editing Edwards's Letters Over Thirty-Five Years." In *The Legacy of Jonathan Edwards*, edited by Sean Michael Lucas, D. G. Hart, and Stephen J. Nichols. Grand Rapids: Baker, 2003.

Clark, David Edward. "Leveling Mountains, Drying Up Rivers: Jonathan Edwards' Historiography Applied." Ph. D. diss., Westminster Theological Seminary, 2001.

Clebsch, William A. *American Religious Thought: A History*. Chicago: University of Chicago, 1973.

Cobb, John B. *Process Theology as Political Theology*. Philadelphia: Westminster, 1982.

Coffey, John. "Puritan Legacies." In *The Cambridge Companion to Puritanism*. Edited by John Coffey and Paul C. H. Lim. Cambridge: Cambridge University, 2008.

Cole, Graham A. "Doctrine of God." In *Dictionary for Theological Interpretation of the Bible*, edited by Kevin J. Vanhoozer. Grand Rapids: Baker, 2005.

The Concise Dictionary of the Christian Tradition, edited by Walter A. Elwell J. D. Douglas, and Peter Toon. Grand Rapids: Zondervan, 1989.

Concise Dictionary of Christianity in America, edited by Daniel G. Reid. Downers Grove, IL: InterVarsity, 1995.

Conforti, Joseph A. *Jonathan Edwards, Religious Tradition, and American Culture*. Chapel Hill, NC: University of North Carolina, 1995.

Coolidge, John S. *The Pauline Renaissance in England: Puritanism and the Bible*. Oxford: Clarendon, 1970.

Copan, Paul. "Jonathan Edwards' Philosophical Influences: Lockean or Malebranchean?" *Journal of the Evangelical Theological Society* 44 (March 2001): 107–24.

Corfield, Penelope J. *The Time and Shape of History*. New Haven: Yale, 2007.

Crisp, Oliver D. "How 'Occasional' Was Edwards's Occasionalism?" In *Jonathan Edwards: Philosophical Theologian*, edited by Paul Helm and Oliver D. Crisp. Burlington, VT: Ashgate, 2003.

Cromwell, Oliver. *Oliver Cromwell's Letters and Speeches*. Edited by Thomas Carlyle. Vol. 2. New York: Harper and Brothers, 1851.

Cross, F. L., and E. A. Livingston, eds. *Oxford Dictionary of the Christian Church*. 2nd ed. Oxford: Oxford University, 1974.

Cunningham, William. *The Reformers and the Theology of the Reformation*. 1862. Reprint, Edinburgh: Banner of Truth, 2000.

Cutter, William Richard. *New England Families, Genealogical and Memorial*. Vol. 1. New York: Lewis, 1913.

Danaher, William J. *The Trinitarian Ethics of Jonathan Edwards*. Columbia Series in Reformed Theology. Louisville: Westminster John Knox, 2004.

Daniel, Stephen Hartley. *The Philosophy of Jonathan Edwards: A Study in Divine Semiotics*. Bloomington, IN: Indiana University, 1994.

———. "Postmodern Concepts of God and Edwards's Trinitarian Theology." In *Edwards in Our Time*, edited by Sang Hyun Lee and Allen C. Guelzo. Grand Rapids: Eerdmans, 1999.

Davidson, Edward H. *The Narrative of the Puritan Mind*. Boston: Houghton Mifflin Co., 1966.

de Saussure, Ferdinand. *Course in General Linguistics*. Translated by Roy Harris. Reprint, Peru, IL: Open Court, 1983.

Delattre, Roland A. *Beauty and Sensibility in the Thought of Jonathan Edwards*. New Haven: Yale, 1968.

Delbanco, Andrew. *The Puritan Ordeal*. Cambridge: Harvard University, 1989.

deWinter, Jennifer Fredale. "The Rhetorics of Context: An Ethics of Belonging." Ph.D. diss., University of Arizona, 2008.

Dockery, David S. "Review of *The American Pietism of Cotton Mather* by Richard F. Lovelace." *Grace Theological Journal* 2, 2 (Fall 1981): 341–43.

Doddridge, Phillip. *Practical Discourses on Regeneration and on the Scripture Doctrine of Salvation*. 1742. Reprint, Glasgow: William Collins, 1829.

Dodds, Elizabeth. *Marriage to a Difficult Man: The Uncommon Union of Jonathan and Sarah Edwards*. Westminster Press, 1971.

Doriani, Daniel M. "A Redemptive-Historical Model." In *Four Views on Moving Beyond the Bible to Theology*, edited by Stanley N. Gundry. Grand Rapids: Zondervan, 2009.

Dorrien, Gary J. *The Remaking of Evangelical Theology*. Louisville: Westminster John Knox, 1998.

Dwight, Sereno Edwards. "Memoirs of Jonathan Edwards." In *The Works of Jonathan Edwards*, edited by Edward Hickman, vol. 1. 1834. Reprint, Edinburgh: Banner of Truth, 2003.

Edelstein, Alan. *Everybody's Sitting on the Curb: How and Why America's Heroes Disappeared*. Westport, CT: Praeger, 1996.

Edwards, Jonathan. "Born Again." In *Sermons and Discourses: 1730–1733*, edited by Mark Valeri. The Works of Jonathan Edwards, vol. 17. New Haven: Yale, 1999.

———. "Diary." In *Letters and Personal Writings*, edited by George S. Claghorn. The Works of Jonathan Edwards, vol. 16. New Haven: Yale, 1998.

———. "Distinguishing Marks of a Work of the Spirit of God." In *The Great Awakening*, edited by C. C. Goen. The Works of Jonathan Edwards, vol. 4. New Haven: Yale, 1970.

———. "A Divine and Supernatural Light." In *Sermons and Discourses: 1730–1733*, edited by Mark Valeri. The Works of Jonathan Edwards, vol. 17. New Haven: Yale, 1999.

———. "Entry 782. IDEAS. SENSE OF THE HEART. SPIRITUAL KNOWLEDGE OR CONVICTION. FAITH." In

The "Miscellanies" 501–832, edited by Ava Chamberlain. The Works of Jonathan Edwards, vol. 18. New Haven: Yale, 2000.

———. "Ephraim Williams to Jonathan Ashley, May 2, 1751." In *Correspondence by, to, and About Edwards and His Family*. The Works of Jonathan Edwards Online, vol. 32. New Haven: Jonathan Edwards Center at Yale University, 2008. Accessed February 18, 2012. http://edwards.yale.edu/.

———. "A Faithful Narrative of the Surprising Work of God." In *The Great Awakening*, edited by C. C. Goen. The Works of Jonathan Edwards, vol. 4. New Haven: Yale, 1970.

———. *Freedom of the Will.* Edited by Paul Ramsey. The Works of Jonathan Edwards, vol. 1. New Haven: Yale, 1957.

———. *The Great Christian Doctrine of Original Sin Defended.* Edited by Clyde A. Holbrook. The Works of Jonathan Edwards, vol. 3. New Haven: Yale, 1970.

———. "Hope and Comfort Usually Follow Genuine Humiliation and Repentance." In *The Works of Jonathan Edwards*, edited by Edward Hickman, vol. 1. 1834. Reprint, Edinburgh: Banner of Truth, 2003.

———. "An Humble Inquiry Into the Rules of the Word of God, Concerning the Qualifications Requisite to a Complete Standing and Full Communion in the Visible Christian Church." In *Ecclesiastical Writings*, edited by David D. Hall. The Works of Jonathan Edwards, vol. 12. New Haven: Yale, 1994.

———. "Images of Divine Things." In *Typological Writings*, edited by Wallace E. Anderson. The Works of Jonathan Edwards, vol. 11. New Haven: Yale, 1993.

———. "Letter to the Reverend Benjamin Coleman, May 22, 1744." In *Letters and Personal Writings*, edited by George C. Claghorn. The Works of Jonathan Edwards, vol. 16. New Haven: Yale, 1998.

———. "Letter to the Reverend Joseph Bellamy, January 15, 1747." In *Letters and Personal Writings*, edited by George S. Claghorn. The Works of Jonathan Edwards, vol. 16. New Haven: Yale, 1998.

——. "Letter to Thomas Gillespie, April 2, 1750." In *A Treatise Concerning Religious Affections*, edited by John E. Smith. The Works of Jonathan Edwards, vol. 2. New Haven: Yale, 1959.

——. "Letter to Thomas Gillespie, September 4, 1747." In *A Treatise Concerning Religious Affections*, edited by John E. Smith. The Works of Jonathan Edwards, vol. 2. New Haven: Yale, 1959.

——. *The Life of David Brainerd.* Edited by Norman Pettit. The Works of Jonathan Edwards, vol. 7. New Haven: Yale, 1985.

——. "Memoirs." Letter to Sir W. Pepperell. In *The Works of Jonathan Edwards*, edited by Edward Hickman, vol. 2. 1834. Reprint, Edinburgh: Banner of Truth, 2003.

——. "The Mind." In *Scientific and Philosophical Writings*, edited by Wallace E. Anderson. The Works of Jonathan Edwards, vol. 6. New Haven: Yale, 1980.

——. *The "Miscellanies" a–500.* Edited by Thomas A. Schafer. The Works of Jonathan Edwards, vol. 13. New Haven: Yale, 1994.

——. *The "Miscellanies" 501–832.* Edited by Ava Chamberlain. The Works of Jonathan Edwards, vol. 18. New Haven: Yale, 2000.

——. "Mysteries. Concerning Reason's Being Superior to Revelation." In *"Controversies" Notebook.* The Works of Jonathan Edwards Online, vol. 27. Jonathan Edwards Center at Yale University, 2008.

——. "Personal Narrative." In *Letters and Personal Writings*, edited by George S. Claghorn. The Works of Jonathan Edwards, vol. 16. New Haven: Yale, 1998.

——. *The Salvation of Souls.* Edited by Richard A. Bailey and Gregory A. Wills. Wheaton, IL: Crossway Books, 2002.

——. *Scientific and Philosophical Writings.* Edited by Wallace E. Anderson. The Works of Jonathan Edwards, vol. 6. New Haven: Yale, 1980.

——. "Some Thoughts Concerning the Revival." In *The Great Awakening*, edited by C. C. Goen. The Works of Jonathan Edwards, vol. 4. New Haven: Yale, 1970.

——. *A Treatise Concerning Religious Affections*. Edited by Edward Hickman. The Works of Jonathan Edwards, vol. 1. 1834. Reprint, Edinburgh: Banner of Truth, 2003.

——. *A Treatise Concerning Religious Affections*. Edited by John E. Smith. The Works of Jonathan Edwards, vol. 2. New Haven: Yale, 1959.

——. "Unpublished Letter of May 30, 1735." In *The Great Awakening*, edited by C. C. Goen. The Works of Jonathan Edwards, vol. 4. New Haven: Yale, 1970.

Elwood, Douglas. *The Philosophical Theology of Jonathan Edwards*. New York: Columbia, 1960.

Erdt, Terrence. *Jonathan Edwards, Art, and a Sense of the Heart*. Amherst, MA: University of Massachusetts, 1980.

Erickson, Millard J. *Christian Theology*. 2nd ed. Grand Rapids: Baker, 1998.

——. *The Word Became Flesh*. Grand Rapids: Baker, 1991.

——. "Exegesis." In *Concise Dictionary of Christian Theology*. Grand Rapids: Baker, 1994.

Eversley, Walter V. L. "The Pastor as Revivalist." In *Edwards in Our Time*, edited by Sang Hyun Lee and Allen C. Guelzo. Grand Rapids: Eerdmans, 1999.

Fanning, Buist M. "Theological Analysis: Building Biblical Theology." In *Interpreting the New Testament Text: Introduction to the Art and Science of Exegesis*, edited by Darrel L. Bock and Buist M. Fanning. Wheaton, IL: Crossway, 2006.

Felt, Joseph Barlow. "Solomon Stoddard to Samuel Sewall, 1701." In *The Customs of New England*, 3:183–84. Boston: Marvin, 1853.

Ferré, Frederick. *Language, Logic, and God*. New York: Harper, 1961.

Fiering, Norman. *Jonathan Edwards' Moral Thought and Its British Context*. Chapel Hill, NC: University of North Carolina, 1981.

———. "The Rationalist Foundations of Jonathan Edwards's Metaphysics." In *Jonathan Edwards and the American Experience*, edited by Nathan O. Hatch and Harry S. Stout. Oxford: Oxford University, 1988.

Flavel, John. *A Discourse of the Occasions, Causes, Nature, Rise, Growth, and Remedies of Mental Errors*. 1691. In *The Whole Works of the Reverend Mr. John Flavel*, vol. 1. Reprint, London: D. Midwinter, 1740.

———. *Husbandry Spiritualized*. 1669. In *The Whole Works of the Reverend Mr. John Flavel*, vol. 2. Reprint, London: D. Midwinter, 1740.

———. *Preparation for Suffering*. 1681. In *The Works of John Flavel*, vol. 6., Reprint, Edinburgh: Banner of Truth, 1968.

———. *Sacramental Meditations*. 1679. Reprint, Paisley, Scotland: A. Weir and A. M'Lean, 1770.

———. *The Touchstone of Sincerity: Or the Signs of Grace, and Symptoms of Hypocrisy*. 1679. In *The Whole Works of the Reverend Mr. John Flavel*, vol. 2. Reprint, London: D. Midwinter, 1740.

Fleming, Robert. *The Fulfilling of the Scripture*. London: Sprint, Ward, Ford, and Oswald, 1726.

Foster, Frank Hugh. *A Genetic History of the New England Theology*. Chicago: University of Chicago, 1907.

Frame, John M. *The Doctrine of the Knowledge of God*. Phillipsburg, NJ: Presbyterian and Reformed, 1987.

———. "Westminster Confession of Faith." In *Evangelical Dictionary of Theology*. Edited by Walter A. Elwell. 2nd ed. Grand Rapids: Baker, 2001.

Frost, R. N. "Puritanism." In *The Dictionary of Historical Theology*. Edited by Trevor A. Hart. Grand Rapids: Eerdmans, 2000.

Gale, Theophilus. *The Court of the Gentiles*. 1671. Reprint, Oxford: T. Gilbert, 1672.

Gallagher, Shaun. *Hermeneutics and Education*. Albany, NY: State University of New York, 1992.

German, James D. "The Political Economy of Depravity: The Irrelevance (and Relevance) of Jonathan Edwards." In *Jonathan Edwards at Home and Abroad: Historical Memories, Cultural Movements, Global Horizons*, edited by David W. Kling and Douglas A. Sweeney. Columbia, SC: University of South Carolina Press, 2003.

Gerstner, John H. *Jonathan Edwards: A Mini-Theology*. Reprint, Morgan, PA: Soli Deo Gloria, 1996.

———. *The Rational Biblical Theology of Jonathan Edwards*. 3 Vols. Powhatan, VA: Berea, 1993.

———. *Steps to Salvation: The Evangelistic Method of Jonathan Edwards*. Philadelphia: Westminster Press, 1960.

Gerstner, John H, and Jonathan Neil Gerstner. "Edwardsian Preparation for Salvation." *Westminster Theological Journal* 42, 1 (Fall 1979).

Gillespie, Thomas. "Letter to Jonathan Edwards, November 24, 1746." In *A Treatise Concerning Religious Affections*, edited by John E. Smith. The Works of Jonathan Edwards, vol. 2. New Haven: Yale, 1959.

———. "Letter to Jonathan Edwards, September 19, 1748." In *A Treatise Concerning Religious Affections*, edited by John E. Smith. The Works of Jonathan Edwards, vol. 2. New Haven: Yale, 1959.

Goen, C. C. "Editor's Introduction." In *The Great Awakening*, edited by C. C. Goen. The Works of Jonathan Edwards, vol. 4. New Haven: Yale, 1970.

———. *Revival and Separatism in New England, 1740–1800: Strict Congregationalists and Separatist Baptists in the Great Awakening*. New Haven: Yale, 1962.

Grenz, Stanley J. "Articulating the Christian Belief-Mosaic: Theological Method After the Demise of Foundationalism." In *Evangelical Futures: A Conversation on Theological Method*, edited by John G. Stackhouse. Grand Rapids: Baker, 2000.

Grenz, Stanley J., and John R. Franke. *Beyond Foundationalism: Shaping Theology in a Postmodern Context*. Louisville: Westminster John Knox, 2001.

Griffin, Edward M. *Old Brick: Charles Chauncy of Boston, 1705–1787*. Minneapolis: University of Minnesota, 1980.

Grudem, Wayne. *Systematic Theology*. Grand Rapids: Zondervan, 1994.

Guelzo, Allen C. "Review of *Jonathan Edwards: A New Biography* by Iain H. Murray." *Fides et Historia* 21 (June 1989): 81–83.

——. "Unpalatable to Modern Sensibilities." *Books and Culture* September–October 2005. Accessed November 28, 2011. http://www.booksandculture.com/articles/2005/sepoct/7.16.html.

Gura, Philip F. *Jonathan Edwards: America's Evangelical*. New York: Hill and Wang, 2005.

——. "Lost and Found: Recovering Edwards for American Literature." In *Jonathan Edwards at 300: Essays on the Tercentenary of His Birth*, edited by Harry S. Stout, Kenneth P. Minkema and Caleb D. J. Maskell. Lanham, MD: University Press of America, 2005.

Hall, Michael G. *The Last American Puritan: The Life of Increase Mather, 1639–1723*. Hanover, NH: Wesleyan University, 1988.

Hall, Richard A. S. "Did Berkeley Influence Edwards? The Common Critique of the Moral Sense Theory." In *Jonathan Edwards's Writings: Text, Context, Interpretation*, edited by Stephen J. Stein. Bloomington, IN: Indiana University, 1996.

Haller, William. *The Rise of Puritanism*. New York: Harper, 1938.

Hambrick-Stowe, Charles. "All Things Were New and Astonishing: Edwardsian Piety, the New Divinity, and Race." In *Jona-*

than Edwards at Home and Abroad: Historical Memories, Cultural Movements, Global Horizons, edited by David W. Kling and Douglas A. Sweeney. Columbia, SC: University of South Carolina Press, 2003.

——. "Review of John H. Gerstner *The Rational Biblical Theology of Jonathan Edwards, Volume 1.*" *Fides et Historia* 25, 2 (Summer 1993): 132–34.

——. "The 'Inward, Sweet Sense' of Christ in Jonathan Edwards." In *The Legacy of Jonathan Edwards*, edited by Sean Michael Lucas D. G. Hart, and Stephen J. Nichols. Grand Rapids: Baker, 2003.

Hansen, Collin. *Young, Reformed, and Restless.* Wheaton, IL: Crossway, 2008.

Hardman, Keith J. *Seasons of Refreshing: Evangelism and Revivals in America.* Grand Rapids: Baker, 1994.

Harris, Harriet A. *Evangelicalism and Fundamentalism.* Reprint, Oxford: Oxford University, 2008.

Harrison, Douglas. "Toward a Theology of Experience: Belief and Incapacity in Edwards, Emerson, and William James." Ph. D. diss., Washington University, 2005.

Hart, D. G. "Jonathan Edwards and the Origins of Experimental Calvinism." In *The Legacy of Jonathan Edwards*, edited by Sean Michael Lucas D. G. Hart, and Stephen J. Nichols. Grand Rapids: Baker, 2003.

Haskell, Thomas L. *Objectivity is Not Neutrality.* Baltimore: Johns Hopkins, 1998.

Hawkes, R. M. "The Logic of Assurance in English Puritan Theology." *Westminster Theological Journal* 52, 2 (Fall 1990): 247–61.

Haykin, Michael A. G. "Evangelicalism and the Enlightenment: A Reassessment." In *The Advent of Evangelicalism*, edited by Michael A. G. Haykin and Kenneth J. Stewart. Downers Grove, IL: InterVarsity, 2008.

——. *Jonathan Edwards: The Holy Spirit in Revival.* Darlington, England: Evangelical Press, 2005.

Heal, Felicity. *Reformation in Britain and Ireland.* Oxford: Oxford University Press, 2003.

Hedges, Paul. *Controversies in Interreligious Dialogue and the Theology of Religions.* London: SCM, 2010.

Helm, Paul. "A Forensic Dilemma: John Locke and Jonathan Edwards on Personal Identity." In *Jonathan Edwards: Philosophical Theologian*, edited by Paul Helm and Oliver D. Crisp. Burlington, VT: Ashgate, 2003.

——. "The Great Christian Doctrine." In *A God Entranced Vision of All Things: The Legacy of Jonathan Edwards*, edited by John Piper and Justin Taylor, 175–200. Wheaton, IL: Crossway, 2004.

——. "John Locke and Jonathan Edwards: A Reconsideration." *Journal of History and Philosophy* 7 (1969): 51–61.

——. *The Varieties of Belief.* Reprint, London: Routledge, 2002.

Helm, Paul, and Oliver D. Crisp. "Introduction." In *Jonathan Edwards: Philosophical Theologian*, edited by Paul Helm and Oliver D. Crisp. Burlington, VT: Ashgate, 2003.

Helseth, Paul Kjoss. *Right Reason and the Princeton Mind: An Unorthodox Proposal.* Phillipsburg, NJ: P&R Publishing, 2010.

Hemmings, G. A. "The Puritans' Dealings with Troubled Souls." In *Puritan Papers*. Edited by J. I. Packer. Vol. 1, *1956–1959*. Phillipsburg, NJ: P&R Publishing, 2000.

Henry, Matthew. *An Exposition of the Old and New Testaments.* 3 vols. Reprint, New York: H. C. Sleight, 1833.

Hill, Christopher. *Society and Puritanism in Pre-Revolutionary England.* London: Panther, 1964.

Hindson, Edward. *Introduction to Puritan Theology: A Reader.* Grand Rapids: Baker Book House, 1976.

Holdcroft, David. *Saussure: Signs, Systems, and Arbitrariness.* Cambridge: Cambridge University, 1991.

Holifield, E. Brooks. "Edwards as Theologian." In *The Cambridge Companion to Jonathan Edwards*, edited by Stephen J. Stein. New York: Cambridge University, 2007.

——. *Theology in America*. New Haven: Yale, 2003.

Hollister, G. H. *The History of Connecticut, From the First Settlements of the Colony to the Adoption of the Present Constitution*. New Haven: Durrie and Peck, 1855.

Holmes, Stephen R. "Does Jonathan Edwards Use a Dispositional Ontology? A Response to Sang Hyun Lee." In *Jonathan Edwards: Philosophical Theologian*, edited by Paul Helm and Oliver D. Crisp. Burlington, VT: Ashgate, 2003.

——. *God of Grace and God of Glory: An Account of the Theology of Jonathan Edwards*. Grand Rapids: Eerdmans, 2000.

Hooker, Thomas. *The Soules Implantation*. London, 1637.

——. *The Soules Preparation*. London, 1632.

Hunt, Arthur W. III. *The Vanishing Word: The Veneration of Visual Imagery in the Postmodern World*. Wheaton, IL: Crossway, 2003.

Hutcheson, Francis. *An Essay on the Nature and Conduct of the Passions and Affections, with Illustrations on the Moral Sense*. 1728. Edited by Aaron Garrett. Natural Law and Enlightenment Classics. Reprint, Indianapolis: Liberty Fund, 2002.

Innes, Stephen. *Creating the Commonwealth: The Economic Culture of Puritan New England*. New York: Norton, 1995.

Jensen, R. W. *America's Theologian: A Recommendation of Jonathan Edwards*. Oxford: Oxford University, 1988.

——. "The End is Music." In *Edwards in Our Time: Jonathan Edwards and the Shaping of American Religion*, edited by Sang Hyun Lee and Allen C. Guelzo. Grand Rapids: Eerdmans, 1999.

Jinkins, Michael. "'The Being of Beings': Jonathan Edwards's Understanding of God as Reflected in His Final Treatises." *Scottish Journal of Theology* 46, 2:161–90.

Jones, Jeremiah. *A New and Full Method of Settling the Canonical Authority of the New Testament.* 1726. Reprint, Oxford: Clarendon Press, 1827.

Kantzer, Kenneth S. "A Systematic Biblical Dogmatics: What is It and How is It to Be Done?" In *Doing Theology in Today's World*, edited by John D. Woodbridge and Thomas E. McComiskey. Grand Rapids: Zondervan, 1991.

Kilboi, John Michael. "The Assurance of Salvation in the Theology of John Calvin, Jonathan Edwards, and John Wesley: Toward a Cumulative Case Argument." M.A. thesis. University of St. Michael's College, 2005.

Kimnach, Wilson H. "General Introduction, Chapter IV: Literary Theory and Practice." In *Sermons and Discourses: 1720–1723*, edited by Wilson H. Kimnach. The Works of Jonathan Edwards, vol. 10. New Haven: Yale, 1992.

Klauber, Martin I. "Review of *Assurance of Faith* by Randall C. Zachman." *The Sixteenth Century Journal* 24, 4 (Winter 1993): 997–98.

Knight, Henry H., III. "The Relation of Love to Gratitude in the Theologies of Edwards and Wesley." *Evangelical Journal* 6 (Spring 1988): 3–12.

Knight, Janice. *Orthodoxies in Massachusetts.* Cambridge, MA: Harvard University, 1994.

——. "Typology." In *The Princeton Companion to Jonathan Edwards*, edited by Sang Hyun Lee. Princeton, NJ: Princeton University, 2005.

Kugel, James L., and Rowan A. Greer. *Early Biblical Interpretation.* Edited by Wayne A. Meeks. Library of Early Christianity. Louisville: Westminster John Knox, 1986.

Kuhn, Thomas S. *The Structure of Scientific Revolutions.* Chicago: University of Chicago, 1962.

Kuklick, Bruce. *Churchmen and Philosophers: From Jonathan Edwards to John Dewey.* New Haven: Yale, 1985.

——. "Jonathan Edwards and American Philosophy." In *Jonathan Edwards and the American Experience*, edited by Nathan O. Hatch and Harry S. Stout. Oxford: Oxford University, 1988.

Lamborn, James Spencer. "Blessed Assurance? Depraved Saints, Philosophers, and the Problem of Knowledge for Self and State in New England, 1630–1820." Ph. D. diss., Miami University, 2002.

Lee, Sang Hyun. "Does History Matter to God? Jonathan Edwards's Dynamic Re-Conception of God's Relation to the World." In *Jonathan Edwards at 300: Essays on the Tercentenary of His Birth*, edited by Harry S. Stout, Kenneth P. Minkema and Caleb D. J. Maskell. Lanham, MD: University Press of America, 2005.

——. *Edwards in Our Time*. Grand Rapids: Eerdmans, 1999.

——. "Edwards on God and Nature: Resources for Contemporary Theology." In *Edwards in Our Time*, edited by Sang Hyun Lee and Allen C. Guelzo. Grand Rapids: Eerdmans, 1999.

——. "Faith." In *Writings on the Trinity, Grace, and Faith*, edited by Sang Hyun Lee. The Works of Jonathan Edwards, vol. 21. New Haven: Yale, 2002.

——. *The Philosophical Theology of Jonathan Edwards*. Princeton, NJ: Princeton University, 1988.

Lesser, M. X. "Appendix B: Dated Sermons, January 1734–December 1738." In *Sermons and Discourses: 1734–1738*, edited by M. X. Lesser. The Works of Jonathan Edwards, vol. 19. New Haven: Yale, 2001.

——. *Reading Jonathan Edwards: An Annotated Bibliography in Three Parts, 1729–2005*. Grand Rapids: Eerdmans, 2008.

Levy, Babette May. *Preaching in the First Half Century of New England History*. Edited by Matthew Spinka and Robert Hastings Nichols. Studies in Church History, vol. 6. Hartford, CT: American Society of Church History, 1945.

Lewis, Gordon R., and Bruce A. Demarest. *Integrative Theology*. Grand Rapids: Zondervan, 1996.

Lindbeck, George A. *The Nature of Doctrine: Religion and Theology in a Postliberal Age*. Philadelphia: Westminster, 1984.

Lints, Richard. *The Fabric of Theology: A Prolegomenon to Evangelical Theology*. Grand Rapids: Eerdmans, 1993.

Locke, John. *An Essay Concerning Human Understanding*. 1689. Edited by J. A. St. John. The Works of John Locke, vol. 2. Reprint, London: George Bell and Sons, 1877.

———. *An Essay Concerning Human Understanding*. 1689. Edited by Kenneth P. Winkler. Reprint, Indianapolis: Hackett, 1996.

———. *A Letter Concerning Toleration*. 1689. Edited by James H. Tully. Reprint, Indianapolis: Hackett, 1983.

———. *The Works of John Locke*. Vol. 6, *The Reasonableness of Christianity*. 1695. Reprint, London: Rivington, 1824.

Loughridge, Adam. "Westminster Assembly." In *The New International Dictionary of the Christian Church*, edited by J. D. Douglas. Rev. ed. Grand Rapids: Zondervan, 1978.

Lovelace, Richard F. "Review of *The American Pietism of Cotton Mather*." *Grace Theological Journal* 2, 2 (Fall 1981).

Lowance, Mason I. "Review of *The Heart Renewed: Assurance of Salvation in New England Spiritual Life* by Norman Pettit." *The New England Quarterly* 78, 3 (September 2005): 491–93.

Lowery, Kevin Twain. "Constructing a More Cognitivist Account of Wesleyan Ethics." Ph. D. diss., University of Notre Dame, 2004.

Lucas, Sean Michael. "Jonathan Edwards Between Church and Academy: A Bibliographic Essay." In *The Legacy of Jonathan Edwards*, edited by Sean Michael Lucas, D. G. Hart, and Stephen J. Nichols, 228–47. Grand Rapids: Baker, 2003.

Luther, Martin. *Ominum Operum*. Wittenberg: T. Klug, 1558.

MacArthur, John F. *The Gospel According to Jesus*. Grand Rapids: Zondervan, 1988.

Madikon, Michael D. "The Marrow Controversy." *Journal of the Grace Evangelical Society* Autumn 2003: 65–77.

Malefyt, Calvin Sterling. "The Changing Concept of Pneumatology in New England Trinitarianism, 1635–1755." Ph. D. diss., Harvard University, 1966.

Manspeaker, Nancy. *Jonathan Edwards: Bibliographical Synopses.* Lewiston, NY: Edwin Mellen, 1981.

Marsden, George M. "Challenging the Presumptions of the Age: The Two Dissertations." In *The Legacy of Jonathan Edwards,* edited by Sean Michael Lucas D. G. Hart, and Stephen J. Nichols, 99–113. Grand Rapids: Baker Book House, 2003.

———. "Jonathan Edwards in the Twenty-First Century." In *Jonathan Edwards at 300: Essays on the Tercentenary of His Birth*, edited by Harry S. Stout, Kenneth P. Minkema and Caleb D. J. Maskell. Lanham, MD: University Press of America, 2005.

———. *Jonathan Edwards: A Life.* New Haven: Yale, 2003.

———. *The Outrageous Idea of Christian Scholarship.* New York: Oxford University, 1997.

———. "The Quest for the Historical Edwards: The Challenge of Biography." In *Jonathan Edwards at Home and Abroad: Historical Memories, Cultural Movements, Global Horizons*, edited by David W. Kling and Douglas A. Sweeney. Columbia, SC: University of South Carolina, 2003.

Martin, Robert P. *A Guide to the Puritans.* Edinburgh: Banner of Truth, 1997.

Mather, Cotton. *Magnalia Christi Americana.* 1702. Reprint, Edinburgh: Banner of Truth, 1979.

McCann, Hugh J. "Edwards on Free Will." In *Jonathan Edwards: Philosophical Theologian*, edited by Paul Helm and Oliver D. Crisp. Burlington, VT: Ashgate, 2003.

McClymond, Michael J. *Encounters with God: An Approach to the Theology of Jonathan Edwards.* New York: Oxford University, 1998.

———. "Review of *Jonathan Edwards's Philosophy of History*." *The Journal of Religion* 85, 1 (2005): 121–23.

McClymond, Michael J., and Gerald R. McDermott. *The Theology of Jonathan Edwards*. Oxford: Oxford University, 2012.

McDermott, Gerald R. "The Deist Connection: Jonathan Edwards and Islam." In *Jonathan Edwards's Writings: Text, Context, Interpretation*, edited by Stephen J. Stein. Bloomington, IN: Indiana University, 1996.

——. "Jonathan Edwards and the National Covenant: Was He Right?" In *The Legacy of Jonathan Edwards*, edited by Sean Michael Lucas D. G. Hart, and Stephen J. Nichols, Grand Rapids: Baker, 2003.

——. *Jonathan Edwards Confronts the Gods: Christian Theology, Enlightenment Religion, and Non-Christian Faiths*. Oxford: Oxford University, 2000.

——. "The Possibility of Reconciliation: Jonathan Edwards and the Salvation of Non-Christians." In *Edwards in Our Time*, edited by Sang Hyun Lee and Allen C. Guelzo. Grand Rapids: Eerdmans, 1999.

McGinley, Phyllis. "The Theology of Jonathan Edwards." In *Times Three*. New York: Viking, 1961.

McGrath, Allister E. *Christianity's Dangerous Idea*. New York: Harper Collins, 2007.

——. *Studies in Doctrine*. Grand Rapids: Zondervan, 1997.

Miller, Perry. *Errand Into the Wilderness*. New York: Harper and Row, 1956.

——. *Jonathan Edwards*. New York: William Sloan, 1949.

——. *The New England Mind: From Colony to Province*. Boston: Beacon, 1953.

——. *The New England Mind: The Seventeenth Century*. Cambridge: Harvard University, 1939.

Min, Anselm Kyongsuk. *Dialectic of Salvation: Issues in Theology of Liberation*. Albany, NY: State University of New York, 1989.

Minkema, Kenneth P. "A Chronology of Edwards' Life and Writings." The Jonathan Edwards Center. Accessed April 5, 2016. http://edwards.yale.edu/research/ chronology.

——. "Jonathan Edwards in the Twentieth Century." *Journal of the Evangelical Theological Society* 47, 4 (December 2004): 659–87.

——. "Jonathan Edwards's Defense of Slavery." *The Massachusetts Historical Review* 4 (2002). The Massachusetts Historical Society. Accessed August 3, 2006. http://www.historycooperative.org/ journals/mhr/4/minkema.html.

——. "The Other Unfinished 'Great Work': Jonathan Edwards, Messianic Prophecy, and "The Harmony of the Old and New Testament"." In *Jonathan Edwards's Writings: Text, Context, Interpretation*, edited by Stephen J. Stein. Bloomington, IN: Indiana University, 1996.

Mitchell, Alex F., and John Struthers, eds. *Minutes of the Sessions of the Westminster Assembly of Divines.* London: Blackwood and Sons, 1874.

Morgan, Christopher William. "The Application of Jonathan Edwards's Theological Method to Annihilationism in Contemporary Evangelicalism." Ph. D. diss., Mid-America Baptist Theological Seminary, 1999.

——. *Jonathan Edwards and the Doctrine of Hell.* Fearn, Scotland: Christian Focus, 2004.

Morgan, Edmund S. *The Puritan Dilemma.* Edited by Oscar Handlin. Boston: Little, Brown and Co., 1958.

——. *Visible Saints.* Ithaca, NY: Cornell, 1963.

Morison, Samuel Elliot. *The Founding of Harvard College.* Boston: Harvard University, 1935.

Morris, William S. "Review of *The Theology of Jonathan Edwards: A Reappraisal.*" *Church History* 36, 3 (September 1967): 332–33.

Mulholland, Kenneth B. "Moravians, Puritans, and the Modern Missionary Movement." *Bibliotheca Sacra* 156, 622 (April 1999): 221–32.

Murray, Iain H. *Jonathan Edwards: A New Biography.* Edinburgh: Banner of Truth, 1987.

Music, David M. "Jonathan Edwards and the Theology and Practice of Congregational Song in Puritan New England." In *Studies in American Puritan Spirituality*, edited by Michael Schuldiner. Vol. 8, *From Anne Bradstreet to Abraham Lincoln: Puritanism in America*, 103–33. Lewiston, NY: Mellen, 2004.

——. "Jonathan Edwards's Singing Lecture Sermon." In *Studies in American Puritan Spirituality*, edited by Michael Schuldiner. Vol. 8, *From Anne Bradstreet to Abraham Lincoln: Puritanism in America*, 135–46. Lewiston, NY: Mellen, 2004.

Naselli, Andrew David. "D. A. Carson's Theological Method." *Scottish Bulletin of Evangelical Theology* 29, 2 (Autumn 2011): 245–74.

Nash, Ronald H. *Christian Faith and Understanding*. Dallas: Probe Ministries, 1984.

Nichols, Stephen J. *An Absolute Sort of Certainty*. Phillipsburg, NJ: P&R Publishing, 2003.

——. *Jonathan Edwards: A Guided Tour of His Life and Thought*. Phillipsburg, NJ: P&R Publishing, 2001.

——. "Jonathan Edwards: His Life and Legacy." In *A God Entranced Vision of All Things: The Legacy of Jonathan Edwards*, edited by John Piper and Justin Taylor. Wheaton, IL: Crossway, 2004.

——. "Last of the Mohican Missionaries." In *The Legacy of Jonathan Edwards*, edited by Sean Michael Lucas D. G. Hart, and Stephen J. Nichols. Grand Rapids: Baker, 2003.

——. "'An Absolute Sort of Certainty': The Holy Spirit and the Apologetics of Jonathan Edwards." Ph. D. diss., Westminster Theological Seminary, 2000.

Niebuhr, Richard H. "The Anachronism of Jonathan Edwards." *The Christian Century* 113, 15 (May 1 1996): 480–85.

Noble, Paul R. *The Canonical Approach: A Critical Reconstruction of the Hermeneutics of Brevard S. Childs*. New York: Brill, 1995.

Noll, Mark A. *America's God: From Jonathan Edwards to Abraham Lincoln*. Oxford: Oxford University, 2005.

———. "Edwards, Jonathan." In *The Blackwell Encyclopedia of Modern Christian Thought*, edited by Allister E. McGrath. Oxford: Blackwell, 1993.

———. "Jonathan Edwards and Nineteenth Century Theology." In *Jonathan Edwards and the American Experience*, edited by Nathan O. Hatch and Harry S. Stout. Oxford: Oxford University, 1988.

———. "Jonathan Edwards's Freedom of the Will Abroad." In *Jonathan Edwards at 300: Essays on the Tercentenary of His Birth*, edited by Harry S. Stout, Kenneth P. Minkema and Caleb D. J. Maskell. Lanham, MD: University Press of America, 2005.

———. *Old Religion in the New World*. Grand Rapids: Eerdmans, 2002.

———. "The Princeton Theology." In *Reformed Theology in America*, edited by David F. Wells. Grand Rapids: Baker, 1997.

———. *The Rise of Evangelicalism*. Downers Grove, IL: InterVarsity, 2003.

———. "Traditional Christianity and the Possibility of Historical Knowledge." *Christian Scholars Review* 19, 4 (June 1990): 388–406.

Oliphint, K. Scott. "Jonathan Edwards on Apologetics: Reason and the Noetic Effects of Sin." In *The Legacy of Jonathan Edwards*, edited by Sean Michael Lucas D. G. Hart, and Stephen J. Nichols. Grand Rapids: Baker, 2003.

———. "Jonathan Edwards: Reformed Apologist." *Westminster Theological Journal* 57, 1 (Spring 1995): 165–86.

Osborne, Grant R. *The Hermeneutical Spiral*. Rev. ed. Downers Grove, IL: InterVarsity Press, 2006.

Owen, John. *Pneumatologia: Or, A Discourse Concerning the Holy Spirit*. J. Darby, 1674.

Packer, James I. "The Glory of God and the Reviving of Religion: A Study in the Mind of Jonathan Edwards." In *A God Entranced Vision of All Things: The Legacy of Jonathan Edwards*, edited by John Piper and Justin Taylor. Wheaton, IL: Crossway, 2004.

——. "Jonathan Edwards and the Theology of Revival." In *The Puritan Papers: Volume Two, 1960–1962*, edited by J. I. Packer. Phillipsburg, NJ: P&R Publishing, 2001.

——. *A Quest For Godliness*. Wheaton, IL: Crossway, 1990.

Pauw, Amy Plantinga. "Edwards as American Theologian: Grand Narratives and Pastoral Narratives." In *Jonathan Edwards at 300: Essays on the Tercentenary of His Birth*, edited by Harry S. Stout, Kenneth P. Minkema and Caleb D. J. Maskell. Lanham, MD: University Press of America, 2005.

——. *The Supreme Harmony of All: The Trinitarian Theology of Jonathan Edwards*. Grand Rapids: Eerdmans, 2002.

——. "'One Alone Cannot Be Excellent': Edwards on Divine Simplicity." In *Jonathan Edwards: Philosophical Theologian*, edited by Paul Helm and Oliver D. Crisp. Burlington, VT: Ashgate, 2003.

Payne, Richard Karl. *Re-Visioning "Kamakura" Buddhism*. Honolulu: University of Hawaii, 1998.

Perkins, William. *A Treatise Tending unto a Declaration, Whether a Man Be in the Estate of Damnation, or in the Estate of Grace*. London: J. Porter and J. Legate, 1595.

Pettegrew, Larry D. *The New Covenant Ministry of the Holy Spirit*. 2nd ed. Grand Rapids: Kregel, 2001.

Pettit, Norman. *The Heart Prepared: Grace and Conversion in the Puritan Life*. New Haven: Yale, 1966.

Pilario, D. F. *Back to the Rough Grounds of Praxis*. Leuven, Belgium: Leuven University, 2005.

Piper, John. "A Divine and Supernatural Light Immediately Imparted to the Soul by the Spirit of God: An Edwardsean Sermon (2 Corinthians 3:18–4:7)." In *A God Entranced Vision of All Things: The Legacy of Jonathan Edwards*, edited by John Piper and Justin Taylor. Wheaton, IL: Crossway, 2004.

——. "A God Entranced Vision of All Things: Why We Need Jonathan Edwards 300 Years Later." In *A God Entranced Vision of All Things: The Legacy of Jonathan Edwards*, edited by John Piper and Justin Taylor. Wheaton, IL: Crossway, 2004.

——. *God's Passion for His Glory*. Wheaton, IL: Crossway, 1998.

——. *The Supremacy of God in Preaching*. Grand Rapids: Baker, 1990.

Plantinga, Alvin. *Warranted Christian Belief.* New York: Oxford University, 2000.

Plumstead, A. W. *The Wall and the Garden: Selected Massachusetts Election Sermons, 1670–1775*. Minneapolis: University of Minnesota, 1968.

Poole, Matthew. *Synopsis Criticorum Aliorumque Sacrae Scriptures Interpretum et Commentatorum*. 5 vols. 1669–76. Reprint, Frankfurt: J. P. Andreas, 1712.

Preston, John. "Discourses on Paul's Conversion," in *Remains of That Reverend and Learned Divine John Preston*. London: Andrew Crooke, 1634.

——. *The Golden Scepter Held Forth to the Humble. With the Churches Dignitie by her Marriage. And the Church's Duty in Her Carriage. In Three Treatises*. London: N. Bourne, A. Boler, and R. Harford, 1638.

——. *The New Covenant or Saints Portion*. London, 1630.

——. *The Onely Love of the Chief of Ten Thousand: Or, An Heavenly Treatise on the Divine Love of Christ*. John Stafford, 1640.

Proudfoot, Wayne. "Perception and Love in *Religions Affections*." In *Jonathan Edwards's Writings: Text, Context, Interpretation*, edited by Stephen J. Stein. Bloomington, IN: Indiana University, 1996.

Purvis, Thomas L. *Colonial America to 1763*. Edited by Richard Balkin. New York: Facts, 1999.

Ramsey, Paul. "Appendix IV: Infused Virtues in Edwardsean and Calvinistic Context." In *Ethical Writings*, edited by Paul Ramsey. The Works of Jonathan Edwards, vol. 8. New Haven: Yale, 1989.

Ray, Stephen K. *Upon This Rock: St. Peter and the Primacy of Rome in Scripture and the Early Church.* San Francisco: Ignatius, 1999.

Rutherford, Samuel. *A Survey of the Spirituall Antichrist.* London, 1648.

Ryken, Leland. *Worldly Saints.* Grand Rapids: Zondervan, 1986.

Sandeen, Ernest R. *The Roots of Fundamentalism: British and American Millenarianism, 1800–1930.* Chicago: University of Chicago, 1970.

Schafer, Thomas A. "Editor's Introduction." In *The "Miscellanies" a–500.* Edited by Thomas A. Schafer. The Works of Jonathan Edwards, vol. 13. New Haven: Yale, 1994.

Schaff, Phillip, ed. "The Westminster Confession of Faith." In *The Creeds of Christendom*, Vol. 3, *The Evangelical Protestant Creeds.* Reprint ed. Grand Rapids: Baker, 2007.

Shepard, Thomas. *God's Plot: Puritan Spirituality in Thomas Shepard's Cambridge.* Edited by Michael McGiffert. Rev. ed. Amherst, MA: University of Massachusetts, 1994.

———. *The Parable of the Ten Virgins.* 1659. Reprint, Orlando: Soli Deo Gloria, 1990.

———. *The Sincere Convert and The Sound Believer.* 1652, 1671 respectively. Reprint, Morgan, PA: Soli Deo Gloria, 1999.

Sibbes, Richard. *The Bruised Reed and Smoking Flax.* 1630. Reprint, Edinburgh: Banner of Truth, 1998.

Silva, Moisés. *Biblical Words and Their Meaning.* Rev. ed. Grand Rapids: Zondervan, 1994.

Simonson, Harold P. *Jonathan Edwards: Theologian of the Heart.* Grand Rapids: Eerdmans, 1974.

Simpson, Alan. *Puritanism in Old and New England.* Chicago: University of Chicago, 1955.

Sliwoski, Richard S. "Doctoral Dissertations on Jonathan Edwards." *Early American Literature* 14, 3 (Winter 1980): 318–27.

Smith, John. "A Discovery of the Shortness and Vanity of a Pharisaic Righteousness" In *Select Discourses*. 1660. Reprint, London: Rivington and Cochran, 1821.

Smith, John E. "Editor's Introduction." In *The Works of Jonathan Edwards*, edited by Perry Miller. Vol. 2, *Religious Affections*. New Haven: Yale, 1959.

———. "Introduction to Related Writings." In *The Works of Jonathan Edwards*, edited by Perry Miller. Vol. 2, *Religious Affections*. New Haven: Yale, 1959.

———. "The Perennial Jonathan Edwards." In *Edwards in Our Time*, edited by Sang Hyun Lee and Allen C. Guelzo. Grand Rapids: Eerdmans, 1999.

———. "Religious Affections and the 'Sense of the Heart'." In *The Princeton Companion to Jonathan Edwards*, edited by Sang Hyun Lee. Princeton, NJ: Princeton University, 2005.

Spickard, Paul R. and Kevin M. Cragg. *God's Peoples*. Grand Rapids: Baker, 1994.

Spohn, William C. "Chapter One: Jonathan Edwards and Sovereign Beauty." In *Markkula Center for Applied Ethics*. Santa Clara University. Accessed August 17, 2011. http://www.scu.edu/ethics/ publications/submitted/spohn/jonathanedwards.html.

Spurr, John. *English Puritanism*. London: Macmillan, 1998.

Stackhouse, John G. "Evangelical Theology Should Be Evangelical." In *Evangelical Futures: A Conversation on Theological Method*, edited by John G. Stackhouse. Grand Rapids: Baker, 2000.

Stallard, Michael. "A Proposal for Theological Method: Systematic Theology as Model Building." In *Our Hope*. Baptist Bible Seminary. Accessed November 29, 2011.

http://faculty.bbc.edu/mstallard/ biblical-studies/systematic-theology/methodology/ method-4.

Stein, Stephen J. "Eschatology." In *The Princeton Companion to Jonathan Edwards*, edited by Sang Hyun Lee. Princeton, NJ: Princeton University, 2005.

——. "Foreword." In *The Theology of Jonathan Edwards: A Reappraisal*. Bloomington, IN: Indiana University, 1990.

——. "Jonathan Edwards and the Rainbow: Biblical Exegesis and Poetic Imagination." *The New England Quarterly* 47, 3 (September 1974): 440–56.

——. "The Quest for Spiritual Sense: The Biblical Hermeneutics of Jonathan Edwards." *Harvard Theological Review* 70, 1 (January 1977): 99–113.

——. "Review of *Jonathan Edwards: A New Biography* by Iain H. Murray." *Church History* 59, 4 (December 1990): 564–65.

——. "Review of *One Holy and Happy Society: The Public Theology of Jonathan Edwards* by Gerald R. McDermott." *The William and Mary Quarterly* 51, 1 (January 1994): 143–45.

——. "The Spirit and the Word: Jonathan Edwards and Scriptural Exegesis." In *Jonathan Edwards and the American Experience*, edited by Nathan O. Hatch and Harry S. Stout. Oxford: Oxford University, 1988.

Stein, Stephen J., ed., *Jonathan Edwards's Writings: Text, Context, Interpretation*. Bloomington, IN: Indiana University, 1996.

Stein, Stephen J., and Brad Walton, eds. *Jonathan Edwards, Religious Affections, and the Puritan Analysis of True Piety, Spiritual Sensations, and Heart Religion*. Lewiston, NY: Edwin Mellen, 2002.

Stoddard, Solomon. *An Appeal to the Learned*. Samuel Phillips, 1709.

______. *A Guide to Christ: Or, The Way of Directing Souls that are Under the Work of Conviction*. J. Allen, 1714.

——. *The Nature of Saving Conversion*. 1719. Reprint, Grand Rapids: Reformation Heritage, 1999.

______. *A Treatise Concerning Conversion*. J. Franklin, 1719.

______. "The Way to Know Sincerity and Hypocrisy." In *A Treatise Concerning Conversion*. J. Franklin, 1719.

Stoever, William K. B. "The Godly Will's Discerning: Shepard, Edwards, and the Identification of True Godliness." In *Jonathan Edwards's Writings: Text, Context, Interpretation*, edited by Stephen J. Stein. Bloomington, IN: Indiana University, 1996.

——. *'A Faire and Easie Way to Heaven': Covenant Theology and Antinomianism in Early Massachusetts*. Middleton, CT: Wesleyan University, 1978.

Storms, C. Samuel. "Open Theism in the Hands of an Angry Puritan: Jonathan Edwards on Divine Foreknowledge." In *The Legacy of Jonathan Edwards*, edited by Sean Michael Lucas D. G. Hart, and Stephen J. Nichols. Grand Rapids: Baker, 2003.

——. "The Will: Fettered Yet Free." In *A God Entranced Vision of All Things: The Legacy of Jonathan Edwards*, edited by John Piper and Justin Taylor. Wheaton, IL: Crossway, 2004.

Stout, Harry S. "Jonathan Edwards' Tri-World Vision." In *The Legacy of Jonathan Edwards*, edited by Sean Michael Lucas D. G. Hart, and Stephen J. Nichols. Grand Rapids: Baker, 2003.

——. "The Puritans and Edwards." In *Jonathan Edwards and the American Experience*, edited by Nathan O. Hatch and Harry S. Stout. Oxford: Oxford University, 1988.

Studebaker, Steven M. *The Trinitarian Vision of Jonathan Edwards and David Coffey*. Amherst, NY: Cambria, 2011.

Studebaker, Steven M., and Robert W. Caldwell III. *The Trinitarian Theology of Jonathan Edwards: Text, Context, and Application*. Burlington, VT: Ashgate, 2012.

Sweeney, Douglas A. *The American Evangelical Story*. Grand Rapids: Baker Book House, 2005.

——. *Edwards the Exegete: Biblical Interpretation and Anglo-Protestant Culture on the Edge of the Enlightenment.* New York: Oxford University, 2016.

——. *Jonathan Edwards and the Ministry of the Word.* Downers Grove, IL: InterVarsity Press, 2009.

——. "Jonathan Edwards, the Harmony of Scripture, and Canonical Exegesis." *Trinity Journal* 34 (2013): 171–207.

——. "Longing for More and More of It? The Strange Career of Jonathan Edwards's Exegetical Exertions." In *Jonathan Edwards at 300: Essays on the Tercentenary of His Birth*, edited by Harry S. Stout, Kenneth P. Minkema, and Caleb D. J. Maskell. Lanham, MD: University Press of America, 2005.

——. *Nathaniel Taylor, New Haven Theology, and the Legacy of Jonathan Edwards.* Oxford: Oxford University, 2002.

——. "Sweeney's Booknotes: Jonathan Edwards's Vision of Reality." *JEC Blog* January 11, 2012. Jonathan Edwards Center at TEDS. Accessed March 28, 2012. http://jecteds.org/blog/2012/01/11/sweeneys-booknotes-jonathan-edwardss-vision-of-reality/

Sweeney, Douglas A., and Brandon G. Winthrow. "Jonathan Edwards: Continuator or Pioneer of Evangelical History?" In *The Advent of Evangelicalism*, edited by Michael A. G. Haykin and Kenneth J. Stewart. Downers Grove, IL: InterVarsity, 2008.

Talbot, Mark R. "Godly Emotions." In *A God Entranced Vision of All Things: The Legacy of Jonathan Edwards*, edited by John Piper and Justin Taylor. Wheaton, IL: Crossway, 2004.

Taves, Ann. *Fits, Trances, and Visions: Experiencing Religion and Explaining Experience from Wesley to James.* Princeton, NJ: Princeton University, 1999.

Thornbury, Gregory Alan. "Prolegomena: Introduction to the Task of Theology." In *A Theology for the Church*, edited by Daniel L. Akin. Nashville: Broadman and Holman, 2007.

Todd, Margo. "The Problem of Scotland's Puritans." In *The Cambridge Companion to Puritanism*, edited by John Coffey and Paul C. H. Lim. Cambridge: Cambridge University, 2008.

Tracy, David. "An Uneasy Alliance Reconceived: Catholic Theological Method, Modernity, and Postmodernity." *Theological Studies* 50, 3 (September 1989): 548–70.

Tracy, Patricia J. *Jonathan Edwards, Pastor.* Hill and Wang, 1980.

Treier, Daniel J. *Introducing Theological Interpretation of Scripture: Recovering Christian Practice.* Grand Rapids: Baker, 2008.

Turretin, Francis. *Institutes of Elenctic Theology.* 1679–85. Edited by James T. Dennison, Jr. Translated by George Musgrave Giger. 3 vols. Reprint, Phillipsburg, NJ: Presbyterian and Reformed, 1997.

Trueman, Carl R. *Histories and Fallacies: The Problems Faced in the Writing of History.* Wheaton, IL: Crossway, 2010.

Valeri, Mark. "Jonathan Edwards in Modernity: A Review Essay." 2003. Institute for Reformed Theology. Accessed October 14, 2011. http://reformedtheology.org/SiteFiles/ SpringSummer2003/ Essay _ JEModernity.html.

——. "Preface to the Period." In *Sermons and Discourses: 1730–1733*, edited by Mark Valeri. The Works of Jonathan Edwards, vol. 17. New Haven: Yale, 1999.

Van de Craen, Piet. "Hermeneutics." In *Philosophical Perspectives for Pragmatics*, edited by Marina Sbisá, Jan-Ola Östman, and Jef Verschueren. Philadelphia: John Benjamins, 2011.

Van Mastricht, Petrus. *Theoretica-Practica Theologia.* Utrecht: Thomas Appels, 1699.

Vanhoozer, Kevin J. *The Drama of Doctrine: A Canonical-Linguistic Approach to Christian Theology.* Louisville: Westminster John Knox, 2005.

——. *First Theology.* Downers Grove, IL: InterVarsity, 2002.

Vincent, Nathaniel. "The Conversion of a Sinner." In *The Puritans on Conversion*. Edited by Don Kistler. Ligonier, PA: Soli Deo Gloria, 1990.

Vogt, Philip. *John Locke and the Rhetoric of Modernity*. Lanham, MD: Lexington, 2008.

von Rohr, John. "Covenant and Assurance in Early English Puritanism." *Church History* 34, 2 (June 1965): 195–203.

Wainwright, William J. "Jonathan Edwards." In *Stanford Encyclopedia of Religion*, edited by Edward N. Zalta. August 2009. Metaphysics Research Lab, Center for the Study of Languages and Information, Stanford University. Accessed October 26, 2011. http://plato.stanford.edu/archives/fall2009/entries/edwards.

———. "Jonathan Edwards and the Doctrine of Hell." In *Jonathan Edwards: Philosophical Theologian*, edited by Paul Helm and Oliver D. Crisp. Burlington, VT: Ashgate, 2003.

Walton, Brad. *Jonathan Edwards, Religious Affections, and the Puritan Analysis of True Piety, Spiritual Sensations, and Heart Religion*. Lewiston, NY: Edwin Mellen, 2002.

Ward, Wayne E. "New Testament Theology: Retrospect and Prospect." *Review and Expositor* 78, 2 (Spring 1981): 153–67.

Warfield, Benjamin Breckinridge. *The Printing of the Westminster Confession*. Philadelphia: MacCalla & Co., 1901.

Weber, Donald. "The Recovery of Jonathan Edwards." In *Jonathan Edwards and the American Experience*, edited by Nathan O. Hatch and Harry S. Stout. Oxford: Oxford University, 1988.

Weber, Timothy P. "The Two-Edged Sword: The Fundamentalist Use of the Bible." In *The Bible in America: Essays in Cultural History*, edited by Nathan O. Hatch and Mark A. Noll. New York: Oxford University, 1982.

Wells, David F. *Reformed Theology in America*. Grand Rapids: Baker, 1997.

Wesley, John. *The Works of the Rev. John Wesley*. Vol. 14. London: Wesleyan Conference, 1872.

Wheeler, Rachel. "Lessons From Stockbridge: Jonathan Edwards and the Stockbridge Indians." In *Jonathan Edwards at 300: Essays on the Tercentenary of His Birth*, edited by Harry S. Stout, Kenneth P. Minkema and Caleb D. J. Maskell. Lanham, MD: University Press of America, 2005.

Whittemore, Robert Clifton. "Jonathan Edwards." In *Makers of the American Mind*. New York: William Morrow, 1964.

Williams, Garry J. "Enlightenment Epistemology and Eighteenth-Century Evangelical Doctrines of Assurance." In *The Advent of Evangelicalism*, edited by Michael A. G. Haykin and Kenneth J. Stewart. Downers Grove, IL: InterVarsity, 2008.

Williamson, Clark M. "The Human Question." In *Essentials of Christian Theology*, edited by William C. Placher. Louisville: Westminster John Knox, 2003.

Wilson, John F. "Review of *Jonathan Edwards's Moral Thought and Its British Context* by John F. Wilson." *Review in American History* 11, 2 (June 29 1983): 190–94.

Winiarski, Douglas L. "Jonathan Edwards, Enthusiast? Radical Revivalism and the Great Awakening in the Connecticut Valley." *Church History* 74, 4 (December 2005): 683–739.

——. "Seeking Synthesis in Edwards Scholarship." *The William and Mary Quarterly* 61, 1 (January 2004): 135–51.

Winslow, Ola. *Jonathan Edwards, 1703–1758*. New York: Octagon Books, 1940.

——. *Jonathan Edwards: Basic Writings*. New York: Meridian, 1966.

——. *Meetinghouse Hill, 1630–1783*. New York: Norton, 1972.

Winthrop, John. "A Modell of Christian Charity." In *The Literatures of Colonial America: An Anthology*. Edited by Susan P. Castillo and Ivy Schweitzer. Oxford: Blackwell, 2001.

Witherington, Ben. *The Problem with Evangelical Theology: Testing the Exegetical Foundations of Calvinism, Dispensationalism, and Wesleyanism*. Waco, TX: Baylor University, 2005.

Woolhouse, R. S. *Locke: A Biography*. Cambridge: Cambridge University, 2007.

Wright, N. T. *The New Testament and the People of God*. Christian Origins and the People of God, vol. 1. Minneapolis: Fortress, 1992.

Yarbrough, Stephen R., and John C. Adams. *Delightful Conviction: Jonathan Edwards and the Rhetoric of Conversion*. Westport, CT: Greenwood, 1993.

Zachman, Randall C. *The Assurance of Faith: Conscience in the Theology of Martin Luther and John Calvin*. Minneapolis: Fortress, 1993.

Zakai, Avihu. "The Age of Enlightenment." In *The Cambridge Companion to Jonathan Edwards*, edited by Stephen J. Stein. Cambridge: Cambridge University, 2007.

———. *Jonathan Edwards's Philosophy of History: The Reenchantment of the World in the Age of Enlightenment*. Princeton, NJ: Princeton University, 2009.

Index of Scripture

Genesis
15:12–13—212n59
20:6–7—196n18, 235
31:24—196n18, 235

Exodus
2:23—212n59

Leviticus
13:45—212n59

Deuteronomy
6:4–5—96
8:2—212n59
8:16—212n59
10:12—96
30:6—97
32:36–37—212n59

1 Samuel
2:2—214n67
16:7—203n39

2 Samuel
23:5—188

1 Kings
18—173
19—212n59

2 Kings
20:3—212n61

Job
19:25—212n61

Psalms
1—255n82
19—255n82
19:7–10—214n67
24:6—219n81
34:11—204n40
65:3—248
69:6—219n81
69:32—219n81
74:4—219n81
76:2—212n59
97:12—214n67
98:1—214n67
99:2–9—214n67
105:15—196n18, 235
116—251
119—204n40, 214n67
119:18—166, 199n29
119:127—214n67

Proverbs
20:27—199

Song of Solomon
8:6—238
9:6—238

Isaiah
6:3—214n67

11:3—203n39
11:6–9—205n43
32—212n59
33:6—219n81
43:22—206n45, 248
52:1—161
55—253n71
64:6—248
65:25—205n43

Jeremiah
3—168n27
3:10—204n40
3:23–25—212n59
4:3–4—204n40
22:15–16—204n40

Ezekiel
9:4—238

Daniel
10—212n59

Malachi
1:13—248

Matthew
7:21–23—154, 253n72
8:24–26—212n59
13—173
13:1–29—253n72
13:36–43—253n72
15:22—212n59
24:10–13—205n42
25:12—152n46

Mark
9:24—207, 253n69

Luke
1:53—219n81
6:44—202n37
8:43–44—212n59
15—212n59
24:32—199n29
24:49—198n24

John
4:14—198n24
4:32—214n67
4:34—214n67, 219n81
5:24—253n67, 253n70, 253n71
5:35—204n42
5:36—237
6:40—203n39
7:37–39—198n24
8:21—253n70
10:35—237
12:44—253n67
12:48—253n70
14–16—198n24, 212n62
14:21—208n49
14:24—253n70
15:11—212n62
16:13—212n62
16:33—212n62
17:17—255n82
20:31—253n67

Acts
1:4—198n24
2:38–39—198n24
2:39—253n71
14:3—237
16:31—253n67

Romans
1:5—253n72
1:9—204n40
2:7—206n45, 248
6—254n79
7—254n79

8—236, 252
8:5—254n76
8:9—253n73, 253n74
8:12—254n76
8:13—253n75, 254n79
8:14—254n76
8:14–16—168
8:15—254n77
8:15–16—19
8:15–17—168
8:16—20, 199, 199n27, 254
8:20—168n27
8:22–23—197n22
10—253n67
10:5–13—253n71
12:11—96
16:26—253n72

1 Corinthians
2:12—253n68
2:13–14—167
2:14—114, 178
9:26—217n76
12—255n84
13—152n46
13:2—196n18, 236

2 Corinthians
1:8–10—212n59
1:12—199n27, 204n40
1:18–20—253n71
1:22—162, 236, 238
3:18—254n80
4:3–4—117n64
4:13—204n40
4:16–17—254n80
5:7—204n40
5:14—204n40
6:4–7—204n40
7:1—253n71

Galatians
2:20—204n40, 212n62
3:1—205n42
3:14—198n24
4:11—205n42
4:15—205n42
5:16–17—254n79
5:24—254n79
6:9—206n45, 248

Ephesians
1:13—198n24, 236
1:13–14—238
1:18–19—177
3:16–19—253n68
4:7–16—255n84
4:13—236, 254n80
5:26—255n82
6:18—255n83
6:24—177

Philippians
1:21—212n62
2:21—205n42
3:7–8—204n40
3:18–19—205n42
4:6–7—255n83

Colossians
3:5—254n79
3:10—254n80

1 Thessalonians
2:2—204n40
2:8–10—204n40

1 Timothy
1:17—40
6:6—219n81

2 Timothy
1:8—212n62
1:12—212n62
4:6–7—204n40

Titus
1:2—253n71
2:12—253n72
3:3—205n43

Hebrews
2:4—237
4:12–13—255n82
5:9—253n72
6:12—253n71
6:17–18—188, 213
6:17–19—253n71
6:18—212n59
9:9—189, 213
10:36—206n45, 248
11—106, 253n67
12:4–17—253n72

James
1:15—178
1:23–25—255n82
2—253n72
3:15—178
3:17—178

1 Peter
1:2—253n72
1:8—89, 98, 177

2 Peter
1—252, 255n81
1:3–4—254n80
1:4—254n78
1:5–8—213
1:5–11—127, 127n80, 217n76, 254n81, 264–65
1:9–11—253n69
1:10—253n68

1 John
1:8–10—254n79
2:25—253n71
3:16–20—254n81
3:18–20—253n69
3:19—199n27
4:13—253n68
4:18—199
5:3—204n40
5:8—238
5:13—253n68, 253n69

2 John
6—204n40

Revelation
1—212n59
3:8—253n70
4:8—214n67
7:3—238
15:4—214n67
2:17—236, 237
21:1—198n24
21:6—198n24
21:17—198n24

Index of Subjects and Names

Abraham, William J., xxviii
Adams, John C., 43, 319
affections, xxii–xxiii, xxvi, 24–25, 37, 47, 89–98, 101–2, 104, 112–14, 118, 122, 124–28, 130, 155, 159, 161–62, 169–70, 174, 182, 201–2, 207, 209, 211, 214–15, 218–19, 239–40, 242, 261, 267, 269–71, 273–74, 276
Ahlstrom, Sydney E., 44, 283
Albro, J. A., 266, 283
Allen, R. Michael, 10, 228–29, 231, 234
Allison, Greg R., 10, 283
Ames, William, 141, 143–44, 153, 156–57, 266, 275–76, 283
anachronism, x, 50, 52, 54–55, 75, 82, 83–85, 261, 307
Anderson, Wallace E., 87
Ankersmit, F. R., 73, 283
anti-intellectualism, 20, 226, 233
antinomianism, 11–12, 28, 149–50, 285, 314
Archer, Kenneth J., 225
Arkin, Marc M., 74
assurance
  and the evidence of sanctification, 7, 18, 21–24, 48, 150, 154, 182, 196, 202–4, 206–11, 213–14, 216–19, 253–56, 259, 263–64
  and the problem of doubt, 11, 21, 23, 38, 91, 155, 188, 192–95, 198, 211, 213, 252, 259, 263
  and the testimony of the Holy Spirit, 21–22, 197, 253, 259
  ground of, 18, 22, 182, 188, 203, 209, 214, 253, 263
  viewed as the essence of faith, 9, 15, 17, 192, 194, 196, 259, 263
Atchison, Thomas F., xxvii, 284

Baxter, Richard, 141
Beaton, D., 15
Beauchamp, Tom L., 94, 284
Bebbington, David W., 100, 114, 121, 284
Beeke, Joel R., 1–3, 9–10, 13–16, 18–19, 22–24, 284
Bellamy, Joseph, xxv, 75, 142, 285, 292
Benedict, Philip, 13, 285
Bennett, Tony, 52, 285
bodily effects, 44, 134, 161, 215
Bolton, Robert, 137–41
Bombaro, John J., 60, 285
Boss, Rob, 51

Bozeman, Theodore Dwight, 12, 150, 285
Bradley, James E., 53, 69, 285
Bremer, Francis J., 3, 5, 8, 11, 285
Brettergh, Catherine, 137–38
Brooks, Thomas, 17, 20–21, 285
Brown, Robert E., xxiv, 115, 164, 173, 181
Brownson, Orestes, 108, 286
Burgess, Anthony, 24, 143–44, 154, 266, 275, 277, 286
Burr, Aaron, 37
Byassee, Jason, 227, 286

Cailliet, Emile, 74, 286
Calvin, John, xxvi–xxvii, 8–9, 16, 133, 141, 143–44, 154, 156, 172, 224, 227, 229, 231, 266, 275–76, 284, 286, 300, 303, 319
Calvinism, Calvinist, xxvii, xxix, 3, 13, 60, 64,–68, 76, 98, 121, 180, 226, 285, 298, 319
Carrick, John, 179–80, 286
Carson, D. A., 51, 80–82, 202, 230, 251–52, 261, 286–87, 307
Chai, Leon, 88, 103–5, 121, 287
Chamberlain, Ava, xxvi, xxix, 46–47, 105–6, 112, 117, 287, 291–92
Charnock, Stephen, 31, 287
Chauncy, Charles, xii, 44, 94, 121–24, 139–42, 144–45, 147, 149, 157, 159, 161, 262, 287, 296
Cherry, Conrad, 59, 67, 71–72, 74, 76, 85, 87, 180, 288
Claghorn, George S., 36–37, 75, 117, 151, 288, 290, 292–93
Clap, Roger, 138
Clark, David Edward, xxvii
Clarke, William Newton, 230
Cobb, John B., 56
Coffey, John, 12, 288, 316
Cole, Graham A., 226
Coleman, Benjamin, 45, 292
conscience, 10, 22–24, 44, 189, 194–99, 204, 208–11, 213, 237, 255, 263
Coolidge, John S., 2
Copan, Paul, 88
Corfield, Penelope J., 53, 55, 289
Crisp, Oliver D., 60, 65, 71, 289, 298, 299, 304, 309, 317
Cromwell, Oliver, 3, 4, 133, 289
Cunningham, William, 10, 15–16, 289
Cutter, William Richard, 138, 289

Danaher, William J., 62, 90, 289
Daniel, Stephen Hartley, 70–71, 183
de Saussure, Ferdinand, 52, 289
decontextualization, 70, 73–74, 85, 180, 223, 231, 256, 260–61
Delattre, Roland A., 70, 289
Delbanco, Andrew, 2, 11, 290
Demarest, Bruce A., 51, 78–79, 224, 302
Distinguishing Marks, x, xii, 25, 42, 46–47, 121, 131–32, 134–35, 260, 290
Dockery, David S., 39, 290
Doddridge, Phillip, 143, 144, 157, 266, 275–76, 290
Doriani, Daniel M., 231–34, 290
Dorrien, Gary J., 231, 290
Dwight, Sereno Edwards, 35, 290

Edelstein, Alan, 16, 290
Edwards, Jonathan

conversion, 35, 40, 42
exegesis of, 4, 163, 173, 176, 177–79, 189
his daughter, Sarah, 205
his father, Timothy, x, 33–35, 38, 39, 41, 43, 138, 260
his mother, Esther, 38, 138
his wife, Sarah, 151
use of allegory, 164, 177
use of typology, 58–59, 164–65
Edwards, Sarah (Pierpont), 151
Elwood, Douglas, 70, 293
empiricism, empiricist, 34, 46, 78, 79, 99, 108, 114, 121, 200, 201, 261
Enlightenment, xxi, xxx, 32, 54, 60, 64, 74, 87, 88, 90, 94, 99, 100, 104, 114–15, 120–21, 142, 176, 287, 298, 300, 305, 315, 318, 319
enthusiasm, 34, 44, 90, 94, 139
epistemology, 3, xxi, xxv, xxviii–xxx, 8, 58, 60, 63, 68, 80–84, 88–89, 99, 101–3, 107–8, 112, 118–19, 120, 125, 128, 130, 261
Erdt, Terrence, xxviii, 293
Erickson, Millard J., 51, 77–79, 176, 224–25, 293

Faithful Narrative, x, 45–47, 109, 117, 291
Fanning, Buist M., 227, 294
Ferré, Frederick, 78, 294
Fiering, Norman, 61, 70–71, 74, 85, 87, 114, 115, 294
Flavel, John, viii, xv, 138, 141, 143–44, 153–57, 266, 273, 294
Fleming, Robert, 139
foundationalism, 82, 234, 261
Frame, John M., 14, 51, 229, 232, 234, 295, 332
Franke, John R., xxix, 51, 234, 296
Frost, R. N., 8, 295

Gale, Theophilus, 143–44, 156, 266, 275, 277, 295
Gallagher, Shaun, 81, 295
Gerstner, John H., xxviii–xxix, 31, 75–76, 295, 297
Gillespie, Thomas, xiv, 168, 192–94, 209, 211, 217, 221–22, 248–51, 255–56, 292, 295
Goen, C. C., xxviii, 45–46, 109–10, 132, 135, 138, 140, 161, 290–91, 293, 296
Great Awakening, 1, x, xxii, xxviii, 42–47, 90, 92, 109–10, 132, 135, 161, 210, 215, 251, 256, 290–91, 293, 296, 318
Greer, Rowan A., 227, 301
Grenz, Stanley J., xxix, 51, 234, 296
Griffin, Edward M., 95, 122, 125, 142, 296
Grudem, Wayne, 80, 296
Guelzo, Allen C., 66, 67, 72–73, 183, 289, 293, 296, 300–301, 305, 312
Guide to Christ, 153, 156, 271, 313
Gura, Philip F., 72, 296
Gurnall, William, 141
Guyse, John, 45

Half-Way Covenant, 4, 6, 28
Hall, Michael G., 12
Hall, Richard, 51, 285
Haller, William, 2, 297
Hambrick-Stowe, Charles, 297

Hansen, Collin, xxix, 297
Harris, Harriet A., 233
Harrison, Douglas, xxvii, 297
Hart, D. G., 88, 121, 288, 297–98, 303–4, 307–8, 314
Haskell, Thomas L., 69, 298
Hawkes, R. M., 17, 21–23, 25, 298
Haykin, Michael A. G., 13, 100, 114, 142, 284, 298, 315, 318
Heal, Felicity, 26, 298
Hedges, Paul, 232, 298
Helm, Paul, 60, 65, 71, 116, 172, 289, 298–99, 304, 309, 317
Helseth, Paul Kjoss, 118, 299
Hemmings, G. A., 11, 299
hermeneutics, 80, 163, 176, 223, 231–32, 238
Hill, Christopher, 2
historiography, 16, 52–55, 63, 66–69, 73, 83
  diachronic, 52, 54–55, 88
  synchronic, 52,–55, 88
Holdcroft, David, 52, 299
Holifield, E. Brooks, 58–59, 63–64, 67, 223, 299
Holmes, Stephen R., 60–62, 64–65, 67, 71, 73–74, 299
Hooker, Thomas, 30–31, 299
Hopkins, Samuel, 36, 63, 142
Hutcheson, Francis, 93, 112, 114, 300
hypocrite, hypocrisy, 3, 105–6, 108, 124, 127, 153, 155–57, 161, 173, 195, 202, 204, 216, 219, 240, 245, 248, 249, 250–51, 259, 268–71, 294, 314

Image of God
  Imago Dei (Image of God), 332

Jonathan Edwards Society, 51, 285
Jones, Jeremiah, 143, 266, 275

Kantzer, Kenneth S., 234, 300
Kilboi, John Michael, xxvi, 300
Kimnach, Wilson H., 174, 179, 300
Klauber, Martin I., 8, 300
Knight, Henry H. III, xxviii
Knight, Janice, 165
Kugel, James L., 227, 301
Kuhn, Thomas S., 69, 301

Lamborn, James Spencer, xxvii, 301
Lee, Sang Hyun, 53, 60–61, 70–71, 73–74, 116, 164–65, 183, 286, 289, 293, 299, 300–302, 305, 312, 313
Lesser, M. X., xxv–xxvi, xxviii, 66, 152, 183, 302
Levy, Babette May, 89, 302
Lewis, Gordon R., 51, 79, 224
Lindbeck, George A., 56, 302
Lints, Richard, 226, 302
Locke, John, 1, xi, 60, 63, 87, 89–90, 98–101, 103–4, 108, 111–12, 114–16, 118, 120, 126, 261, 298, 302, 317, 319
Loughridge, Adam, 13, 303
Lovelace, Richard F., 39, 290, 303
Lucas, Sean Michael, 3, 88, 121, 288, 297–98, 303–4, 307–8, 314
Luther, Martin, 8, 143–44, 156, 206, 224, 266, 275, 277, 303, 319

MacArthur, John F., xxix, 303

Malebranche, Nicholas, 61, 63, 88, 94
Malefyt, Calvin Sterling, xxvi–xxvii, 303
Manspeaker, Nancy, 303
Marsden, George M., 6, 32, 34, 38–39, 42–43, 66–67, 69, 83, 94–95, 121, 124, 303
Mather, Cotton, 39, 290, 303
Mather, Increase, 12, 141, 297
McClymond, Michael J., xxix, 54, 60, 61–62, 64, 67, 70–71, 73, 76, 85, 88, 91, 99–100, 110, 111, 116, 121, 130, 164–65, 172, 176, 191, 304
McDermott, Gerald R., xxix, 54, 58, 76, 121, 130, 164–65, 176, 191, 223, 304, 313
McGrath, Allister E., 9, 180, 228, 305, 307
means of grace, 8, 43, 214, 218–19, 255
metaphysics, metaphysical, 57–59, 62–63, 89–92, 95–98, 100–101, 108, 114, 118–20, 122, 124–26, 129–30, 153, 222–23, 261, 267, 275
Miller, Perry, 3, xxv, 2, 4–5, 11, 18–19, 20, 25, 29–32, 46, 59, 62, 65, 67, 71, 76, 87, 99–100, 108, 114, 116, 118, 141–43, 206, 221, 286, 305, 312, 332
Min, Anselm Kyongsuk, 56, 305
Minkema, Kenneth P., 35, 66, 76, 151, 164, 297, 301, 304–5, 308–9, 315, 318
Miscellanies, 111–12, 117, 150, 176, 191, 291–92, 311
Morgan, Christopher, 85
Morgan, Edmund S., 2, 30
Morison, Samuel Elliot, 141, 306
Morris, William S., 71, 306
Muller, Richard A., 53, 69, 285

Naselli, Andrew David, 81, 307
Nash, Ronald H., 69, 307
New Lights, 44, 46, 47, 106–7, 128, 136–37, 149–50, 154, 158, 160–62, 166, 172, 180, 183, 186, 196, 200–201, 204
new sense, 40, 46, 99, 101–2, 104, 109–10, 112–19, 125, 128–30, 167, 170, 203, 209, 214, 245, 261
Nichols, Stephen J., xxvii–xxviii, 62, 88, 90–91, 121, 172, 223, 288, 297–98, 302–4, 307–8, 314
Noble, Paul R., 68
Noll, Mark A., 44, 69, 77, 120, 230, 307, 318
Northampton, xxi, 32, 39, 45, 66, 109, 151, 287

object/eye distinction, xi, 102, 104–5, 108, 125, 127, 261
Old Lights, 44, 46, 47, 94, 125, 137, 141, 158–59, 166, 172, 180, 200–201
Oliphint, K. Scott, 121, 308
ordo salutis, 26–27, 28
Osborne, Grant R., 81, 308
Owen, John, 20, 143–44, 156–57, 172, 248, 266, 275–76, 308

Packer, James I., 3, 7, 11, 15, 17–18, 20, 21, 299, 308–9
Parable of the Ten Virgins, 105, 148, 149–50, 209, 267, 311
Parsons, Elihu, 205
passions, 3, xi, 90, 93–94, 97, 122, 300

Pauw, Amy Plantinga, 62, 309
Pederson, Randall J., 2, 3, 284
perception, xi–xii, xiii, xx, 90, 99, 101–3, 105, 107–10, 112, 116, 119, 127–28, 130, 153–56, 161, 240, 260–62, 283, 310
perseverance, 39, 155, 182, 184, 206, 245, 248–49, 264, 268, 270, 272, 274
Personal Narrative, x, 36, 40, 42–43, 117, 293
Pettegrew, Larry D., 80, 309
Pettit, Norman, xxviii, 117, 292, 303, 309
Pilario, D. F., 56, 309
Plantinga, Alvin, 88
Plumstead, A. W., 4, 310
postmodernity, xxi, xxv, xxix, 51, 56, 69, 72, 82, 183, 234, 289, 296, 299, 316
preaching, 3, 10, 27, 31, 64, 122, 139–40, 151, 218–19
preparation, -ism, xxvii, 1, 23, 26, 28–32, 34–35, 37–39, 48, 148, 153, 155, 157, 182, 184–86, 189, 201, 211, 259–60, 267–68, 272, 276
Preston, John, 20, 21, 143–44, 157, 266, 275–76, 310
proof-texting, 152, 173, 176, 179–82, 189, 222, 225–36, 238, 256, 263
Proudfoot, Wayne, 118–19, 310
psychology, 3, 78, 122, 124, 226
Puritanism, 1, vii, ix, xxvii–xxviii, 1–8, 10–14, 17–30, 33–34, 42, 48, 59, 64, 74, 89, 100, 116, 128, 133, 135, 138, 141–43, 144, 147, 150, 154, 156–57, 163, 179, 182, 184, 190, 196, 200, 211, 258–59, 262–63, 284–86, 288–90, 295, 297–300, 306–7, 309, 311–14, 316–17
Puritan theology, 22, 25

Ramsey, Paul, xxi, 75, 169, 291, 311
rationalism, rationalist, 20, 51, 88, 121, 200, 294
reductionism, 70–71, 85, 137, 223, 225, 260–61
relativism, 69, 81–82, 261
Richard Karl, 52–53, 309
Rome, Roman Catholicism, 8–9, 16, 19, 56, 132, 212, 227, 311, 316
Rutherford, Samuel, 143–44, 154, 206, 266, 275, 277, 311

Sandeen, Ernest R., 231, 311
Satan, 10, 154–55, 160, 175, 195, 197, 199, 268, 271, 274, 277
Schafer, Thomas A., 111, 292, 311
Scripture
- clarity of, 161, 169
- self-authentication of, xiii, 83, 169, 171–72, 204, 262
- sufficiency of, 159–61, 169, 182, 184, 186

Seasonable Thoughts, xii, 94, 122, 124, 139, 140–41, 144–45, 147, 161, 287
self-deception, 3, xxvii, 1, 10, 22, 32, 34, 102, 105–8, 128, 152–54, 253, 259, 261, 268, 271–73, 276
self-examination, 10, 32, 35, 102, 152, 202, 214, 216–17, 220, 255, 263
Shepard, Thomas, vii, xii, xv, 10–11, 105, 108, 141–43, 146–51,

153–57, 209, 249–51, 262, 266–67, 283, 311, 314

Sibbes, Richard, 19, 143, 144, 156, 266, 275, 277, 311

Silva, Moisés, 52, 311

Simpson, Alan, 2–3, 6–7, 12, 29–30, 311

Sincere Convert, 148, 156, 266–67, 283, 311

singing, 161, 218, 307

Sliwoski, Richard S., xxvi, 312

Smith, John (non-conformist scholar), 266, 275

Smith, John E. (editor for Yale edition of *Religious Affections*), xxv, xxx, 46, 62, 68, 74, 89, 92, 116, 142–43, 159, 169, 192–93, 221, 235, 249, 284, 292–93, 295, 296

Some Thoughts Concerning the Present Revival, x, xii, 47, 110, 117, 121, 123, 131, 135, 137–40, 145, 157, 161, 260, 293

Sound Believer, 153–54, 156–57, 266–67, 283, 311

spiritual sight, 106–7, 109, 116, 153, 155, 157, 268–69, 272, 276–77

Spurr, John, 18

Stackhouse, John G., 52, 77, 296, 312

Stallard, Michael, xxxi, 51, 77–78, 312

Stein, Stephen J., xxiv, 53–54, 59–60, 62, 66, 71, 74, 119–20, 148, 164, 176, 209, 251, 287, 297, 299, 304, 306, 310, 313–14, 319

Stoddard, Esther, 138

Stoddard, Solomon, vii, xv, 28, 32, 39, 134, 136, 138, 142–43, 151, 153–57, 201, 248–49, 266, 271, 294, 313

Stout, Harry S., 88, 164, 294, 296, 301, 304, 308–9, 313–15, 317, 318

Studebaker, Steven M., 72, 314

Swain, Scott R., 228, 283

Sweeney, Douglas A., 4, 61, 66, 114, 115, 121, 164–65, 176, 287, 295, 297, 304, 315

syllogism, 1, 9, 23–25, 48, 194, 209
- mystical syllogism, 24
- practical syllogism, 24

Synod of 1662, 4, 6

Taves, Ann, 92, 162, 315

the mind (faculty of), 2, xxi, 10–11, 17, 68, 90, 92–93, 96, 99–100, 111, 113, 117, 124–26, 129–30, 136, 150, 155, 166–67, 170–71, 173, 178, 183, 185, 197, 213, 236–37, 242, 261

the will (faculty of), 10, 90–93, 122, 126, 208, 276

theological method, xxv, xxviii–xxx, 42, 48, 50–52, 55–57, 60–62, 64, 70–71, 76–77, 80–82, 84–86, 89, 96–97, 101, 108, 131, 158, 181, 189–90, 201, 204, 223, 234, 258, 260–61, 263
- central interpretive motif, xxx, 51, 53, 62, 70–72, 74, 76, 78, 80, 82, 222–25, 256, 260–61, 263
- descriptive, 56, 77, 82–83
- prescriptive, 55–56, 77, 82–83, 260
- regulated matrix, xi, 51, 76, 80–85, 223, 261

stratified, xi, 77, 79, 80, 84
Theses Sabbaticae, 150
Thornbury, Gregory Alan, 77–78, 316
Touchstone of Sincerity, 153, 156, 273, 294
Tracy, David, 56
Treier, Daniel J., 226, 316
Turretin, François, 75, 143–44, 154, 266, 275, 277, 316

Valeri, Mark, 112, 117, 290–91, 316
Van de Craen, Piet, 80, 316
Vanhoozer, Kevin J., 52, 226, 288, 317
Vincent, Nathaniel, 31, 317
Vogt, Philip, 108, 317
von Rohr, John, 18, 20, 317

Wainwright, William J., 58, 223, 317
Walton, Brad, 100, 147, 313, 317
Ward, Wayne E., 140, 227, 294, 317
Warfield, Benjamin Breckinridge, 231, 233, 317, 332
Watts, Isaac, 45
Weber, Timothy P., 230
Wesley, John, xxvi, 91, 300, 318
Westminster Confession, 6, 14, 15, 16, 24, 127, 141, 180, 191, 192, 197, 233, 249, 259, 295, 311, 317
Whittemore, Robert Clifton, xxviii, 318
Williams, Garry J., 99
Williamson, Clark M., 226, 318
Winiarski, Douglas L., 74, 318
Winslow, Ola, 65, 318
Winthrop, John, 5, 319
Witherington, Ben, 226, 319
witness of the Spirit, 23, 153, 154, 155, 168, 196, 197, 198, 235, 236, 237, 238, 255, 268, 272, 274
Woolhouse, R. S., 99, 319
Wright, N. T., 227

Yarbrough, Stephen R., 43, 319

Zachman, Randall C., 8, 300, 319
Zakai, Avihu, 74, 120, 319

Eric Lehner is a graduate of Detroit Baptist Theological Seminary (M.Div.), Virginia Beach Theological Seminary (Th.M.) and Baptist Bible Seminary (Ph.D.). Beginning in 1994, he taught for two years on the faculty of the Hungarian Baptist Theological Seminary in Cluj, Romania, assisted with the planting of Cornerstone Bible Church in Virginia Beach, VA, served on the pastoral staff of Providence Baptist Church in Westerville, OH, and taught as a short-term instructor in Russia, Ukraine, and the Philippines. In 2006, Eric Lehner joined the faculty of Virginia Beach Theological Seminary, where he now serves as Academic Dean and Professor of Theology.

Available in the Reformed Academic Dissertation Series

◆

How Should We Treat Detainees? An Examination of "Enhanced Interrogation Techniques" under the Light of Scripture and the Just War Tradition,
by J. Porter Harlow

Marks of Saving Grace: Theological Method and the Doctrine of Assurance in Jonathan Edwards's A Treatise Concerning Religious Affections,
by Eric J. Lehner

Forthcoming

From Inscrutability to Concursus: Benjamin B. Warfield's Theological Construction of Revelation's Mode from 1880 to 1915,
by Jeffrey A. Stivason

It Has Not Yet Appeared What We Shall Be: A Reconsideration of the Imago Dei *in Light of Those with Severe Cognitive Disabilities*,
by George C. Hammond

Preaching with Biblical Motivation: How to Incorporate the Motivation Found in the Inspired Preaching of the Apostles into Your Sermons,
by Ray E. Heiple Jr.

The Triune God of Unity in Diversity: An Analysis of Perspectivalism, the Trinitarian Theological Method of John Frame and Vern Poythress,
by Timothy E. Miller